# THE EVOLUTION OF THE GILGAMESH EPIC

JEFFREY H. TIGAY

# THE EVOLUTION OF THE GILGAMESH EPIC

UNIVERSITY OF PENNSYLVANIA PRESS
*Philadelphia* 1982

Translations of selected ancient Near Eastern texts, often in modified form, are cited *passim* from James B. Pritchard, *Ancient Near Eastern Texts Relating to the Old Testament*, 3d ed. with Supplement. Copyright © 1969 by Princeton University Press. Extracts reprinted by permission of Princeton University Press.

The selection from the inscription of Naram-Sin in chapter 7 is from O. R. Gurney, *Anatolian Studies* 5:106–9, and is reprinted by permission.

Selections from Sumerian temple hymns in chapter 7 are from Å. Sjöberg and E. Bergmann, *The Collection of the Sumerian Temple Hymns*, and G. G. Gragg, *The Keš Temple Hymn*. TCS 3 (Locust Valley, N.Y.: Augustin, 1969) and are reprinted by permission.

Designed by Adrianne Onderdonk Dudden



---

**Library of Congress Cataloging in Publication Data**

Tigay, Jeffrey H.
The evolution of the Gilgamesh epic.

Bibliography: p.
Includes index.
1. Gilgamesh. I. Title
PJ3771.G6T5 892′1 81-51137
ISBN 0-8122-7805-4 AACR2

---

Printed in the United States of America

*For my mother and father*
Philo, *On the Decalogue*, §§ 107, 118–20

# Contents

# *Preface*

The fact that *The Gilgamesh Epic* has attracted popular attention, even to the extent of being produced as a play and adapted to the form of a children's book, has encouraged me to hope that this volume will be of some interest to the nonspecialist as well as the professional student of the ancient Near East. For this reason I have not hesitated to spell out things that are commonplace knowledge to Assyriologists and to repeat arguments in support of positions established by others. For much in this book I make no claim to originality, but only to have applied methods developed by predecessors and to have gathered together in a single place much of what one needs to know in order to understand how *The Gilgamesh Epic* developed.

Readers who wish to read a translation of the epic before or while reading the present study are referred to any of the following: Speiser and Grayson in *ANET,* Heidel, or the more popular presentation of Sandars (English); Labat, *Religions* (French); Schott and von Soden (German); Böhl (Dutch). (For complete references, see "Works Cited.") In this volume passages of the epic are quoted in a revised translation I have made, based on more recent studies; these revisions are explained in the Appendix.

# *Acknowledgments*

This study grew out of my association with the ancient Near East faculties of Yale University (1965–71) and the University of Pennsylvania (1971 to the present). It began with my doctoral dissertation, submitted to Yale in 1971, parts of which appear here in revised form. These were revised and several other parts prepared during the academic year 1975–76 at the Hebrew University in Jerusalem, where I spent the year on scholarly leave from Pennsylvania. Since that time the entire manuscript has been revised twice and, to the extent that time permitted, brought up to date.

Whatever shortcomings may be found in this volume are my own responsibility. However, there would have been many more had it not been for the generous assistance I have received from many people. I am especially indebted to a number of scholars who were kind enough to read and comment on drafts. Valuable suggestions were made at the outset by the members of my dissertation committee at Yale: W. W. Hallo as director, H. A. Hoffner, and the late J. J. Finkelstein. Professor Hallo, whose article "New Viewpoints on Cuneiform Literature" first suggested such a study, was also kind enough to read and comment on the 1975–76 draft, as were M. Greenberg, H. Tadmor, and my colleagues at Pennsylvania, whose advice was indispensable in the further development of this study: B. L. Eichler, E. V. Leichty, and Å. W. Sjöberg. E. V. Leichty was also kind enough to collate tablets for me at the British Museum and the University Museum. B. L. Eichler very generously reviewed a large number of linguistic questions with me. Å. W. Sjöberg was unstinting in making the resources of the University Museum's Babylonian Section available to me. Professors T. Jacobsen and W. L. Moran each read the penultimate draft with great care and were kind enough to send me their detailed suggestions on many issues and passages dealt with in the book. I am particularly touched that all these scholars were willing to devote so many hours to the book. They have saved me from many errors and offered many new insights.

Several other friends and colleagues were kind enough to discuss particular issues with me. I am indebted for especially helpful suggestions to T. Abusch, J. C. Greenfield, A. Haydar, S. A. Kaufmann, P. Michalowski, I. L. Seeligmann, A. Shaffer, and R. Stefanini. E. Reiner and the late A. L. Oppenheim were kind enough to respond to several queries about data in the files of *The Chicago Assyrian Dictionary.* E. Sollberger kindly collated two tablets in the British Museum. For access to unpublished works, I wish to acknowledge the courtesy of T. Abusch, S. Cohen, M. de J. Ellis, H. A. Hoffner, S. D. McBride, A. Shaffer, and A. Westenholz. For translation of a passage in Italian I am indebted to A. Rofé. The writings of Gilgamesh that appear on the jacket, title page, and chapter opening pages were expertly drawn by Dr. Darlene Loding (cuneiform script) and by Eytan Tigay (alphabetic scripts).

Mrs. Teresa Torelli of the Department of Oriental Studies, University of Pennsylvania, kindly took responsibility for the typing of this difficult manuscript, with assistance in the final stages from Ms. Peggy Guinan. I submitted the manuscript to the University of Pennsylvania Press at the suggestion of my colleague Professor Judah Goldin, and I have had many occasions to be grateful for this advice. Mr. M. English, director of the press, and Mrs. I. Hjelm, managing editor, and the rest of the staff, have made every stage of the publication process a pleasant and helpful experience. The indexes were carefully prepared by Ms. Linda Cooper and Ms. Lee Ann Draud. The contributions of my editor, Dr. Christie A. Lerch, to my clarity of thought as well as expression, have been immense.

For help of a different sort I wish to express my gratitude to Yale

University, the Memorial Foundation for Jewish Culture, and the National Foundation for Jewish Culture for fellowships during the years 1968 through 1971; to the University of Pennsylvania and Professor Norman Oler, director of the University's Israel Exchange Program, for grants-in-aid in 1975; to the American Council of Learned Societies for a research fellowship in 1975–76; and to the A. M. Ellis Foundation and Robert H. Dyson, dean of the College of Arts and Sciences, University of Pennsylvania, for grants that helped cover indexing and publication costs. It was this support that made possible most of the work in connection with this volume.

The greatest thanks of all I owe to my wife, Helene. Not only did she undertake many tasks in connection with my dissertation, but she has served as my most valued adviser on this and all other projects I have undertaken. She and our sons, Eytan, Hillel, Chanan, and Yisrael, have cheerfully accepted the inconveniences my research has required and have made it possible for me to devote my career to teaching and research.

# *Abbreviations: Terminology*

| | |
|---|---|
| acc. | accusative |
| Akk. | Akkadian |
| *apud* | cited by |
| AV | anniversary volume (used for *Festschriften*) |
| B.C.E. | Before the Common Era (same as B.C.) |
| C.E. | Common Era (same as A.D.) |
| col. | column |
| dat. | dative |
| DN | divine name |
| frag. | fragment |
| GN | geographical name |
| Gr. | Greek |
| Heb. | Hebrew |
| Hit. | Hittite |
| Hur. | Hurrian |
| lex. | lexical text section of entry in *CAD* |
| lit. | literally |
| MA | Middle Assyrian |
| MB | Middle Babylonian |
| MS | manuscript |
| NA | Neo-Assyrian |
| NB | Neo-Babylonian |
| OB | Old Babylonian |
| obv. | obverse |
| par. | paragraph |
| pl. | plate; plural |
| PN | personal name |

| | |
|---|---|
| RN | royal name |
| rev. | reverse |
| SB | Standard Babylonian |
| *sub* | under the heading |
| Sum. | Sumerian |
| var. | variant |
| vs. | versus |
| Vs. | verso |

# *Symbols and Special Characters*

| | |
|---|---|
| a, b | following line numbers refer, respectively, to the first and second parts of a line; e.g., l. 12a, l. 72b |
| a, b, c, d | following a page number refer to the quarters of a two-column page in the order: upper left, lower left, upper right, lower right; e.g., p. 72c |
| x | refers to a cuneiform sign of uncertain reading; the number of x's represents a rough estimate of the number of signs in an illegible or broken passage; additional x's within parentheses indicate that the number of signs may be higher by approximately the number of additional x's |
| . . . | omission of material that is irrelevant, illegible, or untranslatable |
| . . . . | (1) in transliterations, indicates a break of undetermined length in the text |
| | (2) in translations, indicates a break of any length (even if roughly determined) in the text |
| [ ] | enclose restorations of material that is completely obliterated in the cuneiform text |
| ⌜ ⌝ | enclose restorations of material that is partly obliterated |
| ( ) | (1) in translations, indicates elements not in the original but added for explanatory purposes |
| | (2) in transliterations, indicates material which may or may not have been present in the cuneiform text |
| > | became (separates an original reading [on left] from a secondary or erroneous reading [on right]) |

| | |
|---|---|
| < | came from (same as above, with original reading on right) |
| < > | enclose material accidentally omitted by an ancient copyist |
| ?, (?) | after a transliteration or translation indicate that a reading or meaning is uncertain |
| / | in translations indicates alternative translations |
| ? | in line numbers, refers to a line the exact number of which is uncertain since it is lost in a break; e.g., ll. ?–17 |
| | after line numbers is used when the beginning of a column is lost in a break and the modern numbering begins after the break; e.g., l. 5′ |

## FOREIGN CONSONANTS

| | |
|---|---|
| ʾ | aleph (glottal stop) |
| ʿ | ayin |
| ḫ | hard velar ch, as in Bach |
| ḥ | laryngeal h pronounced with tightened throat muscles |
| j | y |
| ṣ | ts |
| š | sh |
| ṭ | emphatic t (Hebrew ṭeth) |

Following scholarly convention, Akkadian and other Semitic languages are transliterated in italic type, Hittite in lower-case Roman, and Sumerian in widely spaced lower-case Roman; Roman type in superscript is used for determinatives; upper-case Roman is used for signs of uncertain value in Sumerian texts, Sumerograms in Akkadian texts, and Sumerograms and Akkadograms in Hittite texts. In translations, italics indicate that the meaning is uncertain.

# *Mesopotamian Chronology*

Unless otherwise specified, all dates in this study are B.C.E. except for those referring to modern scholarly research. Third-millennium dates are based on *ANEH.* Dates of individual kings follow Brinkman, "Mesopotamian Chronology."

| **Period** | **Approximate Dates** |
| --- | --- |
| Early Dynastic I | 2900–2700 B.C.E. |
| Early Dynastic II | 2700–2500 B.C.E. |
| Fara | 26th or 25th century B.C.E. |
| Early Dynastic III | 2500–2300 B.C.E. |
| Akkadian (Sargonid) | 2300–2160 B.C.E. |
| Post-Akkadian (Gutian) | 2160–2110 B.C.E. |
| Ur III (Neo-Sumerian) | 2100–2000 B.C.E. |
| Old Babylonian | 2000–1600 B.C.E. |
| Middle Babylonian and Middle Assyrian | 1600–1000 B.C.E. |
| Cassite | 16th–12th centuries B.C.E. |
| Neo-Assyrian and Neo-Babylonian | 1000–400 B.C.E. |
| Persian (Achaemenid) | 538–331 B.C.E. |
| Hellenistic | 331–126 B.C.E. |
| Seleucid | 312–126 B.C.E. |
| Arsacid (Parthian) | 126 B.C.E.–227 C.E. (N.B., Arsacid *era* begins 247 B.C.E.) |

# *Introduction*

## THE AIM OF THE PRESENT STUDY

This volume is a study of the evolution of *The Gilgamesh Epic,* tracing its development through all of its known written stages over a period of at least 1,500 years down to the manuscripts of its final version. The methodology employed here differs from that developed for the study of ancient literature in the seventeenth through early twentieth centuries primarily in that it is based on documented forms of each stage of the epic. By comparing texts of the epic from each attested stage, we can identify and classify the various kinds of changes introduced at each stage, note the methods by which these changes were introduced, and seek to recognize what is distinctive about each stage. The changes range from stylistic and verbal alterations to major thematic, structural, and theological ones. In the process, an attempt is made to relate the changes to factors which may have prompted them, such as developments in political geography and religion, canons of literary taste, linguistic developments, and subjective artistic preferences of the epic's author and subsequent editors. We seek to identify the sources of themes in the epic—biographical, historical, literary, and folkloric—and to suggest what the author and editors may have intended by the use of these themes.

While this study focuses on a Mesopotamian text, it was undertaken in response to a methodological problem shared by students of many ancient literary traditions. The hallmark of the critical approach to the history of ancient literature (biblical and classical, as well as Mesopotamian), developed in the seventeenth through early twentieth centuries, has been its necessary reliance on critical analysis of late, usually final, versions of compositions. By analysis of the received texts, critics have attempted to find embedded within them signs (contradictions, thematic and stylistic variants) of earlier stages of the traditions or the literary sources which were combined to produce those texts, then to hypothetically reconstruct those earlier stages, and, finally, to infer the processes by which the texts reached their present form. Since actual copies of these earlier stages were almost never available for consultation, the results, though impressive, remained hypothetical. For this reason biblical and classical scholars have remained acutely aware of the need to gain some empirical perspective on the hypothetical critical methods which have come to dominate their fields.

In the twentieth century, the field of Assyriology has begun to escape this handicap. Since cuneiform literature was written on durable clay tablets (rather than the perishable materials of biblical and classical literature), copies of earlier as well as later stages in the history of cuneiform compositions have survived to be recovered by archaeologists, and we are now in a position to trace the history of certain compositions through several stages over a span of nearly two millennia. Most significantly, these stages are documented, not hypothetically reconstructed.

It is this situation which, I believe, makes the history of cuneiform literature a subject of interest to those engaged in the literary criticism of other ancient literatures. Biblical scholars have been in the forefront of those calling for just such studies of Mesopotamian literature for the sake of learning their implications for biblical studies. By showing what happened in a field where the history of a composition can be documented, such studies suggest what may also have happened—allowing for differences—in fields where the history cannot be documented, and they may show scholars in these fields whether their hypotheses at all resemble the literary realia of the ancient world.

*The Gilgamesh Epic* is an ideal specimen for such a study. No other Mesopotamian epic is so well attested from so many different periods. When this epic was first unearthed in the mid-nineteenth century, the tablets discovered were from its latest and best-known version, that of the first millennium B.C.E. (often termed the "late" or "Standard Babylonian" version).[1] Analysis of this version shows it to be, on the whole, coherent, integrated, and well structured. Still, enough inconsistencies were noticeable for scholars to hypothesize about diverse origins for different parts of the epic. In subsequent decades, increasingly earlier forms of the epic and texts of related literary compositions were discovered, until ultimately it became possible to identify several different compositions which appeared to have served as sources for the epic. Earlier stages could thus be studied empirically, rather than hypothetically, and comparison of the earlier stages and sources with the final version made it possible to document and describe the processes by which the epic reached its earliest and, later, its final form.

Since the aim of the present study is to show how the epic developed from its earliest to its latest form, the late version will be a constant point of reference as we proceed. We will begin in the next section with a description of the epic based on that version.

## THE STORY AND ITS STRUCTURE

*The Gilgamesh Epic* is an epic poem covering twelve tablets in its latest version and written in Akkadian, the main Semitic language of ancient Babylonia and Assyria. It describes the exploits of Gilgamesh, king of the Sumerian city-state Uruk (biblical Erech, Gen. 10:10). As we shall see, there apparently really was a king of Uruk by this name, who lived sometime between 2700 and 2500 and was

1. Different forms of a composition are referred to as follows in the present study: 1) Forms which differ from each other substantially in wording or content are termed *versions.* 2) Forms of a version which differ from each other insubstantially in wording or orthography, where the differences appear to be the result of deliberate and somewhat systematic revision, are termed *recensions.* 3) Forms of a version which differ from each other insubstantially in wording or orthography, where the differences do not appear to be deliberate or systematic, are termed *manuscripts* (i.e. tablets). 4) Where a decision between *recension* or *manuscript* is either not possible or not intended, the terms *copy* and *text* are used. 5) Forms which differ from each other chiefly in format (size of tablet, number of lines and columns, and the like) are termed *editions.* The term *form* is used neutrally to refer to any of the above.

later remembered for building the city's inimitable walls and temple. The epic portrays Gilgamesh and his adventures in legendary and mythological colors. It describes him as two-thirds divine and irresistible in battle. At the beginning of the epic, Gilgamesh was tyrannizing his subjects, who cried out to the gods for relief. The gods created Enkidu, Gilgamesh's equal, to rival Gilgamesh and distract him. Enkidu was at first an uncivilized brute, roaming the steppe with wild animals, until he was seduced by a harlot who introduced him to human ways. Following the harlot to Uruk, Enkidu encountered and fought with Gilgamesh. After the battle, Gilgamesh and Enkidu became inseparable friends (Tablets I–II).

Aware that man's days are numbered, Gilgamesh sought to make an enduring name for himself by traveling with Enkidu to the Cedar Forest near Lebanon, conquering its divinely appointed guardian, the monstrous Humbaba ("Huwawa," in earlier versions of the story), and then felling its cedars (Tablets III–V). Upon the friends' successful return from the adventure, the goddess Ishtar, taken by Gilgamesh's handsomeness, proposed marriage. But Gilgamesh scorned the proposal, recounting Ishtar's ill-treatment of all her former lovers. Furious, the scorned goddess sent the Bull of Heaven to wreak vengeance upon Gilgamesh and his city, but Gilgamesh and Enkidu slew the bull, and Enkidu threw its thigh at Ishtar. The friends then rode in triumph through the streets of Uruk, while Gilgamesh proclaimed himself the most glorious among men (Tablet VI).

The friends' hybris was to prove their downfall. That very night, in a dream, Enkidu witnessed the decision of the council of the gods that one of the two, Enkidu himself, must die for their slaying of Humbaba and the Bull of Heaven. When Enkidu succumbed to illness, Gilgamesh was shattered by his "dear brother's" death (Tablets VII–VIII) and realized that death awaited him, too, someday.

Fear of death drove Gilgamesh to seek Utnapishtim the Faraway, who lived "at the mouth of the rivers," in order to learn the secret of immortality which, alone among humans, Utnapishtim and his wife had attained. Gilgamesh roamed the steppe and crossed mountains and seas, and, after much difficulty and several warnings that his hope was futile, he reached his destination. But Utnapishtim's message was the same: Nothing is permanent (Tablets IX–X). His own apotheosis had been granted by the gods after his deliverance from the flood (which Utnapishtim recounted in detail); who would convene the divine council to do the same for Gilgamesh? To drive his message home, Utnapishtim challenged Gilgamesh to stay awake for a week, but the hero who sought to escape death was unable to resist even sleep.[2] At the urging of his wife, Utnapishtim told Gilgamesh of a rejuvenating plant found at the bottom of the sea. Gilgamesh retrieved the plant and planned to eat it upon returning to Uruk, but on the way home the plant was snatched by a serpent, and Gilgamesh's quest came to naught. Gilgamesh was brought back to Uruk by Utnapishtim's boatman and resignedly pointed out to him the city's inimitable walls and its layout (Tablet XI), echoing the epic's beginning.

The twelfth and final tablet of the epic contradicts the rest of the epic in several details. When it opens, Enkidu is still alive, and Gilgamesh is bemoaning the fall of certain cherished implements (possibly a wheel, or a puck and a stick used in a game) into the netherworld. Enkidu volunteered to retrieve them, but, ignoring Gilgamesh's advice to conceal the fact that he was an alien to the netherworld, Enkidu was seized and held there. Gilgamesh's attempts to secure Enkidu's release succeeded only in calling up Enkidu's spirit, which described the order of the netherworld and the condition of various classes of the deceased. Because of the contradictions between Tablet XII and the rest of the epic, most scholars regard it as a late and inorganic appendage, rather than part of the original epic (see chap. 2).

As we shall see, before any of the versions of this epic existed, several separate tales about Gilgamesh circulated. The epic was created—to oversimplify for the moment—by uniting these into a single composition. Though one might expect that the product of such a process would seem disjointed, the fact is that, apart from Tablet XII, the epic reads as a consistent and well-ordered whole, with unified structure and themes. The unity of the first eleven tablets is expressed, among other ways, by their prologue and intro-

2. In the *Babylonian Talmud,* "sleep is one-sixtieth of death" (tractate *Berakot,* p. 57b), and in classical literature it is death's brother (*Iliad* 14:231; *Aeneid* 6:278). Sleep is a frequent metaphor for death in the Hebrew scriptures (e.g., Job 3:13) and the New Testament (e.g., 1 Cor. 15:6). According to one debated interpretation, *GE* X, vi, 33 refers to the similarity of the sleeping and the dead (taking SAL-*lu* as intended somehow for *ṣal-lu,* "sleeping"; Jensen, KB 6(1): 477–78; Schott, *ZA* 42: 136; the SAL is shaded in Haupt's copy: Haupt, p. 66, l. 3).

ductory hymn, which look ahead to events at the end of the epic (I, i, 5–7, 38–40); by the repetition of part of the prologue at the end of Tablet XI (XI, 303–7 = I, i, 16–21); and by retrospective summaries of important incidents of the epic in various speeches by Enkidu and Gilgamesh (VII, VIII, X). The episodes follow each other in a meaningful sequence, gradually developing the main theme of the epic, Gilgamesh's quest for immortality.[3] The building of the walls of Uruk and the temple Eanna, mentioned in the prologue (I, i, 9–19), is represented as having taken place before the events of the epic begin, since their existence is presupposed throughout (I, iv, 37, 44 [cf. Gilg. P. ii, 16, 18]; VI, 157; XI 303–7).[4] The building of elaborate structures such as these, with their accompanying inscriptions, served to perpetuate the name of their builders and were a conventional royal means of securing a form of immortality.[5] Gilgamesh's achievement along these lines was extraordinary, since the wall of Uruk was "inimitable" (I, i, 12–15). The events leading to Gilgamesh's friendship with Enkidu were to culminate in another attempt of a conventional type to perpetuate his name, the performance of a great deed.[6] But this, too, was to be no ordinary attempt, for Gilgamesh would defeat the fearsome Humbaba and thereby banish what was baneful[7] from the land.[8] So daring was this attempt that Gilgamesh's name would endure because of it, even if he should fall (*GE* IV, vi, 39; Gilg. Y. iv, 13–15; Gilg. Har. B, 17). But the moment of Gilgamesh's greatest glory, the triumphal procession through Uruk after the slaying of the Bull of Heaven, was

3. Cf. Jacobsen, *Treasures,* p. 217.

4. The meaning of I, ii, 7 is unclear.

5. See pp. 146–47. Note the reference to the foundation inscription in *GE* I, i, 22–25.

6. Cf. the claim of Shulgi, king of Ur (2094–2047), in one of his hymns, that he ran from Nippur to Ur and back in a single day, "that my name be established unto distant days, that it leave not the mouth of men, that my praise be spread wide in the lands, that I be *eulogized* in all the lands" (*ANET,* p. 585, ll. 36–37).

7. For this translation of *mimma lemnu* (usually taken to mean "all that is evil" in translations of *Gilgamesh*), see pp. 79–80.

8. How Gilgamesh first conceived of this project is not clear from the fragmentary *GE* II, iv and Gilg. Y. ii. One suggestion is that living in Uruk, Enkidu was losing his strength (cf. Reiner, "City Bread," pp. 118–19; Hallo, *JCS* 23:57) and was depressed over the fact, which led Gilgamesh to propose that they undertake a strenuous adventure (Hecker, p. 39; Jacobsen, *Treasures,* p. 199). In any case, since Enkidu has knowledge of Humbaba and the Cedar Forest, we may suppose that his coming has something to do with Gilgamesh's idea (see Gilg. Y. iii, 12–20, 36–44; iv, 1–2; vi, 23–24; *GE* III, i, 6–7; cf. *GLL* A 95–102). In this way Enkidu helped to shift Gilgamesh's attention from oppressing Uruk to other projects and thereby further fulfilled the purpose for which he was created.

followed by Enkidu's dream portending his death as punishment for the friends' having killed Humbaba and the Bull of Heaven. Once the passing of his beloved friend had given Gilgamesh a firsthand experience of death and brought home his own mortality, he began to seek a new way by which to transcend death. Shattered and grief-stricken, Gilgamesh would no longer be satisfied with the conventional methods; now, as other texts put it, he "sought life like Zisudra"[9] (a form of the Sumerian name of Utnapishtim)—that is, literal immortality, or eternal life. Gilgamesh first sought to learn the secret of immortality from Utnapishtim himself; finally he placed his hopes in the plant of rejuvenation.[10] When all of this failed, Gilgamesh returned to Uruk and accepted once again the conventional means by which kings can, though only indirectly, overcome death—the building of enduring structures—an achievement to which Gilgamesh called attention at the end of the eleventh tablet and in a didactic inscription that he wrote after his return (*GE* I, i, 8).[11] Thus the epic "exemplifies, through a single legendary figure, the various attitudes to death that humans tend to adopt."[12]

The thematic and structural integrity of the epic is supplemented by a number of motifs and phrases which echo through it. For example, one passage from the "frame" (formed by lines appearing both in the prologue and in Tablet XI), "Go up onto the wall of Uruk and walk about" (I, i, 16 and XI, 303) is echoed in VI, 157: "Ishtar went up onto the wall of Uruk (of?) the sheepfold."[13] Early in the epic, Enkidu "roamed the steppe" *(ṣēra rapādu),* as Gilgamesh did at the end.[14] The reaction of the hunter when he first saw Enkidu and the appearance of Gilgamesh while he wandered the steppe are described in partly identical terms: "Woe in his belly;/ his face like that of a wayfarer from afar" *(nissatu ina*

9. *KAR,* no. 434, rev. 7, an omen text quoted in *GSL,* p. 44; cf. *GE* I, i, 39, and the Sumerian text quoted by Civil, *JNES* 28:72, no. 18.

10. Oppenheim, *Or.* 17:55–56, detects two more attempts in XI; cf. also Gressman and Ungnad, p. 140; Böhl, *Ar. Or.* 18:118; Reiner, "Akkadische Literatur," p. 171.

11. Cf. David, p. 155. For such inscriptions as a means of obtaining posthumous benefit, see pp. 144–46.

12. Kirk, pp. 144–45.

13. Cf. Hecker, p. 61.

14. *GE* I, iv, 35; VII, iii, 48; VIII, iii, [7]; IX, i, 2, 5; X, i, [45, 52]; iii, [14]; v, 5 (*GETh.,* pl. 41); cf. *CT* 46, no. 30, i, 45 (*GETh.,* p. 56, n. 4, l. 13). Cf. Gilg. Meg. rev. iv, 5; Gilg. O.I. obv. 16; for other phrasing, see *GE* I, iii, 5, 32; Gilg. P. ii, 13; Gilg. Y. iii, 15; Gilg. Me. ii, 11.

*karšišu/ ana ālik urḫī rūqūti pānūšu mašlū).*[15] Early in the epic, Gilgamesh is warned about "going down" into Humbaba's forest *(arādu ana qištišu),* while later he "goes down" into a forest to cut punting poles.[16] Several attempts are made to dissuade Gilgamesh from this journey, and later several characters attempt to make him realize that his quest for immortality will fail.[17] The stages of Gilgamesh's journeys from and back to Uruk are regularly marked with all or part of the following formula, or variations of it:

*ana 20 bēr iksupū kusāpa*
*ana 30 bēr iškunū nubatta*
*50 bēr illikū kal ūmi*
*mālak arḫi u šapatti*
*ina šalši ūmi iṭḫû ana* GN
*maḫar* $^{d}$*Šamaš uḫarrû būra*[18]

At twenty leagues they broke off a morsel,
At thirty (further) leagues they prepared for the night;
Fifty leagues they traveled in one (lit. the whole) day,
A journey of a month and fifteen days.
On the third day they approached GN.
Before Shamash they dug a well.

Gilgamesh's voyages with Utnapishtim's boatman also employ another formula:

$^{d}$*Gilgameš u* $^{I}$*Uršanabi irkabū* $^{giš}$*elippa*
$^{giš}$*magilla iddû-ma šūnu irtakbū*[19]

Gilgamesh and Urshanabi boarded the boat.
They launched the vessel and they sailed away.

15. *GE* I, ii, 49–50; IX, i, 4–5; X, i, 8–9, 35–36, 42–43; iii, 4–5, 11–12; v, 2–3, 37 (*GETh.,* pl. 42), cf. 29. Hecker, p. 51, n. 1, thinks that I, ii, 47–50 refer to Enkidu, but cf. I, iii, 8, 35. Note that Gilgamesh compares himself to a hunter in Gilg. Me. ii, 11.

16. *GE* II, v, 4, 6; GEH vi, 9; Gilg Y., iii, 17; v, 15; *GE* X, iii, 41, 45.

17. Gilg. Y. iii, 12–24, 36–iv, 2; v, 8–19; *GE* II, v, 1–6; GEH rev.; in Gilg. Y. this warning is epitomized in the question "Why have you come to desire to do this thing?" *(ammīnim taḫšiḫ anniām epēšam);* Gilg. Me. i, 5–8; ii, 14–iii, 5; *GE* XI, 197–98; in Gilg. Me. this warning is epitomized in the question "Gilgamesh, to what end (lit. where) do you roam?" *(êš tadâl).*

18. *GE* IV: *LKU,* no. 39: i, 1–5; ii, 1–4; *LKU,* no. 40:9–12; *CT* 46, no. 21: obv. 2′–5′; *CT* 46, 22: rev.(?) 2′–6′ (for collations of *LKU* 39, see Landsberger, *RA* 62:92, n. 3, p. 99; Shaffer, *EI* 9:159–60); *GE* V, iii, 44–46; XI, 283–84 (cf. 285), 300–301. Cf. also I, iii, 48 and X, iii, 49. For *Hit. Gilg.,* see Friedrich, *Or.* 30:90–91.

19. *GE* X, iii, 47–48; XI, 256–57. Note how in X, iii, 49 (cf. *Hit. Gilg.* no. 10, rev. iii, 21) this formula is joined by the fourth and fifth lines of the preceding formula.

Gilgamesh and Enkidu frequently grasp *(ṣabātu)* each other or each other's hands as they go off to another place, to sleep, and so forth.[20] Gilgamesh regularly "takes/lifts the axe in his hand/to his side, draws the dirk from/of his belt" (OB: *ilqe ḫaṣṣinam ina qātišu/išlup namṣaram ina šibbišu;* late version: *išši ḫaṣṣinam ana idišu/ išlup namṣari šibbišu*)[21]; Enkidu is symbolized by an axe in one of Gilgamesh's dreams, and Gilgamesh eulogizes him as "the axe at my side, . . . the dirk in my belt" *(ḫaṣṣin aḫīya . . . namṣar šibbiya).*[22] Enkidu and later Gilgamesh undergo week-long "suspensions" from normal activity (as when Gilgamesh falls asleep for a week)[23] and the same period of time figures in the flood narrative.[24] Several scenes begin "with the first glow of dawn" *(mimmû šēri ina namāri).*[25] The epic makes extensive use of dreams.[26] There are frequent crowd scenes,[27] frequent references to the heroes' washing, dressing, and the like,[28] to weeping[29] and to facial reactions.[30] A stylistic device especially favored in this epic is the characterization of various individuals by compound phrases with "man" *(amēlu)* as the second element and with the first element

20. *GE* II, iv, 12–13; III, i, 19; VI, 177; Gilg. Bo. obv. 5. The same verb is used earlier of their struggle (*GE* II, ii, 48; Gilg. P. vi, 15–16).

21. Gilg. O.I. rev. 2–3; Gilg. Mi. iv, 11; *GE* IX, i, 15–16; X, ii, 33–34; iii, 40, 44; cf. *Hit. Gilg.* I, rev. iv, 3 (*ANET,* p. 83c); *Hit. Gilg.* no. 10: rev. iii, 11, 14; cf. the fragment of *GE* VII (K3588) in *ANET,* p. 86b, l.48.

22. Gilg. P. i, 29, 31; *GE* I, vi, 9, 18; *GE* VIII, ii, 4–5; cf. the weapon metaphors for Gilgamesh's onslaught in *GE* IX, i, 17–18; X, ii, 35.

23. Gilg. P. ii, 6ff.; Gilg. Me. ii, 8ff.; *GE* I, iv, 21; X, ii, [4]; iii, [23]; v, [14] (traces of the latter two lines are preserved in *GETh.,* pls. 40, 42); XI, 199–288. See Wolff, p. 393, n. 2.

24. *GE* XI, 127–29, 141–45; cf. the Sumerian *Deluge* v, 3 = *ANET,* p. 44, l. 203.

25. Gilg. Ur obv. 1 = *GE* VII: *STT,* no. 14: rev. 8b; *GE* VIII, i, 1; ii, 23; iii, 8; v, 45; XI, 48, 96; cf. *Hit. Gilg.* no. 8: i, 1 (*ANET,* p. 85d). See chap. 12, n. 49. For other formulas, cf. *gamir/gimir emūqī* with different meanings in III, i, 2 and VI, 51, and similar addresses by Gilgamesh to the elders at the beginning of his speeches: *šima'inni eṭlūti,* GEUW vi, 7; *GE* VII, ii: *STT,* no. 15: rev. 2.

26. Gilg. P. i, 1–ii, 1 // *GE* I, v, 25–vi, 29; Gilg. Har. B; Gilg. Bo. obv.; *GE* V, iii–iv; VI, 189–92; *Hit. Gilg.* no. 8; *GE* VII, iv, 14ff. // Gilg. Ur rev. 60ff. // Gilg. Meg. obv. i, 10ff.; *GE* VII, vi, 5–6; XI, 187. Cf. Oppenheim, *Dreams,* p. 187 and passim.

27. Gilg. P. i, 10, 30 // *GE* I, v, 31–35; vi, 10–13; Gilg. P. ii, 35; v, 10, 13 // *GE* II, ii, 38–42; Gilg. Y. iv, 38; *GE* VI, 179; XI, 161.

28. Gilg. P. ii, 28; iii, 22–26; Gilg. Me. i, 2; *GE* VI, 1–5; VII, iii, 38, 48; VIII, iii, 7; X, i, 6; v, 30–32; XI, 239–52; cf. Gilg. Me. iii, 10–11; *GE* III, ii, 3–5 (and IV, v, 44–45).

29. Gilg. Y. ii, 26, 29, 34–35, 40; vi, 1; Gilg. Me. ii, 5; *Hit. Gilg.* I, rev. iv, 32; *Hit. Gilg.* no. 8, obv. i, 18; *GE* II, iv, 9(?)–10; VI, 82–83 (see *GSL,* p. 117 ad iii, 14–17), cf. 47, 57; VII: *STT,* no. 14: obv. 16, rev. 9–10 (= Gilg. Ur 2–3); VIII, i: *STT* no. 15: obv. 5ff.; VIII, ii, 1–3 = *STT,* no. 15: rev. 1–4; IX, i, 2; X, ii, 5; iii, 23; v, 14; XI, 124–25, 136–37, 290–91. On the formulas used to describe weeping, see Hecker, pp. 178–79.

30. *GE* I, ii, 45–48, 50; IX, ii, 10–11; X, i, 9, 33–37, 40–44; v, 1–4; iii, 2–5, 9–12; Gilg. P. iii, 4–5, 21; iv, 39 (cf. *GLL* B 125–26 in *JCS* 1:42, n. 245, ll. 8–9).

functioning adjectivally (e.g., *ḫābilu amēlu,* "trapper-man;" *lullû amēlu,* "primordial [a noun]-man").[31] Several of these motifs make their final appearance in rapid succession at the end of the eleventh tablet (199–307) as Gilgamesh sleeps for a week, bathes and changes his clothing, and travels home with Urshanabi, until the eleven-tablet form of the epic culminates with the repetition of part of its prologue (XI, 303–7 = I, i, 16–21).[32]

Behind this integrated and well-structured epic lies a long and complex process of development.

## THE VERSIONS OF THE EPIC

The merits of *Gilgamesh,* which a modern authority aptly called "the most significant literary creation of the whole of ancient Mesopotamia,"[33] were appreciated by literate people in the ancient Near East. This we may gather from the epic's wide distribution, its long life, and its translation into other languages.[34] The Akkadian

31. I, ii, 42; iii, 18(?); iv, 6; v, 14; IX, ii, 6, 13, 15; iii, 6; iv, 37. On such compounds in the epic and elsewhere, cf. Oppenheim, *Or.* 17:25, n. 4; 19:129, n. 1; Speiser in *ANET,* pp. 72ff., nn. 19, 23, 126, 170; *CAD* $A_2$, p. 52d; Nougayrol et al., *Ugaritica V,* p. 283, cf. p. 305, n. 1; Hallo, *EI* 9:66; see chap. 11, n. 15.

32. A week's sleep (XI, 199–228), bathing and dressing (239–55), the boat-boarding formula (256–57), the twenty leagues . . . thirty leagues formula (283–84, 300–301). Note also the echoes of I, i, 7 and 26 in XI, 259, 264 (cf. 293).

33. Kramer, *HBS,* pp. 180–81. Other scholars have expressed themselves similarly.

34. A further index of the epic's popularity would be allusions to it in other texts. Part of *GE* I, ii, 35 is quoted in a commentary to a diagnostic omen text (Hunger, *Spätbabylonische Texte,* no. 27:5′). A number of allusions have been proposed in the *Dialogue of Pessimism: BWL,* p. 149, l. 76 (*OBS,* p. 363; contrast *BWL,* pp. 140–41); *BWL,* p. 149, ll. 83–84 (though this adage may go back originally to Sumerian wisdom literature; see Kramer, *JCS* 1:35, n. 215; *OBS,* p. 363; *BWL,* p. 327; Hallo, *IEJ* 12:20, n. 33; Hallo and van Dijk, p. 31, ll. 123–24 and pp. 60–61; see below chap. 8, "Wisdom Sayings"); *BWL,* p. 145, l. 33 (Lambert, *BWL,* p. 325, mentions *GE* IX, ii, 16; cf. *GE* I, ii, 1, and then *SKL* iii 18 [*SKLJ,* pp. 90–91, l. 18, and n. 131; *ANET,* p. 266; cf. *GETh.,* pp. 9–10]). For a suggested allusion in the Mari letters, see Finet, p. 40. Cf. also *BWL,* p. 200, col. IV, 1 and Landsberger, *RA* 62:113; Oppenheim, *Dreams,* pp. 213–14. These suggestions must be evaluated cautiously. We shall see more than once in the course of this study (see esp. chap. 8) how difficult—some would say foolhardy—it is to distinguish between the use of an idiom, cliche, or topos and an allusion to or quotation from a particular text, and to determine the direction of borrowing. Indeed, Oppenheim, *AM,* pp. 256–57, denied that other texts alluded to the epic or that Mesopotamian scribes took an interest in it. (Some of the evidence cited by Nougayrol, "L'épopée," p. 853, attests to the popularity of Gilgamesh himself, but not necessarily to that of the epic). On the question of Gilgamesh and art, see below, n. 63.

version of the first millennium, or "late version," upon which the summary in the preceding section is based, was the first version to become known to scholars in the second half of the nineteenth century. It was deciphered from tablets found in the remains of the library of Ashurbanipal, the Assyrian king (668–627) who assembled the greatest library of the pre-Hellenistic Near East in his capital, Nineveh.[35] Other subsequently discovered first-millennium copies from the earlier capitals at Assur and Calah, from Babylonia in the south, and from Sultantepe in the far north of Mesopotamia (southern Turkey today),[36] are substantially identical to the Nineveh texts, whereas those from the second millennium, although textually related to the Nineveh texts, differ from them considerably. The latest of these second-millennium texts, from the Middle Babylonian Period (ca. 1600–1000), stem from Ur in southern Mesopotamia, from Megiddo in Canaan, and from the Hittite capital Hattusha (Boghazköi) in Asia Minor[37]; the latter site has also yielded translations into the Indo-European Hittite language and into Hurrian, the language of the Mitanni empire in Central Mesopotamia (ca. 1400).[38] The earliest Akkadian copies from the Old Babylonian Period (ca. 2000–1600), when (as we shall see) the earliest version of the epic appears to have been composed, come from several sites in and around Babylonia.[39] Finally, there are the individual tales about Gilgamesh mentioned above. These are in Sumerian, and copies of them dating to the Old Babylonian Period have been

35. The history of publication of *Gilgamesh* is reviewed briefly by Kramer, *JAOS* 64:8, n. 2; the Akkadian versions are surveyed and compared by Kupper in *GSL,* pp. 97–102. The Nineveh texts are published in *GETh.* Cf. the list of texts in Hecker, pp. 26–30.

36. For Assur, see *KAR,* no. 115 and perhaps 319, 320 (cf. von Soden, *ZA* 53:225–26); *GSL,* pp. 113–22. For Calah, see Wiseman, *Iraq* 37:157–62 and pl. 37. For Babylonia, see the NB texts listed by Wiseman in *GSL,* p. 123, those published by him on pp. 124–35, the additional texts published by Lambert and Millard in *CT* 46, and the Uruk fragment published by von Weiher in *ZA* 62:222–29. For Sultantepe, see *STT,* nos. 14–15 (Gurney, *JCS* 8:87–95 and pls. 1–2). See also chap. 6, n. 1.

37. Ur: Gilg. Ur; Megiddo: Gilg. Meg.; Hattusha: Gilg. Bo. For a newly discovered text from Syria, see chap. 6, n. 1.

38. Hittite: *Hit. Gilg.;* Hurrian fragments: see Kammenhuber, pp. 47–48.

39. Texts of known provenance are from Harmal (ancient Shaduppum; Gilg. Har. A and B) and Ishchali (Gilg. O.I.), both in the Diyala River region, and from Nippur (Gilg. Ni., if it is OB; see chap. 2, n. 1). The others were acquired from antiquities dealers in Iraq and were thought by their original publishers to come from Larsa or Uruk (Gilg. P. and Y.; see Langdon, PBS 10[3]:207; Jastrow and Clay, p. 18) and Sippar (Gilg. Me., and therefore Gilg. Mi.; see Meissner, MVAG 7[1]:4).

found at several Babylonian sites. Some, but not all of them, correspond to episodes in the Akkadian epic. These Sumerian tablets are generally regarded as transcriptions of older tablets of the outgoing third millennium.[40]

Mesopotamian tradition credited this epic to an exorcist-priest named Sîn-leqi-unninnī.[41] Although a late roster of scholars, copied in the second century, lists him as a contemporary of Gilgamesh[42] (which would place him somewhere between 2700 and 2500), other evidence suggests that Sîn-leqi-unninnī lived in Uruk during the Middle Babylonian Period.[43] This period seems to have marked an important turning point in the development of the epic. The Akkadian forms of the epic attested in the second-millennium texts disappear by the end of this millennium, to be replaced in the first millennium by a version of the epic that is basically standardized wherever it is found and is characterized by a distinctive style.[44] How many transitional stages the epic went through between the original Old Babylonian version and the latest version we cannot say. However, the conclusion seems inescapable that Sîn-leqi-unninnī's achievement was not the original version, but some im-

40. The Sumerian texts come from Nippur, Kish, Ur, Larsa, and Uruk; see Kramer, *JCS* 1:7; *JAOS* 64:11–12; van Dijk, in *GSL*, p. 70; Falkenstein, *JNES* 19: 65–66; Gadd and Kramer, no. 60. The Akkadian and Sumerian versions are compared by Kramer in *JAOS* 64:7–23, 83, and Matouš, in *GSL*, pp. 83–94, and in chap. 1 of the present study. For the generally accepted view on the date of composition of the Sumerian texts, at least in their presently known forms, see Falkenstein, CRRAI 2:12ff. Note, however, the comment of Klein, *JAOS* 91:297, that this view will have to be modified when Ur III duplicates of a number of texts are published. Klein informs me that he has in mind such texts as the Ur III copy of *Lugalbanda*, cited by Cohen, *Enmerkar*, pp. 10–13, n. 22, which diverges considerably from the OB text.

41. See below, pp. 246–47.

42. Van Dijk, *UVB* 18:44, l. 12; contrast Böhl in *RLA* 3:369a.

43. Lambert traces the name Sîn-leqi-unninnī back to the MB Period, when Babylon was ruled by the Cassites (from some time after 1595 until shortly after 1160); see *JCS* 11:1–9; cf. *JCS* 16:77. The name means "O Sin (the moon-god), accept my prayer!" (Stamm, *Namengebung*, p. 167); cf. *CAD* L, p. 136d.

44. For the Akkadian texts, see nn. 35, 37, 39 above. The standardized first-millenium version *(GE)*, found in several copies, is usually termed the *canonical* version. The phenomena which this term is intended to express are described by Oppenheim, *AM*, pp. 17–22; Hallo, *IEJ* 12:21–26; *JAOS* 88:73–74; *ANEH*, p. 156; however, this use of the term does not have much basis in its semantic history, and it creates the need to deny that the word is being used in the theological sense in which the reader is most likely to understand it (cf. Lambert, *JCS* 11:9). Since the writers cited indicate that they refer primarily to the standardization of the wording of the text and the inclusion of the text in the curricula of scribal schools, we shall use the terms *standard(ized)*, and *curricular* or *academic*.

portant Middle Babylonian version or, as is more often assumed, the late version, and that he produced it some time in the last half or quarter of the second millennium.[45]

## THE HISTORICAL BACKGROUND

The Sumerian tales, the earliest known literary embodiment of Gilgamesh's adventures, are separated from his lifetime by several centuries. According to the *Sumerian King List,*[46] Gilgamesh was the fifth king of the first dynasty of Uruk, which historians place in the Second Early Dynastic Period of Sumer (ca. 2700–2500).[47] His name is of a type which is characteristic of this approximate period.[48] Although Gilgamesh's existence is not confirmed directly by any contemporary inscriptions of his own which mention him, the likelihood that there was a king of this name has been enhanced by the discovery of inscriptions of contemporaneous rulers of Kish and Ur with whom Gilgamesh is associated in epic and historical tradition[49]; their existence, at least, is confirmed. Nonliterary texts indicate that by the Fara Period (ca. twenty-sixth or twenty-fifth century), Gilgamesh was regarded as a god[50] and that offerings were made to him in Early Dynastic Lagash (before the middle of the twenty-fourth century) and in several towns under the third

45. Von Soden, *MDOG* 85:23; *ZA* 40:187; 41:129–30; Lambert, *JCS* 11:1–14; Böhl, *Gilgamesj-Epos,* p. 16; *RLA* 3:364; Landsberger, in *GSL,* p. 34; Matouš, in *GSL,* pp. 93–94; Hallo, *IEJ* 12:15–16.

46. *SKLJ,* pp. 84–91; *ANET,* p. 266.

47. *ANEH,* pp. 42–46.

48. *SKLJ,* pp. 187–90; Lambert, in *GSL,* p. 49.

49. For the chronological and military connection of Gilgamesh with Enmebaragesi of Kish and his son Agga, and the chronological correlation with Mesannepadda of Ur and his sons Aannepadda and Meskiagnunna, see Klein, in *Kramer AV,* pp. 273, 278–79, ll. 58–60 (text cited below, pp. 158–59); *GA* 1ff.; Kramer, in *GSL,* pp. 60–63; for inscriptions of all but Agga, see Edzard, in *GSL,* p. 57; *ZA* 53:9; Gordon, *BASOR* 132:28; *SKLJ,* pp. 92–94, nn. 144–46. Cf. *ANEH,* p. 45; Lambert, in *GSL,* pp. 48–49.

50. Lambert, in *GSL,* p. 48. For the problematic date of this period, see Hallo, *Or.* 42:228–38; *ANEH,* p. 48 (for another view, cf. Edzard, "Early Dynastic Period," pp. 52–57). That Gilgamesh was deified within a century or two of his lifetime may not be surprising if this is viewed as an antecedent of the later deification of kings in Mesopotamia. The kings of Ur III regarded Gilgamesh as something like their personal god, and this is the very relationship in which deified kings seem to have stood toward their realms (Jacobsen, *ZA* 52:138; *ANEH,* p. 61). Kings were sometimes accorded this status in their own lifetimes (*ANEH,* p. 61), and conceivably this was the case with the historical Gilgamesh (cf. Jacobsen, *Treasures,* p. 209).

dynasty of Ur (Ur III, ca. twenty-first century),[51] whose kings claimed Gilgamesh as their brother.[52] By the Ur III Period, he was regarded as king and judge of the netherworld, the role in which he was best known in Mesopotamian magic and religion in the first millennium.[53] The interest shown in Uruk and its first dynasty by the kings of the Ur III dynasty has, along with other factors, suggested that the Sumerian narratives dealing with Gilgamesh and other kings of Uruk's first dynasty were composed, or at least given their present form, during the Ur III Period, or twenty-first century.[54]

In their exclusive concentration on Gilgamesh as a god, the nonliterary texts down through the Ur III period give no information of a biographical nature. For such, we are dependent on later sources. Apart from the *Sumerian King List,* an inscription from the end of the Ur III Period or the early Old Babylonian Period states that Gilgamesh rebuilt a shrine of the god Enlil in Nippur.[55] A slightly later Sumerian inscription refers to his constructing the wall of Uruk.[56] Although this inscription is nearly a thousand years later than the event, its claim is made plausible by archaeological evidence that the wall of Uruk was built in Early Dynastic times, with the widespread appearance of great city walls characterizing precisely the Second Early Dynastic Period.[57]

Gilgamesh is also mentioned in omen literature, beginning with

51. Lambert, in *GSL,* pp. 47–48; Edzard, *ZA* 53:24; Thureau-Dangin, *RA* 10: 101; Sollberger, UET 8:21; cf. Jacobsen, *Treasures,* pp. 211–12.

52. Falkenstein, *ZA* 50:73–77; Lambert, in *GSL,* p. 47; Hallo, *JCS* 20:136–37; Klein, in *Kramer A V,* pp. 271–92. Earlier, Utu-hegal of Uruk described Gilgamesh as the "divine deputy" sent to accompany him in liberating Sumer from the Gutians (Thureau-Dangin, *RA* 9:115: iii, 1–3; *RA* 10:100, l. 7; Jacobsen, *Treasures,* pp. 86, 211).

53. Kramer, *JCS* 21:112ff., ll. 94, 142–43 (assuming this text reflects the Ur III period; cf. Kramer, p. 104, n. 1); the text cited by Jacobsen, *Treasures,* p. 211 and p. 257, n. 348, may be an earlier example of this. For the first millennium see pp. 80–81, 186–87.

54. Matouš, *Bi. Or.* 21:5; Hallo, *JCS* 20:137; Wilcke, *Lugalbandaepos,* pp. 1–4; Landsberger, in *GSL,* p. 32; Matouš, in *GSL,* p. 93; Klein, in *Kramer A V,* p. 271; cf. n. 40, above.

55. Lambert, in *GSL,* p. 48; Kramer, in *GSL,* pp. 59–63; Sollberger, *JCS* 16: 40–47.

56. Inscription of AN-àm, king of Uruk (ca. 1821–1817: see Falkenstein, "Inschriftenfunden," pp. 18–22); for the text, see *SAKI,* p. 222, no. 2b; Edzard, *Zweite Zwischenzeit,* p. 156, n. 831; Tournay, "Inscription."

57. Lambert, in *GSL,* p. 49; von Soden, "Sumer," p. 541; Jacobsen, PAPhS 107:479; *ZA* 52:120.

the Old Babylonian Period.[58] The single example from this period describes him simply as having no equal. Later omens, from the first millennium, describe him as "the strong king who had no rival." Whether "strong" connotes "mighty" or "harsh" is debated.[59] Another omen is described as "omen of Gilgamesh, who ruled the land, (meaning) there will be a ŠÚ king in the land," with the untranslated word connoting either "despotic" or "universal."[60] The late omens mention a number of episodes known from the epic and may depend upon it, rather than independent historical tradition. A few other episodes they mention are not known from the epic, but whether the Gilgamesh omens possess any historical value at all is doubted.[61]

This is the extent of the historical and biographical information about Gilgamesh available outside of the epic and its Sumerian forerunners. It tends to support his existence, his date, and therefore his association with certain historical figures, his reconstruction of a shrine, and the epic's statement that he built the wall of Uruk (*GE* I, i, 9–10). It may be that other details in the Sumerian and Akkadian narratives have a historical basis, but on these we can only speculate.[62]

For the centuries between Gilgamesh's lifetime (between 2700 and 2500) and the earliest literary texts about him (2100–2000) or their forerunners, the narratives about him are generally presumed to have undergone a process of oral development and transmission.[63] Since the publication of the Old Sumerian texts from Abu Salabikh (ca. twenty-sixth or twenty-fifth century), this presumption seems less self-evident than it once did, for these texts include

58. Lambert, in *GSL,* pp. 43–47.

59. Lambert, in *GSL,* p. 45, translates "mighty," but *CAD* D, p. 98a and Leichty, *Šumma Izbu,* p. 46, l. 1, understand *(šarru) dannu* in other omens as "despotic" or "harsh." Cf. Isa. 19:4.

60. Leichty, *Šumma Izbu,* p. 46, l. 6 (cf. l. 9 and the commentary on p. 211, ll. 8–9; note also the Alu commentary cited in *CAD* $A_1$, p. 210b lex.); contrast *CAD* K, p. 458a; *AHw,* p. 492c.

61. Lambert, in *GSL,* pp. 45–46; cf. Finkelstein, PAPhS 107:461–72, esp. p. 465, nn. 13, 17.

62. See "The Historical Background of the Sumerian Tales" in chap. 1.

63. Laessøe, "Literary Tradition," pp. 210–11; Matouš, *Bi. Or.* 21:5. Certain third-millennium artistic motifs which have been thought to represent Gilgamesh (and which would, if so, reflect early and possibly oral traditions about him) actually antedate his lifetime by centuries and can hardly be connected with him. See Calmeyer, p. 373. For possible later artistic representations of Gilgamesh and other characters in the epic, see ibid.; Amiet; Nougayrol, "L'épopée," pp. 852–53.

forerunners, and in at least one case a virtually identical version, of other works previously known only in later copies.[64] But at least for the present, no such narrative texts about Gilgamesh are known,[65] and the traditions about him in this period, whether oral or written, are equally beyond our reach.

## CRITICAL METHODS IN THE STUDY OF *THE GILGAMESH EPIC*

As mentioned above, this study was prompted by the possibility of gaining new perspectives on the development of ancient literature by comparing the texts of a composition from different periods over the course of several centuries. This approach was not yet possible when cuneiform literature was first deciphered in the late nineteenth century from late texts in the library of Ashurbanipal. Since only one, late version of any particular composition was available for study at that time, it was impossible to trace its development empirically, that is, to base descriptions of earlier stages on copies of those stages. But this was the heyday of biblical and Homeric criticism, which had honed the theoretical study of ancient literature to impressive methodological sophistication, and since cuneiform studies were dominated by scholars well versed in biblical

64. See Biggs, *Inscriptions,* pp. 30–33. With one or two exceptions (see Sjöberg and Bergmann, p. 7), the oldest Sumerian literary texts known come from this period. Although no texts about Gilgamesh have been identified among these, there is one about the goddess Ninsun and one of Gilgamesh's predecessors, Lugalbanda (Biggs, *JCS* 20:85; *Inscriptions,* p. 91, no. 327), the couple identified as Gilgamesh's parents in the epic and its Sumerian forerunners (contrast, however, Sjöberg, *Or. Suec.* 21:101, cited below, chap. 4, n. 10). This text is interpreted by Bing as a dialogue between Lugalbanda and Inanna which is similar to Ishtar's proposal of marriage to Gilgamesh in *GE* VI (*JANES* 9:1–4); Biggs, *Biblical Archaeologist* 43:79, agrees with the reading of the names and the interpretation of the text as a dialogue, but expresses reservations about the rest of the interpretation.

65. There may be an exception among the texts from Ebla in northern Syria, of perhaps the twenty-fifth century. According to Pettinato, Ebla texts nos. 2093 and 2094 are copies of a composition about Gilgamesh and Aratta, a city-state in northern Iran. See Pettinato, *Catalogo,* p. 198; *Ebla,* p. 257. Pettinato reads the opening words of this composition as g u$_4$. a n. g í r. The first two words can be translated as "the bull (of) heaven." While this calls to mind the episode of the Bull of Heaven in *GE* VI and its Sumerian forerunner *GBH* (see chap. 1), this does not necessarily mean that the Ebla text is related to that episode; the Bull of Heaven is known in other compositions that are not about Gilgamesh (see Kramer, in *ANET,* p. 647; *CAD* A$_1$, p. 377; Edzard, "Mythologie," p. 79).

criticism, cuneiform literature was soon studied in the same way. Critically analyzing late versions of cuneiform compositions, scholars found inconsistencies, redundancies, and other clues which might point to divergent underlying traditions and stages through which a composition had passed. Although cuneiform scholars did not usually go so far as to reconstruct documentary sources by chapter and verse,[66] conclusions similar to those of biblical criticism were soon reached: Many cuneiform literary compositions were described as the composite products of a long evolution.

A leading exponent of this approach to cuneiform literature was Morris Jastrow, Jr. (1861–1922), who was active in biblical as well as cuneiform studies. In 1898, Jastrow published an analysis of the entire *Gilgamesh Epic,* based on the late version.[67] He discerned five main elements in the epic, which he held were originally separate from each other. 1) The first was a group of stories about Gilgamesh's heroic adventures: the conquest of Uruk, the victory over Humbaba, the killing of the Bull of Heaven, and the strangling of a lion (an episode alluded to later in the epic, X, i, 51[31], etc.).[68] The other elements were episodes originally unrelated to the epic: 2) the story of Enkidu, the harlot, and the hunter[69]; 3) the story of Gilgamesh's wanderings and his encounter with Utnapishtim[70]; 4) Utnapishtim's narrative of the flood, itself a combination of two elements: a local tale about the destruction of Utnapishtim's city by a rainstorm, and a nature myth symbolizing the inundation of the land by the annual overflow of the Euphrates[71]; and 5) Tablet XII, which Jastrow considered a scholastic addition to the epic and really a doublet of Gilgamesh's wanderings in the earlier tablets.[72] Jastrow concluded that Gilgamesh was "a favorite personage, to whom floating traditions were attached, in part by popular fancy and in part by the deliberate efforts of literary compilers."[73]

Two decades later, following the discovery of the Meissner, Pennsylvania, and Yale Tablets of the Old Babylonian version, Jas-

66. Cf. Koschaker's analysis of *LH.*
67. *RBA,* chap. 23; cf. his study of *EnEl,* "Composite Character."
68. *RBA,* pp. 514–15.
69. Cf. YOR 4(3):39–47 and *AJSL* 15:193–214.
70. *RBA,* pp. 514–15.
71. *RBA,* pp. 493–94.
72. *RBA,* p. 513.
73. *AJSL* 15:198; cf. *RBA,* pp. 494, 513.

trow revised his analysis.[74] Even then his reasoning was guided by certain critical presuppositions, such as that "when a tale associates two figures in one deed, one of the two has been added" and (referring to what he thought were Enkidu's dreams about the battle with Humbaba) that "the person who dreams is always the one to whom the dream applies."[75] Following these assumptions and certain hints which he found in the Old Babylonian tablets, Jastrow now concluded that Enkidu was the original hero of the Humbaba/Huwawa and Bull of Heaven episodes and the allusion to lion-strangling, all of which were, he thought, transferred to Gilgamesh only secondarily. Gilgamesh and Enkidu were both fabled conquerors of parts of Babylonia. Once-independent tales about each of them had been combined into a single epic, with Gilgamesh made the main character. The new epic was augmented by episodes which Jastrow considered originally independent nature myths and a didactic tale. In all, Jastrow outlined in 1920 "four main currents that flow together" in *The Gilgamesh Epic:* 1) the adventures of Enkidu (now including the Humbaba and Bull of Heaven episodes), which once had existed in the form of an Enkidu epic, partly based on traditions about the civilizing of primitive man; 2) the adventures of Gilgamesh (now limited to the conquest of Uruk, the building of its wall, and his tyrannizing Uruk); 3) nature myths and a didactic tale which were not originally about Gilgamesh and Enkidu (the myth about the incident with Ishtar and that about Gilgamesh's fear of death and his wanderings, in both of which Jastrow took Gilgamesh to represent the sun-god; the flood story, a myth about the rainy season; the rejuvenating plant episode; and the didactic tale about the netherworld in Tablet XII); and 4) the process of weaving all these together, in the course of which Gilgamesh became the main hero.

Although P. Jensen registered a brief objection to Jastrow's original analysis of the epic of 1898,[76] analyses of the same type were offered subsequently by other scholars.[77] The methodology of Jastrow and his successors was identical to that being followed at the time in pentateuchal and Homeric criticism. But unlike those fields,

74. YOR 4(3):32–55.
75. Ibid., pp. 36–37.
76. *OLZ* 24:268.
77. *GETh.*, pp. 7–8; Oppenheim, *Or.* 17:17–58, passim (e.g., p. 24, n. 3).

cuneiform studies have been enriched in the twentieth century by the discovery of versions of literary works and literary sources which are centuries older than those versions which were first subjected to critical analysis. The flood story, for example, has been discovered in a Sumerian version, *The Deluge,* and a classic Akkadian version, *The Atrahasis Epic,* both attested in copies as early as the Late Old Babylonian Period (seventeenth century) and neither of which was part of a text about Gilgamesh. The study of *Gilgamesh* has been advanced immeasurably by the discovery of parts of the Middle and Old Babylonian forms of the epic and of the Sumerian sources upon which important parts of the epic appear to have been based. Later in 1898, Jastrow was able to cite *Atrahasis,* and, by 1920, *The Deluge,* in support of his contention that the flood story was originally independent of *Gilgamesh.*[78] The full significance of the Sumerian sources was first made clear by S. N. Kramer in his essay "The Epic of Gilgameš and Its Sumerian Sources" (1944).[79] It was Kramer who first showed empirically that *Gilgamesh* was based on a number of originally unconnected tales, written in Sumerian, which did not constitute a single epic. These tales, in Akkadian adaptations, were first joined together into a literary whole with a unified theme and meaningful plot sequence by later hands. Although differing greatly in detail from Jastrow's reconstruction of the prehistory of the epic (see chap. 1), Kramer's study confirms Jastrow's general conception of the diverse origins of different elements of the epic. But the persuasiveness of Kramer's study, as he himself stressed, lay in the actual availability of copies of the earlier sources, so that it was unnecessary to rely solely upon critical analysis of the final epic, an approach which remains hypothetical no matter how rigorously argued.[80]

It is not the aim of the present study to criticize the theoretical approach in principle. As we learn from Kramer's results, empirical research can often confirm at least the general conceptions reached by the theoretical approach. Furthermore, the documentation which permits more empirical suggestions is not yet, and may never be, so abundant that we will be able to dispense with critical hy-

78. *ZA* 13:288–301; YOR 4(3):50–51; cf. Poebel, PBS 4(1):51, n. 2, and Laessøe, *Bi. Or.* 13:90–102.
79. *JAOS* 64:7–23, 83.
80. *BASOR* 94:3, n. 3; cf. Matouš, *Bi. Or.* 21:5, n. 22.

potheses that are not based on empirical evidence, nor will we able to avoid such hypotheses entirely in the present study. My aim, however, is to explore the extent to which one can invoke empirical evidence in the solution of literary-historical problems and, incidentally, the extent to which empirical solutions support the results of the older, more theoretical approach to ancient Near Eastern literature. The dividend of such an exploration is not merely the satisfaction of curiosity, for the more experience we can gain with empirical literary history where the documentation permits it, the more we will be able to frame realistic suggestions in cases where the documentation is deficient.[81]

Now that it is possible to study the history of *The Gilgamesh Epic* through various periods, it becomes necessary to decide how to arrange the evidence in the most meaningful way and what questions to pose. Students of ancient literature have, in the past, seen their task primarily as the identification of sources or the reconstruction of earlier, or even original, versions. This was based on a predisposition to view what was early as pure, and what was late as degenerate. For better or worse, however, each writer, compiler, or editor who worked on the epic and its forerunners must have had something in mind when he did so. Therefore it seems to me that historical study demands that each version be taken seriously as a piece of literature in its own right, and that wherever possible an attempt be made to discern the aims and methods of those who produced it. The best procedure for bringing out the aims and methods of each version is comparison and contrast of texts. Chapter 1 is based on the pioneering work of S. N. Kramer. Once Kramer had reconstructed the texts of the Sumerian narratives about Gilgamesh, he saw that they were separate compositions, rather than a single integrated epic, and that they shared with the Akkadian *Gilgamesh Epic* only broad plot outlines, not an overall conception or message. By comparing and contrasting the Sumerian and Akkadian versions, Kramer was able to discern the distinctive contributions of the Akkadian version. In Chapter 2, I argue that the Akkadian epic had become an integrated whole by the Old Babylo-

81. I hope to publish in the near future a collection of studies by myself and several others following this approach; the tentative title is "Comparative Models for the Literary Criticism of the Hebrew Bible." See, in the meanwhile, Hallo, *IEJ* 12:13–26; Tigay, *JBL* 94:330–31 and literature cited in nn. 9–11 there; "Stylistic Criteria"; and "Some Aspects," pp. 374–78.

nian Period. This argument is based on a comparison of the old Babylonian fragments with the Sumerian narratives and the late version, showing that the elements which unify the Akkadian epic are present in the Old Babylonian fragments. The subsequent development of the Akkadian epic, from the Old Babylonian version through the late version, is traced in Chapters 3 through 6. For this purpose I have found it best, when specific passages are being compared, to lay out the texts of the versions in parallel columns, as in the Appendix. By reading horizontally, one can easily spot how the text was or was not changed from one version to another, while reading each column vertically enables one to see how each reading fits into the context of its own version. Once the similarities and differences between versions have been highlighted in this way, we can try to identify characteristic phenomena in each version, to assess how each version relates to those earlier and later than itself, and to determine how each was produced. We can also pose, and hopefully sometimes answer, the more elusive question of what caused the changes from one version to the next. The causes seem to include such diverse phenomena as historical, religious, and linguistic developments in Mesopotamia and other regions where texts of the epic were inscribed, changing canons of literary style, textual corruption and confusion, as well as the literary taste of the original author and subsequent editors of the Akkadian epic and their own sense of the significance of Gilgamesh's story as presented by tradition.

Once we have traced the evolution of the epic from Sumerian narratives through all the versions of the Akkadian epic currently available, we turn to a different type of evolutionary question. Not everything in the epic goes back to sources which were originally connected with Gilgamesh. Some elements are borrowed from literary or even nonliterary sources which originally had nothing to do with Gilgamesh. Only rarely, as in the case of the flood story, is the relationship between the source and the derivative in Gilgamesh so detailed as to bear close textual comparison (see chap. 12). There is no way of knowing in advance that the source of any particular element can be found outside of literature about Gilgamesh. If an element is lacking in presently available Sumerian literature about Gilgamesh, one may, if he suspects an external source, search through whatever other cuneiform or ancient Near Eastern literature is presently available, or may even search farther afield, in the hope of discovering parallels which might be sources. As often as not, however, the discovery of parallels is not based on a methodical search, but on a scholar's happening to spot similarities between texts he is familiar with. The real methodological problem is in deciding whether a parallel might be, or point to, a source, and in deciding which of two parallel texts is the source and which is derivative. Apart from the flood story, in most cases I have not found it possible to identify a particular text as the source of an element in *The Gilgamesh Epic;* the kind of exclusive detailed similarities that might permit such an identification are not present. At best I can point to a circle of traditions about a particular subject or to a type of situation in life from which an element may be drawn. Studies of this type are the basis of Chapters 7 through 11. These studies differ from those of earlier generations in two ways. First, their basis is more empirical, in that enough cuneiform literature is now known so that we can often document the existence of specific types of compositions and circles of traditions, and we do not have to simply hypothesize about their existence in ancient Mesopotamia. Second, I do not think that the study of external sources is finished once a possible type of source has been identified. The more important question, admittedly not always answerable, is why a source was drawn upon, how it was used in the epic, and what it contributed to the epic.[82] This brings us once again to the mind of the author and subsequent editors of the epic.

Both main lines of research thus lead back to the mind of the writers. Ultimately this must have been the decisive factor in the shaping of the epic, but it is the most elusive factor of all. We cannot really "explain" why these writers presented the epic as they did. At most we can try to describe some of the raw materials each had to work with and some of the possibly relevant conditions of the world in which they worked, and we can describe what appear to be the literary effects of changes they introduced. But why they chose to use these materials and respond to these conditions precisely as they did, and whether they really intended the effects we sense, are questions upon which we can only speculate.

82. Cf. Jacobsen, *Treasures,* pp. 208–9.

# 1

# *The Sumerian Sources of the Akkadian Epic*

## THE KNOWN SUMERIAN SOURCES

The discovery of Sumerian tales related to *The Gilgamesh Epic* was ultimately to open a new chapter in its study. By 1920, as we have seen, Jastrow realized that the Sumerian *Deluge,* like the earlier-discovered fragments of the Akkadian *Atrahasis Epic,* confirmed that the flood story was originally independent of *Gilgamesh.*[1] But the full implications of the Sumerian compositions were slow to be realized. In 1932, Langdon simply took it for granted that, like the Akkadian epic, the Sumerian texts also constituted a single epic with the episodes in a fixed order.[2] It remained for Kramer, in 1944, to argue that the Sumerian compositions were in fact separate tales.[3] Kramer surveyed all of the Sumerian texts known to him at the time which were about Gilgamesh or corresponded to parts of the epic. These comprised six compositions: *Gilgamesh and the Land of the Living; Gilgamesh and the Bull of Heaven; The Deluge; The Death of Gilgamesh; Gilgamesh and Agga;* and *Gil-*

1. YOR 4(3):50–51.
2. *JRAS* 1932:912; cf. *SRT,* p. 35, cited by Shaffer, "Sources," p. 4. For more recent advocacy of a Sumerian Gilgamesh epic, see Bing, *JANES* 7:1–10, and the literature cited by him on p. 2, n. 7.
3. *JAOS* 64:7–23, 83.

*gamesh, Enkidu, and the Netherworld.*[4] Since then, two further Sumerian texts about Gilgamesh have become known, one a hymn of Shulgi, king of Ur (2094–2047 B.C.E.), which contains two short hymns addressed by Shulgi to Gilgamesh, and the other a narrative about Gilgamesh which has not yet been edited.[5] The known copies of all these texts are from the Old Babylonian Period (2000–1600), but are presumed to be based on originals of the Ur III Period (twenty-first century).[6]

In comparing the plots of the first two tales with their later Akkadian counterparts in the epic, the episodes concerning the journey to the Cedar Mountain and the Bull of Heaven (*GE* III–VI), Kramer concluded that the Sumerian compositions were undoubtedly sources of the Akkadian epic, but that the similarities were limited to the broad outlines of the plot, with details varying so widely that the basic relationship is at times difficult to recognize. For example, the fifty Urukites who set out with Gilgamesh and Enkidu in the Sumerian version of the journey to the Cedar Mountain *(Gilgamesh and the Land of the Living)* are absent in the epic, while the council of elders with whom Gilgamesh debated about the journey in the epic is not mentioned in the Sumerian tale.[7] In *Gilgamesh and the Bull of Heaven,* according to Kramer, the gifts offered Gilgamesh by the goddess Inanna (the Sumerian counterpart of Ishtar) are quite different from those that Ishtar offers in the epic; scholars have since come to doubt that Inanna proposed to Gilgamesh at all in the Sumerian tale.[8] In order to induce the sky-god An (the Sumerian form of Anu) to place the Bull of Heaven at her disposal, Inanna does not threaten to bring the dead up from

4. For publication data on each of these texts, see the list of abbreviations for ancient texts in this volume, pp. 304–7 under "Sumerian Gilgamesh Texts," for *GLL, GBH, DG, GA,* and *GEN,* and under "Other Ancient Texts" for *The Deluge.*

5. The hymn is edited by Klein, in *Kramer AV,* pp. 271–92 (Klein's translation of the hymns to Gilgamesh is quoted below at the end of chap. 7). The narrative is published in Gadd and Kramer, no. 60.

6. See Introduction, n. 40.

7. Kramer, *JAOS* 64:14–15. Böhl notes that the consultation with the elders does have a counterpart in *GA,* where Gilgamesh consults with the elders and men of Uruk (MVEOL 7:170; cf. Shaffer, "Sources," p. 6, n. 1). However, this does not necessarily imply literary dependence of the Akkadian epic on *GA* for this theme.

8. Falkenstein, *RLA* 3:361. According to Falkenstein, the only agreements between *GBH* and *GE* VI are in the goddess's sending the bull in anger at Gilgamesh and in Gilgamesh and Enkidu's killing the bull.

the netherworld, as she does in the epic; she threatens simply to cry out, and when she does, her cry reaches heaven and earth, and An becomes frightened.[9] While the third Sumerian composition, *The Deluge,* corresponds to the report of the flood heard by Gilgamesh in Tablet XI, Kramer noted that the story had, just as Jastrow believed, no original connection with traditions or literature about Gilgamesh. It was, instead, part of a separate narrative beginning with creation and continuing through the flood to the immortalization of the hero.[10] It has since become clear that this Sumerian composition is actually a counterpart of the Akkadian *Atrahasis Epic,*[11] and that the flood narrative came to *Gilgamesh* through *The Atrahasis Epic,* rather than directly from *The Deluge.*[12] In the version in Tablet XI, the material on creation is omitted, and the third-person style of the Sumerian tale and *The Atrahasis Epic* is replaced by first-person narrative, so that the flood-hero himself is the narrator, as required by the plot of *Gilgamesh.*[13] The fragmentary remains of the fourth Sumerian composition, *The Death of Gilgamesh,* include a statement made to Gilgamesh by an unknown speaker saying that kingship, heroism, and the like had been granted to Gilgamesh, but not eternal life; the text then describes Gilgamesh's death. Kramer concluded that while the Akkadian epic says nothing of Gilgamesh's death, *The Death of Gilgamesh* displayed "an indisputable source relationship to portions of [*GE* IX–XI] which contain Gilgamesh's plea for eternal life, and the

9. Kramer thought that Inanna threatened to call upon the gods (*JAOS* 64:15), but according to Prof. Jacobsen, the correct reading of the passage in question is mà-⌜e gù⌝ ba-an-dé an-ki-bé ⌜im⌝-⌜da⌝-⌜te⌝/ní [b]a-d[a]-te ní ba-da-te (VAS 10, no. 196, ii edge; variant CBS 1039, 4′–5′:[mà-e gù] ba-dé-en an-ki-šè a-ba-da-te / [ní ba]-da-an-te ní ba-da-an-te), "I shall cry out! It (i.e., the cry) drew near unto both heaven and earth (var. after it had managed to draw near to heaven and earth), he became afraid of her, he became afraid of her." (Private communication)

10. Named Ziusudra ("life of long days") in the Sumerian text, Atrahasis ("exceedingly wise") in the epic of that name (and once in *Gilgamesh, GE* XI, 187), and Utnapishtim (generally understood as "he found life"; see pp. 229–30) in *Gilgamesh.* Berossus reproduced the Sumerian name as Xisuthros (Lambert and Millard, pp. 135–36).

11. Laessøe, *Bi. Or.* 13:90–102; cf. Lambert and Millard, p. 14, and the remarks of Civil, ibid., p. 139, and especially p. 171 on line 202, where Civil implies that the Sumerian is based on an Akkadian version, rather than vice versa.

12. See below, chap. 12.

13. See below, chap. 12. For further differences between the Sumerian and Akkadian accounts, see Kramer, *JAOS* 64:15–16.

rejoinder that it is death, not immortality which is man's fate."[14] However, apart from this rejoinder, little else in the Sumerian tale corresponds to anything in the Akkadian epic; the preserved portions of the tale do not contain an explicit plea or search for immortality. If these themes in the Akkadian epic owe something to *The Death of Gilgamesh,* they may have been derived from it only by the Akkadian author's inferring from the rejoinder that Gilgamesh had wished for immortality.[15] The fifth Sumerian composition, *Gilgamesh and Agga,* deals with a conflict between Gilgamesh and the king of the city-state Kish. As Kramer noted, this poem has no counterpart in the epic.[16] Finally, Kramer noted that the sixth Sumerian composition, *Gilgamesh, Enkidu, and the Netherworld,* was the forerunner of Tablet XII, but with these differences: Tablet XII begins only in the middle of the original story, the first half being omitted, except for one incident which survived elsewhere in the epic[17]; and Tablet XII was a literal translation of the Sumerian text, rather than a creative adaptation like other parts of the epic.[18] Knowledge of this composition in its entirety, with its

14. *JAOS* 64:16–17; similarly, Matouš speaks of "la recherche de l'immortalité" in *DG* A (*GSL,* pp. 88, 90). Because he originally believed that Gilgamesh was seeking immortality in *GLL* (see *JAOS* 64:13–14; contrast *JCS* 1:4, n. 2), Kramer believed that *DG* might be the sequel to *GLL* (*JAOS* 64:16, n. 62; *BASOR* 94:3, n. 4; *ANET,* p. 50, n. 1; cf. Matouš in *GSL,* pp. 85–87). The publication of the end of *GLL* showed subsequently that neither *DG* nor any other composition is part of *GLL* (van Dijk, in *GSL,* pp. 69–81; cf. Matouš's acknowledgment, *GSL,* p. 87, n. 2).

15. In Jacobsen's view, there is no known Sumerian prototype for the "Quest for Life" episode (*Treasures,* p. 214).

16. *JAOS* 64:17–18; compare, though, n. 7, above. Kramer supposed *GA* to have been omitted from the Akkadian epic in part because its characters were exclusively human (*HBS,* p. 192). Whether Gilgamesh or Agga prevailed in the encounter described in *GA* is debated (Kramer, *JAOS* 64:17–18; *AJA* 53:15–16; Jacobsen, *ZA* 52:116–18, n. 55; *Treasures,* p. 213), but Gilgamesh's ultimate recognition of Agga's authority was hardly a heroic outcome. Since the epic stressed the futility of even heroic achievements in overcoming death, there was no point in including a less than heroic episode. Another theme from the Sumerian tales omitted by the epic is, as we have noted, Gilgamesh's death (an omission regarded by Ranke, p. 49, n. 3, as one of the epic's finest features). This omission forces Gilgamesh to live with what he has learned, an apt conclusion for a text whose prologue gives that learning so prominent a place (though the prologue was added later; see chaps. 2 and 7). The epic's complete silence on Gilgamesh's role as king of the netherworld, of which the author must have been aware, may reflect similar purposes, for its inclusion would have deprived Gilgamesh's resignation of its poignancy.

17. *JAOS* 64:20, 22; see below, chap. 9. For another possible parallel between *GEN* and the epic, see n. 26.

18. *JAOS* 64:23, n. 118. Some modifications appearing in the Akkadian translation are noted below, pp. 106–7.

contradictions of the epic (Gilgamesh is friendly to Inanna/Ishtar; though Enkidu died in Tablet VII of the epic, he is alive at the beginning of Tablet XII; Enkidu is usually termed Gilgamesh's servant, rather than friend) supported Jastrow's view that Tablet XII was an inorganic appendage to the eleven tablets which constituted the original form of the late version.[19] Shulgi's hymns to Gilgamesh, published since Kramer's study, mention Gilgamesh's victory over another king of Kish, Agga's father Enmebaragesi, and the Cedar Mountain episode. Generically these hymns are similar to the hymn to Gilgamesh which appears at the beginning of the Old Babylonian version of the epic and is part of the introduction to the late version. However, Shulgi's hymns share with that in the epic only a few vaguely similar epithets and allusions and show no special relationship with any part of the epic.

On the basis of the Sumerian tales, Kramer was able to answer three questions: 1) Was there a Sumerian original of the Akkadian *Gilgamesh* as a whole? 2) Can we identify those episodes in the Akkadian epic which go back to known Sumerian prototypes? 3) Are portions of the Akkadian epic for which no Sumerian prototypes are yet available of later, Babylonian origin, or do they, too, go back to Sumerian sources? Kramer answered the first question by saying that the Akkadian epic drew upon several of the Sumerian tales, but that the varying lengths of the Sumerian tales and their character as "individual, disconnected episodes" showed them to be independent narratives which were not parts of a single epic. He concluded that the integration of these tales into a unified whole, with an unfolding plot linking the episodes, was first achieved in the Akkadian epic. These arguments were not in themselves decisive, for differences in length are not a proof of separateness, and the statement that the episodes were disconnected still required substantiation. The necessary evidence was adduced in a subsequent study by Matouš.[20] Matouš noted that *Gilgamesh, Enkidu, and the Netherworld* and *The Deluge* begin with mythological introductions, a feature which typically appears at the

19. Cf. below, pp. 105, 138. On the other hand, some scholars take *GE* XII seriously, at least to the extent of seeking to understand its role in the edition at whose end it appears. See Jastrow and Clay, pp. 12, 51; Oppenheim, *Or.* 17:20; Dossin, "Enkidou," pp. 587–88; Sasson, *Studies in Philology* 69:275; Komoróczy, *Act. Ant.* 23:54–60.

20. *GSL,* pp. 87–88.

beginning of a composition,[21] and that *Gilgamesh and the Land of the Living, Gilgamesh and Agga,* and *Gilgamesh, Enkidu, and the Netherworld* were listed by their opening phrases (functioning as titles) as separate entries in Sumerian literary catalogues.[22] These facts showed that none of these episodes was preceded by another.[23] That the latter three compositions, and fragment B of *The Death of Gilgamesh,* were not followed by any other episode is shown by the doxological formula "Oh DN, (your) praise (is good)" (DN zà-mí(-zu du$_{10}$-ga-àm)) with which they end, since this formula typically appears at the end of a composition.[24]

In considering the second and third questions, Kramer showed how episodes of the Akkadian epic were based on some of the Sumerian tales and stressed that these episodes were not incorporated into the later epic as simple reproductions of their sources, but rather as creative adaptations sharing only broad outlines of plot with the originals, only the bare nucleus of which remains recognizable. Kramer suggested that some episodes in the epic for which no Sumerian prototypes had been discovered might well go back to various Sumerian motifs not necessarily connected with Gilgamesh. Other elements of the Akkadian epic seemed to be original with it, the most important being the chain of events culminating in the friendship of Gilgamesh and Enkidu. Since this plot sequence is intended to motivate the friendship, which is absent in the Sumerian tales (where Enkidu is Gilgamesh's servant, not his friend), Kramer argued that this chain of events is not likely to have existed in Sumerian Gilgamesh texts, even if some of its individual elements may go back to Sumerian literature (as we shall see below, in chaps. 9–11). In addition, noting that the Akkadian epic's version of Enkidu's death differs completely from that related in *Gilgamesh, Enkidu, and the Netherworld,* Kramer concluded that the Akkadian version of Enkidu's death was created for the epic in order to provide dramatic motivation for Gilgamesh's quest for immortality.

In sum, Kramer argued convincingly (with support from

21. See Castellino, SVT 4:117–18, for a list of texts, and cf. the comment of Speiser, *Genesis,* p. LVII.

22. Catalogues P, L, and B. See Kramer, *BASOR* 88:10–19; UET 5:86 (Bernhardt and Kramer, *WZJ* 6:393, n. 4); Gadd and Kramer, p. 123 (Kramer, *RA* 55:169–76).

23. This type of argument is challenged by Wilcke, *Lugalbandaepos,* p. 8.

24. *GLL* 191–92 (*GSL,* p. 71, ll. 119–20); *DG* B 42; *GA* 114–15; *GEN* 303; the same is true of Gadd and Kramer, no. 60, l. 17.

Matouš) that the raw material of the Akkadian epic was taken over from Sumerian sources, but that the elements which give the Akkadian epic its distinctive character and significance were the achievement of the author of the Akkadian epic.

In a subsequent study of Enkidu in the epic, Dossin observed that the "unity [of the epic] is assured for it as much, if not more, by the role given to Enkidu as by that of Gilgamesh."[25] Indeed, it seems that converting Enkidu into Gilgamesh's friend was the seminal change by which the Akkadian author lent unity to the materials which he used in the epic. The epic is not a study of friendship per se. The motif of friendship serves as a device whereby Enkidu's death can be made to shock Gilgamesh into an obsessive quest for immortality, an effect which would probably have been less plausible had Enkidu been only a servant. In the Sumerian tales, where Enkidu was Gilgamesh's servant[26] (though once or twice affectionately termed his friend, Sum. k u - l i [27]), Gilgamesh's response to death was not as strong. In *Gilgamesh and the Land of the Living,* the sight of people dying upset Gilgamesh and prompted his journey to the Cedar Mountain to establish his and the gods' names (possibly by erecting inscriptions which might keep his name alive).[28] In *Gilgamesh, Enkidu, and the Netherworld,* Gilgamesh grieved over Enkidu's capture by the netherworld; he had truly cared for Enkidu, servant though he was,[29] and he tried to recover him. But in neither case was Gilgamesh's emotional response one of distraction, as it is in the epic, and it did not issue in an attempt to escape death himself. To enable Enkidu's death to turn Gilgamesh from

25. "Cette unité lui est assureé autant, sinon davantage, par le rôle prête à Enkidou que par celui de Gilgameš" ("Enkidou," p. 588; cf. Shaffer, "Sources," pp. 21–25; Kramer, *JAOS* 64:18–19). Note that the origin and death of Enkidu and Gilgamesh's adventures with him are described not only in their proper places, but also in retrospective speeches later in the epic (*GE* VII–VIII, X).

26. E.g., *GLL* 3, 8–9, 95–96, 103, 153; *GBH* rev. "II," 17; *GEN* 177–78, 206, 241; *GA* 42. For š u b u r as "servant," see *CAD* $A_2$, p. 243d lex. and the variants š u b u r and ì r in *GA* 42, cited by Wilcke, *Lugalbandaepos,* p. 44, l. 116. Note, however, the similarity of *GEN* 250 (= *GE* XII, 93, 95) to Gilg. P. i, 20, 32–34.

27. *GBH:* VAS 10:196, rev. "II," 11; *GEN* 247 (237 in Wilcke's citation of the passage, *ZA* 59:71; Wilcke's restoration of k u - l i in the previous line seems ruled out in Shaffer's edition, p. 86). Jastrow's references to Enkidu as Gilgamesh's brother in Sumerian texts are erroneous (YOR 4(3):33): The first involves Ishtar, not Enkidu, and in the second the sign is l u g a l, not š e š.

28. See Kraus, *JNES* 19:127–32. According to variants in lines 7 and 33, Gilgamesh wants to establish his own name and that of his god, i.e., his personal god. On the concept of the personal god, see Jacobsen, *Treasures,* pp. 155–60.

29. Cf. Shaffer, "Sources," pp. 22–23.

the pursuit of lasting fame to a literal quest for immortality, the Akkadian author seized upon the sporadic hints of friendship in the Sumerian tales and applied them across the board, consistently terming Enkidu Gilgamesh's friend (Akk. *ibru, tappu*), brother *(aḫu),* and equal *(mašil, kīma),*[30] whom he loves and is to caress.[31] Enkidu's new status as Gilgamesh's friend and equal created a need to account for Enkidu's origins, which led to the account of Gilgamesh's high-handedness in Uruk and the story of Enkidu's creation and early life, based partly on other Sumerian literary motifs. As we shall argue in Chapter 11, the description of Enkidu's early life, in turn, was used by the author to highlight the benefits life offers short of immortality. Thus the literary changes which give the Akkadian epic its distinctive features were set in motion by the author's raising the status of Enkidu from servant to friend.

## THE POSSIBILITY OF UNKNOWN FORMS OF THE SUMERIAN SOURCES

As Kramer noted, it is theoretically conceivable that some of the developments underlying the Akkadian epic appeared in Sumerian forerunners which differed from those known to us.[32] We do know that in the Old Babylonian Period, when the Akkadian epic was probably created (see chap. 2), a number of Sumerian compositions existed in more than one recension or version.[33] For example, several versions or recensions of *Gilgamesh and the Land of the Living*[34] (two of which are listed simultaneously in some Sumerian literary catalogues)[35] and two of *Gilgamesh, Enkidu, and the Ne-*

30. For "friend," see *GE* I, iv, 41; vi, 1, 21; II, vi, 3, 6, 9; etc. For "brother," see *GE* VI, 156 (also XII, 81, 87; contrast 54).

31. *GE* I, v, 36, 47; vi, 4, 14, 19; X, ii, 3, 12; iii, 20–21; v, 21 (see *GETh.*, pl. 42, for v, 21, on which restorations earlier in X are based). On "caress," see Appendix, no. 5, note to Gilg. P. i, 34.

32. This possibility was considered and ruled out by Kramer, *JAOS* 64:16, n. 20.

33. See Falkenstein, *JNES* 19:65, 70–71; "Sumerische und akkadische Mythos," pp. 96–110; Hallo, *JCS* 20:92–93 (a royal hymn); CRRAI 17:123–33 (a divine hymn). For historiographic texts, note the differences in texts of *SKL:* Finkelstein, *JCS* 17:39–51; Hallo, *JCS* 17:52–57; Kraus, *ZA* 50:31–33); and the *Tummal Inscription* (Sollberger, *JCS* 16:40–41). For Gilgamesh texts, see the next note.

34. Kramer, *JCS* 1:7; *GSL,* p. 64; van Dijk, in *GSL,* pp. 69–81; Matouš, in *GSL,* p. 91; Falkenstein, *JNES* 19:65–66; see also *HKL* 2:143; M. Ellis, "Gilgamesh' Approach." Excerpts of these are compared by Falkenstein and by Limet, pp. 8–9.

35. Kramer, *BASOR* 88:15 (catalogue P, ll. 10, 14), 17–18 (catalogue L, ll. 10, 39); *RA* 55:173, ll. 9–10; Bernhardt and Kramer, *WZJ* 6:394, n. 4 (catalogue B, ll. 14, 16).

*therworld*[36] were still in existence. The differences between these versions or recensions make it plausible that some of the details in the Akkadian epic that differ from the known Sumerian sources derive from a Sumerian textual prototype *(Vorlage)* different from those hitherto known. For example, in two versions of *Gilgamesh and the Land of the Living* (A and B), Gilgamesh and Enkidu debate releasing Huwawa,[37] after they have captured him, in terms which differ almost completely[38]:

| *GLL* A, 153–61 | *GLL* B, rev., iv, 2–22 |
|---|---|
| (Gilgamesh) says to his servant Enkidu: | (Gilgamesh) says to his servant, to E[nkidu]: |
| "Enkidu, let the caught bird go to its place, | "Come, let us set free the warrior, let him be our informant |
| Let the caught young man return to the lap of his mother." | Against highwaymen who will see us, let him be our informant. |
| Enkidu answers Gilgamesh: | His servant Enkidu answers: |
| "The tallest, who has not judgment, | |
| Namtar will devour, Namtar will not regard. | |
| (If) the caught bird goes to its place, | "A captured warrior set free, a captured en-priest returned to the gipar (priestly residence), |

36. Both texts are edited in Shaffer, "Sources"; cf. Gadd and Kramer's remarks in the introduction to nos. 58–59.

37. The Sumerian and OB form of Humbaba's name.

38. For texts and notes, see the Appendix, no. 1. The same passage in the Kish MS (Kramer's "F") basically agrees with *GLL* A, but Endiku's response includes an additional 6-line passage praising Gilgamesh (see Kramer, *JCS* 1:44, n. 251). Of these lines, 5 also appear in Huwawa's exchange with Gilgamesh in *GLL* A (Shaffer's reconstruction, ll. 127–31), 4 at the beginning of *GLL* B, and 3 in *GBH* (Kramer, *JCS* 1:45, n. 251). In TLB 2, no. 4 (van Dijk, in *GSL,* p. 71), ll. 85–91, Gilgamesh's proposal to release Huwawa agrees with the phrasing of his proposal in *GLL* A, ll. 154–55, while Enkidu's reply agrees with the phrasing of his reply in *GLL* B (TLB 2, no. 4, l. 87, is a variant of *GLL* A 161 = *GLL* B rev. iv, 21). (Since literary catalogues show both versions A and B to have been present simultaneously in certain collections, it is plausible that the part of this dialogue in TLB 2, no. 4 represents an intentional compromise version.) As a result, the themes expressed in *GLL* A, 157–58, are not present in this version. The omission of a transitional "Enkidu said to Gilgamesh" in TLB 2, no. 4, between lines 86 and 87 is a common phenomenon (see chap. 6, n. 30). Coincidentally, the late version of *GE* also conflates —in a different way—two replies by Enkidu, both of which are present separately in the OB version. See Appendix, no. 8.

| | |
|---|---|
| (If) the captured young man returns to the lap of his mother, | A captured gudu-priest returned to (his priestly) headdress—since ancient times, who has ever seen (such a thing)? |
| | The mountain road he will *confuse* for you, |
| | The mountain path he will confound for you, |
| You will not return to the city (uru) of the mother who gave birth to you." | (And) we will [not] return to the [city] of the mother who gave birth to you." |

There are also structural differences between the versions of this poem. For example, in version A, Gilgamesh's opening statement to Enkidu (4–7) includes only a brief statement of his motivation in proposing to journey to the Cedar Mountain to establish his own and the gods' names (possibly by erecting inscribed monuments), while the occasion for his proposal and the reasoning behind it are expressed only in his subsequent prayer to Shamash (23–33). But in version B, the occasion and reasoning appear at the beginning of the proposal to Enkidu.[39]

Given these differences between versions of the same Sumerian tale, it is plausible that differences between a given Sumerian tale and the epic are due to the fact that the episode in the epic had a different (unknown) Sumerian textual prototype. For example, the description of Huwawa in version A of *Gilgamesh and the Land of the Living* differs from the description of him in the Akkadian epic (Old Babylonian version) as follows[40]:

| ***GLL* A 99–102** | **Gilg. Y. iii, 18–20** |
|---|---|
| The warrior, his teeth are the teeth of a dragon, | |
| His face is the face of a lion, | |
| His breastbone is the onrushing floodwater. | Huwawa, his roaring is the floodstorm, |

39. *GLL* B 5ff. (partly cited in Kramer, *JCS* 1:31, n. 205).

40. For the text of *GLL* A 99–102, see Kramer, *JCS* 1:16–17. For "breastbone," in line 101, see $^{uzu}$giš-gaba = *šitiq irti,* cited by Kramer, *JCS* 1:40, n. 233; *AHw,* p. 1251d (*CAD* I–J, p. 183d: uzu.PA.gaba). Line 102 reads sag-ki-ni giš-gi-izi-kú-a lú nu-mu-un-te-gá-dam. For the text of Gilg. Y. iii, 18–20, see Appendix, no. 8.

| | |
|---|---|
| His forehead is a reed thicket consumed by fire, which none can approach. | His mouth is fire, |
| | His breath is death. |

In fact, version B, at this point, does have an additional line not present in version A, although it is no closer to the Akkadian text.[41]

However, details such as these seem a matter of indifference in the creation of the unified Akkadian epic. One might concede that they favor the existence of a different textual prototype behind certain details of the Akkadian text, but this need not imply that its variants included the kind of changes by which the Akkadian epic, with its distinctive unifying themes, was created. What is decisive is that none of the variant Sumerian texts shows the latter changes —Enkidu as Gilgamesh's equal and brother, the quest for literal immortality, and the like—nor any other large differences in theme. Even a structural difference, such as that between versions A and B of *Gilgamesh and the Land of the Living* described above, is not the kind of major difference in theme and structure, reflecting a unified artistic purpose, which characterizes the Akkadian epic.

An example of the latter type of difference is the position of Gilgamesh's proposal to take on Huwawa, and Enkidu's warnings against this, in *Gilgamesh and the Land of the Living* and in the Akkadian epic. In the Sumerian tale, the proposal and warnings appear late in the plot, after the two heroes have reached the Cedar Mountain. They have no place in Gilgamesh's original plan of traveling to the Cedar Mountain and establishing his and the gods' names, to which Enkidu raises no objection, and are in fact unrelated to his original plan (which disappears from sight after the introduction). But in the epic, Gilgamesh's proposal to battle Huwawa, and Enkidu's warnings, appear from the beginning, presenting an opportunity to stress repeatedly Gilgamesh's motive of seeking to establish a reputation which will survive beyond his death and to magnify his achievement by having him resist several attempts at dissuasion.[42]

41. *GLL* B, ed. Shaffer, l. 85: gù?-da-ni ur-maḫ máš-kú-a-gin$_x$/ BAD nu-ub-ra-ge-dam, "his . . . like a lion devouring a kid,/ . . ."

42. Note how the OB version appends to Enkidu's description of Huwawa (and the elders' identical description) the question "Why have you come to desire to do

In sum, the variant versions or recensions of this Sumerian tale lend color to the possibility that different Sumerian textual prototypes underlie certain details of the Akkadian text, but offer no support to the possibility that the essential changes by which the integrated epic was created were found in such prototypes.

## THE HISTORICAL BACKGROUND OF THE SUMERIAN TALES

A gap of several centuries separates the Sumerian tales about Gilgamesh (presumed to have been written in the twenty-first century) from his lifetime (between 2700 and 2500). By the time of the Sumerian texts, Gilgamesh had already assumed mythic proportions, and there is little direct empirical evidence to help us isolate a historical kernel in the narratives. To bridge this gap we are thrown back on conjecture, though some conjectures can invoke more historical evidence than others.

By applying to the historical Gilgamesh what has been learned about early Mesopotamian political development, Jacobsen has suggested that the themes of the Sumerian tales go back to the magical and martial roles that the historical Gilgamesh would have played as ruler of Uruk: *The Death of Gilgamesh* and *Gilgamesh, Enkidu, and the Netherworld* arose from his role as priest-king embodying the dying fertility-god Dumuzi-Amaushumgalanna, while *Gilgamesh and the Land of the Living, Gilgamesh and the Bull of Heaven,* and *Gilgamesh and Agga* arose from his role as military leader.[43]

Others have conjectured that aspects of the Sumerian tales are not rooted in events of Gilgamesh's lifetime but project later events back onto him. For example, the tradition about Gilgamesh's expedition to the Cedar Mountain *(Gilgamesh and the Land of the Living)* has been thought to reflect the expeditions of later kings, Sargon of Akkad (2334–2279) or the rulers of Ur III.[44]

this thing?" (Gilg. Y. iii, 21–22; v, 18; cf. i, 13–14). Cf. the observation of Oppenheim, *Or.* 17:30–31.

43. Jacobsen, *Treasures,* pp. 209–11. Jacobsen also notes that some themes based on these roles are preserved only in nonliterary traditions.

44. Falkenstein, CRRAI 2:18; Matouš, in *GSL,* p. 93; *Bi. Or.* 21:5; Malamat, in *Landsberger AV,* p. 373, n. 42.

Although the mountain is located near Lebanon in the Akkadian versions, a considerable body of evidence has led scholars to suppose that the Sumerian versions located it in the Zagros range, thus implying a geographical modification of the episode in the course of its transmission (see pp. 76–78). Wilcke has recently suggested that Gilgamesh's quarrel with Inanna and the defeat of the Bull of Heaven in *Gilgamesh and the Bull of Heaven* reflect the Sumerian struggle for freedom from Akkadian domination in the Akkadian Period.[45]

Other suggestions arise from noticing certain constants in the literature about Gilgamesh. For example, *Gilgamesh and the Land of the Living* mentions Gilgamesh's concern about death, while in *The Death of Gilgamesh* he is consoled over not being granted immortality, and *Gilgamesh, Enkidu, and the Netherworld* reflects his interest in the condition of the dead. The persistence of his preoccupation with death in these compositions and in the later Akkadian epic, coupled with evidence that he was regarded early as a god, has led Lambert to theorize that if it could be accepted that Gilgamesh's position as ruler of the netherworld "was from the beginning considered a compensation for missing eternal life, then the tradition of his fear of death would be almost proved."[46]

There is much that is plausible in these suggestions, and some of them may ultimately be confirmed as the discovery and decipherment of third-millennium texts progresses. But given the paucity of direct evidence currently available from Gilgamesh's own lifetime, it may be a long time, if ever, before we will be in a position to know which details in the literary texts truly reflect the historical Gilgamesh.

## THE FUNCTION OF THE SUMERIAN TALES

While much has been written about the new meaning imparted to the tales about Gilgamesh in the Akkadian epic, little attention has been given to the meaning or function of these tales in their original Sumerian form. Like the Akkadian epic, the Sumerian sources do

45. "Politische Opposition," pp. 57–59; contrast Lambert, "Forschungsstand," p. 72, n. 4.

46. Lambert, in *GSL*, p. 51.

reflect attitudes toward death,[47] but they seem to be more interested in Gilgamesh as a person than in any message based on his life. One may hazard a guess that the function of the Sumerian compositions is indicated by their concluding hymnic doxologies.[48] While such endings appear in several genres of Sumerian literature which, by our definitions, are not hymns, and while it is true that the Gilgamesh texts are running narratives, rather than strings of epithets as in many Sumerian hymns, it is nonetheless possible that the Gilgamesh texts were recited as hymns in the cult of Gilgamesh in the Ur III Period (see pp. 13–14). Royal hymns often contain a good deal of narrative content, and they "add up to a kind of hymnic biography of the monarch."[49] It is plausible that just as hymns were recited in honor of reigning Sumerian kings in the Ur III Period, some long-dead kings were honored in a similar way, and that the epic "hymns" about Gilgamesh were the liturgy for just such occasions. The similarity in content and, possibly, structure between *The Death of Gilgamesh* and *The Death of Ur-Nammu* noted by Wilcke seems to imply just such a parallelism between the cults of contemporary and ancient kings.[50] The ceremonies in honor of Gilgamesh in the month of Ab reflected in *The Death of Gilgamesh* (see below, pp. 186–87) may have been one possible occasion for reciting the texts about the hero. It has been suggested that Shulgi's hymns to Gilgamesh may have been recited on the occasion of the introduction of a statue of Gilgamesh into the temple complex of Ur or during a visit by Shulgi to such a statue.[51] Given the absence of liturgical notations in the narrative texts about Gilgamesh, they were perhaps recited in royal palaces, rather than temples,[52] just as has elsewhere been presumed for royal hymns ending with hymnic doxologies but lacking liturgical notations.[53] Whether this was the function of the Sumerian Gilgamesh texts or not, the point to keep in mind is that they must have had both a meaning and a function

47. Jacobsen, *Treasures,* pp. 213, 215.

48. See n. 24. On such doxologies and the distinction between hymnic and scribal doxologies, see Wilcke, in *Jacobsen AV,* pp. 246–48.

49. See Hallo, CRRAI 17:118. For an example of narrative in a royal hymn, see *ANET,* pp. 584–86.

50. Wilcke, CRRAI 17:82, 84.

51. Jacobsen, *BASOR* 102:15–16; Klein, in *Kramer AV,* p. 272.

52. Kramer, "Sumerian Literature, a General Survey," p. 342, n. 6; cf. *JCS* 1:6, n. 3d.

53. See Hallo, CRRAI 17:117 and *Bi. Or.* 23:241.

of their own, and that these were not necessarily identical to those of the integrated Akkadian epic.

## THE THEORETICAL APPROACH IN THE LIGHT OF THE EMPIRICAL EVIDENCE

The empirical evidence of the Sumerian tales lends support to the concept that *The Gilgamesh Epic* is based on several independent sources, a concept which Jastrow developed on the basis of his theoretical approach. In fact, the sources of the epic appear to be even more numerous than Jastrow had imagined. The Sumerian tales confirmed that two of the elements in the late version that Jastrow held to be originally unrelated to the epic were indeed independent. *The Deluge,* like *Atrahasis,* was an independent account of the flood, as Jastrow himself later realized; both compositions were, in their complete forms, histories of mankind from the creation down through the flood and its immediate aftermath. The full Sumerian version of the story, which appears in Tablet XII of *Gilgamesh*, also proved to be an independent composition, though still involving Gilgamesh. What is more, other episodes which Jastrow had not thought to separate from each other—the Cedar Mountain and Bull of Heaven episodes—now also turned out to have once circulated separately. Kramer could only speculate on the ultimate origin of the chain of events culminating in Gilgamesh's and Enkidu's friendship, which largely overlaps Jastrow's putative story of Enkidu, the harlot, and the hunter, but we shall offer evidence below that parts of this chain are indeed based on traditions about the first men, as Jastrow suggested (see chaps. 10–11). For some of Jastrow's suggestions (such as a story about Gilgamesh's wanderings or an Enkidu epic) no further evidence has surfaced.[54] Neither, however, has any of his basic suggestions been disproved.

54. Apart from the empirical evidence of cuneiform texts, the original independence of some motifs is suggested by their appearance as folklore motifs outside of Mesopotamia. For Jastrow's view that the rejuvenating plant episode was originally independent, one may compare the widespread motif of how the means of rejuvenation was snatched from man by animals that shed their skins (Frazer, pp. 26–31; Gaster, *Myth,* pp. 36–39; *MI* A 1335.5).

The empirical evidence presently available to us still leaves many questions unanswered in addition to that of possible sources for other elements of the Akkadian epic. The Sumerian tales seem to give no clear indication of their purpose or function, and the historical basis of the Sumerian tales is not illuminated by any direct evidence from Gilgamesh's lifetime. At least for the time being, these questions can only be answered by educated guesses based on a much fuller knowledge of early Mesopotamian history and culture than was available to nineteenth-and early twentieth-century scholars.

# 2

# *The Integrated Epic in the Old Babylonian Period*

## THE OLD BABYLONIAN TEXTS

The earliest known Akkadian narratives about Gilgamesh come from the Old Babylonian Period (ca. 2000–1600).* Currently seven or eight Old Babylonian *Gilgamesh* texts are known and their contents understood. They cover the meeting of Gilgamesh and Enkidu (the Pennsylvania tablet [Gilg. P.], whose colophon describes it as the second tablet of its series); parts of the journey to the Cedar Mountain (the Yale tablet [Gilg. Y.], Harmal fragments A and B [Gilg. Har. A, B], and the Oriental Institute fragment [Gilg. O.I.]); and Gilgamesh's encounters with the sun-god, the barmaid, and Utnapishtim's boatman during his quest for Utnapishtim after Enkidu's death (the adjoining Meissner and Millard fragments [Gilg. Me. + Mi.]). A fragment from Nippur (Gilg. Ni.), which has often been considered Old Babylonian, describes the creation of Enkidu, and therefore belongs to the first tablet of the version which it represents; however, whether it is really Old Babylonian is uncer-

*This chapter is a revised version of an essay entitled "Was There an Integrated Gilgamesh Epic in the Old Babylonian Period?" that appeared in M. de Jong Ellis, ed., *Essays on the Ancient Near East in Memory of Jacob Joel Finkelstein,* Memoirs of the Connecticut Academy of Arts and Sciences 19 (1977):215–18. Material from that essay is reprinted here with the publisher's permission.

tain.[1] Unfortunately, apart from the nearly complete Gilg. P. and Y., most of these texts are fragmentary, which makes their interconnections uncertain. Incomplete as these remains are, however, they parallel or refer to the contents of most of the tablets of the late version (Tablets I–V and VII–X).

The Old Babylonian tablets differ from each other in size and number of columns and lines,[2] which indicates that there were different editions of the epic in this period. Whether the texts of these editions differed from each other to any extent—in which case we might have to speak of more than one Old Babylonian version or recension—we cannot tell, since at present there is no overlap to speak of between the known tablets.[3]

## THE DERIVATION OF THE OLD BABYLONIAN NARRATIVES FROM THEIR SUMERIAN FORERUNNERS

Of the Sumerian tales surveyed in Chapter 1, *Gilgamesh and the Land of the Living* is the most extensively paralleled in the Old Babylonian material (the journey to the Cedar Mountain), while themes known from *Gilgamesh, Enkidu, and the Netherworld* (Enkidu's death and Gilgamesh's grief) and *The Death of Gilgamesh* (the denial of immortality for Gilgamesh) also play an important role. There is a certain affinity to *The Deluge* or a related flood story in the idea of Utnapishtim as the source of knowledge about immortality, which is reflected in the Old Babylonian version, and a generic similarity to Shulgi's hymns to Gilgamesh in the hymnic introduction reflected in the colophon to Gilg. P. (see below).

1. Prof. T. Jacobsen, on stratigraphic grounds, and Prof. P. Michalowski, on grounds of paleography and tablet appearance, independently raised the possibility that Gilg. Ni. could be post-OB (private communications). There are two additional, practically useless OB fragments which may repeat information known from those listed here; see n. 3.

2. See Jastrow and Clay, pp. 17–18; Kupper, in *GSL*, pp. 100–101.

3. A small OB Gilgamesh fragment (identified by M. Civil) in the University of Pennsylvania Museum (UM 29-13-570) contains on its obverse (a left-hand column) the beginnings of eleven lines which are close, but not identical, to Gilg Y. i, 26–43. To judge from van Dijk's remarks in the "Summary Catalogue" to TIM 9, text No. 46 of that volume could contain a variant of part of Gilg. O.I., but perhaps the passage in question is simply a reference from elsewhere in the epic to the same events. On the question of variant texts of the epic in the OB Period, cf. pp. 65–66. For variant texts of another Akkadian epic in the OB Period, see Lambert and Millard, pp. 33–34, 54, and below, chap. 3, n. 25.

Whether the contents of *Gilgamesh and the Bull of Heaven* formed part of the Old Babylonian Akkadian material is not yet known. Since nothing of *Gilgamesh and Agga* appears in any version of the epic,[4] we may presume that it was already passed over in the Old Babylonian material.

Just how the Akkadian Gilgamesh narratives are related to the Sumerian tales is a matter of conjecture. Verbal similarities between the Sumerian and Akkadian versions are so few[5] that one could assume that whoever wrote the Akkadian texts never saw the Sumerian ones, but had only heard of their themes or rough outlines.[6] Conceivably the Akkadian narratives were not based on written Sumerian narratives at all, but were derived independently, perhaps prior to the Old Babylonian period, from the same oral tradition on which the Sumerian texts were based. Hecker raises the possibility that the Old Babylonian Akkadian copies known to us may not have been the earliest Akkadian versions, but that the Sumerian sources or their forerunners were taken over into Akkadian as early as the Sargonid Period (twenty-third and early twenty-second centuries) or the early second millennium (2000–1800). Under these circumstances, even if the original Akkadian versions adhered more closely to their Sumerian prototypes than do the extant Old Babylonian texts, a few centuries of transmission might have allowed the differences to develop.[7] However, it is hard to believe that even many centuries of textual transmission would have obliterated the similarities so thoroughly. In any case, the fact that virtually all of the earliest known Akkadian narrative composi-

4. See chap. 1, n. 16, but cf. n. 7.

5. Cf. Hecker, p. 192. Excluded from this discussion are *GEN* and its translation in *GE* XII, which was probably not part of the OB version (see below in this chapter).

6. Cf. Lambert, "Forschungsstand," p. 67. On the question of whether these differences could be based on Sumerian forerunners unknown to us, see chap. 1. If we do not assume that the Sumerian texts were seen by the Akkadian writers, we might consider the possibility that the Akkadian was composed orally by an illiterate poet. Since Mesopotamian society was largely illiterate, oral literature seems likely to have existed. But we know next to nothing about possible connections between academic scribal literature and oral literature. That scribes did not have access to bards who knew the texts of epics by heart is suggested by that fact that in copying epics (and other types of texts), when they came upon a break in a tablet from which they were copying, scribes could sometimes only record the presence of the break; in other words, they had no oral source for restoring the break (see apparatus to OB *Atr.* II, i, 12 and the NA MS *Atr.* U obv. 11, rev. 4, 9). Arguments for oral composition based on supposedly oral features found in written texts are, in my view, unpersuasive. See pp. 102–3, below.

7. Hecker, pp. 192–93, 195; cf. Diakonoff, p. 66.

tions, including those about Gilgamesh, are from the Old Babylonian Period suggests that this is probably when the Akkadian Gilgamesh texts were first composed. Scribes in this period, and perhaps in earlier periods, are likely to have studied the Sumerian Gilgamesh texts as part of their training. Sumerian literary texts were studied closely in Old Babylonian scribal schools, and Sumerian narratives about Gilgamesh, including school tablets, were current in this period.[8] It seems most plausible, therefore, that whoever first rendered the tales about Gilgamesh into Akkadian—whether the author of the epic or an earlier Akkadian paraphraser or paraphrasers (see immediately) did know the Sumerian texts, but took the liberty of rewording them completely.

## THE AUTHOR

Whether the Akkadian rendition was the work of one writer or several we cannot definitively say. However, in this chapter it will be argued that the Akkadian episodes about Gilgamesh were united into an integrated epic in the Old Babylonian Period, and that the known Old Babylonian fragments are parts of that integrated epic. It will be argued, further, that the integration was not simply an act of compilation, whereby separate episodes about a single character were mechanically placed together in sequence, but rather, as Kramer held, a careful process of revision. In this process, the original episodes were modified by certain deliberate changes that cemented them together in the service of a particular theme that the epic develops. The plan of the integrated epic thus testifies to the working of a single artistic mind, and the work of this person is so creative that he deserves to be considered an *author,* rather than an editor or compiler.[9]

8. See Sjöberg, in *Jacobsen AV,* pp. 170–72 (curriculum); for the geographical distribution of Sumerian Gilgamesh texts in this period, see the Introduction, n. 39, and for references to them in literary catalogues, see chap. 1, n. 25; for Sumerian Gilgamesh texts as school texts, see, for example, Falkenstein, *JNES* 19:66, n. 3, and Ellis, "Gilgamesh' Approach," p. 1 of unpublished MS of article to appear in *AfO* (in press).

9. The terms *editor* and *redactor* will be used to refer to those scribes responsible for the post-OB forms of the epic (see chaps. 3–6). Where a distinction between *author* and *editor/redactor* is either not possible or not intended, the terms *writer* and *scribe* will be used.

If it was this author who first rendered the Sumerian tales freely into Akkadian, then the Akkadian was ipso facto the work of one writer. However, it is possible that the Sumerian tales were put into Akkadian form earlier by one or more scribes, and that the author of the epic worked from these free Akkadian renditions, rather than directly from the Sumerian originals. If this is the case, some of the differences in wording and content between the Sumerian and Akkadian texts which are not part of the integration process could be the work of Akkadian *paraphraser(s)* (just as some could be based on Sumerian textual prototypes not presently known), rather than of the author who produced the integrated epic. Because these questions cannot be answered, it will be safest to distinguish, at least in theory, between the Akkadian paraphraser(s) of the Sumerian tales and the author of the epic, even though it is possible that these were one and the same person.

## THE INTEGRATION OF THE EPIC

As we have seen, the late, standardized version of *Gilgamesh* was a single, integrated composition with episodes arranged in meaningful sequence and held together by recurrent themes, unlike the independent, unconnected Sumerian tales. It is clear that the transition from separate tales to an integrated epic took place prior to the late version: As later discussion will show, the integrated epic is already present in the Akkadian and Hittite *Gilgamesh* texts of the Middle Babylonian Period (ca. 1600–1000) unearthed at Hattusha. But these texts cannot be cited as indirect evidence for the state of affairs in the Old Babylonian Period, since it is still an open question whether the Hattusha Akkadian texts[10] and the Hittite versions of Babylonian literature go back to Old Babylonian prototypes or only to earlier Middle Babylonian ones.[11]

Whether the integrated epic already existed in the Old Babylo-

10. Cf. Oppenheim, "A New Prayer," p. 292.

11. Güterbock, "Hittite Mythology," 154; Otten, in *GSL,* p. 139; cf. Hecker, p. 200, and n. 4; Kammenhuber, pp. 46, 55. Otten, in *GSL,* p. 140, and Kammenhuber, p. 47, have raised the possibility that the Hurrian Gilgamesh material still consisted of separate episodes. However, the reference to Enkidu as Gilgamesh's brother (Kammenhuber, *loc. cit.*) implies the integrated epic, as we shall see later in this chapter.

nian Period is debated, and scholars have taken positions on both sides of the issue. It was, for a long time, assumed that the Old Babylonian Akkadian fragments, like their first-millennium counterparts, constituted an integrated epic,[12] just as it was first taken for granted that the Sumerian Gilgamesh texts constituted one. Now that the separateness of the Sumerian tales has been established, a number of scholars have asked whether the Old Babylonian Akkadian fragments might not also represent separate tales not yet drawn together into an integrated epic.[13] One scholar has gone further and inferred that the use of different formulas for introducing speeches in the different Old Babylonian tablets demonstrates that these tablets represent independent poems.[14] However, the use of different formulas is not incompatible with an integrated epic. If we assume that the Old Babylonian Akkadian renditions are the work of the "author," the use of different formulas could simply indicate either secondary recensional differences between manuscripts[15] of the epic that he created or his lack of concern for formulaic consistency between episodes.[16] If, on the other hand, we assume that the Akkadian renditions are older than the integrated version, varying formulas could stem from different Akkadian paraphrasers for each episode; in other words, if the Old Babylonian version is directly based on older Akkadian sources, the different formulas reflect different sources. This is precisely the case with the different formulas in Tablet XI of the late version, as we shall see,[17] and is a phenomenon well known in biblical criticism.

While different formulas are thus not incompatible with an integrated epic, what can be said in favor of the assumption that the

12. Heidel, p. 15; Jacobsen, "Mesopotamia," p. 223; Speiser, in *ANET,* p. 73; Bauer, *JNES* 16:261; Landsberger, in *GSL,* pp. 33–34; Kupper, in *GSL,* p. 102.

13. Gadd, *Teachers,* pp. 7–8; Edzard, "Mythologie," p. 72; Jacobsen, *Treasures,* p. 195, and p. 257, n. 340; Jacobsen and Hallo *apud* Wolff, p. 393, n. 2; cf. Komoróczy, *Act. Ant.* 23:52.

14. Hecker, p. 196. Gilg. Me. + Mi. and Gilg. O.I. (and Gilg. P. once) use "A said to him, to B," whereas Gilg. P. and Y. use "A opened his mouth, saying to B."

15. For the provenances of the different OB *Gilgamesh* texts, see the Introduction, n. 39. However, recensional differences are not necessarily a function of provenance; see chap. 6, n. 33.

16. The OB version is less concerned with consistency than the late version is; see below, pp. 96–100.

17. See pp. 233–34, 238–39. Note also the different wording of formulas in the originally independent ante- and post-diluvian sections of *SKL;* see *SKLJ,* pp. 61–64, and Tigay, "Stylistic Criteria," § 4.

epic was in fact integrated by the time of our Old Babylonian texts?[18] Explicit evidence bearing on this question is meager, owing to the incomplete preservation of the Old Babylonian material. Only Gilg. P. and Y., to judge from their appearance and script, demonstrably belong to one and the same edition. Since the former (as indicated by its colophon) is tablet two of its series and the latter, to judge from the location of the same contents in the late version, is its sequel,[19] this edition contained at least four tablets, the first not extant, the second dealing with the advent of Enkidu, and the third with preparations for the journey to the Cedar Mountain; the latter implies at least one more tablet describing the journey itself. While this evidence points to a composition which contains more than a single episode, it does not prove the existence of the entire integrated epic known from the late version. None of the other Old Babylonian texts demonstrably belongs to this edition, and most, with their different appearances, number of columns, and provenances, clearly do not.[20] Their mere existence, in itself, implies nothing about the possible integration of the epic in this period.

Despite the paucity of explicit evidence for the integration of the epic, the content of the Old Babylonian fragments provides ample implicit evidence to this effect. A comparison of the late version with its Sumerian forerunners reveals certain features in the late version which constitute the cement unifying the episodes

18. Wolff, *JAOS* 89:393, n. 2, attempted to adduce some evidence which might overcome doubts about the epic's early unification. She noted the use of a "week-long suspension" followed by a "change of character and outlook in the person concerned" twice, at strategic points, in the OB version, and inferred that this indicates "the work of an author pursuing a specific line of thought." She concluded, however, that this implies at most a single author (not necessarily a single composition) and is, in addition, subjective. Cf. Sasson, *Studies in Philology* 69:272.

In reviewing an earlier version of this chapter, Lambert asks: "Surely [Gilg. Me. and Mi.] presume the outline of the story as known from the late version?" (*JNES* 39:173). But these fragments do not explicitly refer to any events prior to Enkidu's death. While their references to Gilgamesh's love for Enkidu and the hardships they shared (Gilg. Me. ii, 1–3) could have in mind Gilgamesh's dreams about Enkidu and the Cedar Mountain or the Bull of Heaven episodes, this is not necessarily so. One reader suggested the possibility that a separate tale about the friends might have begun with Enkidu dead and Gilgamesh grieving. Some years ago, von Soden expressed uncertainty as to whether or not Gilg. Me. was part of the same poem as Gilg. P. and Y. (*MDOG* 85:21). Given such doubts, more extensive signs of the epic's integration are called for.

19. Jastrow and Clay, pp. 17–18.

20. Note also the different spellings of Huwawa's name in Gilg. Y. ($^{d}$ḪU.PI.PI), Gilg. O.I. (ḪU.PI.PI), and Gilg. Har. A (ḪU.BI.BI); cf. Wilcke in *RLA* 3, p. 530, a, b, g.

of the integrated version and are either unique to the Akkadian epic or play a unique role in it.[21] These features, all concerning the character and role of Enkidu, were noted in Chapter 1 (pp. 29–30). They are: 1) The role of Enkidu as Gilgamesh's friend; 2) Gilgamesh's reaction to Enkidu's death; and 3) the description of Enkidu's beginnings. All of these developments in the character and role of Enkidu, which, as noted, constitute decisive integrating factors in the epic, are already present in the Old Babylonian fragments and tablets. Gilg. Ni.—though irrelevant if it is post–Old Babylonian—describes the creation of Enkidu to contend with Gilgamesh, a role which he plays in Gilg. P. as well,[22] and bring relief to Uruk. This role presupposes an account of Gilgamesh's tyranny over Uruk, which is also mentioned in Gilg. P.[23] Enkidu's primitive ways and his introduction to civilization are partly narrated in the same tablet.[24] Throughout the Old Babylonian material, Enkidu is called Gilgamesh's friend[25] and is "like" him,[26] and Gilgamesh loves, and is to caress him.[27] The Old Babylonian version of Gilgamesh's journey to Utnapishtim has the journey motivated by grief over Enkidu's death.[28]

Theoretically, these features of the Old Babylonian material could have developed separately prior to the integration of the epic. Perhaps, for example, one writer made Enkidu a friend of Gilgamesh's under the influence of new social concepts or an Amorite literary taste for adventures shared by equals. Enkidu's role as Gilgamesh's equal could have led another writer to create an account of his origins, and yet another writer to describe how deeply the death of his friend affected Gilgamesh, whom tradition had

21. Gilgamesh's quest for some form of immortality, the epic's main and recurrent theme, which appears in some of the OB fragments (Gilg. Y. iv, 13–15; Gilg. Me., i, 8, 11–15; ii, 13; iii, 2) also contributes to the epic's unity, but it does so only with the help of the features mentioned in this paragraph. This theme was adumbrated in some of the Sumerian Gilgamesh tales (see p. 35), but, unaccompanied by these other features, it constituted at most a common denominator, without lending these tales literary coherence.

22. Gilg. P. v–vi.

23. Col. iv.

24. Cols. ii–iii.

25. Gilg. Y. ii, 40; iii, 14; iv, 5, 26; v, 21–22; vi, 27; Gilg. Har. B 3, 10; Gilg. O.I. obv. 14; rev. 5 (cf. 1); Gilg. Me. ii, 7; Gilg. Mi. iii, 4′.

26. Gilg. P. i, 17; v, 15.

27. Gilg. P. i, 21, 33–34; Gilg. Me. ii, 2.

28. Gilg. Me. ii; Gilg. Mi. iii.

already shown to be upset about Enkidu's death and concerned about mortality. But if we are right in arguing that these features are the cement unifying the integrated epic, their independent development would make the epic's unity almost a matter of coincidence. The process by which it was created would be reduced to not much more than putting the various separate episodes together into a single series. The role of these features in the epic seems too deliberate to have resulted from such a procedure. Had the story of Enkidu's origins, for example, developed independently of the epic, there would have been no special reason for modeling Enkidu's early life on that of animals, as is done in the integrated epic. In Chapter 11, I argue that this model was chosen for thematic reasons, to highlight the contrasting benefits of human culture which the integrated epic urges in place of immortality as the best man can hope for. This message, and the contrasting description of Enkidu's early life, are both found in the Old Babylonian fragments.[29] The story of Enkidu's origins and the other features surveyed above receive a single, clear explanation if they are recognized as being the result of the design of the integrated version, rather than independent developments.

Lambert has suggested that only some of the Old Babylonian fragments reflect the integrated version. In his view, there were different versions of *Gilgamesh* in the Old Babylonian Period, some ending after the Cedar Mountain episode, while others continued further in accordance with the plan of the integrated version. According to Lambert, since the continuation is reflected in Gilg. Me. + Mi., the integration must have been accomplished by the middle of the second millenium.[30] However, while it is conceivable that some of the Akkadian episodes were copied independently before, or even after, the epic was integrated,[31] there is no textual evidence (such as a final colophon[32]) to show that this is true of the known fragments. Indeed, all of the Old Babylonian fragments contain the features which are, in my view, indicative of the integrated epic.

29. Gilg. Me. iii; Gilg. P. ii–iii.
30. Lambert, "Forschungsstand," p. 68.
31. As was the prologue to *LH* long after it was joined to the laws; see Wiseman, *JSS* 7:161–72; Tigay, "Stylistic Criteria," § 3.
32. Like that at the end of OB *Atr.;* see Lambert and Millard, p. 32.

## THE CONTENTS OF THE OLD BABYLONIAN VERSION

Whether the Old Babylonian version contained all of the episodes known from the later *Gilgamesh Epic* is mostly a matter of conjecture, since many, such as the Bull of Heaven episode and the flood story, are not attested in the Old Babylonian fragments discovered to date. We know that the Old Babylonian version to which Gilg. P. belonged must have opened with a hymnic line beginning *šūtur eli,* "Surpassing. . . ." The introduction to the late version contains such a line (27) describing Gilgamesh, "[Sur]passing the rulers, renowned, possessing stature." When this line (in GENim) was published recently, A. Shaffer recognized that the same two words appearing in the colophon of the Old Babylonian Gilg. P. must have been the title, and hence the opening phrase, of the series to which that tablet belonged.[33] Thus the first tablet of the Old Babylonian version must have begun with a version of that hymn. If so, at least the first twenty-six lines of the late version are a later addition. How much of lines 27ff., apart from the opening phrase, was already present in the Old Babylonian version, we cannot say, lacking the first tablet of this version.

The Bull of Heaven episode is not yet attested in the Old Babylonian version (it is first attested in the Akkadian and Hittite texts from Hattusha).[34] It could be presupposed by Enkidu's death (Gilg. Me. ii), but not necessarily, for in the Sumerian *Gilgamesh and the Land of the Living,* Enlil was angered at the two friends for the killing of Huwawa,[35] and conceivably the Old Babylonian version offered that as the reason for Enkidu's condemnation.[36] It is true that the Bull of Heaven episode is based on a Sumerian original, but

33. *Apud* Wiseman, *Iraq* 37:158, n. 22. The hymn introduced by this phrase was either modeled on or borrowed from royal hymns and inscriptions, possibly from an independent hymn about Gilgamesh himself. See chap. 7.

34. Gilg. Bo. rev.; *Hit. Gilg.* no. 8.

35. See van Dijk, in *GSL,* p. 71, ll. 105ff.; cf. Kramer, in *GSL,* pp. 65–66.

36. It is a little strange that in the integrated epic the gods delay announcing a punishment for the slaying of Huwawa until after the Bull of Heaven is slain (*Hit. Gilg.* no. 8). This would be compatible with a theory that the latter episode is a secondary interpolation. Does the seeming redundancy in the wording of the gods' reason suggest that the first phrase is interpolated? Note: "Because the Bull of Heaven they have slain and Huwawa they have slain" (*Hit. Gilg.* no. 8, ll. 6–7; contrast ll. 12–13, where the verb is given only once).

to judge from *GE* XII, Sumerian Gilgamesh texts were also available to later editors of *Gilgamesh* and might have been drawn into the epic later than the Old Babylonian period.

Since Gilgamesh reaches Utnapishtim's boatman in the Old Babylonian version (Gilg. Me. + Mi.), he presumably reached Utnapishtim as well, but stylistic considerations suggest that this version did not have Utnapishtim retell the entire flood story, as does the late version.[37]

Lacking the end of the Old Babylonian version, we cannot document a claim that it lacked the equivalent of the late version's Tablet XII, but everything argues against the presence of that episode in the original Old Babylonian version: The episode contradicts the rest of the epic in having Enkidu still alive at its beginning and in describing him as Gilgamesh's servant, and it is, unlike the rest of that version, a literal translation from the Sumerian, rather than a creative adaptation.[38] It was probably added to the epic at a later date.

## THE OUTLINE AND MESSAGE OF THE OLD BABYLONIAN VERSION

Apart from the exceptions noted, the episodes of the Old Babylonian version were evidently arranged in the same order as those of the late version.[39] The opening phrase of the Old Babylonian version, *šūtur eli,* "Surpassing . . . ," indicates that it began with a version of the hymn which appears in Tablet I of the late version. Since Enkidu is already a known character in Tablet II of the Old Babylonian version (Gilg. P.), the account of his origins must have been found in Tablet I, as in the late version, whether Gilg. Ni. is Old Babylonian or not. The meeting of Gilgamesh and Enkidu takes

37. See chap. 12, pp. 238–39.

38. Hallo notes that *GE* XII constitutes "the principal exception to the general rule that straightforward Akkadian translations of Sumerian originals (outside the area of wisdom literature) appear only in the form of bilinguals, that is, in combination with their Sumerian originals" ("Sumerian Literature," pp. 189–90). Note also Shaffer's comment that the Akkadian of *GE* XII is linguistically no earlier than the Cassite period ("Sources," p. 43; cf. his comment on l. 193), though one may concede the possibility that the late features could be due to a revision of earlier language.

39. Within episodes, there were sometimes structural variations between the versions; see chap. 4.

place in Tablet II of the Old Babylonian version, as in the late version. The journey of Gilgamesh and Enkidu to the Cedar Mountain (Gilg. Y., Gilg. Har. A and B, Gilg. O.I.) obviously took place after their meeting, as in the late version (*GE* III–V). Enkidu's death is mentioned in the account of Gilgamesh's journey to Utnapishtim (Gilg. Me. + Mi.), and his death therefore took place before that journey, as in the late version (*GE* VII). On that journey Gilgamesh meets the barmaid (Gilg. Me. + Mi. ii–iii), Utnapishtim's boatman (Gilg. Me. + Mi. iv), and then presumably Utnapishtim, all in the same order as in the late version (*GE* X).

The Old Babylonian version also agrees with the late version in stressing the futility of Gilgamesh's hope for literal immortality. Gilgamesh is informed by both the sun-god (Gilg. Me. i) and the barmaid (iii) that he cannot attain immortality. While the sun-god's statement deals only with Gilgamesh's current situation, the barmaid's advice is formulated in a way that seems addressed to the epic's audience, as well as to Gilgamesh. Gilgamesh had told the barmaid that: 1) Enkidu, whom he loves, is dead; 2) he mourned Enkidu for seven days and nights; and 3) he has not found the immortality he seeks. In reply, the barmaid tells Gilgamesh:

> The life you pursue you shall not find.
> When the gods created mankind,
> Death for mankind they set aside,
> Life in their own hands retaining.
> As for you, Gilgamesh, let your belly be full,
> Make merry day and night.
> Of each day make a feast of rejoicing,
> Day and night dance and play!
> Let your garments be sparkling fresh,
> Your head be washed; bathe in water.
> Pay heed to a little one that holds on to your hand.
> Let a spouse delight in your bosom,
> For this is the task of [woman].
> (Gilg. Me. iii, 2–14)[40]

In this advice, the barmaid responds to Gilgamesh's plaint in inverse order: 3) You will never find immortality, because it is reserved for the gods; 2) eat, bathe, put on fresh garments and rejoice (the opposite of what mourners do); and 1) let your family fill the

40. For the Akkadian text and further discussion, see chap. 8, pp. 167–68.

void left in your life by Enkidu's death. In sum: Embrace reality. But this advice goes beyond an ad hoc response to Gilgamesh's present situation. The phrases "day and night" and "each day" indicate that the barmaid is referring to a permanent way of life. Indeed, as we shall see in Chapter 8, her advice is a well-known wisdom topos in ancient Near Eastern literature, where it is often coupled with the observation that life ends in death.[41] What the barmaid offers Gilgamesh is a conventional philosophy of life, of which Gilgamesh sorely needs to be reminded. Presumably this advice is intended for the epic's audience as well.

The fragmentary state of the Old Babylonian version makes it difficult to grasp its message more completely. Much of what is said about the message of the late version in the Introduction to this volume and Chapter 8 undoubtedly applies to the Old Babylonian version, but because we are so dependent on the late version for our understanding of the earlier ones, there is a real possibility of our seeing in them more of the late version than they really contain.

## THE FUNCTION OF THE OLD BABYLONIAN VERSION

In Chapter 1, we speculated about the possible cultic use of the Sumerian Gilgamesh texts. The hymnic introduction implied for the Old Babylonian version by the colophon of Gilg. P. raises the question of whether this version was once used in the course of worshipping or honoring Gilgamesh.[42] Later, the Hittite version of *Gilgamesh* was entitled *The Song* (ŠÌR) *of Gilgamesh,*[43] which could imply hymnic use, However, several Akkadian myths and epics are termed *zamāru,* "song," just as a Hittite myth was known as *The Song* (ŠÌR) *of Ullikumi.*[44] While the terms *zamāru* and ŠÌR

41. See chap. 8, nn. 15–16.

42. As god of the netherworld, Gilgamesh continued to play a role in magical rituals in the first millennium, and he was invoked in ceremonies in the month of Ab. See pp. 80–81, 186–87; Pfeiffer, *State Letters,* no. 269, obv. 7–rev. 6; Lambert, in *GSL,* pp. 39–46; Abusch, *JNES* 33:259–61. Cf. chap. 9, this volume, "Athletic Contests."

43. For *Hit. Gilg.,* see p. 111, n. 5.

44. For the Akkadian epics, see OB *Atr.* III, viii, 15; *Erra* V, 49, 59; *EnEl* VII, 161 (see Wilcke, *ZA* 67:172–74; *EnEl* was read liturgically; see Sachs, in *ANET,* p. 332); Heidel, *Babylonian Genesis,* p. 16; cf. Lambert and Millard, p. 7. For the Hittite myth, see below, p. 111, n. 5.

were also used for hymns,[45] it remains to be determined whether these terms mean anything more than "song" or "poem" when applied to myths and epics. The hymnic introduction to the epic may have been merely a stylistic convention.[46] While a cultic use of the epic is not out of the question, it is equally possible that it was used in the Old Babylonian period solely for entertainment and edification.

## THE OLD BABYLONIAN VERSION AND THE SUMERIAN COMPOSITIONS

Assuming, as we do, that the sources available to the author of *Gilgamesh* included versions of the Sumerian compositions known to us, he seems to have used each of them in a different way. The source drawn upon most extensively was *Gilgamesh and the Land of the Living;* four of the Old Babylonian fragments correspond to that episode.[47] The wording of the Old Babylonian version is completely different from that of the Sumerian tale; the Akkadian is not a literal translation. We have already seen an example of this different wording in Chapter 1, in Enkidu's description of Huwawa (pp. 32–33), and in Chapter 8 we shall note different formulations of proverbs that are quoted in both versions (pp. 164–67). Changes such as these have no discernable connection with the integration of the epic, and could therefore be the work of an Akkadian paraphraser who was not the author of the integrated version. A paraphraser's contributions need not have been limited to wording, but might also have included changes in content that reflect the conditions of his time. The location of the Cedar Mountain in the west, for example, rather than the east as was probably the case in the Sumerian version, may be something that any writer in the Old Babylonian Period would have taken for granted, given the western orientation of the dynasties that dominated Babylonia in that period (see pp. 76–78).

On the other hand, certain changes in content and structure

45. See Hecker, p. 69, n. 3; *CAD* Z, p. 36.
46. Cf. Wilcke, *ZA* 67:153–216, esp. 177ff.
47. Gilg. Y., Gilg. Har. A. and B, and Gilg. O.I. The fragments mentioned in n. 3 may also belong to this episode.

discussed in Chapters 1 and 4 seem to emphasize the themes which integrate the epic and are therefore plausibly credited to its author, although it is hard to be confident in every case. One example is the elevation of Enkidu from the status of servant to friend, as we have seen. Certain themes are moved from a location late in the episode to its beginning, apparently to give Gilgamesh's motives a more prominent position and to emphasize the magnitude of his achievement.[48]

From two or three other Sumerian compositions, the Old Babylonian author drew only themes, not their plots. *Gilgamesh, Enkidu, and the Netherworld* supplied the theme of Enkidu's death and Gilgamesh's grief. However, in the Old Babylonian version the circumstances of Enkidu's death are changed completely[49] and with Enkidu now changed from servant to bosom friend, Gilgamesh's grief is magnified to the point of distraction. *The Death of Gilgamesh* provided the idea that Gilgamesh was told that he could not have immortality (Gilgamesh himself had spoken of man's mortality in *Gilgamesh and the Land of the Living*), and it may be that the Old Babylonian author inferred from this that Gilgamesh had wished or asked for immortality. This theme the author made into a central factor in the epic, and the story of Gilgamesh's adventures became the story of how he sought immortality, first by reputation and later, after Enkidu's death, literal immortality, until he was told that this possibility is foreclosed. The late version, and perhaps already the Old Babylonian, omitted the description of Gilgamesh's death which is found in *The Death of Gilgamesh,* and thereby forced Gilgamesh to go on living with this knowledge. The idea of having Gilgamesh travel to Utnapishtim to learn the secret of immortality may have been prompted by *The Deluge* or a related account of the flood, since this composition states that the survivor of the flood was granted "eternal life, like a god" (*Deluge* 256–57).[50]

As indicated above, we do not know whether the Old Babylo-

48. See pp. 33, 79. The elimination of the fifty Urukites who accompanied Gilgamesh and Enkidu (p. 24) has the same effect, by depriving the friends of assistance, as does the addition of a debate with the elders (ibid.), since the latter warn Gilgamesh about the dangers of Huwawa.

49. Gilg. Me. ii suffices to show this, though we are dependent on *GE* VII–X for details.

50. Cf. the MB flood fragment from Ras Shamra, rev. 4 (Lambert and Millard, pp. 132–33).

nian author incorporated the contents of *Gilgamesh and the Bull of Heaven* into his epic, and he presumably did not include *Gilgamesh and Agga.*

We will see in later chapters that the Old Babylonian author also made use of themes from other compositions which, like *The Deluge,* were not connected with Gilgamesh. This author was a creative adaptor of a good part of his literary heritage. But the themes of mortality and immortality which he allowed to dominate his epic were neither taken from those other texts nor made up of whole cloth. They had already been important in some of the Sumerian Gilgamesh texts, and in this respect the author remained true to his sources even while he transformed them.

We have seen that in all likelihood the integrated version of *The Gilgamesh Epic* was composed in the Old Babylonian Period and that the Old Babylonian Akkadian texts about Gilgamesh are parts of this version. The author who composed the epic based his work on several older compositions known to us in Sumerian. We cannot tell whether he worked directly from the Sumerian originals, rendering them freely into Akkadian as he worked, or whether he worked from free Akkadian paraphrases already made by others. Whereas the Sumerian tales seem to have been interested primarily in Gilgamesh himself, this author and later editors of the epic appear to have been more interested in the message they saw in Gilgamesh's life. This author saw that his sources touched on people's attitudes toward death. He realized that by judicious revision and integration of these sources he could tell an entertaining tale and at the same time explore these attitudes and make a statement about how one ought to live one's life knowing that death is inescapable. In so doing, this author created a new and profound work of art whose originality is in no way compromised by its indebtedness to earlier sources.

# 3

# *The Old Babylonian Version and the Late Version: Smaller Changes*

The most fully preserved version of *The Gilgamesh Epic* is the late, or Standard Babylonian, version. Produced apparently during the last half or quarter of the second millennium B.C.E., this version became the standard version in the first millennium. It differs from the Old Babylonian version in many respects, although it appears, as shown in Chapter 2, that the differences did not affect the epic's basic form or plot. Furthermore, despite extensive revision of the wording, we shall see that enough similarities remain to show that the late version is textually related to the Old Babylonian version. Unlike the Old Babylonian paraphrasing of the Sumerian sources, which ignored the wording of the Sumerian versions completely, the wording of the late version is based on that of the Old Babylonian version. In wording and plot, then, the late version represents a revised form of the Old Babylonian version, not a new composition, and the writers responsible for these revisions will therefore be described as *editors* or *redactors.* These terms are not meant to deny that real creative work went into the late version, both in the poetic rephrasing of older poetic passages and in the composition of new lines and sections. The writers responsible for these changes could well be described as *poets* or *author-editors,* as they sometimes are. However, we shall adhere to the terms *editors* and *redactors,* both for simplicity and to make clear that we are referring to writers who were transmitting in revised form a text that was essentially the work of an earlier author.

We have no way of knowing how many different editorial stages the epic went through between the Old Babylonian version known to us and the late version. Revision could have begun as early as the Old Babylonian Period. We shall argue in Chapter 5 that changes took place in the Middle Babylonian Period. The Middle Babylonian fragments of the epic may represent two or three intermediate stages, and there may have been more. Therefore, the changes that will be described in this and the following chapter may not all have taken place simultaneously. The fact that they are all discussed together should not be allowed to obscure the likelihood that the process was gradual and complex.

The differences between the Old Babylonian version and the late version are of the types usually categorized as textual and literary, the study of which is usually divided between two separate disciplines, "lower," or textual, criticism and "higher," or literary, criticism. This and the next chapter correspond roughly to these two categories. However, it is difficult to draw a clear line of demarcation between these categories, since a small textual change can sometimes have considerable literary significance. We are not primarily concerned with superficial differences in orthography, grammar, word order within lines, the forms of the protagonists' names,[1] and column and tablet division.[2] From a literary point of view, it is changes in vocabulary, style, structure, and content which are most significant. Such changes can be traced by comparing sections which are attested in both the old Babylonian and the late versions.[3] These sections concern: Gil-

1. Jastrow and Clay, pp. 23–32, 55; Kramer, *JAOS* 64:11, n. 15; *GETh.*, pp. 8–10; Gadd, *Iraq* 28:116–17; Speiser, in *ANET,* p. 90, n. 163.

2. See Kupper, in *GSL,* pp. 97–102, and the dispute between Kinnier Wilson, in *GSL,* p. 105, and Landsberger, *RA* 62:104–5, n. 27.

3. It is perfectly possible that differences between nonequivalent passages in the two versions are also characteristic differences between the versions. For example, differences in strophic structure, style, or vocabulary between, say, Tablet II of the OB version and Tablet X of the late version could actually be typical of each version throughout the epic. By limiting the present investigation to equivalent passages, we of course forego investigating differences which show up only in passages which are

gamesh's dreams of the coming of Enkidu and their interpretation; Enkidu's arrival in Uruk and challenge to Gilgamesh; Enkidu's and the elders' warnings about Humbaba/Huwawa; Gilgamesh's departure from Uruk on his journey to the Cedar Mountain; and parts of his meetings with the barmaid and Utnapishtim's boatman Urshanabi/Sursunabu.[4]

The differences between equivalent passages in the two versions should be viewed against the backdrop of their similarities. Although only a handful of lines are verbally identical in both versions,[5] the differences are often small. In the following pages, types of differences between the Old Babylonian version and the late version are illustrated (the list is not exhaustive), the least extensive differences being presented in this chapter and the more extensive ones in Chapter 4. The Old Babylonian version is in the left-hand column, with the late version to its right. The difference or feature being illustrated in each passage is underlined in the text (some examples could be cited under several categories).[6]

not available in two separate versions. But the alternative, comparing the OB version of one passage with the late version of a different passage, runs the risk of viewing as a difference between versions what may have been only an internal difference within one and the same version. In other words, what appears in Tablet II of the OB version might also have been found in the equivalent passage of Tablet II of the late version had it been preserved, in which case there would be an internal inconsistency in the late version between Tablet II and Tablet X. Cf. the comment about Oppenheim in n. 4. This danger can be minimized when compared phenomena are extensively attested in the versions in which they are found. For some examples of differences between earlier and later versions of *Gilgamesh* inferred from nonequivalent passages, see Hecker, pp. 119, 141, 172, 202, and in general his chap. 8.

4. A few other equivalent passages are preserved only in scraps in one or the other version, such as the creation of Enkidu (*GE* I, ii, 30ff. and Gilg. Ni.) and the harlot's instructing him (GEUW obv. 1–11; Gilg. P. ii, 11–32); Enkidu's meeting with the shepherds (Gilg. P. ii, 35–iii, 3 and perhaps 12 or 15, matched in GEUW obv. and GEH obv.); Enkidu's assistance to the shepherds (if *GE* II, ii, 1–7 [K8574] is really the counterpart of the last lines of Gilg. P. iii; see *GETh.,* p. 17). Oppenheim treated the descriptions of the aftermath of the seduction scene in *GE* I, iv, 22ff. and Gilg. P. ii, 9ff. as equivalent (*Or.* 17:26–27; cf. Kupper, in *GSL,* p. 102), but the description in Gilg. P. could be only a brief recapitulation of a description perhaps present in the mostly missing first OB tablet, which might have been fuller and more similar to the late version.

5. For example, Gilg. P. i, 1–2 = *GE* I, v, 25; Gilg. Y. iii, 18–20 = *GE* II, v, 3; Gilg. Y. v, 10, 16–17 = GEH rev. vi, 4, 6–7.

6. Restored passages are cited only when the restoration is virtually certain; evidence is cited in the philological notes in the Appendix.

## A. DIFFERENT GRAMMATICAL AND LEXICAL FORMS OF THE SAME WORD

| | |
|---|---|
| 1. ^d^*Gilgameš e-re-ba-am u-ul id-din*<br>He did not allow Gilgamesh to enter<br>(Gilg. P. vi, 14) | ^d^*Gilgameš a-na šu-ru-bi ul i-nam-din*<br>He does not allow Gilgamesh to be brought in<br>(*GE* II, ii, 47) |
| 2. *na-am-ma-áš-te-e*<br>wild creatures (fem.)<br>(Gilg. P. ii, 12) | *nam-maš-še-e*<br>wild creatures (masc.)<br>(*GE* I, iv, 35) |
| 3. *li-ib-ša-am,* garment<br>(Gilg. P. ii, 27, 29; iii, 26) | *lu-bu-šu,* garment<br>(GEUW, obv. 9, 10) |

See also the verb in the next example.

## B. SYNONYMS OR WORDS FUNCTIONING SIMILARLY

| | |
|---|---|
| 1. *im-qu-ut a-na ṣe-ri-ia*<br>descended upon me<br>(Gilg. P. i, 7) | *im-ta-naq-qu-ut e-li ṣērīa*<br>keeps descending toward me<br>(*GE* I, v, 28) |
| Cf.: *ip-ḫur um-ma-nu-um a-na ṣe-ri-šu*<br>the populace gathered around him<br>(Gilg. P. v, 10) | Cf. *i-ṭàp-pi-ir um-man-ni* [*eli ṣērišu*]<br>the populace jostles toward him<br>(*GE* II, ii, 40) |
| 2. *aš-ši-šu-ma ik-ta-bi-it e-li-ia*<br>I raised it, but it became too heavy for me<br>(Gilg. P. i, 8) | *aš-ši-šu-ma da-an e-li-ia*<br>I raised it, but it was too mighty for me<br>(*GE* I, v, 29)[7] |
| 3. *Uruk re-bi-tim*<br>broad-marted Uruk<br>(Gilg. P. i, 28 and passim) | *Uruk su-pu-ri*<br>Uruk (of?) the sheepfold<br>(*GE* I, vi, 9 and passim) |
| 4. *am-mi-nim it-ti na-ma-áš-te-e ta-at-ta-*[*n*]*a-la-ak ṣe-ra-am* | [*a*]*m-me-ni it-ti nam-maš-še-e ta-rap-pu-ud ṣēram* |

7. On the reason for the change to *dan* and its translation as "mighty" in this context, see below, pp. 87–88, and Appendix, no. 5, note on *GE* I, v, 29.

| | | |
|---|---|---|
| | Why with the wild creatures (fem.) do you keep ranging over the steppe? (Gilg. P. ii, 12–13) | [W]hy with the wild creatures (masc.) do you roam over the steppe? (*GE* I, iv, 35) |
| 5. | *zi-ik-ra u-ti-ir-ru a-na* $^{d}$*Gilgameš* | *[ṭ]è-e-mu ú-tar-ri* ⸢*a*⸣-[*na* $^{Id}$*Gilgameš*] |
| | they replied (with this) word to Gilgamesh (Gilg. Y. v, 9) | they reply (with this) instruction to Gilgamesh (GEH vi, 3) |
| 6. | *mi-im-ma ša te-te-ni-pu-šu la ti-di* | *u* ⸢*mim-ma*⸣ *šá ta-ta-ú ul ti-di* |
| | of that which you would do you know nothing (Gilg. Y. v, 11) | of that about which you speak[8] you know nothing (GEH vi, 5) |
| 7. | [*a-lik*] *maḫ-ra tap-pa-a u-ša-lim* | *a-lik maḫ-ri tap-pa-a u-še-ez-z*[*ib*] |
| | [He who goes] in front protects (lit. protected) the companion (Gilg. Y. vi, 27) | He who goes in front saves the companion (*GE* III, i, 4) (Cf. I, vi, 1; contrast III, i, 9: *tap-pa-a li-šal-lim*) |
| 8. | [*le-q*]*é-e-ma* $^{d}$*Gil*[*gameš*] *ḫa-ṣi-na-am i-na qa-ti-ka* | *i-ši* $^{d}$*Gilgameš ḫa-ṣi-in-na a-na i-*[*di-ka*] |
| | Gilgamesh, take the axe in your hand (Gilg. Mi. iv, 11) | Gilgamesh, lift the axe to your side (*GE* X, iii, 40)[9] |

## C. ADDED WORDS OR PHRASES

At times the late version simply adds a word or phrase (often epithets or descriptive terms) to a line which is otherwise identical to its Old Babylonian counterpart[10]:

8. Cf. Lambert, *MIO* 12:49 *sub* 7, 8; *GAG,* § 106x; cf. Heidel, *JNES* 11:143 *ad loc.*

9. For other examples of the formulations in example 8, see Introduction, n. 21. Another passage of Type B is Gilg. Y. v, 15 = GEH rev. vi, 9. For Gilg. P. i, 6–7 = *GE* I, v, 27–28, cf. von Soden, *ZA* 53:210; for Gilg. P. i, 9 = *GE* I, v, 30, cf. *ANET,* p. 76, n. 36.

10. Cf. Hecker, pp. 116–17.

| | |
|---|---|
| 1. *ana bītim [el-l]im mu-ša-bi ša A-nim* | *a-na bītim el-lim mu-[ša]b $^{d}$A-nim u $^{d}$Ištar* |
| to the pure temple, abode of Anu (Gilg. P. ii, 16) | to the pure temple, abode of Anu and Ishtar (*GE* I, iv, 37) |
| Cf. 18: *a-na É-[an-n]a mu-[š]a-bi ša A-nim,* to E[ann]a, the abode of Anu. | Cf. 44: *a-na bītim el-lim qud-du-si,* etc., to the pure holy temple, etc. |
| 2. *um-mi $^{d}$Gilgameš mu-di-a-at ka-la-ma* | *um-mi $^{d}$Gilgameš em-qet mu-da-at ka-la-ma i-di* |
| the mother of Gilgamesh, knowing all (Gilg. P. i, 15, 37) | the mother of Gilgamesh is wise, knowing, she knows all (*GE* I, v, 39; vi, 16) |
| 3. *ma-li-[ki]-šu,* his counselors (Gilg. Y., v, 20) | *mālikī rabûti*, the great counselors (GEH vi, 13) |
| 4. *[e t]a-at-kal $^{d}$Gilgameš a-na e-[mu]-qi-ka* | *[l]a ta-tak-kil $^{d}$Gilgameš a-na gi-mir e-mu-q[i-ka]* |
| Trust [not], Gilgamesh, in your own strength (Gilg. Y. vi, 21) | Do not trust, Gilgamesh, in all [your] own streng[th] (*GE* III, i, 2) |
| 5. *a-na 60 bēr til-ma-at qištum* | *i-šem-mé-⸢e-ma a-na* 60⸣ *bē[r] ri-ma-at qišti-šú* |
| At sixty leagues | He can hear at (a distance of) sixty leagues |
| the forest is encompassed (Gilg. Y. v, 14; iii, 16) | rustling in his (the) forest (*GE* II, v, 4; GEH rev. vi, 8) |

## D. CHARACTERISTIC AND NONCHARACTERISTIC VARIANTS

A few of the variants are characteristic of the version in which they appear, such as those in example B, 8: The formula quoted from the late version there never occurs in the Old Babylonian version, nor does the formula quoted from the Old Babylonian version ever occur in the late version. However, this is not always the case. Sometimes what appears in only one version's wording of a particular passage does appear in the other version, but in a different passage. A case in point is some of the formulas introducing direct speech. Each of the versions employs several different formulas for introducing speeches. Sometimes both versions of a passage may use the same formula.[11] In others, they differ, as in the following:

| | |
|---|---|
| A *pi-šu/ša i-pu-ša-am-ma*<br>*iz-za-kar-am a-na* B | A *a-na ša-šu izzakkara*<br>*ana* B |
| A opened his / her mouth,<br>Saying to B | A says to him,<br>To B |
| (Gilg. P. ii, 9–10;<br>Gilg. Y. iii, 25–26) | (*GE* I, iv, 33; II, v, 7) |

The formula quoted here from the late version is also known in the Old Babylonian version.[12] There are passages, however, where the late version uses a formula which is exclusively found in late texts[13] (the Old Babylonian version of these passages is not attested).

## E. EXPANSION BY PARALLELISM

At times variants are simply the result of the fact that a line in the Old Babylonian version has been expanded in the late version into a group of parallel, synonymous lines,[14] with the original components of the line divided among the several lines of the late version. Thus:

| | |
|---|---|
| *Uruk ma-tum pa-ḫi-ir e-li-šu* | *Uruk ma-a-tum iz-za-az eli-*[*šu*]<br>[*ma-a-tum pu-uḫ-ḫu-rat*] *ina muḫ-ḫi-šu*<br>[*i-ṭàp-pi-ir um-ma*]*-nu e*[*li ṣēri-šu*]<br>[*eṭlūtu uk*]*-tam-ma-ru eli-šu* |
| Uruk-land was gathered about it | Uruk-land stands about [it],<br>[The land is gathered] around it,<br>[The popula]ce [jostles] t[oward it],<br>[The men ma]ss against it. |
| (Gilg. P. i, 10) | (*GE* I, v, 31–34)[15] |

11. For example, Gilg. Mi. iv, 6 = *GE* X, iii, 36; cf. Gilg. Mi. iii, 2, 11 = *GE* X, ii, 15, 20.

12. See the OB texts cited in n. 11 and Sonneck, p. 228, no. 8.

13. *GE* I, iii, 1, etc. See Sonneck, pp. 225–35.

14. On the creation of parallel lines from single lines, cf. OB *Anzû* II, 11–12 and NA *Anzû* I, ii, 31–34 (*ANET,* pp. 111, 113). On *GE* XI and *Atr.* III, see chap. 12.

15. Cf. *GE* I, vi, 9–12, similarly expanded from Gilg. P. i, 30; *GE* II, ii, 38–41, expanded from Gilg. P. v, 10, 11(?), 13 (cf. Gilg. Y. iv, 38–39). Note that Gilg. P. v may contain three parallel lines. For other cases in *Gilgamesh* of expansion by the addition

## F. TELESCOPING OF PARALLEL LINES

The reverse also happens, though less commonly: Parallel Old Babylonian lines are telescoped into a single line containing components of each of the original two:

| | |
|---|---|
| *al-kam lu-ur-di-ka a-na libbi*<br>*[Uruk] re-bi-tim*<br>*a-na bītim [el]-lim mu-ša-bi*<br>*ša A-nim*<br>*dEn-ki-du ti-bi lu-ru-ka*<br>*a-na É-[an]-na mu-šá-bi*<br>*ša A-nim* | *al-ka lu-u(?)-ru-ka [ana] lib-bi*<br>*Uruk su-pu-ri*<br>*a-na bītim el-lim mu-[ša]b*<br>*dA-nim u dIš-tar* |
| Come, let me lead you to<br>Broad-marted Uruk,<br>To the pure temple, the abode<br>Of Anu,<br>Enkidu, arise, let me direct you<br>To Eanna, the abode<br>Of Anu. | Come, let me direct you to<br>Uruk (of?) the sheepfold,<br>To the pure temple, the abode<br>Of Anu and Ishtar |
| (Gilg. P. ii, 14–18) | (*GE* I, iv, 36–37) |

## G. REFORMULATION WITH NEGLIGIBLE CHANGE IN MEANING

We also find extensively or completely different formulations in the two versions. At times the meaning is hardly affected:

| | |
|---|---|
| 1. *aš-ši-a-šu-ma at-ba-la-aš-šu*<br>*a-na ṣi-ri-ki* | *[u a]t-ta-di-šu*<br>*ina šap-li-[ki]* |
| I raised it and brought it<br>To you | And I placed it<br>At your feet |
| (Gilg. P. i, 14) | (*GE* I, v, 37) |
| 2. *iš-me a-[w]a-az-za*<br>*im-ta-gàr qa-ba-ša*<br>*mi-il-[ku]m ša sinništim*<br>*im-ta-qu-ut a-na libbi-šu* | *i-ta-ma-aš-šum-ma*<br>*ma-gir qa-ba-ša* |

of parallel lines, see Gilg. P. i, 15 = *GE* I, v, 39 // 40; vi, 39 // 40; vi, 16 // 17; Gilg. Mi. iii, 10 = *GE* X, ii, 18, with the addition of an antithetic parallel, line 19.

| | |
|---|---|
| He hearkened to her words,<br>Agreed with what she said;<br>The woman's counsel<br>Reached (lit. fell upon) his heart.<br>(Gilg. P. ii, 24–26) | As she speaks to him,<br>He is in agreement<br>with what she says.<br>(*GE* I, iv, 40) |

## H. REFORMULATION WITH NEW IDEA ADDED

| | |
|---|---|
| 1. *ki-ib-sam ku-ul-li-mi*<br>[x x x x] | [*e-nin-na*] *sa-bit mi-nu-ú*<br>*ḫar-ra-an šá* $^{d}$*Ut-napiš*[*tim*]<br>[*mi-nu-u i*]*t-ta-šá ia-a-ši id-ni*<br>*id-nim-ma it-ta-šá ia-a-ši*[16] |
| Show (me) the path [ . . . ]<br>(Gilg. Mi. iii, 9) | [Now], barmaid, what is<br>The road to Utnapish[tim]?<br>[What is] its [l]andmark?<br>Give me,<br>O give me its landmark!<br>(*GE* X, ii, 16–17) |
| 2. *eṭ-lu-tum*<br>*ú-na-ša-qú še*$_{20}$*-pi-šu* | [*ki-i šèr-ri la*]*-'i-i*<br>*u-na-šá-qu šēpī-šu* |
| The men<br>Kiss his feet.<br>(Gilg. P. i, 11) | [Like a ba]by, an [in]fant,<br>They kiss his feet<br>(*GE* I, v, 35) |

## I. REFORMULATION WITH MEANING CHANGED COMPLETELY

| | |
|---|---|
| 1. *pu-ul-ḫá-tim* 7 [x x x x x] | *ana pul-ḫa-a-ti ša nišī* . . . |
| Seven terrifying haloes<br>(Gilg. Y. iv, 2) | As a terror to people . . .<br>(*GE* II, v, 2, 5; cf.<br>GEH rev. vi, 12) |
| 2. *iṣ-ṣa-ab-tu-ma*<br>*ki-ma le-i-im i-lu-du* | *iṣ-ṣab-tu-ma*<br>*ina bāb bīt e-mu-ti* |
| They grappled with each other,<br>like champions (lit. victors) they<br>bent the knee<br>(Gilg. P. vi, 15–16) | They grappled with each other<br>in the gate of the marital<br>chamber<br>(*GE* II, ii, 48) |

16. Restored from *GE* X, iii, 33–34.

3. Sursunabu/Urshanabi's response to Gilgamesh's request for directions to Utnapishtim:

| | |
|---|---|
| *šu-ut ab-nim-ma* $^{d}$*Gilgameš mu*!-*še-bi-ru-ú-ia* | *qa-ta-a-ka* $^{d}$*Gilgameš ik-la-a* [x x x (x)] |
| *aš-šum la a-*⌜*la*⌝*-ap-pa-tu me-e mu-tim* | *tuḫ-tap-pi šu-ut abnī ta-*⌜*ab*⌝*-ta-*⌜*qa*⌝-[*an ur-na*] |
| *i-na uz-zi-*[*k*]*a tu-uḫ-te-ep-pi-šu-nu-ti* | *su-ut abnī ḫu-up-pu-ma* |
| [*š*]*u-ut ab-nim* [*aš-š*]*um šu-bu-rim šu-nu it-ti-ia* | [*ba* (?)*-a*]*q* (?)*-nu ul-*[*tu* x (x)] |
| The Stone Things, O Gilgamesh, (were what) carried me across, | Your hands, O Gilgamesh, have hindered [the crossing (?)]! |
| That I might not touch the waters of death. | You have smashed the Stone Things, Have pulle[d up(?) the *urnu*-cedar]. |
| In your anger you smashed them. | The Stone Things are smashed, |
| I kept those [S]tone Things with me [t]o carry (me) across! (Gilg. Mi. iv, 7–10)[17] | [Pul]led up (?) fr[om . . . . ] (*GE* X, iii, 37–39)[18] |

17. On the Stone Things, see the literature cited in *ANET,* p. 91, n. 173; von Soden, *ZA* 58:192; Heidel, p. 74, n. 157; *CAD* $A_1$, p. 61. Note also the interesting theory of A. D. Kilmer, cited by Stefanini, *Ausonia* 25 (2–3): 31 (kindly translated from the Italian by Dr. A. Rofé):

> The "stones" and the *urnu* snakes (the latter possibly a metaphor for lianas or ropes made of twisted lianas) may hint at another method of navigation in the swamps ("rope-ferry")—a raft advances across still water by being pulled manually along a rope which is stretched horizontally between two counterbalances, i.e., two "stones," probably worked and sculptured. The two "stones" were presumably situated at the two ends of the crossing place, at a certain height from the ground, upon forks or trees.

In light of the suggestion in the next note that *urnu* refers to a cedar, the *urnu* would be one of the trees or poles that supported the rope, rather than a metaphor for the rope itself.

18. For the text see von Soden, *ZA* 53:231. Note the addition in this version of *urnu* as a counterpart to the Stone Things (the restoration is based on *GE* X, ii, 29). This is usually taken as *urnu* I, a type of serpent (see von Soden, ibid., and Speiser, in *ANET,* p. 91, n. 174), but the verbs *qatāpu* (in X, ii, 29) and *baqāmu* in our passage, both meaning "pluck, pick," seem most favorable to *urnu* II, a small cedar (*AHw,* pp. 1431–32).

In the sequel to this passage, the two versions differ on the number and preparation of the punting poles Gilgamesh is instructed to cut; for details, see Appendix, no. 12.

## THE SIGNIFICANCE OF THE CHANGES IN WORDING

Evaluating the significance of these types of variants for the textual history of the epic is not as simple as one could wish. On the face of it, one would assume that the variants found in the late version are secondary and late. But in many cases, this seems impossible to demonstrate on linguistic grounds. For example, alternations between such pairs as *qātu/idu* (type B, no. 8), *kibsu/ḫarrānu* (H, 1), and *ušallim/ušezzib* (B, 7) are chronologically indifferent, each member of the pair occurring in both early and late texts, sometimes in both versions of *Gilgamesh.*[19] The same is true of most of the formulas for introducing direct speech (D), though one of those used in the late version is found exclusively in late texts.[20]

If readings in the late version that differ from those in the Old Babylonian texts available to us are not demonstrably late, they could, theoretically, go back to unknown originals in the Old Babylonian Period and could even be more original than readings attested in our Old Babylonian manuscripts.[21] If these readings do go back to the Old Babylonian Period, this would imply the existence of more than one recension or version of the epic in this period. That is a possibility which we cannot evaluate empirically, since there are virtually no known *Gilgamesh* texts preserved in two Old Babylonian copies.[22] The case of the Old Babylonian *Atrahasis Epic* indicates that at least one Akkadian[23] literary text in the Old Babylonian period existed in more than one recension or version.[24] However, the number of variants between these was minimal, compared to those between the early and late versions of *Gilgamesh.* The apparatus in the Lambert and Millard edition of *Atrahasis* cites only eight nonorthographic textual variants between Old Babylonian manuscripts, and only one is a true lexical

19. See simply *CAD* and *AHw* on these words.
20. See n. 13, above.
21. Cf. Jastrow, YOR 4(3):55–59; Kupper, in *GSL,* p. 101.
22. See chap. 2, n. 3.
23. The case of the Sumerian texts cited in chap. 1, n. 33 cannot be invoked as an analogy, since their presumably greater antiquity allowed much more time for the development of variants.
24. See Lambert and Millard, pp. 34, 54, and see the next note.

variant.[25] A few seemingly variant speeches and scenes noted by Lambert and Millard are difficult to evaluate, since in one case they consider it possible that the variant passage really belongs in a gap in the main recension, and the others are traces of lines which cannot be identified. The small number of Old Babylonian variants in *Atrahasis* is undoubtedly due to the fact that the epic was composed in that period, and the texts also date from that period, leaving little time for variants to have developed. Although the case of the Old Babylonian *Gilgamesh* should properly be judged in its own right, it is reasonable to suppose that its various manuscripts also displayed only a small number of minor variants, and that the large number of variants found in the late version are mostly secondary.

In some cases, the wording of the variants in the late version does seem demonstrably secondary. A study of the late version's variants in the light of the chronological distribution of words and phrases cited in the Akkadian dictionaries suggests that some of these variants involve language which is especially prevalent in late sources.[26] For example, the alternation OB *Uruk rebītim*/SB *Uruk supūri* (B, 3) corresponds with the fact that the only other example cited in von Soden's *Akkadisches Handwörterbuch* of a city termed "(city) *rebītim*" is also Old Babylonian, while the only other example of "(city) *supūri*" is also late.[27] In the alternation OB

25. $^{d}$*bēlet-ilī* for $^{d}$*Nintu šassūru* (OB *Atr.* I, 295; note the alternation between OB and NB copies of the prologue to *LH* cited by Wiseman, *JSS* 7:171 *sub* iv, 19′; cf. OB *Atr.* III, iii, 33 with *GE* XI, 117, quoted in Appendix, no. 13). The variant in OB *Atr.* I, 290 is a phonetic alloform of the same word (cf. von Soden, *AfO* 18:119–21); the variant in II, ii, 18 differs only in the assimilation of a consonant; that in I, 105–6 is the apparent omission of a formula introducing a speech (see below, p. 136, nos. 19–20 and chap. 6, n. 30). The other variants look like cases of textual corruption (I, 162, 298; II, i, 10; ii, 23–24 [accidentally assimilated to 9–10]; note the ancient breaks recorded in II, i, 12). The picture is made clearer, but not changed materially, by von Soden's study of OB *Atr.* I in *ZA* 68:50–86. Note there: lines 212–13 (word order); 215, 217 *(Edimmu* vs. *Widimmu);* 285, instead of the variant cited in Lambert and Millard for line 290; 298 (no variant).

26. It goes without saying that new discoveries or examples omitted by the dictionaries could upset the following examples, especially in cases where the dictionaries cite only a small number of occurrences. The dictionaries themselves upset two such examples: see Goetze, *Or.* 16:247–49 on *kūdanu* and contrast *CAD* K, pp. 491–92; *AHw,* pp. 498–99; see also von Soden *Or.* 38:432 on *sapannu* and contrast *AHw,* pp. 1025c; on the study of linguistic modernization, cf. the comments of von Soden, *MDOG* 85:17.

27. *AHw,* pp. 964c (Akkad *rebītim*), 1061b (Uruk *supūri*). The word *supūru* itself occurs in OB; e.g., Gilg. P. vi, 33.

*nammaštê* (fem.)/SB *nammaššê* (masc.) (A, 2), the feminine form is found in all periods, but the masculine form is attested, outside of lexical texts, only in late sources.[28] In the alternation *ana ṣēri* or *ina ṣēri / eli ṣēri* (B, 1) the Old Babylonian version uses compound prepositions which are common in Old Assyrian and Old Babylonian and last appear in the fourteenth-century Amarna letters,[29] while the late version replaces them with a compound which is restricted to the Standard Babylonian literary dialect, first created in the Cassite Period (between the sixteenth and twelfth centuries).[30] In the alternation *libšu/lubūšu* (A, 3), the Old Babylonian version uses a form attested only in Old Babylonian texts, while the late version uses a form that was still current in later times.[31] In the alternation OB *tattanallak ṣēram* /late *tarappud ṣēram* (B, 4), the late version uses a phrase which is commonly attested in the Middle Babylonian Period and later (although it has approximate counterparts in the Old Babylonian Period).[32] In the formula for Gilgamesh's taking up the axe (B, 8), the alternation of the verbs in OB *leqû,* "take (the axe)," and SB *našû,* "lift (the axe)," corresponds to the distribution of examples in the dictionaries: All examples cited for "*leqû* a weapon" are Old Babylonian and Old Assyrian, while those cited for "*našû* a weapon" are late.[33] Finally, as noted (D), the late version sometimes introduces direct speech with a formula found only in late texts.

These examples suggest a measure of linguistic and stylistic updating in the late version. It is difficult to estimate the extent of such modernization, owing to the small number of passages attested in both versions and available for comparison. A first impression, however, is that modernization was not extensive: The number of variants demonstrably using language prevalent in later literature is

28. See *AHw,* p. 728ab.

29. *CAD* Ṣ, pp. 140–41; *AHw,* pp. 1094b, which cites a single later example (*sub* B, 1, c).

30. *CAD* Ṣ, p. 141a *sub* 4′; *AHw,* p. 1094b, *sub* B, 2; cf. von Soden, *ZA* 41:143; on SB, cf., *BWL,* p. 14.

31. See *CAD* L, pp. 181a, 236; cf. pp. 232–33.

32. *AHw,* p. 954; *CAD* Ṣ, pp. 144b, 145d; cf. Nougayrol, *JCS* 2:203–8, passim. The verb *rapādu* appears in Gilg. O.I. obv. 16; it is used with other nouns *(kīdātum, eqlum, kupātum)* in similar contexts in the OB Period (*AHw,* p. 954; *CAD* K, p. 345c).

33. For the use of *leqû,* see *CAD* L, p. 132a; K, pp. 51–52; *AHw,* p. 544c, *sub* G, 1, a; for the use of *našû,* see *AHw,* p. 762c, *sub* I, 1, d, and p. 763c *sub* II, 1, b, α.

much smaller than the total number of variants studied. It appears that even when the editor(s) modified their sources, they usually relied upon ancient or "classical" vocabulary.[34] Conceivably, revisions with ancient vocabulary and those with late vocabulary were the work of different editors, perhaps of earlier and later periods, respectively.

Other passages in the late version suggest corruption or the misunderstanding of uncommon words. For example, in the alternation OB *pulḫātim* 7, "seven terrifying haloes" / SB *ana pulḫāti ša nišī,* "as a terror to people" (I, 1), the Old Babylonian reading is supported by other references to Huwawa's sevenfold terrifying halo; the corruption of seven to *šá,* "to" (literally "of"), was made possible by the graphic similarity of the cuneiform signs for each (  or  versus  ), and perhaps abetted by the fact that the late version uses a different word for Huwawa's haloes (*naḫlapātu,* "coats").[35] The variants OB *kīma lē'îm ilūdu,* "like champions they bent the knee" / SB *ina bāb bīt emūti,* "in the gate of the marital chamber" (I, 2), may have occurred because the word *lâdu* is relatively uncommon; the fact that the phrase is replaced in the late version by a phrase of different meaning, rather than a more common equivalent, suggests that the late editor did not understand thc word.[36]

In addition to the factors we have discussed so far, there are some changes which could be the result of changing religious ideology. The late version refers to the temple Eanna in Uruk as the "abode of Anu and Ishtar," whereas the Old Babylonian version termed it only the "abode of Anu" (C, 1, from Gilg. P. ii, 16, 18 and *GE* I, iv, 37, 44).[37] The omission of Ishtar in the Old Babylonian

34. According to Lambert, the literary style of the first millennium permitted very few neologisms, even in texts which originated in that millennium (*JAOS* 88:124).

35. See Kinnier Wilson, in *GSL,* pp. 107–11; Klein, in *Kramer AV,* p. 290.

36. Note the uncertainty over the word's meaning in *CAD* L, p. 36c; *AHw,* p. 527a; Oppenheim, *Or.* 17:29, n. 3; note also that the late version's *ina bāb bīt emūti* repeats a phrase from two lines earlier and is parallel to a phrase in the following line—all of which may have helped the editor create this substitute for the original reading. On example C, 5, see Appendix, no. 8, note to *GE* II, v, 4.

37. Note also the disputed reading of Gilg. Me. iv, 9 according to Schott, *ZA* 42:134–35, followed by Heidel, p. 71; but contrast the reading by Speiser in *ANET,* p. 90, n. 165.

version seems strange, for by the Old Babylonian Period the Eanna was preeminently Ishtar's temple. It is true that this temple is usually presumed to have been originally Anu's,[38] since its name seems to mean "House of Anu" (É-an-na(k)),[39] and there are a few Old Babylonian sources outside of *Gilgamesh* which refer to the Eanna of Uruk as the temple of both Anu and Ishtar, just as in the late version of *Gilgamesh* (*GE* I, iv, 37, 44).[40] However, explicit references to this temple as belonging to Anu are rare in any period,[41] while references to it as Ishtar's (Inanna's) are numerous in a variety of compositions from Neo-Sumerian literature on.[42] It is therefore startling that a scribe of the Old Babylonian Period should omit Ishtar and attribute Eanna to Anu alone.

The omission of Ishtar's name does not seem accidental. The phrase "abode of Anu" occurs twice in the Old Babylonian passage (Gilg. P. ii, 16, 18), and it is unlikely that Ishtar's name would have been omitted twice if the cause were merely a mechanical scribal error. The omission seems to have been deliberate, and may perhaps be related to an antipathy toward Ishtar/Inanna reflected in her unfavorable portrayal in the Bull of Heaven episode and its Sumerian forerunner *(Gilgamesh and the Bull of Heaven).*[43] It has been suggested that this antipathy reflects a theological or cultic

38. That Inanna's place in the Eanna was not original is perhaps reflected in a group of texts which state that she was introduced into Eanna during the reign of Enmerkar (one of Gilgamesh's predecessors). See, for example, *ELA* 233–34; Reiner, *Or.* 30:2–4, ll. 10′–13′; van Dijk, *UVB* 18:44–45, ll. 8–9 (but note van Dijk's translation and his comment on p. 49, n. 120, which would eliminate the latter two texts from consideration).

39. Contrast Jacobsen, *Treasures,* p. 17, for a different etymology, and North, pp. 232–33, for the view that Eanna was Inanna's from the outset.

40. *LH,* prologue, ii, 37–47; cf. the inscription of AN-ám, Clay, no. 36, edited by Falkenstein, *Inschriftenfunden,* p. 53; cf. also the hymn to AN-ám, Falkenstein, ibid., pp. 80–81, ll. 6–7, and the date formulas, nos. 10, 12, 31, ibid., pp. 10–11, 14. For early references to Inanna's sharing An's throne, cf. Hallo and van Dijk, pp. 50, 53, 60–61, 86–87, 97, and Hruška, p. 501. Later, in the *Erra Epic,* Uruk is referred to as the dwelling of Anu and Ishtar (*Erra* IV, 52).

41. Cf. North, pp. 231–32. For an early reference, see *Exaltation of Inanna* 85–86 (Hallo and van Dijk, pp. 24–27; translated by Kramer, in *ANET,* p. 581).

42. See, for example, *Inanna's Descent* 7 (*ANET,* p. 53); *Self-Laudatory Hymn of Inanna* 22 (*ANET,* p. 579); *Lamentation Over the Destruction of Sumer and Ur* 153–54 (*ANET,* p. 614); Sjöberg and Bergmann, no. 16. Cf. North, p. 232. Earlier references, such as inscriptions of Enannatum I of Lagash, are uncertain, since they do not specify that it is the Eanna *of Uruk* to which they refer (some temples of Inanna in other cities bore the same name).

43. Cf. Edzard, "Mythologie," p. 84, *sub* 1.

struggle such as may have underlain Inanna's eclipsing Anu in the Eanna,[44] or a political struggle.[45] Such an explanation may be valid for the Sumerian version of the episode, but it is not clear whether such struggles were still living issues in the Old Babylonian Period. In the Akkadian *Gilgamesh,* the Bull of Heaven episode (which entered the Akkadian epic either in the Old or Middle Babylonian Period)[46] may simply mirror the antipathy to Ishtar expressed in its Sumerian source. Similarly, the presence of the episode in the late version would not necessarily reflect an attitude to Ishtar still alive when that version was created, but could merely reflect the fact that by the time of the late version the episode was an inalienable part of the epic, its original significance perhaps long forgotten.

With respect to the Old Babylonian version, however, one wonders whether a dead theological issue could account for the reading which omits Ishtar from the phrase "abode of Anu." It is one thing for an entire episode, once it has entered an epic tradition, to outlive the conditions which created it, but this hardly accounts for a specific reading in another part of the Old Babylonian version separate from the Bull of Heaven episode, especially since we know that the Old Babylonian version adapted its Sumerian sources freely. Such an omission would be more plausibly explained by a struggle still alive.

There is another piece of evidence which suggests that there was still literary hostility to Ishtar in the Old Babylonian Period, or possibly as late as the Middle Babylonian Period. The Bull of Heaven episode, which entered the epic in one of these two periods, describes how Ishtar sent the Bull of Heaven against Uruk. The occasion given for her action in the Akkadian versions, her spurned proposal of marriage to Gilgamesh, may have been original with the Akkadian versions. According to Falkenstein, the Sumerian *Gilgamesh and the Bull of Heaven* may have had an entirely different beginning from the episode in the Akkadian versions.[47] If the writer of an Akkadian version created the theme of Ishtar's spurned proposal on his own, this may reflect a hostility to Ishtar still alive at the time he wrote. If this happened in the Old Babylonian period or

44. Cf. Schott in *UVB* 1:5, 46; North, pp. 232–33.
45. Wilcke, "Politische Opposition," pp. 55–63, esp. pp. 57–59.
46. See above, pp. 48–49.
47. In *RLA* 3:361.

later, it would imply that the kind of hostility that could lead to Ishtar's omission from the description of Eanna as the "abode of Anu" was still alive in the Old Babylonian Period.

While we can only speculate about this omission in the Old Babylonian version, we can speak with more confidence about the fuller phrase "abode of Anu and Ishtar" in the late version. There is no doubt that after the Old Babylonian Period the Eanna was chiefly Ishtar's sanctuary, and while a few other deities were sometimes worshipped there, these did not include Anu, whose cult seems to have had little if any significance again until Seleucid times.[48] When the editor who composed the prologue to the late version of *Gilgamesh* described the Eanna, he called it simply "the dwelling of Ishtar" (*šubat* ᵈ*Ištar, GE* I, i, 14),[49] omitting Anu altogether, and in revising the text of the older version this or a different editor added "and Ishtar" to his prototype's description of Eanna as "abode of Anu" (*GE* I, iv, 37, 44). These formulations brought the text into line with long-standing cultic reality.

## CHANGES DUE TO EDITORS' TASTE

The influence of later language and style, scribal error, misunderstanding of uncommon words, and later religious conditions, are objective factors which to some extent impelled later scribes and redactors to introduce variants of the kinds we have been discussing. But most of the variants in the late version cannot be explained as the result of impelling objective factors, even though the variants are presumably secondary in most cases. Variants whose language or style is no less ancient than that of the Old Babylonian version, which do not add clarity or more familiar words to a difficult passage, or stem from error, or update a passage theologically—in short, variants not attributable to objective factors—would seem to be based on the subjective artistic judgement or taste of later edi-

48. Note the rarity of personal names with Anu as the theophoric element (contrast Ishtar) until this period: see the chart presented by Stamm, *Namengebung,* p. 68.

49. Cf. "hallowed Eanna, the pure storehouse" in I, i, 10, and the description of Inanna as "Lady of Eanna, the hallowed storehouse" in the hymn to Ishtar, Reiner and Güterbock, p. 260, l. 28 (a late copy of which is translated in *ANET,* p. 384, l. 28); cf. also Jacobsen, *ZA* 52:108, n. 32.

tors.[50] While basing their version on whatever derivative of the Old Babylonian version had come down to them, these editors felt free to alter its wording and style in accordance with their own sense of clarity and aesthetics.

The differences noted in this chapter indicate that the text of the epic underwent considerable revision between the Old Babylonian and the late version. While telling the same story, the late version adheres to the exact wording of the Old Babylonian version only sporadically. Usually lines are reworded, sometimes negligibly, sometimes completely. Some lines are dropped, but more often new lines are added. In a few cases the reformulation is due to simplification, misunderstanding, or corruption of the older text. Sometimes the reformulation brings the language of the text into line with later linguistic usage. In one case, the change may reflect later theological notions. In most cases, however, the editors seem to have revised simply in accordance with their own taste in vocabulary or style. There are enough similarities between the two versions to indicate that they are textually related, but beyond that, the editors seem to have felt free to revise the wording of the epic as they saw fit.

50. Cf. Hecker, p. 185.

# 4

# The Old Babylonian Version and the Late Version: Larger Changes

In addition to the smaller changes that differentiate the late version from the Old Babylonian version, larger changes are also apparent. These include the restructuring of entire sections, the assimilation of similar passages, large additions of new material, and theological changes.

## J. RESTRUCTURED SECTIONS

Entire sections are restructured in the late version.[1] When the elders ([*ši-b*]*u-tum*) of Uruk accede to Gilgamesh's plan to battle Huwawa/Humbaba, the Old Babylonian version (Gilg. Y. vi) contains a long speech in which they advise him to rely upon Enkidu, pray that the sun-god Shamash and Gilgamesh's father Lugalbanda will aid him in achieving his desire, and advise him to make nightly offerings to Shamash and be mindful of Lugalbanda. This is followed by a short speech by Enkidu saying, basically, "Follow me!" After this comes a short speech by Gilgamesh, and then the young men (*eṭlūtu,* KAL.MEŠ)[2] address him. In what appears to be the late

1. In addition to the following example, see the description of Enkidu's arrival in Uruk, Gilg. P. v–vi = *GE* II, ii.

2. For the reading, see Stephens *apud* Pohl, *Or.* 25:273, n. 1. Compare Gilgamesh's consultation of the elders and then the younger men in *GA* 3ff., 19ff.

version's counterpart to the elders' speech (*GE* III), an authoritative body, presumably the elders, advises Gilgamesh to rely on Enkidu, but makes no mention of Shamash and Lugalbanda; the speakers add a charge to Enkidu to bring Gilgamesh back safely (*GE* III, i, 1–12). This speech is followed, not by a speech of Enkidu's, but by Gilgamesh's speech summoning Enkidu to join him in consulting Ninsun, Gilgamesh's mother, and by Gilgamesh's address to Ninsun (i, 13ff.), ending in a break in the text. When the text resumes, Ninsun addresses Shamash, laments the fact that he endowed Gilgamesh with a restless heart and has inspired him to battle Humbaba, and implores Shamash to aid him (*GE* III, ii). After a long break, there is a scene in which Ninsun is thought to have adopted Enkidu (*GE* III, iv), and after another long break we come upon the end of a speech which is identical to at least the end of the elders' earlier speech, advising Gilgamesh to rely on Enkidu and charging Enkidu to bring Gilgamesh back safely (*GE* III, vi, 8–11 = i, 9–10).[3] Only this second speech is followed by a speech of Enkidu's to Gilgamesh, as in the Old Babylonian version (Gilg. Y. vi, 44ff.), but most of Enkidu's speech is lost in a break. The remainder of Tablet III, vi of the late version or the beginning of Tablet IV must have included the final farewell, since in Tablet IV we are already into the journey.[4]

For ease of comparison, we may represent the structure of the two versions of the departure section as follows:

| **Gilg. Y.** | ***GE* III** |
| --- | --- |
| Elders bless Gilgamesh and advise him to rely on Enkidu and be attentive to Shamash and Lugalbanda (vi, 19–43). | A group (elders?) advises Gilgamesh to rely on Enkidu (i, 1–10). |
| | Group charges Enkidu (i, 11–12). |
| | Gilgamesh summons Enkidu to Ninsun (i, 13ff.). |
| | [Break] |

3. The traces of *GE* III, vi, 7 on Ki. 1904-10-9,19 (*GETh.*, pl. 13) may be [*qa*]*b-l*[*um*!], in which case the line equals III, i, 8, especially as written on K 8558.

4. Whether the journey began at the beginning of *GE* IV is unclear, because of uncertainty about the beginning of the tablet; see Speiser in *ANET*, p. 81d; contrast Landsberger, *RA* 62:97–102.

| | |
|---|---|
| | Ninsun's prayer (ii). |
| | [Break] |
| | Ninsun adopts (?) Enkidu (iv). |
| | [Break] |
| | Group advises Gilgamesh to rely on Enkidu[5] and charges Enkidu (vi, ?–11). |
| Enkidu addresses Gilgamesh (vi, 44–?). | Enkidu addresses Gilgamesh (vi, 12ff.). |
| Final farewell from young men (vi, ?–64) | [Final farewell from Uruk (end of III or beginning of IV)]. |

From this comparison it is clear that the late version has inserted more than four columns of material in between the speech of the elders and the speech of Enkidu, which followed one another immediately in the Old Babylonian version. There appears to be no plausible place anywhere in the Old Babylonian text for any of this material, including the repetition of the elders' speech in GE III, vi. This means that the material is new, at least in this location. If the speech in vi, ?–11 is by the elders,[6] repeating part of their earlier speech, its position at the end of the interpolation constitutes a resumptive repetition *(Wiederaufnahme),* a literary device whereby the compiler, after an interpolation, returns to the point of interruption and, before continuing, first repeats part of what immediately preceded the interruption.[7] Following the repetition,

5. Assuming what is said in n. 3, above.

6. This speech, like that in the first column, is by a body which has the authority to place Gilgamesh in Enkidu's charge (*paqādu,* i, 11; vi, 10), unless this is just a figurative way of saying "We're counting on you." Speiser translated *ina puḫrinima* in these lines as "we, the assembly," which is certainly not precise; at most the phrase could mean "in our assembly," but it could also mean simply, "we, collectively." If the speech in col. vi is not by the elders, it may represent, not a newly created resumptive repetition, but an assimilation of a speech already present in Gilg. Y. vi (perhaps that of the young men in Gilg. Y. vi, 58ff.) to that in *GE* III, i, 2ff. On such assimilation, see below, § L.

7. For another example of this device in the epic, see below in this chapter, "Enkidu's Arguments against Challenging Huwawa." Another apparent example appears in the *Vassal Treaties of Esarhaddon,* § 4 (*ANET,* p. 535a; see Frankena, *Oudtestamentliche Studien* 14:132–33. For literature and other examples in ancient Near Eastern literature, see Talmon and Fishbane, pp. 35–38; Tigay, *JBL* 94:338, n. 28. The practice is by no means universally followed; cf. the interpolations in NA *Anzû* I, ii, 38–42 (Assyrian version) with OB version II, 14–15 (*ANET,* pp. 113, 111).

the narrative then continues according to the plot of the original version (i.e., with a speech of Enkidu to Gilgamesh, *GE* III, vi, 12ff., corresponding to Gilg. Y. vi, 44ff.).

## K. CHANGES IN THE ROLES OF CHARACTERS

Apart from the restructuring of the departure pericope, the role of one of its characters, the sun-god Utu/Shamash, appears to have undergone a change from the early versions to the late one. In the late version, Ninsun states that Shamash inspired *(talpussuma)* Gilgamesh's desire to journey to Humbaba's abode (*GE* III, ii, 10ff.).[8] The sun-god seems to have played a different role in each of the earlier versions.

### *Sumerian Version*

In the Sumerian version of the story, *Gilgamesh and the Land of the Living,* Gilgamesh's journey to the Cedar Mountain is undertaken on his own initiative. He wishes to establish his name (possibly by erecting inscribed monuments),[9] since he will eventually die. Gilgamesh asks Utu to be his helper (á-daḫ) in this undertaking. He turns to Utu because of the latter's connection with the Cedar Mountain.[10] The Cedar Mountain is implicitly located in the east,

8. Cf. the translation of line 11 in *CAD* L, p. 85d; note also *lapātu,* with the meaning "assign," *CAD* L, p. 87d *sub* k.

9. Kraus, *JNES* 19:127–32.

10. kur-ra dím-ma-bi ᵈUtu-kam, "the mountain, it's *charge* is Utu's" (*GLL* A, l. 11). The precise nuance of the word translated "charge" (dím-ma) is uncertain, but the genitive form of Utu implies some sort of possession. One possibility is dím-ma = *ṭēmu,* "disposal, order," etc. (see the lexical equation in *AHw,* p. 1385d, s.v. *ṭēmu*). Another factor, in addition to that specified in *GLL* A, 11–12, may have contributed to Gilgamesh's reliance on Utu in this episode. According to Edzard, "Mythologie," p. 126, the epics about Gilgamesh and Lugalbanda constitute the principal exceptions to the generally modest role played by the sun-god in Sumerian religious literature. Gilgamesh and Lugalbanda were kings of the first dynasty of Uruk, a dynasty whose lineage was traced back to the sun-god (*SKLJ,* p. 151). Note that in the OB version, Gilgamesh's father Lugalbanda is associated with the sun-god in the role of Gilgamesh's helper, strengthening the impression that at one point in the history of the tradition the sun-god was also invoked as an ancestor. Cf. Sjöberg, *Or. Suec.* 21:101.

as is typically the case with the Cedar Mountain connected with the sun in Sumerian texts.[11] Utu at first seems to have reservations about Gilgamesh's request,[12] but once Gilgamesh explains that he is motivated by his concern over death, Utu consents. At no point in describing his original intentions does Gilgamesh mention Huwawa or a desire to cut down cedar trees; these ideas seem to develop only late in the story.

## *Old Babylonian Version*

In the Old Babylonian version, the initiative for the journey is still Gilgamesh's alone. It is consistently represented as something Gilgamesh "has come to desire" *(taḫšiḫ),*[13] and this is underscored by the use of cohortative verbs in stating his plans.[14] The motive Gilgamesh expresses is his own: to leave an enduring name after he dies (Gilg. Y. iv, 13, 25; v, 5, 7),[15] a motive he is able to explain with a proverbial saying about man's mortality (iv, 5–8).[16] Shamash's role is still that of helper, rather than instigator, of the journey (cf. Gilg.

11. Note such passages as "like Utu when he comes forth from the mountain perfumed by cedars" (ᵈUtu kur-šim-ᵍⁱˢeren-na-ta è-a-ni/gim, Falkenstein, *ZA* 48:105, ll. 27–28 = *SAHG,* pt. 1, no. 10, ll. 27–28); cf. the Nabonidus inscription quoted by Sjöberg, *Mondgott,* p. 88, n. 6: "As Shamash, the supreme lord, when he shines forth from the cedar mountain" *(kīma ištu šadî* ᵍⁱˢ*erēni* ᵈ*Šamaš bēlu šurbû ina napāḫišu);* cf. Castellino, *Or. Ant.* 8:6–7, ll. 17–18; *EWO* 313–14, translated in Kramer, *Sumerians,* p. 181 (Mt. Ḫašur is located in the east, in the vicinity of Aratta and Mt. Sabum; see Wilcke, *Lugalbandaepos,* p. 38; Rowton, *JNES* 26:268). For cedar mountains in the east, see also Kinnier Wilson, *JSS* 7:174; *ZA* 54:86–87; Gelb, pp. 35–36, with n. 94; cf. also Kramer, *BASOR* 96:18–28; *Sumerians,* pp. 281–82; Gurney, *JCS* 8:92; von Soden, "Sumer," p. 563. In the view of van Dijk, the eastern location is confirmed by a reference to the road to Aratta (in Iran) in *GLL* B (*Or.* 44:74; text in *JCS* 1:36, n. 217). The eastern location of the Cedar Mountain is not contradicted by the fact that it is a "mythical" place of inexact location (Bauer, *JNES* 16:260; *BWL,* p. 11) (See now Hansman; Marszewski).

12. Cf. *GLL* A, 19–20 and the comments of Kramer in *JCS* 1:4, 32, and *ANET,* p. 47.

13. Gilg. Y. i, 13–14; iii, 21–22; v, 18; cf. vi, 30.

14. Gilg. Y. iii, 27; iv, 13, 25; v, 1, 3, 5–7.

15. This motive survives in the late version, *GE* IV, vi, 39; cf. K 7224 (*GETh.,* p. 18 and pl. 10), l. 4, in light of Gilg. Y. iv, 16.

16. Cf. Oppenheim, *Or.* 17:32, n. 1. The first line of the saying echoes its counterpart in the Sumerian version (*GLL* A, 28–29; *GLL* B, MS a, i, 6–8, 11–12 [Kramer, *JCS* 1:31, n. 205]; note that in *GLL* B this is addressed to Enkidu, as in Gilg. Y.; in *GLL* A it is addressed to Utu). For the proverbial character of the first line, see below, chap. 8, "Who Can Scale Heaven."

Har. B, 12–13, and see below), and in this version, too, he seems to have had reservations at first.[17] But, unlike his role in the Sumerian version, the sun-god's involvement is not related to a special connection he has with the Cedar Mountain. In the Akkadian versions, the Cedar Mountain is explicitly located in the northwest, in or near Lebanon (Gilg. O.I. rev. 13; *GE* IV: *LKU* 39:4),[18] a change presumably influenced by the western orientation of the West Semitic dynasties which came to dominate Mesopotamia in the Old Babylonian period and the campaigns of certain kings of that period to the west.[19] With Gilgamesh's destination removed from the east, the original reason for turning to the sun-god was also eliminated.

How, then, was the role of Shamash in this episode understood in the Old Babylonian version? In part, the elders seem to trust in Shamash in his capacity as protector of travelers (Gilg. Y. vi, 31–33; cf. v, 32–34).[20] But Shamash does more than help Gilgamesh arrive at his destination. The elders pray that Shamash will enable Gilgamesh to realize his ambition, and the dream in Gilg. Har. B promises Shamash's help in distress. (In *Hit. Gilg.* No. 4, Shamash stirs up eight winds to immobilize Huwawa before Gilgamesh,[21] and No. 8 also

17. Cf. the comments of Speiser, *ANET,* p. 80, and Heidel, p. 38, at the end of Gilg. Y. v; contrast Jastrow, YOR 4(3):36.

18. For *LKU* no. 39, l. 4 see Landsberger, *RA* 62:99. According to Shaffer, the reading KUR *Lib-na-nu* was confirmed by collation (*EI* 9:160). The western location of the Cedar Mountain may also be reflected in references to the god Wer as the guardian of the Cedar Forest (Gilg. Y. iii, 40, 42), which give the impression of identifying Wer with Huwawa. Although the origin of this storm-god is obscure, he was popular in Syria under several forms of this name. See Rosenthal in *ANET,* pp. 655–56 (Ilu-wer); Edzard, "Mythologie," pp. 135–36 ("Wettergott"); *APNM,* p. 272 (Mer); and Roberts, p. 36 ([Ilu]mer). Van Dijk suggests that the eastern location of the Cedar Mountain is still reflected in *GE* VIII: *STT* 15, i, 11–12, which would represent a different Akkadian version of the episode (*Or.* 44:74). Both versions, according to van Dijk, come from Sumerian versions. However, the allusion in *GE* VIII is too vague to interpret. Cf. Lambert, in *GSL,* p. 47, n. 2.

19. Cf. Malamat. Coincidentally(?), the closest parallel to Gilgamesh's expedition cited by Malamat is the campaign of Iaḫdun-Lim described in his inscription to Shamash (*ANET,* p. 556). Cf. also *BWL,* p. 12, [See also Hansman, pp. 32–33; van Dijk, *Or.* 44:74.]

20. Cf. Gordon, *Bi. Or.* 17:124, n. 23; Castellino, *Or. Ant.* 8:6–7, l. 13, and the note thereto on p. 30; Cooper, *ZA* 62:70, l. 7; 77, l. 7; *Shamash Hymn,* ll. 65–68, 135, 138–39, 169–70 (*BWL,* pp. 130–37); *KAR* 7 (Ebeling, MVAG 23(1):37–40), l. 7. Cf. Lichtheim, p. 230, n. 8. Note the antithesis of the blessing of Gilg. Y. vi, 31–33 in the covenant curse of OB *Etana* A-2, 1–3; late version C-2, 14 (*ANET,* pp. 114, 116). For prayer and divination about the outcome of journeys, note also *ANET,* p. 391a, l. 12; Reiner, *JNES* 19:33, ll. 71–76 (cf. p. 27); Vanstiphout, *JCS* 29:52–56; the omens quoted in *CAD* $A_1$, p. 313c, and *CAD* Ḫ, p. 109 *sub* 2 and b; Falkenstein, in *RLA* 3:159a.

21. Cf. Kinnier Wilson, in *GSL,* p. 109.

assigns the god a role, but we cannot infer from the Hittite texts that Shamash played these roles in the Old Babylonian version.) The reason for this active role seems to be suggested by a fragmentary passage which can be restored on the basis of the late version: "... fierce Huwawa we/I slay, and banish from the land what is baneful" (Gilg. Y. iii, 5–7, restored from *GE* III, ii, 17–18). It is noteworthy that the prominence of the intention to slay Huwawa in Gilgamesh and Enkidu's original discussions about the campaign is an innovation in the Old Babylonian version, and therefore deserving of attention; as we noted, in the Sumerian version Gilgamesh's intention was simply to travel to the Cedar Mountain and establish his name, with Huwawa figuring only as an obstacle who first appears when Gilgamesh and Enkidu have reached the mountain. In the Old Babylonian version, slaying Huwawa becomes the means by which Gilgamesh intends from the outset to establish his name.[22] In the passage from Gilg. Y. just quoted, Huwawa appears as the personification of "what is baneful" *(mimma lemnu).* The late version characterizes "what is baneful" as "that which (Shamash) hates" (*GE* III, ii, 18). There is apparently not enough room on the line in Gilg. Y. iii, 7 for this phrase, but it only makes explicit what is already implicit in the Old Babylonian version, for Shamash is in any case the opponent of what is *lemnu.* In the present passage, the word is usually translated as "evil" and construed in a moral sense, in agreement with Shamash's role as god of justice.[23] However, the full phrase *mimma lemnu* normally refers to supernatural evil.[24] Huwawa does appear in magical and demonic contexts as a demonic being to whose charge other demons may be banished,[25] a role played in other passages by Namtar, the vizier of the netherworld, by the doorkeeper(s) of the netherworld, by the netherworld itself, and by

22. Although establishing his name may have referred to erecting inscribed monuments in *GLL,* in the OB version Gilgamesh is explicitly seeking fame (Gilg. Y. iv, 13–15; v, 4–7; on the first of these passages, see von Soden, *ZA* 53:213–14).

23. See *ANET* and Heidel for the translation, and Bauer, *JNES* 16:260 and *CAD* L, p. 121b, for the moral sense "thoughts, words, etc." A proverb characterizes certain immoral acts as n í g - g i g $^{d}$U t u, "an abomination to Utu" (Young, p. 132).

24. What *CAD* L terms "magically evil and dangerous"; see the references cited there, pp. 121d–122a, and in *AHw,* p. 543c. *CAD* L, p. 121b *sub* 3′ hints that the use of *mimma lemnu* in a moral sense is exceptional.

25. In an incantation, Dumuzi is asked to consign a demon "to the mighty Humbaba, the merciless demon" (*gallî la bābil panī,* variant adds at beginning *lemni,* "evil"); see Thureau-Dangin, *RA* 22:23–26; *SAHG,* p. 345, no. 70.

other beings.[26] Since such a role is beneficial to humans, it would not account for Gilgamesh's desire to kill Huwawa, but some of the other beings who play this role are elsewhere antisocial in character, playing a helpful role only when their power is employed against other antisocial powers.[27] Presumably this is the case with Huwawa: In the epic he personifies what is baneful, while in incantations he is invoked against other baneful forces. If this is the significance of Huwawa in the epic, Shamash's interest is explained by his own role as opponent of baneful forces.[28] At times, Gilgamesh is associated with Shamash in this role, as in the following incantation calling upon ancestral spirits to intercede on behalf of a person being harrassed by some unknown spirit:

> This day stand before Gilgamesh and Shama[sh]:
> Judge my case, give a decision concerning me!
> That which is baneful (NÍG ḪUL = *mimma lemnu*), which is in my body, my flesh, my sinews,
> Place in the charge of Namtar, vizier of the netherworld . . .[29]

In an earlier passage in the same text, an incantation calling upon Shamash is followed by one calling upon Gilgamesh, the operative part of which reads:

> Illness has come upon me. That my case be judged,
> That a decision be given concerning me—I bow before you.
> Judge my case, [gi]ve a decision concerning me.
> Remove the illness of my body,
> Drive away that which is baneful *(mimma lemnu),* which comes to cut off my life,
> The illness which is in my body, my flesh, my sinews.[30]

26. See *TuL,* p. 130, ll. 22–24; p. 131, ll. 40–43; p. 128, l.5*; p. 141, l. 15; Lambert, *AfO* 19:117, l. 24; Meier, p. 146, ll. 122–25; *STT,* no. 215: col. III, l. 9.

27. E.g., Namtar (Edzard, "Mythologie," p. 108); Thureau-Dangin cites Pazuzu (*RA* 22:26; cf. Thureau-Dangin, *RA* 18:194, and literature cited by Edzard, "Mythologie," p. 48). In Lambert, *AfO* 19:117, l. 27, even the "great devils" *(gallê rabûti)* are among those to whom the baneful forces are handed over.

28. Schollmeyer, p. 7; Jacobsen, PAPhS 107:480–81, n. 22 = Moran, ed., *Image of Tammuz,* pp. 330–31, n. 22. For some examples, see Castellino, *Or. Ant.* 8:16–17, ll. 103ff.; Goetze, *JCS* 9:11, 17; Cooper, *ZA* 61:5 (n. 21), 10; *ZA* 62:65ff.; Ebeling, *MVAG* 23(1), Shamash incantations b, c, f, g; Schollmeyer, nos. 1–2; Reiner, *Šurpu,* p. 52, ll. 28–29; *ANET,* p. 387a, l. 12.

29. *TuL,* p. 131, ll. 40–43; Heidel, pp. 156–57.

30. *TuL,* p. 128, ll. 18–23, translated from Abusch's unpublished edition of *Maqlû.* The invocation immediately preceding the incantation is translated by Lambert in *GSL,* p. 40; note also the incantations cited there, pp. 41–43.

Such passages raise the possibility—about which one can only speculate—that the Cedar Mountain episode was thought to express Gilgamesh's role in exorcistic rituals, and perhaps its etiology as well.[31]

### *Late Version*

In the late version, as noted, Shamash appears for the first time[32] as the initiator of the campaign against Huwawa. This seems to be a final and logical development of his role: Now that Gilgamesh intends from the outset to battle against an embodiment of baneful forces, he is thought to have been not only aided but inspired by a god who banishes what is baneful *(muḫalliq raggim).*[33]

To sum up: After events in the Old Babylonian period led to a shift in the geographic context of this episode, making Shamash's original role in the Cedar Mountain episode meaningless, the Old Babylonian version understood his role in accordance with his role in Mesopotamian religion as banisher of baneful forces. Further reflection based upon this understanding resulted in the late version's crediting Shamash with the very conception of the campaign against Huwawa/Humbaba. A historical stimulus, followed by theological reflection, have thus combined to transform the role of the god who in the Sumerian version may have initially questioned the proposal.

## L. ASSIMILATION

A number of differences between the Old Babylonian and late versions are the result of assimilation of related passages to each

31. Another motif in the same episode, digging wells and libating water to Shamash, is reminiscent of a ritual discussed in chap. 7, p. 152. For other possible ritual reflexes of the epic, see below, pp. 106–7, and Lambert, in *GSL,* p. 56 (on p. 42 [cf. 46] Lambert cites ritual texts mentioning ships and sailors along with Gilgamesh; this could refer to Gilgamesh and Enkidu's return from the Cedar Mountain with the cedars by boat [cf. Landsberger, *RA* 62:104 (n. 26), 108–9] or to Gilgamesh's voyages on Urshanabi's boat).

32. *Hit. Gilg.* no. 8 states that Gilgamesh and Enkidu slew Huwawa and the Bull of Heaven at Enlil's command. This is generally emended to refer to Shamash's command (see Heidel, p. 56, n. 113). See, however, Stefanini, *JNES* 28:40–47. The initiative in this version is, in any case, not Gilgamesh's.

33. Schollmeyer, no. 2, l. 15.

other in the late version. Unlike modern authors, who strive for variety and economy of expression, the editor(s) responsible for the late version sought to minimize variety and to create or increase correspondences between sections of the epic. The result is a much more homogenized version.

At times this assimilation takes the form of a harmonization of vocabulary. For example, the Old Babylonian version of the elders' warning to Gilgamesh calls them "elders" *(šībūtu)* before their speech and "counselors" *(mālikī)* afterwards (Gilg. Y. v, 8, 20; cf. vi, 20). The late version uses "counselors" in both passages (GEH vi, 2, 13).[34]

More often, such assimilation involves conforming entire passages to one another, as in the next four examples.

## *Gilgamesh's Dreams of the Coming of Enkidu*

In both the Old Babylonian and the late version, Gilgamesh has two dreams portending Enkidu's arrival. In the Old Babylonian version, the two dreams differ from each other and appear to portend different qualities of Enkidu and of the friends' future relationship: The first emphasizes their initial struggle, the second their friendship.[35]

| **First Dream, Gilg. P. i, 3–23** | **Second Dream, Gilg. P. i, 26–ii, 1** |
|---|---|
| 3. "My mother, in the time of night | i. 26–27a. "My [mot]her, I saw another (dream). |
| 4. I was striding about proudly | 27b. [*At the gate*] of my marital [chamb]er, in the street |
| 5. Among some men. | 28. [Of] broad-marted [Uru]k. |
| 6. The stars of the heavens appeared, (and) | |
| 7. A ⌜meteor (?)⌝ of Anu descended upon me. | 29. There lay an a[x]e, and |

34. Cf. also the sequence " . . . the forest . . . its midst" in Gilg. Y. iii, 16–17, becoming " . . . the forest . . . his forest" in *GE* II, v, 4 (below, pp. 93–94); and the change of *ikabbit* to *dan* in Gilgamesh's first dream (Gilg. P. i, 8 and *GE* I, v, 29, below, pp. 84, 87–88).

35. Cf. Oppenheim, *Dreams,* p. 215; Jacobsen, *Ac. Or.* 8:70. Text and notes in Appendix, no. 5.

| | |
|---|---|
| 8. I raised it, but it became too heavy for me! | |
| 9. I tried to dislodge it, but dislodge it I could not! | |
| 10. Uruk-land was gathered about it, | 30. About it they were gathered. |
| 11. While the men kissed its feet. | 31. That axe, strange was its appearance. |
| 12. As I set my forehead, | 32. As soon as I saw it, I rejoiced. |
| 13. They loaded (it on) me. | 33. I loved it, and like a wife |
| | 34. I caressed(?) it. |
| 14. I raised it and brought it to you." | 35–36. I took it and placed it at my side."[36] |
| 15. The mother of Gilgamesh, knowing all, | 37. The mother of Gilgamesh, knowing all, |
| 16. Says to Gilgamesh, | 38. [Says to Gilgamesh,] |
| 17. "Perhaps, Gilgamesh, one like you | [" . . . (break of a few lines)] |
| 18. Was born on the steppe, | |
| 19. And the hills have reared him. | |
| 20. When you see him [(. . . . ?)], you will rejoice. | |
| 21. The men will kiss his feet; | |
| 22. You will embrace [(him. . . . and . . . . ?)] him; | |
| 23. You will lead him to me." | ii. 1. Because he shall compete with you." |

In this version, the similarities between the two dreams are mostly thematic: A symbolic object appears; people gather about it (identical but inverted phraseology, ll. 10 and 30); Gilgamesh takes

36. The Akkadian words for "side" and "brother" are homonyms *(aḫu),* so that a double entendre may be intended here (Schott, *ZA* 42:103; Hecker, p. 112, n.1): The line could also be translated, "I . . . made him my brother" (as it is actually taken in *AHw,* p. 545c). For references to Enkidu as Gilgamesh's brother later in the epic, see chap. 2, nn. 11, 30. Note that in the late version of the formula for taking up the axe, *idu,* "side," is sometimes written with the sign Á, which can also be read *aḫu,* "side" (*GE* X, iii, 44; contrast 40).

it and does something with it. In her interpretation of the first dream, Ninsun predicts that Gilgamesh will rejoice over his new friend when he sees him (20), and in the second dream Gilgamesh rejoices over the symbol itself when he sees it (32, identical phraseology). Note that in the first dream, Gilgamesh brings the symbol to his mother (14, 23), while in the second he places it at his own side (35–36). Note also that correspondence between the first dream and its interpretation are limited to the nobles' kissing the symbol's feet (identical phraseology, ll. 11 and 21) and Gilgamesh's bringing it to Ninsun.

In the late version, the two dreams resemble each other much more, though not to the point of monotony. The similarity is achieved by lines from each dream now appearing in both. The interpretations also resemble the dreams more. Here, for purposes of comparison, are the first and second dreams from both versions.[37]

| **Old Babylonian, Gilg. P. i, 3–ii, 1** | **Late Version, *GE* I, v, 26–vi, 27** |
|---|---|
| ***First Dream*** | ***First Dream*** |
| 3. "My mother, in the time of night | 26. "My mother, in the dream I saw last night |
| 4. I was striding about proudly | |
| 5. Among some men. | |
| 6. The stars of the heavens appeared, (and) | 27. The stars of the heavens appeared, (and) |
| 7. A ⌜meteor(?)⌝ of Anu descended upon me. | 28. (Something) like a meteor(?) of Anu keeps descending toward me. |
| 8. I raised it, but it became too heavy for me! | 29. I raised it, but it was too [m]ighty for me! |
| 9. I tried to dislodge it, but dislodge it I could not! | 30. I tried to move it away, but I could not dislodge it! |
| 10. Uruk-land was gathered about it, | 31. Uruk-land stands about [it], |
| | 32. [The land is gathered] aro[und it], |
| | 33. [The popula]ce [jostles] t[oward it], |

37. Text and notes in Appendix, no. 5.

| | |
|---|---|
| | 34. [The men ma]ss against it. |
| 11. While the men kissed its feet. | 35. [Like a baby, an in]fant, they kiss its feet. |
| 12. As I set my forehead, | |
| 13. They loaded (it on) me. | |
| | 36. [I loved it, and lik]e a wife I caressed it. |
| 14. I raised it and brought it to you." | 37. [And I] placed it at [your] feet, |
| | 38. [(And) you m]ade it compete with me." |
| 15. The mother of Gilgamesh, knowing all, | 39. [The mother of Gilgamesh is wise, kn]owing; she knows all; She says to her lord; |
| 16. Says to Gilgamesh | 40. [Rimat-Ninsun is wise], knowing; she knows all; She says to Gilgamesh: |
| | 41. "[As for your having se]en(?) the stars of heaven, |
| | 42. [(Something) like a meteor(?) of A]nu which fell upon you, |
| | 43. [You raised it, but it was too mi]ghty for you; |
| | 44. [You tried to move it away, but] could [not] move it; |
| | 45. [You place]d it at my feet; |
| | 46. [I made] it [com]pete with you; |
| | 47. [You loved it, and like a wife] you car[essed(?)] it. |
| 17. "Perhaps, Gilgamesh, one like you | vi, 1. [A mighty com]rade who rescues [(his) friend will come to you]. |
| 18. Was born on the steppe, | 2. [He is the mightiest in the land]; strength he h[as]. |
| 19. And the hills have reared him. | 3. [Like a meteor(?) of Anu, his might is [s]trengthened. |
| 20. When you see him [(. . . . ?)], you will rejoice. | |

| | |
|---|---|
| 21. The men will kiss his feet; | |
| 22. You will embrace [(him. . . . and . . . . ?)] him; | 4. [You will love him and like a wife] you will care[ss(?)] him, |
| | 5. [And he will al]ways rescue yo[u]. |
| 23. You will lead him to me." | |
| | 6. Your dream is [favorable, most preci]ous." |
| ***Second Dream*** | ***Second Dream*** |
| 27b."[*At the gate*] of my marital [chamb]er, in the street | 9. "[At the gate of my marital chamber], |
| 28. [Of] broad-marted [Uru]k, | |
| 29. There lay an a[x]e, and | there lay an axe, and |
| 30. They were gathered about it. | they were gathered about it. |
| | 10. [Uruk-la]nd stands about it, |
| | 11. [The land is gather]ed around it, |
| | 12. [The popula]ce [jostles] toward it. |
| | 13. [I] placed it at your feet. |
| 31. That axe, strange was its appearance. | |
| 32. As soon as I saw it, I rejoiced. | |
| 33. I loved it, and like a wife | 14. [I loved it, and] like a wife |
| 34. I caressed(?) it. | I caressed(?) it. |
| 35. I took it and placed it | |
| 36. At my side." | |
| | 15. [You] made it compete with me." |
| 37. The mother of Gilgamesh, knowing all, | 16. The mother of Gilgamesh is [wise], knowing; she knows all; She says to her lord; |
| | 17. Rimat-Ninsun is wise, knowing; she knows all; |
| 38. [Says to Gilgamesh,] | She says to Gilgamesh: |
| 39. [". . . . (break of a few lines)] | 18. "The axe which you saw is a man. |

| | |
|---|---|
| | 19. You shall love him, and [li]ke a wife you shall caress (?) him, |
| ii.1. Because he shall compete with you." | 20. And I shall make him compete with you. |
| | 21. A mighty comrade who rescues (his) friend will come to you. |
| | 22. He is the mightiest in the land; strength he has. |
| | 23. Like a meteor(?) of Anu, his might is strengthened." |
| | 24. Gilgamesh speaks to her, his mother: |
| | 25. "[To me], by the command of Enlil, may a counselor descend! |
| | 26. A [fri]end and counselor may I gain! |
| | 27. [May I g]ain a friend and counselor!" |

In the late version, these dreams and their interpretations are considerably expanded. Much of the elaboration consists of passages which assimilate the dreams to each other; the interpretations of the dreams are also assimilated to the dreams and to each other. The elaborations and variants, and their sources, are as follows.[38]

**FIRST DREAM**

**GE *I, v, 29.*** "mighty" *(dan).* This wording, replacing the Old Babylonian version's "became heavy" *(iktabit),* corresponds to the threefold stress on Enkidu's might in the interpretation of the dream (*dannu, dan, dunnunā,* vi, 1–3, 21–23). Derivatives of *danānu* and *kabātu* are often used synonymously[39]; the late ver-

38. The following was written independently of Cooper's "Gilgamesh Dreams of Enkidu," but agrees with it fully.

39. See *CAD* D, p. 93b lex., and *CAD* K, p. 25c lex., as well as the interchanging use of *dannu* and *kabtu/kabātu* as medical symptoms in *CAD* D, pp. 6c, 93d, 94b; *CAD* K, pp. 15d, 31b. In the present context, *dan* undoubtedly refers to heaviness, but I have translated "mighty" to bring out the text's intentional use of a word which echoes other passages.

sion's choice of the former seems intended to echo the frequent descriptions of Enkidu which use this root (Gilg. Ni. 3′; *GE* I, iii, 3–4; v, 3; and the interpretation of the dream).

***v, 31–34.*** Expanded by parallel lines; same as second dream, vi, 9 (end) to 12.

***v, 36.*** From the Old Babylonian version of the second dream (Gilg. P. i, 33–34); in the late version, this line is found in both dreams and both interpretations (v, 36, 47; vi, 4, 14, 19). In the first dream it replaces a different formulation of Gilgamesh's emotional response to Enkidu (Gilg. P. i, 20, cf. 32).

***v, 38.*** From the interpretation of the second dream in the Old Babylonian version (Gilg. P. ii, 1); in the late version, this line is found in both dreams (v, 38, 46; vi, 15, 20).

***v, 39–40.*** Expanded by parallel lines; same as second dream, vi, 16–17. Note how the components of the original lines are divided among the two new lines: "The mother of Gilgamesh . . . " (Gilg. P. i, 15) goes with *GE* I, v, 39, while "says to Gilgamesh" (Gilg. P. i, 16) goes with *GE* I, v, 40. Cf. Chapter 3, E.

***v, 41–47.*** These lines repeat details of the dream (27–30, 36–38) as a prelude to interpreting it. In the Old Babylonian version, Ninsun did not repeat the dream. Repetition of a dream or details thereof in the course of interpreting it is found in other interpretations of symbolic dreams, both early and late.[40] Note how the order of lines 45 through 47 differs from that of the dream in ll. 36–38; the order in vi, 13–15 differs from both.[41]

***vi, 1–3.*** See comments on v, 29. Lines 2 and 3 are from *GE* I, iii, 3–4, 16, 30–31. This version of the interpretation concentrates more on the nature and actions of the character portended in the dream, whereas the Old Babylonian version focused mostly on Gilgamesh's response to him.

40. See Oppenheim, *Dreams,* pp. 245–47, nos. 1, 2, 4 (cf. p. 248, no. 5).

41. Cf. the variant order of Gilg. Y. ii, 16–20 and v, 14–17 in *GE* II, v, 3–4 and GEH rev. vi, 6–9.

***vi, 4.*** If we are correct in reading this as future tense, it is a part of the interpretation which corresponds to a detail of the dream (v, 36, 47).

**SECOND DREAM**

***vi, 9 (end) to 12.*** Corresponds to first dream, vi, 31–34.

***vi, 13.*** "I placed it at your feet" corresponds to the first dream, v, 37, unlike the Old Babylonian version in which Gilgamesh treated the two symbols differently, bringing the meteor(?) to Ninsun, but placing the axe at his own side (Gilg. P. i, 14, 35–36). The treatment of the axe in the Old Babylonian version is still reflected elsewhere in the late version, in *GE* VIII, ii, 4, where Gilgamesh calls Enkidu "the axe at my side" *(ḫaṣṣin aḫija).*[42]

***vi, 15.*** From the interpretation (Gilg. P. ii, 1); corresponds to the first dream and its interpretation (see on v, 38).

***vi, 16–17.*** See comments on v, 39–40.

***vi, 18.*** Mentions a detail of the dream in the course of interpreting it; see comments on v, 41–47.

***vi, 19.*** See comments on vi, 4; corresponds to vi, 14 = Gilg. P. i, 33–34 and possibly to this line's more immediate counterpart, the (missing) Old Babylonian version of the interpretation of the second dream.

***vi, 21–23.*** Identical to part of the interpretation of the first dream, vi, 1–3. The missing Old Babylonian interpretation of this dream must have been shorter.

The reasons for the late version's omission of details from the dreams in the Old Babylonian version are less obvious. Brief mise-en-scènes (Gilg. P. i, 4–5, 27a) are dropped in both dreams, perhaps to get directly to the symbols. On the other hand, the omission of Gilg. P. i, 21 eliminates a correspondence between the first dream

42. Cf. n. 36, above.

(11 = *GE* I, v, 35) and its interpretation, while the omission of Gilg. P. i, 20 and 32 eliminates correspondences between the first dream and the second. Since the late version strives to create correspondences, these omissions are most plausibly credited to an earlier stage in the transmission between the Old Babylonian period and the late version. A similar explanation may apply to the omission of Gilg. P. i, 12–13, which describes Gilgamesh's efforts to lift the meteor and the help which enabled him to succeed. This help was necessary, since Gilgamesh had earlier been unable to move the meteor by himself (8–9). The late version thus describes Gilgamesh's earlier failure (*GE* i, v, 29–30) and ultimate success (37), but leaves the success unexplained by omitting the help he received.[43] Conceivably this help was omitted because even in the Old Babylonian version it had not been mentioned either in Ninsun's interpretation of the dream or in the realization of the dream in Gilg. P. v–vi. Again, this change probably took place prior to the formulation of the late version, which would have been more likely to resolve the inconsistency by adding help for Gilgamesh to the interpretation and realization of the dream.

## *Enkidu's Arrival in Uruk*

More drastic abridgement, combined with assimilatory expansion, appears in the account of Enkidu's arrival in Uruk.[44]

| **Old Babylonian, Gilg. P. v, 9–vi, 23** | **Late Version, *GE* II, ii, 35–50** |
| --- | --- |
| v, 9. He entered the hea[rt] of broad-marted Uruk. | |
| | ii, 35. . . . . in the street of Uruk (of?) the sheepfold. |

43. Jastrow (YOR 4[3]: 56–57) explained omissions in the late version on the ground that *GE* I is ostensibly anticipating the dreams, while Gilg. P. i narrates them directly; the implication is that *GE* II also narrated the dreams directly *and fully*. This assumption cannot currently be tested, since the relevant portion of *GE* II is missing, but even if it should be correct, it is irrelevant, since the late version omits lines throughout the epic where no such claim of anticipation, as opposed to direct narration, can be made.

44. Text and notes in Appendix, no. 7.

| | |
|---|---|
| | 36. . . . . strength. . . . |
| | 37. He barred the way [. . . . ] |
| 10. The populace gathered around him. | 38. Uruk-land stands [about him], |
| 11. (As) he/they stood in the street | 39. The land is gathered [around him], |
| 12. Of broad-marted Uruk, | |
| 13. The people were gathered, | 40. The populace jostles [towards him], |
| | 41. The men mass [against him]. |
| | 42. Like a baby, an infant, they k[iss his feet]. |
| 14. Speaking about him, | |
| 15. Saying: "He is like Gilgamesh in build! | |
| 16. Though [sh]orter in height, | |
| 17. He is [st]rong(er?) in body! | |
| 18. . . . . was [bo]rn, | |
| 19. He a[te] spring grass. | |
| 20. The milk o[f wild] creatures | |
| 21. He was wont to suck." | |
| 22. Continually in Uruk are sacrifices (offered). | |
| 23. The men were celebrating. | |
| 24. A/the *lušanu*-instrument was set up. | |
| 25. For the man of f[a]ir appearance, | 43. Before the handsome man [arrives(?)], |
| 26. For Gilgamesh, as (for?) a god, | 44. For Ishhara the bed [of marria]ge |
| 27. A/the *meḫrum* was set up. | is laid out. |
| 28. For Ishh[a]ra the bed | 45. For Gilgamesh, as (for?) a god, |
| 29. Is laid out. | a/the . . . is set up. |
| 30. Gilgamesh wi[th the y]ou[ng wom]an | |

31. (Is to) jo[in] at night.

32. As he approa[ch]ed,

33. [Enkidu] stoo[d] in the street,

34. He ba[rred the w]ay

35. To Gilgamesh.

36. . . .
(about seven lines missing)

vi, 6. Gilgamesh [. . . .]

7. On the steppe/against [. . . .]

8. [. . . .] sprouts(?)

9. [Enkidu] rose up and [. . . . (?)]

10. Before him.

11. They confronted each other in the Market-of-the-Land.

| | |
|---|---|
| 12. Enkidu blocked the gate | 46. Enkidu blocked, in the gate of the marriage chamber, [his (i.e., Gilgamesh's)] feet. |
| 13. With his foot. | |
| 14. He did not allow Gilgamesh to enter. | 47. He does not allow Gilgamesh to be brought in. |
| 15. They grappled with each other, like champions (lit. victors) | 48. They grappled with each other in the gate of the marriage chamber. |
| 16. They bent the knee. | |
| | 49. In the street they attacked each other, in the Market-of-the-Land. |
| 17. They shattered the doorpost, | 50. The [d]oor[p]osts trembled, |
| 18. The wall shook. | the wall *shook*. |
| 19. Gilgamesh and Enkidu | (remainder missing) |
| 20. Grappled with each other, | |
| 21. Like champions (lit. victors) they bent the knee. | |
| 22. They shattered the doorpost, | |
| 23. The wall shook. | |

One gains the impression that in the late version the narrative has been pared down[45] to leave just those elements which more or less corresponded with the dreams in which the scene was foretold, namely the crowd in the market square of Uruk and the struggle between Gilgamesh and Enkidu. The additions indicate the same assimilatory purpose: The expansion of the crowd scene in lines 38 through 42 is identical to that in the first dream, including the kissing of Enkidu's feet, which has no equivalent in the Old Babylonian version of this passage. (Note in contrast that in *GE* VI, 179, which is not related to this scene and was not foretold in the dreams, the description of the crowd is not expanded.) Apparently the lines about Enkidu's blocking Gilgamesh's way in the street (Gilg. P. v, 33–35) have been moved up to the beginning of the scene in the late version (*GE* II, ii, 36–37) to match the first dream, where the meteor(?), which represents Enkidu, constitutes an obstacle for Gilgamesh at the beginning of the dream (*GE* I, v, 28b–30).

## *Enkidu's Arguments against Challenging Huwawa*

Another case of assimilation is found in Enkidu's attempts to dissuade Gilgamesh from challenging Huwawa. In the Old Babylonian version, Enkidu makes at least two such attempts, phrased in different ways. First, Gilg. Y. iii, 14–24[46]:

14. "I found it out, my friend, in the hills,
15. As I was roaming with the wild beasts:
16. At sixty leagues the forest is encompassed;
17. [Who is there th]at would go down into its midst?
18. [Huwa]wa—his roaring is the flood-storm,
19. His mouth is fire,
20. His breath is death!
21. Why have you come to desire

45. Such abridgment is an exception to the general rule often stated that ancient Near Eastern literary works tended to expand, rather than contract, with time. Cf. Albright, *Stone Age,* pp. 79–80; *AM,* p. 249; cf. also Laessøe, "Literary and Oral Tradition," p. 210. For other cases of material dropped in the late version, note its apparent lack of room for much of what was narrated in Gilg. Me.+Mi.: the dialogue with Shamash (Gilg. Me. i), the barmaid's carpe diem speech (Gilg. Me. iii), and the introduction to Gilgamesh's request for directions from her (Gilg. Mi. iii, 3–6).

46. Text and notes for this and the next two passages in Appendix, no. 8.

22. To do this thing?
23. Irresistible in (his) onslaught
24. Is the [*ba*]*ttering ram,* Huwawa."

Lines 16 through 24 are repeated later in the elders' warning (v, 13–19) in different order. But prior to this, after Gilgamesh's response to his first warning, Enkidu adds another (Gilg. Y. iii, 38–iv, 2):

iii, 38. How can we go. . . .
39. To the [Cedar] Forest?
40. Its keeper is (the god) Wer.
41. He is mighty, never res[ting].
42. Huwawa, We[r]. . . .
43. Adad has. . . .
44. He. . . .
iv, 1. To safeguar[d the Cedar Forest]
2. A sevenfold terror [Enlil gave him(?)].

A fragment of the late version of Enkidu's warning incorporates parts of both of these warnings (*GE* II, v, 1–6)[47]:

| | |
|---|---|
| 1. To safeguard the Cedar [Fores]t,<br>2. As a terror to mortals has Enlil appointed him. | = Gilg. Y. iv, 1–2 (corrupted)[48] |
| 3. Humbaba—his roaring is the flood-storm, his mouth is fire, his breath is death!<br>4. He can hear (at a distance of) sixty leagues rustling in the forest; who is there that would go down to his forest? | = Gilg. Y. iii, 18–20, 16–17 (corrupted?) |
| 5. To safeguard the cedar(s), as a terror to mortals has Enlil appointed him.<br>6. Weakness seizes him who goes down to his forest. | = Gilg. Y. iv, 1–2 (corrupted) |

47. Conceivably some or all of Gilg. Y. iii, 38–44 was incorporated right before this fragment into the missing end of *GE* I, iv.
48. On the corruptions, see pp. 63, 68 and 282.

The late version of the elders' warning also includes the same combination (GEH, vi, 6–9, 12 = *GE* II, v, 3–5; contrast the Old Babylonian version, Gilg. Y. v, 8–19).

The identity of these warnings with those in the Old Babylonian version is patent, despite some changes in detail. Some of the changes are the result of textual corruption (see n. 48). The late version's "his forest" (also in GEH vi, 9) for the Old Babylonian's "its midst" assimilates the line to its antecedent, though this reading, too, could conceivably stem from scribal error (the ideograms ŠÀ for "midst" and TIR for "forest" are graphically similar). Line 6 has no equivalent in the Old Babylonian version (nor in the late version of the elders' warning, GEH vi, which differs from Enkidu's warnings in other respects as well). It does, however, correspond with what actually happens to Enkidu during the expedition: His hand and arm become weak (*GE* IV, vi, 25, 34).[49]

The repetition in line 5 of lines 1 and 2 in *GE* II, v, from Enkidu's second warning in the Old Babylonian version, frames the excerpt from that version's first warning. This looks like another case of resumptive repetition *(Wiederaufnahme),* with the interpolation followed by repetition of the lines immediately preceding the point at which the interpolation was made.

## *Gilgamesh's Encounters on the Journey to Utnapishtim*

Another case of assimilation in the late version spreads over an entire section. In his quest to reach Utnapishtim, Gilgamesh encounters first "the barmaid Siduri, who dwells by the edge of the sea" (*GE* X, i, 1; restored from IX, catchline) and then Sursunabu/Urshanabi, Utnapishtim's boatman, asking each for directions to reach Utnapishtim. In the Old Babylonian version, Gilgamesh's request is phrased differently in each case. To the barmaid, he says (Gilg. Mi. iii, 9–10):

*ki-ib-sa-am ku-ul-li-mi* [. . . .]
*šum-ma na-ṭú tâmta* [*lu-bi-ir*]

Show (me) the path [. . . .]
If it be possible, [I will cross] the sea.

49. Cf. Gilgamesh's mysterious sleep in *GLL* A 71ff. (cf. Kramer, in *GSL,* pp. 64–65).

To Sursunabu, he says (Gilg. Me. iv, 13):

*ku-ul-li-ma-an-ni U-ta-na-iš-*[*ti*]*m re-qa-am*

Show me Utanaishtim[50] the Faraway.

In the late version, the requests to the barmaid and Urshanabi are identical (*GE* X, ii, 16–19; iii, 33–35):

*e-nin-na sa-bit/*$^{d}$*Ur-šanabi mi-nu-ú ḫar-ra-an šá Ut-napištim*
*mi-nu-ú it-ta-šá ia-a-ši id-ni id-nim/nam-ma it-ta-šá ia-a-ši*
*šum-ma na-ṭu-ma tâm-ta lu-bir*
*šum-ma la na-ṭu-ma ṣēra lu-ur-pu-ud*

Now, barmaid/Urshanabi, what is the road to Utnapishtim?
What is its landmark? Give me, O give me its landmark!
If it be possible, the sea I will cross;
If it be not possible, over the steppe I will range!

Although the requests proper have been reformulated in the late version, the conditional sentence which followed the first request (Gilg. Mi, iii, 10) has been taken over verbatim, expanded with an antithetically parallel line, and incorporated in both requests (see also *GE* X, ii, 31).

The case of this small passage is representative of the late version's treatment of Gilgamesh's journey to Utnapishtim. So far as one can judge from the Old Babylonian fragments Gilg. Me. and Gilg. Mi., Gilgamesh's dialogues with the barmaid and Sursunabu differed from each other in most respects, although they reflected a single concern. The same is true of the preceding dialogue with Shamash in Gilg. Me. i. The relationship between these three dialogues in the Old Babylonian fragments is illustrated in the accompanying comparison (verbal parallels are indicated by underlining).

The comparison shows that each of the verbal parallels indicated by underscoring is shared by only two of the three dialogues, and that the parallels are distributed differently in each. Thus Gilgamesh's plea, "O . . . , now that I have seen your face, show me . . . ," which is part of a single sentence in the dialogue with Sursunabu, is split up into two widely separated speeches in the dialogue with the barmaid. The parallel passages in all three

50. On this form of the name, see chap. 12, p. 229, n. 38.

| Shamash | Barmaid | Sursunabu |
|---|---|---|
| *(Gilg. Me. i)* | *(Gilg. Me. ii–iii; Gilg. Mi. iii)* | *(Gilg. Me. iv; Gilg. Mi. iv)* |
| Unknown speaker addresses Gilgamesh, may tell him of impossibility of crossing sea to Utanaishtim.[51] | | Sursunabu asks Gilgamesh's identity and identifies himself. |
| | [Gilgamesh probably identifies self, perhaps describes adventures with Enkidu.] Describes death of Enkidu and concludes: "Since his passing I have not found life. | Gilgamesh identifies himself and describes his journey: |
| | I have roamed like a hunter in the midst of the steppe. | ". . . (I) have traversed the mountains, a distant journey as the sun rises. |
| | O̲ barmaid, n̲o̲w̲ t̲h̲a̲t̲ ̲I̲ ̲h̲a̲v̲e̲ s̲e̲e̲n̲ ̲y̲o̲u̲r̲ ̲f̲a̲c̲e̲, let me not see the death which I ever dread." | O̲ Sursunabu, n̲o̲w̲ t̲h̲a̲t̲ ̲I̲ ̲h̲a̲v̲e̲ s̲e̲e̲n̲ ̲y̲o̲u̲r̲ ̲f̲a̲c̲e̲, s̲h̲o̲w̲ ̲m̲e̲ Utanaishtim the Faraway." |
| Shamash: "G̲i̲l̲g̲a̲m̲e̲s̲h̲,̲ ̲t̲o̲ w̲h̲a̲t̲ ̲e̲n̲d̲ ̲(̲l̲i̲t̲.̲,̲ w̲h̲e̲r̲e̲)̲ ̲d̲o̲ y̲o̲u̲ ̲r̲o̲a̲m̲?̲ T̲h̲e̲ ̲l̲i̲f̲e̲ ̲y̲o̲u̲ p̲u̲r̲s̲u̲e̲ ̲y̲o̲u̲ ̲s̲h̲a̲l̲l̲ n̲o̲t̲ ̲f̲i̲n̲d̲." | Barmaid: "G̲i̲l̲g̲a̲m̲e̲s̲h̲,̲ ̲t̲o̲ w̲h̲a̲t̲ ̲e̲n̲d̲ ̲(̲l̲i̲t̲.̲ w̲h̲e̲r̲e̲)̲ ̲d̲o̲ y̲o̲u̲ ̲r̲o̲a̲m̲?̲ T̲h̲e̲ ̲l̲i̲f̲e̲ ̲y̲o̲u̲ p̲u̲r̲s̲u̲e̲ ̲y̲o̲u̲ ̲s̲h̲a̲l̲l̲ n̲o̲t̲ ̲f̲i̲n̲d̲." | Sursunabu: (contents lost in break[52]) |

51. Compare line 3 to *GE* X, ii, 21. For another view, see Böhl, *RLA* 3:366.
52. On the possibly small size of the breaks, see Millard, *Iraq* 26:100–101.

| | | |
|---|---|---|
| [Speech ends here.] | She continues with carpe diem advice. | |
| Gilgamesh responds: ". . . must I die?" etc., and asks to see "light" (= life).[53] | Gilgamesh responds (after break) with further statement of grief over Enkidu and asks for directions to cross sea to Utanaishtim: "Show (me) the way [. . .]" | Fragmentary beginning of Gilg. Mi. seems to indicate request by Gilgamesh to be taken to Utanaishtim on Sursunabu's boat.[54] |
| [Perhaps a response by Shamash in break.] | Barmaid responds that sea has never been crossed [and presumably directs Gilgamesh to Sursunabu]. | Sursunabu responds that Gilgamesh has broken the Stone Things, instructs him to cut punting poles.[55] |

dialogues are preceded and followed by dissimilar passages. The speeches also differ in length. Although it is possible that the recovery of the lost parts of this section would show that the dialogues resemble each other more than they currently appear to, these differences would remain. One may, however, venture a guess that the lost material would not have assimilated the dialogues to any great extent, for each of the dialogues as preserved is tailored to the nature or role of the character to whom Gilgamesh is speaking. In his speech to the sun-god Shamash, life is symbolized as light.[56] The barmaid's "hedonistic" counsel befits one of her profession, and what remains of the dialogue with Sursunabu deals with his role as Utnapishtim's boatman. In sum, just as the Old Babylonian version of Gilgamesh's two dreams stressed

53. Contrast *GE* X, vi, 23 (*ANET*, p. 507c).

54. For lines 1–2, omitted in *ANET*, p. 507, see Millard, *Iraq* 26:101–2, and von Soden, *ZA* 58:190.

55. On the Stone Things, *urnu*-cedars, and the punting poles, see chap. 3, nn. 17–18.

56. Cf. Gilg. Y. iv, 6, "only the gods [live] forever with Shamash." For the sun and other celestial bodies as symbols of longevity, cf. Greenfield, pp. 266–67; Paul, *JNES* 31:351–55; Hallo, *apud* Paul, "Heavenly Tablets," p. 353, § 6.

different aspects of Enkidu's role and worded the dreams differently, each of Gilgamesh's encounters in his quest for immortality stressed different aspects of the quest and its futility.

In the late version, the dialogue with Shamash is not preserved.[57] Those with the barmaid and Urshanabi are, and following them is one with Utnapishtim. This last dialogue was presumably present in the Old Babylonian version,[58] since reaching Utnapishtim was the ultimate goal of Gilgamesh's journey. What interests us in these dialogues is the way that they have been conformed to each other in the late version (*GE* X). The manner in which both the barmaid and Utnapishtim spot Gilgamesh approaching from afar is described in identical terms (*GE* X, i, 10–12; iv, 12–14).[59] Although each encounter begins with unique actions and ends with unique instructions or advice, all three contain the same long dialogue in which Gilgamesh is presumably asked who he is (to judge from his answer in X, i, 31ff.) and why he appears so worn and sad, and in response he describes his achievements, his adventures with Enkidu, Enkidu's death, and his own grief and fear of dying.[60] The late version's characteristic use of the same dialogue in all three scenes contrasts markedly with the varying dialogues of the Old Babylonian version. Equally characteristic of the late version is the fact that at least some elements of the dialogue can be identified as coming from the separate dialogues of the Old Babylonian version. The (presumed) request for Gilgamesh's identity is found in the Old Babylonian version of the scene with Urshanabi (Gilg. Me. iv, 5), as is Gilgamesh's answer, though in a very brief and different form

57. This dialogue is certainly not present in *GE* X, nor is there any room for such a dialogue at the end of IX if one assumes that it would have been as long as X's scenes with Siduri and Urshanabi. I am at a loss to explain its apparent omission.

58. Gilgamesh's meeting with Utnapishtim is mentioned in the hymn at the beginning of the epic (*GE* I, i, 40), but although some portion of this hymn was present in the OB version (which opened with what appears as I, i, 27 in the late version), we cannot be certain that the OB version included every line found in the late version of this hymn, and therefore cannot infer from the hymn that the OB version included this meeting.

59. *GE* X, ii, 37–39 (*GSL,* p. 130), involving Urshanabi, is different, but the gap before col. iii could have contained an introduction like those before the scenes with the barmaid and Utnapishtim.

60. Although much of these dialogues is reconstructed from fragmentary remains, it is the similarity of the remains of the three dialogues which suggests that they were identical. See *GETh.*, pp. 55–56; Schott, *ZA* 42:132–33; Wiseman, in *GSL,* pp. 128–31 (I do not understand Wiseman's seeming denial of this, on p. 131, n. 1, with regard to the dialogue with Utnapishtim).

(8–11). Gilgamesh tells of Enkidu's death and his own grief and wanderings in the dialogue with the barmaid (Gilg. Me. ii, 1–11; cf. Gilg. Mi. iii, 3–6). (The description of Enkidu and the friends' common adventures which precedes the latter passage in the late version [*GE* X, i, 46–51] is also found in Gilgamesh's lament [*GE* VIII, ii, 8–12]; whether it was present in the Old Babylonian version, either in such a lament or in the missing portion of the dialogue with the barmaid, is not known.) Gilgamesh's plaint "Must I die?" is found in the dialogue with Shamash (Gilg. Me. i, 10–16). The request for directions to Utnapishtim is found in the dialogues with the barmaid and Sursunabu in two different forms. At the very least, it is clear that all of these elements were not united in a single long speech in the Old Babylonian version, as most were in the late version. Even if the recovery of missing passages in the Old Babylonian version were to indicate greater similarity between the dialogues than is now apparent, the dialogues still could not exhibit the degree of conformity which the late version has imposed upon them.

## THE SIGNIFICANCE OF THE ASSIMILATION

The secondary character of the assimilatory variants in the late version is suggested by the inconsistencies associated with some of them[61] and corroborated by the analogy of other Old Babylonian compositions which underwent similar development in their late versions. In the late version of *The Atrahasis Epic,* for example, Enlil's description of how mankind's noise has disturbed him is conformed, partly by the creation of parallel lines, to the narrator's description a few lines earlier, unlike the Old Babylonian version, where the two descriptions of the same event were somewhat different.[62] Lambert and Millard have noted other cases of the assimilation of related passages in this version, such as those describing the

61. See above, p. 89 (on vi, 13), pp. 89–90.

62. Compare OB *Atr.* I, 352–59 // II, i, 1–8 with the late version, *Atr.* S, rev. iv, 1–8. In the OB version, the narrator's description in I, 354–55 // II, i, 3–4 differs from Enlil's description in lines 358–59 // 7–8; in the late version, the narrator's description in S, rev. iv, 2–3 is identical to Enlil's in lines 7 and 8 (differences remain in other lines). For text and translation, see Lambert and Millard, pp. 66–67, 72–73, 106–7.

second through fourth plagues which the gods visit upon mankind[63] (they also note one case of the avoidance of repetition).[64] In *Anzû,* Anu summons several gods to challenge Anzû and they decline, until finally the mother-goddess orders her son Ningirsu (Ninurta, in the late version) to take up the cause; after initial difficulty, with the advice and encouragement of the god Ea, Ningirsu (Ninurta) succeeds. The Old Babylonian version quotes only the address to (and refusal speech of) Adad, the first of the declining gods, and the later speeches of the mother-goddess and Ea; all of these speeches differ from one another. In the late version of *Anzû, all* of the declining gods are addressed in identical speeches, which are composed mostly of 1) the Old Babylonian speech to Adad plus 2) a couplet from Ea's final speech of encouragement. The speeches of the mother-goddess and Ea retain distinctive features, but have been partly conformed to each other and to the earlier speeches to the declining gods.[65] In the late version of the refusal speeches, the description of Anzû's crime has been reworded to agree with the narrator's description earlier in the myth, which is not the case in the Old Babylonian version.[66]

Although such pedantic homogenization of passages is a common secondary development in Akkadian narratives, internal parallels and repetitions are by no means absent in Old Babylonian compositions. Within the Old Babylonian *Gilgamesh,* we have already noted in this chapter a small number of similarities between Gilgamesh's two dreams, between Enkidu's first warning and that of the elders, and between Gilgamesh's encounters on his journey to Utnapishtim. There are also recurrent motifs in this version, such as crowd scenes, six- or seven-day and seven-night suspensions of normal action followed by a turning point, and repeated instances

63. Lambert and Millard, pp. 6, 38.

64. Ibid., p. 38.

65. Most of this can be seen by simply comparing the passages in *ANET,* pp. 111 (N.B. n. 9), 113, 515. The first tablet of the late version has recently been edited, with new material, by Hallo and Moran in *JCS* 31:65–115; note Moran's comments on pp. 66–68. The phenomenon of assimilation has now been studied, with further examples, by Cooper in *JAOS* 97:508–12. On the reading of the villain's name as *Anzû* instead of $^{d}$*Zû,* see most recently Cooper in *JCS* 26:121.

66. Assyrian version I, ii, 47–49 (*ANET,* p. 113bc) agrees with lines 20–22 (p. 113a), in contrast to the OB version II, 19–20 (p. 111c), which does not agree with line 1 (p. 111b).

of Gilgamesh's taking his axe in his hand and drawing the sword from his belt.[67] On the whole, the phraseological parallels between the passages involved do not extend beyond a couple of lines. The echoes are clear enough to help unify the epic, but monotony is avoided. In this respect, the Old Babylonian *Gilgamesh* contrasts markedly with the Old Babylonian *Atrahasis,* which is filled not only with recurrent motifs (such as *rigmu,* "noise, thunder"), but also with proposals and their execution, messages and their delivery, identical introductions to successive cycles, and instructions to third parties followed by their transmission and execution, all repeated in virtually identical terms.[68] The style of *Atrahasis* is similar to that of Sumerian epic literature as attested in copies of the Old Babylonian period.[69] The Old Babylonian *Gilgamesh,* with its variety and general avoidance of repetition and assimilation, represents a different style in the same period. "In it we find the purity and simplicity of language, the clarity of outline, and the depth of experience that cannot be duplicated."[70] The late version, on the other hand, "contains much that is extraneous to the tale, and it lacks the freshness and vigor of the Old Babylonian fragments."[71]

The repetitiousness and homogenized style typical of epic literature is often explained by theories of oral composition or recitation. It may be that these theories correctly explain the origin of this *style* in Mesopotamia. Some narratives were certainly read or recited aloud, and even private reading was often done aloud.[72] However,

67. See the OB passages cited in the Introduction, nn. 27, 23, and 21.

68. See Hecker, p. 159.

69. These features are described by Kramer, "Sumerian Epic Literature"; cf. Hecker, pp. 188–92, where differences are also noted. Repetition of this sort is, of course, known in epic literature of many cultures.

70. Speiser, in an unpublished paper on the epic.

71. Jacobsen, *Treasures,* p. 195.

72. For the singing or oral recitation of Akkadian epics—unless these statements are literary fictions—see OB *Atr.* III, viii, 18 and the texts cited by Wilcke, *RA* 67:154–55, l. 1; 172–73, ll. 158, 161; 175–76, l. 2; 179, l. 1. Note that *EnEl* was recited at the Babylonian New Year's festival (see *ANET,* p. 332); it or its concluding hymn to Marduk is said in the epic's epilogue to have been spoken by an old scholar and then written and deposited "for the hearing of future generations" (*ištur-ma iš-t[a]kan ana šimē arkūti, EnEl* VII, 158; see Wilcke, *ZA* 67:172–74)—in other words, written to be read or taught aloud (cf. l. 161 as read by Lambert *apud CAD* $M_1$, p. 367d). Cf. also the uses to which the tablets of *Erra* are to be put (*Erra* V, epilogue). For private reading aloud, note that one of the Akkadian verbs for "read" means basically "call" (Akk. *šasû,* like Heb. *qārā';* see Driver and Miles, 2:286), and for other cultures see McCartney; Zwettler, pp. 16–17 and 37, n. 45; R. J. Williams, *JAOS* 92:218.

repetitiousness and homogeneity need not imply oral composition, transmission, or recitation of any particular composition. A narrative style created for oral recitation may well have survived as a norm for centuries after the transition to writing.[73]

Conceivably, the degree of repetitiousness and homogenization that we find in Sumerian myths and epics is also due, in part, to their age. By the Old Babylonian period, from which our earliest copies mostly come, these epics were already several centuries old and may have already undergone a process of expansion and assimilation which conceals a more variegated original style. This process is, in any case, what later happened to Old Babylonian Akkadian literature. Whether a composition was as variegated as the Old Babylonian *Gilgamesh* or already as homogenized as the Old Babylonian *Atrahasis Epic*, it was to become much more homogenized by the time of its late versions. At least on the surface, it appears that the stylistic norm of Sumerian literature as we know it survived and in later centuries was imposed upon Akkadian literature that had earlier escaped it.

## M. MAJOR ADDITIONS

Three major additions in the late version of the epic were mentioned in Chapter 2: the prologue (*GE* I, i, 1–26),[74] the flood story (in *GE* XI), and the whole of Tablet XII. While these were not part of the Old Babylonian version known to us, there is no obvious indication whether the prologue and Tablet XII were first added in the late version or at some intermediate stage[75] (on which see chap. 5; on the flood story, see chap. 12).

73. Cf. Komoróczy, *Act. Ant.* 23:63, n. 88. On the subject of compositions which are "transitional between an oral tradition of verbal art and a written literary tradition," see Zwettler, pp. 15–19.

74. Text and translation in Appendix, no. 3, and chap. 7.

75. The absence of the prologue in *Hit. Gilg.* I cannot be taken as evidence for its absence in the contemporary Akkadian version, since the Hittite version is an abridgement (see chap. 5, "The Hittite Version(s)"). Nor can the possibly hymnic introit of that version (I, i, 1–2) be taken to reflect a hymn at the beginning of the contemporary Akkadian version (such as *GE* I, i, 27ff.), for the Hittite hymnic introit resembles that of the Hittite *Song of Ullikumi* (if correctly understood: see Güterbock, *JCS* 5:141, 160; *JCS* 6:34) and could be an independent Hittite addition. Note that *GE* XII is not limited to the Nineveh MSS, but was present in NB MSS, too (see *GSL,* p. 135).

## *The Prologue*

The addition of introductory and supplementary matter to an existing composition is a known secondary development in ancient Near Eastern literature. As early as the Old Babylonian period, the list of antediluvian kings was prefixed to the *Sumerian King List,* which originally began with the postdiluvian kings.[76] In narrative literature, the late version of *Etana* adds an eight-line introduction to the original prologue.[77] Various types of texts have been supplemented after their original conclusions.[78] The most unambiguous cases[79] involving narrative literature come from non-Mesopotamian sources, such as the additions to Job and Esther found in their ancient translations.[80]

Lines 16 through 21 of the prologue are repeated at the end of Tablet XI (303–7), forming a literary framework for the epic. This

76. *ANET,* p. 265; *SKLJ,* pp. 55–64; Finkelstein, *JCS* 17:39–51; Rowton, *JNES* 19:160–61; Hallo, *JCS* 17:54, 56–57 (with the last, contrast Lambert and Millard, p. 25). According to Finkelstein, the prologue to the *LH* was probably a secondary addition to the laws, although made within Hammurapi's own lifetime (*JCS* 21:42, with n. 5; Addenda, p. 48; cf. Hallo, CRRAl 17 [1970]:121, and in general Paul, *Studies,* pp. 11–26).

77. The late version begins with the fragment translated in *ANET,* p. 517c, followed by *ANET,* p. 115d, which is the late counterpart of the OB version, *ANET,* p. 114b. The late introduction has been restudied by Kinnier Wilson in *Iraq* 31:8–12, and Wilcke *ZA* 67:211–14.

78. E.g., the *Tummal Inscription* (see Sollberger, *JCS* 16:41) and the omen series *Šumma Izbu* (Leichty, *Šumma Izbu,* pp. 20–26). Cf. Lambert in *GSL,* p. 44, and n. 2. For internal supplementation, see Sjöberg and Bergmann, pp. 8 (on no. 9), 24.

79. An ambiguous cuneiform example is the combination of the syllabic alphabet known as "Silbenalphabet A" and a bilingual version of the creation of man. A copy of this text from Assur (*KAR* 4, twelfth to eleventh century) indicates in its colophon that the text is complete, but a seventh-century copy from Nineveh indicates by its catchline that it was somehow "followed" by *Atr.* This is usually taken to imply an enlarged composition consisting of the *Silbenalphabet* plus the bilingual creation story supplemented by *Atr.,* which is another creation story. But it is not certain that the catchline in this case refers to successive tablets of a single series; it could refer simply to proximity on a library "shelf" or in a school curriculum. See the literature cited by Grayson in *ANET,* pp. 512–13. For a translation of the creation story of *KAR* 4, see Heidel, *Babylonian Genesis,* pp. 68–71; for its colophon, see Hunger, no. 50. The catchline of the Nineveh tablet K4175+Sm57 + 80-7-19, 184, and 82-3-23, 146 is closer to the incipit of *Atr.* than is usually realized; it reads *e-nu-ma i-lu*$_4$ *a-w*[*i* . . .]; according to E. Sollberger, who kindly collated the tablet, "the *a-* of *awīlum* and even the beginning of *-wi-* shows clearly on the fragment Sm 57" (letter to the author, 22 Mar. 1971). On the varying functions of catchlines, see Leichty, "Colophon," p. 148; Hallo, *IEJ* 12:24.

80. See Pope, *Job,* pp. 351–54; Moore, *Esther,* pp. LXI–LXIV, 103–13.

device raises a number of questions which cannot presently be answered on empirical grounds. Are both sections of the framework the work of the same hand? If so, the lateness of the prologue implies the lateness of XI, 303–7. But it seems equally possible that a late redactor found XI, 303–7 in his textual prototype and created the framework simply by repeating them in I, i, 16–21. Since frameworks often mark the beginning and end of compositions, the location of this one could imply that I, i, 1–15 and XII were added later than the framework. But this is not necessarily so, for we also know of doublets which appear a short distance from the extremities of a composition.[81] The purpose of the framework and prologue as a whole are discussed separately in Chapter 7.

## *Tablet XII*

Tablet XII, as mentioned earlier, is inconsistent with the rest of the late version and appears as an appendix to the epic, rather than an integral part of it (see above, p. 27, and below, p. 138). The purpose for which it was added is elusive, being hidden behind the words of an older source which the redactor who added this tablet took over practically verbatim (though in translation). Under the circumstances, one must look for indirect clues to the redactor's purpose by examining the relationship of the contents of Tablet XII to the rest of the epic and to what is otherwise known about Gilgamesh, and by examining passages where the redactor has deviated from a literal rendition of the Sumerian source. The tablet does have a number of thematic affinities with passages elsewhere in the epic, but most do not seem important enough to account for a desire to incorporate the episode despite its discrepancies with the rest of the epic.[82] However, there is one entire section of the epic of which Tablet XII, in which Enkidu describes the netherworld, might have been regarded as a doublet or variant, Enkidu's deathbed vision of the netherworld in *GE* VII, iv, 15ff. The vision briefly characterizes the netherworld and the mode of existence there, mentioning the

81. *GA* 30–36, 107–11.

82. Compare 1) *GE* XII, 1, 4, 8 to I, ii, 10 (see below, chap. 9); 2) XII, 14, 16 to Gilg. Me. iii, 10; *GE* VII, iii, 36ff.; XI, 240ff.; 3) XII, 24, 26 to Gilg. Me. iii, 12–14.

people dwelling there who had enjoyed privileged positions in life.[83] Tablet XII complements this information by having Enkidu, when he is temporarily brought up from the netherworld, describe the condition of those distinguished there not by privilege but by family situation, mode of death, and other circumstances.[84] Some have suggested that the aim of Tablet XII is to give Gilgamesh as complete a knowledge of death as possible once he had resigned himself to it.[85] However, it is not precisely a knowledge of death, but of the netherworld and the condition of its inhabitants which is imparted to Gilgamesh, a knowledge which seems appropriate in light of his role as king and judge of the netherworld in Mesopotamian religion.[86] In the Sumerian *Death of Gilgamesh,* it is stated, according to one interpretation,[87] that Gilgamesh's kingship of the netherworld was a consolation for his failure to attain immortality. Has the redactor who added Tablet XII introduced a similar line of reasoning into the epic—namely, that once Gilgamesh was reconciled to his mortality (*GE* XI) he began to obtain the knowledge which would be appropriate to his posthumous role?

That some connection with this role is involved in the addition of Tablet XII seems indicated by the fact that the order of the lines deviates from that of the Sumerian source only in the last ten lines (145–54), so that this version culminates (unlike the Sumerian source) with a reference to the condition of "him whose spirit has no one to tend it" (*ša eṭimmašu pāqida la īšû,* XII, 153–54).[88] In a ritual text, it is just such uncared-for spirits which Gilgamesh is entreated to help satisfy and banish to the netherworld.[89] The ad-

83. Cf. Oppenheim, *Or.* 17:45.

84. There is a line in *GE* XII which has no equivalent in the Sumerian version and which, as restored by Jensen (KB 6(1):262), makes this the explicit purpose for Enkidu's recall: *a-na a-ḫi-*[*šu ur-ti erṣeti i-qab-bi*], "that to [his] brother [he might tell the ways of the netherworld]," *GE* XII, 81, restored on the basis of lines 88, 90. As a line apparently added by the Akkadian redactor (though there exists the possibility of a Sumerian textual prototype unknown to us—see below in this chapter) this would be an important clue for us, but while the restoration is plausible it is still conjectural, and we cannot infer from it with confidence.

85. Cf. Oppenheim, *Or.* 17:20; Dossin, "Enkidou," pp. 587–88; cf. Böhl, *RLA* 3:370.

86. See above, pp. 14, 80–81.

87. Lambert, in *GSL,* p. 51; cf. Kramer, *BASOR* 94:6.

88. Neither in the main recension of *GEN* nor in the differently ordered Ur MS U16878 (UET 6(1), no. 58) is this the last-mentioned class of the dead nor the end of the composition.

89. *TuL,* pp. 132–33. Cf. Finkelstein, *JCS* 20:114–15.

dition of Tablet XII to the epic may thus have been intended to bridge the gap between this role, in which Gilgamesh was so well known in Mesopotamian religion, and the Gilgamesh of the epic.[90]

The translator's treatment of Enkidu's status in Tablet XII is the same as that by the Old Babylonian author of the integrated epic. Where the Sumerian text terms Enkidu Gilgamesh's "servant" (arad, šubur) the Akkadian either drops the word or reads otherwise (*GEN* 177, 241, 243 = *GE* XII, 6, 80, 84); the Akkadian also adds two lines, with no counterpart in the known Sumerian manuscripts, calling Enkidu Gilgamesh's "brother" *(aḫu)* and friend *(ibru)* (*GE* XII, 81, 87, added after the translations of *GEN* 241, 245). On the other hand, Tablet XII retains "my master" (*be-li*, Sum. lugal-mu) in Enkidu's address to Gilgamesh, and line 54 adds to the translation of *GEN* 222 a clause which calls Enkidu Gilgamesh's "servant" (ARAD); even if the latter clause is based on an unknown Sumerian prototype, its retention in Tablet XII is anomalous.

Tablet XII also displays assimilation and expansion based on parallel passages. While the Sumerian merely states that "the wailing of the netherworld seized" Enkidu (*GEN* 221 = *GE* XII, 46), in Tablet XII the description of the capture is expanded in seven additional lines (47–53), based mostly on 1) material that had followed the equivalent of line 46 in Gilgamesh's warning (47–49, based on 29–31 = *GEN* 200–203) and 2) the account of the capture in Gilgamesh's subsequent appeals to the gods (51, 53, based on 59–61 = *GEN* 227–29 and parallel passages). Tablet XII also adds an appeal to the god Sin (62b–69a) which is identical to the appeals to the gods Enlil and Ea. While assimilatory expansions are characteristic of the late version, they are also found in Old Babylonian manuscripts of Sumerian compositions,[91] which means that those in Tablet XII could be based on currently unknown Sumerian prototypes.[92]

90. Keeping in mind that Sîn-leqi-unninnī, to whom the epic is attributed in a literary catalogue (see p. 246), was an incantation/exorcist priest *(mašmaššu)*, one wonders whether this last point might not suggest that *GE* XII was also the contribution of a *mašmaššu* who added the tablet because of his professional interest in its subject matter.
91. Cf. chap. 1, n. 38.
92. Cf. Shaffer, "Sources," pp. 37, n. 2, and 153 *ad* 294.

## ON THEOLOGICAL CHANGES

We have noted two cases of the epic's possible responsiveness to religious-historical developments, one involving the goddess Ishtar (pp. 76–81) and one involving the god Shamash (pp. 68–71). On the other hand, the late version fails to reflect a pair of important religious developments, the "exaltations" of Marduk and Ashur to national and cosmic status.[93] These deities played no role in myths and epics of the Old Babylonian period. *The Gilgamesh Epic* is not alone in making no room for them in its late version. The other Akkadian myths and epics of Old Babylonian origin also give them no role in their late versions. The late version of *Atrahasis,* for example, does not introduce these deities into its account of the creation of man, even though the late myth *Enuma Elish*[94] makes Marduk the creator, and manuscripts of *Enuma Elish* from Assur make Ashur its hero.[95] Similarly, the late manuscripts of *Anzû* have Ninurta, not Ashur or Marduk, as the hero.[96] It is not that late theologians failed to credit Marduk with the defeat of Anzû: A hymn of Ashurbanipal celebrates him as "the one who crushed the skull of Anzû,"[97] but contemporary copies of the myth were not altered in accordance with this declaration.

Lambert has argued that Marduk did not rise to his later preeminence until toward the end of the second millennium.[98] Ashur apparently first began his rise to superlocal prominence around the thirteenth century.[99] These approximate dates accord well with a date in the last half or quarter of the second millennium for the late versions of *The Gilgamesh Epic* and other Akkadian literary texts

93. For the exaltation of gods, see Hallo and van Dijk, chap. 6. There is one possible insignificant reference to Marduk in *GE,* if the text BM 34191 (*GETh.,* pl. 12 and *CT* 46, no. 28) is really part of the epic (Landsberger, *RA* 62:103; note the hesitation of Lambert and Millard, *CT* 46, p. 4).

94. See Lambert, "Reign"; Hallo and van Dijk, pp. 66–67; Grayson, in *ANET,* p. 501; cf. Schott, *MVAG* 30(2):123; Jacobsen, *Treasures,* p. 167 (contrast his earlier view in *JAOS* 88:107–8); contrast van Dijk, *MIO* 12:57–74; cf. Yadin, pp. 82–85; Grafman, pp. 47–49.

95. Labat, *Le Poème,* p. 22; see his notes on *EnEl* I, 81–82; III, 10 (add: III, 138, in *KAR* 173 rev. 19). In other Assur MSS, Marduk remains: *KAR* 5, rev. 9 (*EnEl* II, 95); *KAR* 316:4′ (*EnEl* IV, 20); *KAR* 164:1 (*EnEl* VI, 1), etc.; cf. also Ebeling, *RLA* 1:196–97, and Luckenbill, *Annals,* pp. 140–42.

96. See *ANET,* pp. 111 (n. 12), 113, 514–17; Hallo and Moran.

97. Brünnow, p. 230, l. 15; Gressmann, p. 268, l. 15; quoted in *ANET,* p. 113.

98. Lambert, "Reign."

99. Edzard, "Mythologie," p. 43.

originating in the Old Babylonian period. In other words, these texts reached their final form before Marduk and Ashur were considered important enough to be given a place in them.[100] Once they had been given their classical late formulations, they were not subject to further theological editing.

In this chapter we have seen that the late version fleshes out—some would say pads—the epic considerably. Although the plot remains essentially the same, several episodes are restructured or expanded with new material, although a few are abridged. Much of the new material has a homogenizing effect: Variety in wording is diminished, and dissimilar but related sections become much more repetitious and similar to each other. Recurrent thematic and verbal motifs lend more explicit unity to the epic (see also, in the Introduction, "The Story and Its Structure"). Changes of these types adapt the epic to a stylistic norm well known in epic literature. New sections are added to the epic as introductory and supplementary matter. The role of one character, the sun-god Shamash, is redefined in the light of geopolitical changes and theological reflection. Although the plot of the epic seems to have remained basically unchanged, the post–Old Babylonian editors exercised freedom with regard to its structure and content, just as they had with regard to its wording.

100. Schmöckel, p. 14; Edzard, "Mythologie," p. 97; for a different explanation, cf. Böhl, *RLA* 3:369.

# 5

# *The Fragments of the Middle Babylonian Period*

In Chapters 3 and 4, we have seen how the late version, the last documented stage of the integrated *Gilgamesh Epic,* differs from the epic's earliest documented stage, the Old Babylonian version. However, since a gap of several centuries separates these versions, the question remains whether the final editor is responsible for all the differences or whether he based his work on some intermediate version. The analogy of *Etana* illustrates such an intermediate stage,[1] but different compositions cannot be presumed to have undergone identical development, and the case of *The Gilgamesh Epic* must be determined in its own light.

The gap between the Old Babylonian and late versions is partly bridged by some Hittite, Hurrian, and Akkadian fragments of the Middle Babylonian Period (mostly from about the fourteenth century B.C.E.), but these do not present as clear a picture as one would desire. Most of these texts have come to us from outside of Mesopotamia, and whether they reflect the contemporary Mesopotamian

1. The OB version of *Etana* (*ANET,* pp. 114–18) tells, in two consecutive parallel passages, of a lopsided arrangement whereby the serpent hunts and then shares his prey with the eagle and its offspring (*Etana* A-2, 8–11); the MA version describes the arrangement in three consecutive parallel passages (MA version i, 15–23). The late version describes the arrangement differently, in four consecutive parallel passages, with the eagle sharing the burden of hunting equally with the serpent (*Etana* C-2, 20–27). See now Cooper, *JAOS* 97: 509, 511.

text or earlier (Old Babylonian) prototypes is debated.[2] They are few in number, short, and fragmentary, and they coincide only incompletely with passages attested in the other versions. The Hittite and Hurrian fragments of this period do coincide with some of the Old Babylonian fragments, and some passages in the Hittite version coincide with passages in the late version. The Hittite and Hurrian fragments, however, can be used to reconstruct the epic's inner-Mesopotamian development only with caution, for several reasons: 1) They are translations, with the Hittite possibly translated not directly, but from the Hurrian[3]; 2) they display signs of modification and adaptation to foreign conditions and interests; 3) the Hittite version is certainly an abridgment of the original. The Akkadian fragments of this period[4] cover parts of the epic not currently attested in the Old Babylonian fragments, ruling out a direct comparison between them. On the other hand, the Akkadian fragments do coincide with a few passages in the late version, and this will give us an impression of how close the text was to its final form in this intermediate period.

## THE HITTITE VERSION(S)

Since the Hittite version (or versions: see presently) permits some comparison with the Old Babylonian version as well as the late version, we shall consider it first. This version was known as *The Song of Gilgamesh* (ŠÌR GIŠ.GIM.MAŠ).[5] According to A. Kammenhuber, its fragments date from the second half of the fourteenth century.[6] The Hittite version unquestionably reflects the integrated version of the epic. This is indicated first of all by the fact that a number of its tablets cover several episodes each. The first tablet covers in abbreviated form the events narrated in *GE* I through V. The events of *GE* VI (as well as III–V) are presupposed

2. See above, chap. 2, nn. 10–11. Böhl groups Gilg. Meg. with the OB texts (*RLA* 3:366).
3. Cf. Kammenhuber, pp. 21, 46, 55.
4. Gilg. Bo., Gilg. Meg., and Gilg. Ur.
5. Otten, *RLA* 3:372; cf. ŠÌR Ullikumi, "The Song of Ullikumi" (Güterbock, *JCS* 5:141, 160), the title of the Hittite text translated in *ANET,* pp. 121–25; cf. Otten, *Ist. Mit.* 8:118; *CAD* Z, p. 36 *sub* c.
6. P. 46.

by *Hit. Gilg.* No. 8 and its partially overlapping duplicate No. 9, which include episodes of *GE* VII through X, from Enkidu's dream in which the gods condemn him for his part in killing Huwawa and the Bull of Heaven through Gilgamesh's mourning over Enkidu and his meeting with the barmaid. Furthermore, this version bears the earmarks of the integrated epic as we have defined it on pp. 29–30 and 45–46: Gilgamesh's oppression of Uruk, description of the origins of Enkidu,[7] Enkidu as Gilgamesh's "dear brother,"[8] and Gilgamesh's reaction to Enkidu's death.[9]

On the other hand, the Hittite is a drastic abridgment of the epic, in comparison to both the Old Babylonian and late versions. In its first tablet, it reaches the defeat of Huwawa, a point which the Old Babylonian version (Gilg. Y.) had not reached by the end of its third tablet and which the late version reaches only in its fifth tablet. Another tablet of the Hittite version (represented by *Hit. Gilg.* nos. 8 and 9) covers events related in Tablets VII through X of the late version. What the Hittite version omits is therefore no indication of an omission in its Akkadian prototype. What it adds, however, can show that features otherwise known to us only from the late version are at least older than that version. A case in point is the story of the creation of Gilgamesh. Fragmentary remains of *GE* I, i and ii, indicate the presence of such an account in the late version, and the Hittite version preserves it.[10]

The fidelity with which the Hittite version reflects the Middle Babylonian Akkadian text of this and other episodes is difficult to assess, given the lack of overlap between the extant Akkadian and Hittite fragments of the period.[11] The Hittite fragments bear some indications of local Anatolian adaptation, such as, probably, the inclusion of the storm-god among those who endowed Gilgamesh with his attributes at birth.[12] Otten suggests that the omission of

7. *Hit. Gilg.* I (text in Appendix, no. 1; translation on pp. 153, 179, 193, 199).

8. *Hit. Gilg.* no. 8, ll. 19, 22; on the Hurrian version, see Kammenhuber, p. 47.

9. *Hit. Gilg.* no. 8 (*ANET,* p. 86).

10. See below, pp. 153–56.

11. The dialogue between Gilgamesh and Ishtar in *Hit. Gilg.* no. 7 is generally assigned to the scene in which Ishtar proposes to Gilgamesh (= *GE* VI: see Friedrich, *ZA* 39:49), a scene which is partly preserved in Gilg. Bo. However, the recognizable details are so few that Stefanini is able to doubt the identification (*JNES* 28:47).

12. See *Hit. Gilg.* I, i, 5–6 (see Appendix, no. 4); contrast *GE* I, v, 21–22, and see Otten, *Ist. Mit.* 8:119; cf. Kammenhuber, pp. 21, 56. The addition or outright substitution of gods is a typical feature in the local adaptation of texts. For some examples, see chap. 4, n. 95; *ANET,* pp. 111a, and p. 113d, n. 12; Cooper, *Iraq* 32:51–67; Hallo, *Jacobsen AV;* pp. 184 (n. 24), 188.

scenes relating to Uruk and the relatively extensive attention given to the battle with the guardian of the Cedar Forest reflect special Anatolian interest in episodes which were localized nearby.[13] But such modifications are by no means extensive. The story still begins in Uruk.[14] Although the Euphrates is naturally given its Hittite name, Mala,[15] the names of most of the characters remain the same as those used in the Akkadian epic.[16] None of the Hittite deities who predominate in native Hittite mythology has gained a major role or displaced a Mesopotamian god.[17] Adaptation to local interest was therefore not so thoroughgoing as to modify the epic beyond recognition.

An indirect method for gauging the relationship of the Hittite to the contemporary Akkadian version would be to compare equivalent phenomena which occur in the Old Babylonian, the Hittite, and the late versions. When a phenomenon in the Hittite differs from the Old Babylonian version, it can theoretically be either a local Hittite modification or a reflex of a modification which had taken place in the Mesopotamian prototype on which the Hittite is based. If the same phenomenon is also found in the late version, which is also Mesopotamian, this would tilt the balance in favor of the latter possibility. An example of this is the form of characters' names. In the Hittite version, the characters who were known as Sursunabu and "the barmaid" in the Old Babylonian version are called, respectively, Urshanabi and Ziduri (= Siduri), as in the late version.[18] These changes from the Old Babylonian version may therefore be presumed to have taken place in the Akkadian prototype on which the Hittite version is based. On the other hand, the

13. *GSL*, p. 143; *Ist. Mit.* 8:96, cf. 120; *RLA* 3:372. Uruk is mentioned only to the extent necessary to explain the creation of Enkidu (*Ist. Mit.* 8:98–99 on Vs. I, 11–12). On the location of the Cedar Mountain episode in the Hittite version, see *Ist. Mit.* 8:122, § 9.

14. Cf. the location of *Gurparanzaḫu and the Bow* (Laroche, *Catalogue* no. 233) in Akkad.

15. Kammenhuber, pp. 21, 50.

16. Ibid., pp. 50–57. Two apparent exceptions are Ullu- and Naḫmu-zulen, who are sometimes taken for Utnapishtim and Siduri (cf. Friedrich, *ZA* 39:65; Kammenhuber, pp. 54–57). Kammenhuber speculates that the texts which use, respectively, Naḫmuzulen and Ziduri may represent different Hittite versions (p. 57).

17. But note the presence of Kumarbi in *Hit. Gilg.* no. 13, rev. iv, 15 (cf. Friedrich, *ZA* 39:64–65; Kammenhuber, p. 56). The Hurrian fragments reflect a greater degree of modification; see Kammenhuber, pp. 47, 55.

18. On these names, see Kammenhuber, pp. 54–57; Speiser, in *ANET*, p. 89, n. 152; Gadd, *Iraq* 28:116–17.

Hittite version's retention of the Sumerian and Old Babylonian form Huwawa[19] implies that the Hittite's Akkadian prototype had not yet adopted the form Humbaba, which is used in the late version.

Unfortunately it is hardly possible to compare the wording of all three of these versions, since only a few equivalent lines are preserved in all three.[20] It is, however, clear that the Hittite version has textual affinities with both the Old Babylonian and the late version without being literally identical to either. This may be seen in the account of Gilgamesh's encounter with Urshanabi. One Hittite fragment, from the end of a tablet, corresponds to an Old Babylonian fragment describing part of this scene[21]:

| **OB Gilg. Mi. iv, 1–10** | ***Hit. Gilg.* no. 11, 1–5** |
|---|---|
| 1–4. (Dialogue mentioning, probably, Utanaishtim and boarding the boat) | 1. "[Y]ou cross it. . . . |
| | 2. Which you cross so regularly by day and night." |
| 5. [He(?)] speaks a word to him, | |
| 6. [S]ursunabu says to him, to Gilgamesh: | 3. [T]hus Urshanabi: |
| 7. "The Stone Things, O Gilgamesh, | "Those same two stone images |
| (were what) carried me across, | 4. Always carried me [ac]ross." |
| 8. That I might not touch the waters of death. | |
| | Thus Gilgamesh: "Why |

19. See Wilcke, *RLA* 3:530, b.

20. Urshanabi's instruction to Gilgamesh to take his axe and cut poles is worded differently in Gilg. Mi. iv, 11–14, *Hit. Gilg.* no. 10, rev. iii, 11–12, and *GE* X, iii, 40–42 (see texts in Appendix, no. 12, and translations on pp. 115–16). The wording is partially identical and partially different in all three versions and no clear line of development is discernible.

Owing to the fragmentary state of the material, it is not always clear whether related but dissimilar passages are contradictory or complementary; compare the varying suggestions about the OB and Hittite fragments describing the battle with Huwawa by Bauer, *JNES* 16:261; Otten, *Ist. Mit.* 8:124; Kinnier Wilson, in *GSL*, p. 109.

21. Text and notes in Appendix, no. 11.

| | |
|---|---|
| 9. In your anger you smashed them. | 5. Do you make me angry?" |
| 10. I kept those [S]tone Things with me [t]o carry (me) across! | |

A larger fragment, *Hit. Gilg.* No. 10, preserves more of the scene about Gilgamesh and Urshanabi, but the first part of the dialogue corresponds to a speech attributed in the late version not to Urshanabi, but to the barmaid Siduri[22]:

| ***Hit. Gilg.* No. 10, rev. iii** | ***GE* X, ii, 26–27 and iii, 40–50** |
|---|---|
| 5. From a tree. . . . | |
| 6. They ate them. Urshanabi to Gilgamesh, | |
| 7. The king, answered: | (The barmaid:) |
| 8–9a. "How, O Gilgamesh, over a[cross] the sea will you go? | ii, 26. "Where(?), then, O Gilgamesh, would you cross the sea? |
| 9b–10. When you reach the waters of death, what will you do? . . . . | 27. When you reach the waters of death, what would you do?" . . . |
| | (Urshanabi:) |
| 11a. Grasp the axe in your hand | iii, 40. "Lift, Gilgamesh, the axe to your si[de], |
| 11b. And [cut poles] | 41. Go down to the forest and cut poles |
| 12. Which are forty ells(?) (long) or fifty e[lls(?)] (long). | which are five *nindas* (long) |
| | 42. Trim(?) them and attach *ferrules,* (then) bring [them to the boat]. |
| 13–14a. When Gilgamesh heard Urshanabi's words, | 43. When Gilgamesh [heard] this, |
| 14b. He gr[asped] the axe in his hand | 44. He lifted the axe to his side, D[rew the dirk of his belt], |

22. Text and notes in Appendix, no. 12.

| | |
|---|---|
| 15–16a. And cut poles which were fifty ells(?) (long) . . . . | 45. Went down to the forest and [cut] poles which were five *nindas* (long). |
| 16b. He peeled them. . . . , | 46. He trimmed(?) them and attached *ferrules,* |
| 17. And placed them on the boat. | and he brought (them) [to the boat]. |
| 18–19a. The two of them [boarded] the boat, Gilgamesh and Urshanabi. | 47. Gilgamesh and Urshanabi boarded [the boat]. |
| 19b–20. Ursh[anabi] held the rudder(?) with his hand, while Gilgamesh. . . . | |
| 21a. With his hand. | |
| | 48. They launched the boat and they [sailed away]. |
| 21b. A [journey(?)] of a month and fifteen days. . . . | 49. A journey of a month and fifteen days,<br>By the third day. . . . did/was . . . . |
| | 50. Urshanabi arrived at the waters [of death]. |

The only extant Old Babylonian text which corresponds to part of the Hittite text here is the passage in Gilg. Mi. iv in which Sursunabu instructs Gilgamesh about the punting poles[23]:

| **OB Gilg. Mi. iv, 11–14** | ***Hit. Gilg.* No. 10, rev iii, 11–12** |
|---|---|
| 11. [Ta]ke, O Gilgamesh, the axe in your hand. | 11a. Grasp the axe in your hand. |
| 12. Cut [po]les which are smooth, three hundred (in number), | 11b–12. And [cut poles] which are forty *ells* (long) or fifty *e[lls* (long)]. |
| 13. . . . . attach oarlock ropes, | |
| 14. [(And) bring them(?)] into the boat. . . . | |

23. See n. 22, above.

Comparison of the three versions of this scene shows affinities between the Hittite and each of the other two versions. Apart from the brevity of the Hittite version, its wording is at times quite close to the wording of one of the others. Urshanabi's statement in *Hit. Gilg.* 11:3–4a looks like a nearly literal translation of line 7 (cf. 10) of the Old Babylonian version (a line omitted in the late version), save for the (possibly interpretive) rendering of "Stone Things" as "stone images."[24] Given the similarity of these two lines, the references to anger in line 5 of the Hittite text and line 9 of the Old Babylonian text also seem related, notwithstanding the fact that they are assigned to different speakers in these texts; this suggests that some confusion or modification has taken place in the course of transmission. The frequent differences in wording and detail between the Old Babylonian and Hittite versions show that the Hittite version is mostly not a literal translation of the Old Babylonian.

In other lines, the Hittite fragments show affinity to the late version.[25] The wording of Urshanabi's questions in *Hit. Gilg.* 10 rev. iii, 8–10, is practically identical with the wording of Siduri's questions in *GE* X, ii, 26–27. But there are frequent differences in wording and detail between the Hittite version and the late version in this and other sections of the epic.[26]

Owing to the fragmentary state of both the Old Babylonian and Hittite versions, we cannot say whether the latter's attribution to Urshanabi (in *Hit. Gilg.* no. 10, iii, 8–10) of questions asked in the late version by the barmaid represent a secondary development or a discrepancy between versions. It is conceivable that these questions appeared in speeches of both the barmaid and Sursunabu in the Old Babylonian version, and in speeches of both in the Hittite version.[27]

24. This interpretation is favored by some modern scholars; see the literature cited in chap. 3, n. 17.

25. The affinity of the axe formula in *Hit. Gilg.* is ambiguous; see Appendix, no. 12, note on *Hit. Gilg.* 10, rev. iii, 11. The instruction-followed-by-verbatim-execution-of-that-instruction sequence in lines 11 through 16 of that passage resembles the style of the late version, but lacking the continuation of Gilg. Mi. iv, we cannot be certain that the OB version lacked a verbatim execution.

26. For example, the passages describing the creation of Gilgamesh and that of Enkidu, and Enkidu's early life, on which see below, chaps. 7 and 10.

27. The barmaid's speech in Gilg. Mi. iii, 11′–12′ begins similarly to that in the late version where she asks these questions (*GE* X, ii, 20ff.). There is a missing speech of Sursunabu, beginning in Gilg. Me. iii, 14, which precedes the OB counterpart of the sequel to these questions (Gilg. Mi. iv. 11ff. // *Hit. Gilg.* no. 10 iii, 11ff.). Only a scrap of the scene with the barmaid is preserved in *Hit. Gilg.* no. 10: obv. ii, 6.

In this case, the late version preserved only one of the two passages in which the questions were asked (just as it omitted certain correspondences in Gilgamesh's dreams, as noted already on pp. 89–90. Alternatively, the speech was originally Sursunabu's and was secondarily transferred to the barmaid in the late version, or it was originally the barmaid's and the Hittite version represents either an outright transfer to Urshanabi or an imitation of the barmaid's speech, designed to make the dialogue with Urshanabi more similar to that with the barmaid.

The small Hittite fragment No. 11 abridges and corresponds to a part of Gilgamesh's dialogue with Urshanabi in the Old Babylonian version which was not included in No. 10.[28] Unless we are dealing with a scribal oversight, this indicates that the two fragments belong to different Hittite versions of the epic, as Kammenhuber suspected on stylistic grounds.[29]

To summarize, the Hittite version(s) reflects the integrated epic, but it goes its own way in several respects. It is an abridgment of the epic, and what it preserves of the original is not a literal translation, at least not of any Akkadian text known to us. It displays a little adaptation to local Anatolian interests. Its contents reflect some confusion or modification of the original, though it is unclear whether this is due to the Hittite translation or its source. As for its relationship with the Akkadian epic, it clearly has textual affinities with both the Old Babylonian and the late version. There is insufficient evidence to determine whether the textual affinities with the late version are in passages where the late version deviated from the Old Babylonian version or in passages where the text never changed. In the former case, the Hittite reading would indicate that the change had taken place by the Middle Babylonian period. In the latter case, the agreement with the late version would really be an agreement with the Old Babylonian version. Finally, the Hittite version shows that some, but not all, changes in the forms of characters' names had taken place by the Middle Babylonian period.

28. Friedrich had suggested that no. 11 belongs somewhere between nos. 9, iii and 10, iii, but now that its OB counterpart is available (Gilg. Mi., iv) it emerges that no. 11 represents a passage missing from no. 10, iii right before line 11, in the middle of the dialogue: The last line of no. 11 echoes Gilg. Mi. iv, 9, and the second part of Urshanabi's speech in no. 10, iii, begins (11a) with its counterpart of Gilg. Mi. iv, 11 (Gilg. Mi. iv, 10 may have been thought redundant after l. 7).

29. Pp. 21, 55–56.

## THE HURRIAN FRAGMENTS

The Hurrian texts are so fragmentary that they are practically useless for our purposes. Since these fragments are given differing names in their colophons ("Fourth tablet of Huwawa; incomplete" and ". . . . tablet of Gilgamesh; incomplete"), it has been suggested that they do not reflect the integrated epic but the earlier independent tales.[30] However, the tablet entitled "Huwawa" terms Enkidu Gilgamesh's brother,[31] an epithet which belongs to the integrated epic. The title "Huwawa" may constitute simply a subsection title,[32] or it may be a variant name attached to one version or recension[33] of the epic among the Hurrians, in either case because of local Anatolian interest in the guardian of the Cedar Forest, which was near the Lebanon and Anti-Lebanon ranges. Conceivably, then, the Hurrian fragments do reflect the integrated epic. In any case, the Hurrian fragments do not transmit the epic without modification, for they also introduce Hurrian gods into the narrative.[34]

## THE AKKADIAN FRAGMENTS

There are three Akkadian fragments from the Middle Babylonian Period. Two of them are from outside of Mesopotamia: one from Boghazköi, the site of the Hittite capital in Anatolia (Gilg. Bo.), another from Megiddo in Palestine (Gilg. Meg.).[35] The third is from

30. Otten, in *GSL,* p. 140; Kammenhuber, p. 47. The two fragments also write Gilgamesh's name differently ($^{d}$*Gal-ga-mi-šu-ul* versus $^{d}$*Bil-ga-miš*), but this could reflect only a recensional difference.

31. Kammenhuber, p. 47.

32. An inexact parallel to this would be the subseries titles described by Leichty in *Šumma Izbu,* p. 25.

33. Some texts are referred to alternatively by subject titles and by their incipits (e.g., "The Series Gilgamesh" vs. "Him Who Saw All," "The Series Erra" vs. "King of All Inhabited Places," "The Decree(s)/Laws of Hammurapi" vs. "When Lofty Anum"; see Finkelstein, *JCS* 21:42; M. Ellis, *JCS* 24:74–82), but this is not the same thing as naming the same epic after two different heroes—antagonists at that!

34. Kammenhuber, p. 47. Cf. Otten, in *GSL,* pp. 140–41, for what may be the Hurrian counterpart of *GE* X, i–ii. For the question of the length of the Hurrian version, see Otten, in *GSL,* pp. 140–41.

35. In considering the possible influence of Mesopotamian literature on the Bible, it is important to note that many cuneiform literary texts were known west of Mesopotamia in the MB Period, prior to the Israelite settlement in Palestine. Note, in addition to Gilg. Meg., the Sumerian and Akkadian literary texts found at Ras Shamra (Nougayrol, *Ugaritica V,* chap. 5) and the Akkadian literary texts found at

Ur in southern Mesopotamia (Gilg. Ur). These fragments relate one of Gilgamesh's dreams on the way to the Cedar Mountain (Gilg. Bo. obv.), part of the scene in which Gilgamesh rejects Ishtar's advances (Gilg. Bo. rev.), and parts of Enkidu's deathbed scene (Gilg. Meg., Gilg. Ur), corresponding, respectively, to parts of *GE* V, VI, and VII. Since the scene with Ishtar is part of the Bull of Heaven episode, we can see that this episode was definitely part of the Akkadian epic by the Middle Babylonian Period. Conceivably this episode and parts of Enkidu's deathbed scene, which are not so far attested in the Old Babylonian fragments, were first added to the epic in a Middle Babylonian version, just as the account of the creation of Gilgamesh, preserved in the Hittite version, could have been. However, the absence of these sections from the Old Babylonian material may be due to the accidents of discovery. That the Akkadian fragments reflect the integrated epic is clear from a number of details. Parts of two episodes which were originally separate—the journey to the Cedar Mountain and the Bull of Heaven episode—appear on one and the same tablet, Gilg. Bo.[36] The fragments of Enkidu's deathbed scene, paralleling *GE* VII, allude to the hunter and the harlot who brought Enkidu to civilization in *GE* I and II (Gilg. Ur) and apparently also to the Cedar Mountain episode of *GE* III and V (Gilg. Bo. obv. 4, 7, 8). Gilgamesh and Enkidu are termed friends several times in these fragments.[37]

Differences between these fragments[38] suggest that they do not represent a single Middle Babylonian version, but rather two or three intermediate stages between the Old Babylonian version known to us and the late version. This impression must, however, be regarded as tentative in view of the poor condition of the fragments (especially Gilg. Meg.) and the foreign provenance of two of

Amarna (Knudtzon, *Die El-Amarna-Tafeln,* nos. 356–58; Rainey, *El Amarna Tablets,* no. 359).

36. The reverse apparently skips from Gilgamesh's toilet (=*GE* VI, 1ff.) to Ishtar's indignation (=GE VI, 80ff.), omitting (with the possible exception of rev. 8–9) Ishtar's proposal and Gilgamesh's rejection. Cf. Kupper, in *GSL,* p. 100, and von Soden, *ZA* 53:221.

37. Gilg. Bo. obv. 8, 10, 13, 21; Gilg. Meg. rev. 2, 7, 17; Gilg. Ur. obv. 5, rev. 60.

38. Note also the different orthography of characters' names in the three fragments: $^{d}$GIŠ.GIM.MAŠ (Gilg. Bo.), $^{I}$GIM.MAŠ (Gilg. Meg); $^{d}$*En-ki-du*$_{4}$ (Gilg. Bo.), $^{I}$*En-ki-du* (Gilg. Meg.), $^{d}$*En-ki-du*$_{10}$ (Gilg. Ur). In and of themselves these orthographic differences do not indicate differences in content, but at least those between Gilg. Meg. and Gilg. Ur are accompanied by differences in content (see below in this chapter).

them, which opens the possibility that some differences are due to local, non-Mesopotamian adaptation.

## *The Boghazköi Fragment*

We shall discuss each of the Akkadian fragments separately, beginning with the fourteenth- to thirteenth-century fragment from Boghazköi (Gilg. Bo.). The obverse of this fragment ties in with part of Tablet V of the late version. *GE* V relates three dreams that Gilgamesh had on the way to the Cedar Mountain. An Old Babylonian fragment preserves what is apparently the first,[39] Gilg. Bo. contains the second, and the late version gives the third and a scrap of the second (*GE* V, iii–iv). All three dreams are thus preserved, but direct comparison is rendered practically impossible because of the negligible overlap (despite tantalizing similarities between the dreams). However, an indirect comparison may be based on the introductions to the second dream, preserved in Gilg. Bo., and that to the third dream, preserved in *GE* V, which are similar[40]:

| **Gilg. Bo. obv., 6–12** | ***GE* V, iv, 7–13** |
|---|---|
| 6. Sleep, the outpouring of the night *(mūši),* overcame [him/them]. | 7. [Sl]eep, which is poured on mankind *(nišī),* fell over him. |
| 7. At midnight sleep [left] him. | 8. [In] the middle watch he ended his sleep. |
| 8. A dream he tells Enkidu, [his] fr[iend]: | 9. [H]e arose and said to his friend: |
| 9. "If you did not awaken me, why [am I awake]? | 10. "My friend, did you not call me? Why am I awake? |
| | 11. Did you [n]ot touch me? Why am I startled? |
| | 12. Did [n]ot some god pass by? Why is my flesh numb? |

39. Gilg. Har. B; see Frankena, in *GSL,* p. 119; von Soden, *ZA* 53:215; Grayson, in *ANET,* p. 504.

40. Text and notes in Appendix, no. 9.

10. Enkidu, my friend, I have seen a dream!
11. Did you awaken me? Why . . . . ?
12. Aside from my first dream, a second [(dream) I saw].
13. My [f]riend, I saw a third dream.

It must be kept in mind that these passages are not strictly comparable, since they introduce different dreams. However, the assimilating tendency of the late version would lead one to believe that its lost introduction to the second dream (the dream paralleled in Gilg. Bo.) would not have differed from its introduction to the third, which would make the comparison valid. No line is identical in both of these passages, but the variants are minimal, generally equivalents.[41] The late version has three consecutive parallel lines (10–12) where Gilg. Bo. has two which are interwoven with another pair of parallel lines (9, 11, separated by 10, which is parallel to 12); in other words, the structure in *GE* V is A: A′: A″, while that in Gilg. Bo. is A: B: A′: B′).[42] The differences between the Middle Babylonian and late versions here are similar to the least extensive differences traced earlier between the Old Babylonian and the late version.

Of the second dream itself, only a few lines are preserved in the late version (*GE* V, iii, 32–35). These look different from the Middle Babylonian version of that dream,[43] but a useful comparison is impossible.

Considerable differences from the late version are also found on the reverse of Gilg. Bo. in the passage describing Ishtar's reaction to her rejection by Gilgamesh.[44] There are a few lines of similar content, differently worded,[45] but on the whole the two versions

41. The variants *mūši* / *niši* in the first line could be the result of aural scribal error (cf. *AHw,* p. 969a *sub* 4a); cf. chap. 6, n. 7.

42. Cf. the relationship of *GE* II, ii, 38–41 to Gilg. P. v, 10, 13, separated by 11–12; the latter two lines parallel line 9 (see Appendix, no. 7).

43. Cf. Kupper, in *GSL,* pp. 99–100.

44. While the main part of Gilg. Bo. rev. (11ff.) relates Ishtar's response to Gilgamesh's rejection (corresponding to *GE* VI, 80ff.), what precedes it does not resemble the rejection, but, apparently, Gilgamesh's toilet at the beginning of *GE* VI and Ishtar's proposal slightly later (see von Soden, *ZA* 53:221 and *GETh.,* pp. 81–82). Is this, perhaps, an excerpt tablet?

45. Gilg. Bo. rev. 11–12 and 14a correspond respectively to *GE* VI, 80 and 81.

appear to differ in structure and detail. The text is too poorly preserved to permit detailed comparison.

## *The Megiddo Fragment and the Ur Fragment*

The Megiddo fragment dates to approximately the fourteenth century.[46] It contains part of Enkidu's deathbed scene (*GE* VII in the late version). Although the text is fragmentary, what is preserved reveals a relationship with the late version similar to that of Gilg. Bo. obverse[47]: Lines found in both versions are close (there are exceptions), but not identical; on the other hand, the order of lines sometimes differs, and there are lines and sections which were found in only one of the two versions. For example, the late version's passage enumerating twelve days of Enkidu's final illness and his subsequent address to Gilgamesh (*GE* VII, vi, 7–14)[48] is paralleled in Gilg. Meg. rev. 7 end through 12, but there it cannot have consisted of more than six or seven days (there is no room for more). In addition, the addresses which preceded and followed the enumeration were quite different in the two versions.

The Middle Babylonian fragment from Ur is the only fragment of this period to have been found in Mesopotamia. On paleographic and orthographic grounds, Gadd dated the fragment toward the end of the second millennium, about the early eleventh century. This would make Gilg. Ur the latest Middle Babylonian fragment, but still two or three centuries earlier than any of the known manuscripts of the late version. Since the late version is generally supposed to have been formulated some time in the last half or quarter of the second millennium—a few centuries earlier than its earliest known manuscripts—an eleventh-century date could mean that Gilg. Ur is part of a Middle Babylonian version that continued to be copied for some time after the late version was formulated.

There is a slight overlap between Gilg. Ur, Gilg. Meg., and the

46. See Goetze and Levy, p. 128.

47. For the following, see the comparison by Landsberger, *RA* 62:131–35; note, however, that Gilg. Meg. is heavily restored from the later texts, where its preserved portions seem close to them; this could give a deceptive picture of similarity.

48. Thompson's "IV," vi, 7–14 (see *ANET,* p. 87bc); in *RA* 62:133, Landsberger numbers these lines 4–12.

late version (Gilg. Ur 63–67 = Gilg. Meg. obv. 13b–rev. 1 = *GE* VII, iv, 17–20), which enables us to trace the relationship of the three (see the following comparison of the texts).[49]

| **Gilg. Meg.** | **Gilg. Ur** | ***GE* VII, iv** |
|---|---|---|
| | 60. Hear, my friend, the dr[eam] (I had) [last] night: | 14. Hear, my friend, the dream I saw last night: |
| 9b. This is what he s[aid]: | | |
| 10. "[Go]od and pl[easing is the dream], | | |
| 11. [Valuab]le, good, but ha[rsh]; | | |
| 12. . . . . , harsh. | | |
| | 61. The heavens s[hout]ed, the e[arth r]esponded. | 15. The heavens shouted, the earth responded. |
| | 62. [Between] them I was stan[ding]. | 16. Between them I was standing. |
| In my dream I saw a man, | 63. (There was) a man | 17. (There was) a man |
| 13. Short of stature, large of. . . . | | |
| | whose face was dark. | [whose] face was dark. |
| [Like that of Anzû] 14. His [face] was made. | 64. To the face of Anzû [his] fa[ce was similar]. | 18. [To] the face of Anzû his face was similar. |
| The pa[ws of a lion were his paws]. | 65. The paws of a lion were [his] paws. | 19. The paws of a lion were his paws. |

49. Texts in Appendix, no. 10. The creature described in the following vision resembles a denizen of the netherworld (see *A Vision of the Netherworld, ANET,* p. 110, par. 10), possibly Humut-tabal ("Remove Hastily"), the boatman of the netherworld (*ANET,* p. 109d, par. 5). On "the face of Anzû," see Hallo and Moran, *JCS* 31:70, n. 14.

| | | |
|---|---|---|
| 15. The talons of an eagle were his talons. | 66. The talons of an eagle were [his] talons. | The talons of an eagle were his talons. |
| 16. His face was entirely. . . . | | |
| 17. . . . . [his] paws. | | |
| [He grabbed] | 67. He grabbed | 20. He grabbed |
| rev.1. a tuft of my hair and. . . . | a tuft of my hair (and). . . . | a tuft of my hair and overpowered me. |
| (Dream ends) | (Text breaks off) | (Dream continues) |

The Megiddo text is very fragmentary here, but enough survives to show that its wording is close to that of Gilg. Ur where the two texts run parallel, but that it also possesses lines not found in Gilg. Ur (namely Gilg. Meg. obv. 9–12a, 13a, 16 [possibly = Gilg. Ur 63b, differently located], 17). The differences indicate that Gilg. Meg. and Gilg. Ur, though textually related, represent different versions of the epic. Gilg. Ur and the late version flesh out the beginning of the dream with some atmospherics concerning the sounds of heaven and earth (Gilg. Ur 61–62 = *GE* VII, iv, 15–16, either drawing upon a common topos or related in one direction or the other to Gilgamesh's dream in *GE* V, iv, 15). The Ur text breaks off after the man grabs Enkidu's hair. In the late version, we can see that the dream continued with Enkidu's being taken to the netherworld and a description of what he saw there. In the Megiddo text, however, the dream ends when the man grabs Enkidu's hair and does something to him, and it is followed by a speech of Enkidu's to Gilgamesh (Gilg. Meg. rev. 2ff.), the late version's counterpart of which comes only about a column and a half later (*GE* VII, v, end and vi, 1ff.)[50] The late version has thus expanded the passage. Seven lines of the expansion, describing the netherworld in a series of epithets and brief phrases (*GE* VII, iv, 33–39), are identical to a passage which appears in the myth *The Descent of Ishtar to the Netherworld* and the late version of the myth *Nergal and Ereshkigal.*[51] On the face of

50. See Landsberger, *RA* 62:132–33.

51. *Ishtar* (*ANET,* pp. 107–9) N obv. 4–10 (one MS of *GE* adds an eighth line corresponding to the passage in *Ishtar;* see *GETh.*, p. 46, n. 9); *Nergal and Ereshkigal* ii end–iii, 5 (*ANET,* p. 509).

it one would assume that *The Gilgamesh Epic,* in which the netherworld is a secondary theme, borrowed the passage from one of the other texts, where the netherworld is the main subject. But the question is complicated by several other parallels between *Gilgamesh* and *Ishtar,*[52] especially since part of one of these seems to fit the context of *Gilgamesh* more naturally, and therefore more originally, than it fits the context of *Ishtar.*[53] It is not excluded that *Gilgamesh* was the original source of the passage we are discussing, but reciprocal influence between the texts in the course of their transmission or their reliance upon a common source is also possible. For our purposes, it is sufficient to note that even apart from the possible influence of these parallels, at least some of the epithets for the netherworld used in the late version's expansion were traditional.[54] The list of dwellers of the netherworld (*GE* VII, iv, 40ff.) also appears to be based upon conventional material, rather than being original with the late version of *Gilgamesh.*[55]

Enkidu's dream is the best-preserved section of the Ur tablet. As the parallel passages just cited reveal, the text of this section is identical to that of the late version. Gilg. Ur as a whole is close to the late version when they run parallel, which is usually the case. But enough differences remain to show that we are not yet dealing with the standardized late version. The number of true variant readings between Gilg. Ur and the late version is about 8[56] in the

52. *GE* VI, 99–100 // *Ishtar* obv. 19–20; *GE* VI, 81–82 // *Ishtar* rev. 3–4; *GE* VII, iii, 6a+8, 20, 22 // *Ishtar* rev. 23, 26, 28; note that in place of *Ishtar* N, rev. 23, *Ishtar* A (ll. 19–20) is similar to *GE* VII, iii, 6–7, rather than 6a+8; see *ANET,* p. 108, n. 23, and see the texts below, p. 171.

53. "The besotted and thirsty shall smite your cheek," *GE* VII, iii, 22 // *Ishtar* rev. 28, fits the harlot of *GE* more than Asushunamir of *Ishtar.* For a possible qualification of this argument, see chap. 8, n. 32.

54. "House of Darkness" (cf. *DG* A, 26), "Abode of Irkalla," "Land of No Return," "the road whose traveler returns not" (see *Descent of Inanna, ANET,* p. 54, ll. 82–83); see Tallqvist, pp. 37, 34, 15–16.

55. To *GE* VII, iv, 46–49 (on part of which see *CAD* L, p. 244cd), cf. *The Death of Ur-nammu* 77 (Kramer, *JCS* 21:114/118, l. 77); *DG* frag. B 20, 23–26 (compared to our passage by Kramer, *BASOR* 94:12, n. 32); cf. Job 3:13–19; Isaiah 14:9. Belit-Ṣeri (*GE* VII, iv, 51) = Ningishzida of *DG* frag. B, 13.

56. (Gilg. Ur 7) *ḫariṣ* vs. *ḫa/ulliq;* (10) KAR.KID (usually = *ḫarimtu* in *Gilgamesh:* see Gilg. P. iv, 12 and *GE* VI, 166 with var.) vs. [f]*šamḫat;* (23) *pa-ḫa-ri* vs. KASKAL; line 38 (see Landsberger); (54) *limellâ qātaki*(?) vs. *lu nidinki;* (57) *ašib* vs. *ittālu;* l. 60 apparently lacks the late version's *aṭ-ṭul* (see Landsberger); (61) *ir-*[*mu*]*ma* (with Gadd and the copy) vs. *ilsû.* In line 24, *ma-a-a-la-ki* vs. *m*[*a*]-*ṣal-lu-ka* could be due to scribal confusion (*ṣa* is graphically close to *a*). For two other possible variant readings, see Gadd's commentary on Gilg. Ur lines 9 and 67. Orthographic and grammatical variants are excluded from the discussion here.

approximately 60 lines of this manuscript which are at least partly legible, or a ratio of 1 variant for every 7½ lines. This is a somewhat higher percentage than one normally finds between manuscripts of the late version.[57] Furthermore, there are 3 or 4 additional words or phrases in these passages in the late version,[58] and 5 full lines found only in the late version, 2 lines found only in Gilg. Ur, and an entire section of 5 lines in Gilg. Ur which is replaced by a 16-line section in the late version.[59] Such a high percentage of plusses and minuses within the space of about 60 lines far surpasses anything encountered among manuscripts of the late version.[60]

What emerges from the Ur tablet is first of all that in the last centuries of the second millennium, the wording of the epic was close to that of the late version. But the fact that the text of lines appearing in both versions is close, while at the same time other lines are yet to be added (or, in a few cases, subtracted), reminds us that the wording of verses and the addition or subtraction of verses are separate phenomena which did not necessarily develop together.[61] It seems possible that the main body of the epic attained its final wording first, and later underwent a supplementary elaboration. If so, an important aspect of that elaboration may be indicated by the expanded late version of Shamash's rebuke of Enkidu, in the deathbed scene, for cursing the hunter and the

57. The estimate at the beginning of chap. 6 implies about 100 true variants (i.e., variants not due to scribal error) among about 1,600 fully or partly preserved lines of the late version; in other words, even with its larger number of MSS, the proportion of variants in the late version is only 1 per 16 lines. This ratio is naturally higher in tablets for which a larger number of exemplars is available, but even in *GE* XI the variants do not reach a ratio of 1 per 10 lines, despite the fact that some of its lines are attested in up to four or five MSS (see chap. 6, n. 5).

58. The late version adds [*ṣa-a-a*]-*du* at the beginning of line 6; [x x x]-*ti* at the beginning of line 10 (see *GETh.*, pl. 27:5); -*ka ṣillu* (GIŠ.MI) in line 25; and *ana eb-ri-šu* in line 58.

59. The late version adds lines after its lines 4, 8, 11, 14, and 56, and apparently lacks counterparts to Gilg. Ur 28–29, and possibly 59 (see Gadd, *Iraq* 28:108–13; Landsberger, *RA* 62:122–29). The variant sections are Gilg. Ur 42–46 and *GE* VII, iii, 35–51.

60. In MSS of the late version, in the approximately 1,600 usable lines of the epic, we encounter, excluding particles, prepositions, and pronominal suffixes, plusses and minuses of about 5 single words, 4 or 5 phrases, 5 lines, and possibly 1 section; see chap. 6. The terms *plus* and *minus* are used in their text-critical sense to refer to items present or absent in one MS as compared to another.

61. Landsberger (*RA* 62:122, n. 91) denies that Gilg. Ur represents a penultimate version of the epic and attributes the missing lines to omission by a student scribe, rather than to a shorter version. But this cannot account for the presence in Gilg. Ur of lines not found in *GE*, and especially for the presence of the variant (not simply shorter) version of Shamash's rebuke to Enkidu.

harlot. In the Middle Babylonian version, only the words *ḫa-bi-lam-ma amēlu,* "rogue," and $^{na_4}$ZA.G[ÌN], "lapis lazuli," are recognizable (Gilg. Ur 42, 46).[62] The first had been used of the hunter in Enkidu's curse[63]; the point of the second seems to be that the harlot had led Enkidu to wealth and luxury, as in the first three lines of the late version of the rebuke (*GE* VII, iii, 29–31). In the Ur tablet, then, Shamash's rebuke must have referred to Enkidu's curses of both the hunter and the harlot. The late version of Shamash's rebuke mentions only the curse of the harlot and is worded very differently. The rebuke on the grounds that the harlot brought Enkidu to wealth and luxury fits the context well, but what follows in the late version seems forced[64]: Shamash naturally includes among the benefits to which the harlot brought Enkidu the latter's friendship with Gilgamesh, but he then proceeds to describe (in nine more lines) Gilgamesh's past favors for Enkidu and his future mourning for him. The stress on Gilgamesh's actions, especially his future actions, is not directly to the point in a speech which aims to persuade Enkidu to cancel his curse of the harlot. What is more, the passage listing Gilgamesh's actions is repeated verbatim by Gilgamesh himself in the next tablet (VIII, iii, 1–7). In other words, this expansion is best understood as part of the assimilating process discussed in Chapter 4. It thus appears that the process was, at least sometimes, part of a supplementary elaboration in the late version. This impression parallels a process attested in the history of other ancient Near Eastern compositions.[65] In the case of *The Gilgamesh Epic,* the hypothesis that the elaboration is supplementary must be considered tentative, in view of the current state of the evidence.

Only tentative conclusions can be drawn from our study of the Akkadian fragments of the Middle Babylonian Period, owing to the limitations of the evidence. Differences between equivalent passages in Gilg. Meg. and Gilg. Ur suggest that these two fragments

62. See Landsberger, *RA* 62: 127, n. 104, and Gadd, *Iraq* 28:111, l. 46.
63. Gilg. Ur 4 and the late version; see Gadd, *Iraq* 28:108, l. 4, and Landsberger, *RA* 62:124, l. 4a.
64. Though not pointless; see Oppenheim, *Or.* 17:42.
65. See above, chap. 4, "The Significance of the Assimilation"; cf. Lambert and Millard, pp. 6, 34–35, 38. For related phenomena in Hebrew literature, see Purvis, pp. 71–72; Tigay, *JBL* 94:329–42; for the New Testament, see Metzger, pp. 193, 197; for Homer, see Murray, p. 289.

may represent different, though textually related versions of the epic in this period, and, for all we know, Gilg. Bo. could be from yet another version. A comparison of the Middle Babylonian fragments with the late version suggests that during this period the text developed considerably toward its ultimate Standard Babylonian form. Although the equivalent Old Babylonian passages are not available for comparison with the Middle Babylonian Akkadian fragments, we may reasonably presume that the text of these fragments differs from its Old Babylonian sources. This we infer from the fact that the Middle Babylonian text is so close to the text of the late version, sometimes being identical to it for several lines in a row. If the Middle Babylonian text were equally close to its Old Babylonian source, this would imply an equal similarity between the Old Babylonian and late texts, and such extensive similarity between those two versions would be anomalous in the light of Chapters 3 and 4. Hence we infer that the Middle Babylonian and late texts represent a development beyond the Old Babylonian text. The similarity between the Middle Babylonian and late texts implies that much of the wording of the late version was formulated prior to the work of the editor who produced that version. Comparison of the Middle Babylonian and late texts in some passages indicates that the late editor did not reformulate extensively, but generally replaced some words with their equivalents. In other passages, however, more extensive reformulation is indicated. Apart from the wording, the order of some lines was rearranged in the late version, a few lines were dropped, and lines and entire passages were added. Many additions do not give the impression of originality: They include lines synonymously parallel to those to which they are adjoined, traditional and conventional descriptions, and some material modeled upon or related to other passages in the epic and contributing to its homogenized style.

According to the view that some of the Boghazköi texts reflect Old Babylonian prototypes, differences between those texts and the Old Babylonian texts known to us would indicate that revision of the text of the epic began as early as the Old Babylonian period. In any case, the fragments of the Middle Babylonian period indicate that the emergence of the late Standard Babylonian text was a gradual process that took centuries, rather than something achieved all at once by the final editor.

# 6

# *The Late Version*

Changes in the text of the epic from the Old Babylonian down to the late version show that it did not remain stable. Only with the late version did the text approach stability, and even then its stability was not absolute.

Of all the versions of the epic, the late version is the most fully preserved and is attested in the largest number of manuscripts. Although it is difficult to ascertain precisely how many different copies disconnected fragments come from, some eight to twelve manuscripts are represented by the fragments of the best-attested tablet of the late version, Tablet XI. Most of the manuscripts of the late version were discovered in the remains of Ashurbanipal's library (destroyed in 612) at Nineveh in northeastern Mesopotamia, but others come from different sites: Assur and Nimrud, also in northeastern Mesopotamia; Sultantepe in the northwest; and Uruk and elsewhere in southern Mesopotamia. The dates of these manuscripts span a period from the ninth or eighth to apparently the second or first century.[1]

1. See Introduction, nn. 35–36. The Assur tablet of *GE* VI is generally dated to the ninth or eighth century; see *GETh.*, p. 7; Frankena, in *GSL*, p. 114; Böhl, *RLA* 3:367. The text with the latest date is *CT* 46, no. 30, apparently from the Arsacid era; see Oelsner, pp. 262–264. (Arnaud, "Bibliothèque," p. 380, reports the discovery at Emar [Syria] of "the oldest witness to the canonical version known to date," from about the thirteenth century.)

The version to which these fragments belong was not necessarily created as late as the ninth or eighth century. It may well be an accident of discovery that earlier manuscripts of the late version have not yet been found (see n. 1). Indeed, various considerations arising from the study of Akkadian literature as a whole have led scholars to the conclusion that the late, standardized versions of most Akkadian literary texts, including *The Gilgamesh Epic,* were produced during the last half or quarter of the second millennium. As a rough approximation of the date,[2] 1250 is sometimes given, but it should be kept in mind that the date is conjectural.[3]

The relative stability of the late version is indicated by a comparison of its manuscripts to each other. When we compared the Old Babylonian version to the late version, we found that only a small number of lines were verbally identical. But among manuscripts of the late version, only a few lines are not verbally identical in all the manuscripts, and this is despite the fact that some passages are attested in several manuscripts.[4] A preliminary review of the manuscripts shows fewer than 130 verbal variants among the more than 1,600 fully or partly preserved lines of the late version.[5] Most of these are of the least extensive types of variant surveyed in our

2. See Introduction, n. 45.

3. Theoretically, one could infer from the early eleventh-century date of the MB Gilg. Ur that the late version did not yet exist around 1100. But Gilg. Ur could be a copy of an earlier MS and reflect the text of the epic a century or two earlier than the date when it was copied. The creation of the late version did not necessarily put an immediate end to the copying of earlier versions.

4. This excludes grammatical variants, in which the MSS abound (about 240 cases). The bulk of the grammatical variants involves the status, case, number, and gender of nouns, tense and mode of verbs, phonology, word order, and variant forms of the same word. It appears that the standardization of the wording of the text did not include its grammar, in which scribes continued to exercise considerable freedom (at times influenced by local dialect forms). It should be noted that even individual MSS are often internally inconsistent in their grammar. Many, perhaps most, of these variants reflect the blurring or disuse of certain grammatical distinctions in the first millennium, e.g., the disuse of case endings in the spoken language.

5. For the 307 lines (mostly complete) of *GE* XI, the tablet that is attested in the largest number of examplars (between 8 and 12, with some lines preserved in as many as 4 or 5 of them, e.g., ll. 56–62), the apparatus in *GETh.* cites fewer than 30 variants in wording (in ll. 65, 88, 93, 116, 119–120, 125–126, 128–129, 132, 138–139, 143, 147, 150, 165, 180, 185, 194, 228, 244, 248, 253–55, 278, 282; a few are uncertain; on l. 138, see Haupt, pp. 128, 140 [l. 139]; on lines 147 and 150, see *BAL* 3:118 *ad loc.*). Most of the variants in the other tablets are noted in the apparatus of *GETh.* and by Gurney, *JCS* 8:89–95; Frankena, in *GSL,* pp. 113–18; and Wiseman, in *GSL,* pp. 123–35. In what follows, variants are cited from the apparatus of *GETh.* unless otherwise identified by the abbreviations *Gu, Fr,* or *Wi,* indicating the latter three authors respectively.

comparison of the Old Babylonian and late versions in Chapter 3. More than a quarter, for example, involve simply the presence or absence of the copula or the use of different particles and prepositions (mostly synonymous). Something like one-fifth to one-quarter are scribal errors, rather than true variant readings[6]; such errors abound in the Assur and Sultantepe tablets, the former of which is explicitly the work of an apprentice scribe and the latter of which is so poor as to appear the work of a schoolboy.[7] A description of the types of variants that occur among the manuscripts of the late version follows.

## A. SUBSTITUTION OF SINGLE WORDS

A considerable portion of the true variants involves the substitution of single words, some synonymous or similar in meaning and others with different meanings but functioning similarly in context. Some examples are:

1. The prepositions *ina* (in the meanings "in," "into," "on," "onto") and *ana* (in the meanings "to," "toward," "upon") vary with each other both singly (XI, 248, 254; XII, 22–23) and in compound prepositions (*ana muḫḫi/ina muḫḫi,* "onto," I, i, 16, var. from *CT* 46, no. 17; cf. XI, 303; *ina ṣēr/ana ṣēr,* "toward," I, iv, 23; *ana pāni/ina pāni,* "before," VI, 82–83 [Fr], 132[Fr]; VII, ii, 20 [Gu]; note also *mimmû šēri* *ana* *namāri* in VIII, i, 1[Gu] in place of the usual *ina* *namāri* [Gurney, *JCS* 8:92, n. 20]).
2. *kīma/kî,* "like," I, iv, 34; vi, 19 (Wi).
3. *kīma/akî,* "in the manner of," VIII, i, 13 (Gu).

6. For example: *šu-tum-mi* > *ku-tum-mu* (I, i, 10); *ki-ma a-lit-ti* > *ma-li-ti* (XI, 116; see *BAL* 3:118 *ad loc.*). On XI, 125, see Lambert and Millard, p. 163 *sub* iv, 18–19a. On III, ii, 20, see *ANET,* p. 81, n. 78. Numbers are often corrupted: XI, 65, 139; VI, 124 (Fr). Note also *i'-tal-lak* > *im-tal-lak* in I, i, 16 (cf. XI, 303); *ul-taḫ-ḫi-iṭ* vs. *ul-taḫ-ḫi/ḫa,* I, iv, 26 (see p. 207, n. 44); *il-lik-ma* vs. *i-li,* VI, 82 (Fr); and *i-na pu-uq-qí-šú te-bu-ú* > *ina pu-uk-ki šu-ut-bu-ú* in different MSS of the parallel passages I, ii, 10 and 22 (cf. *ANET,* p. 505d and see below, p. 265). The variant in item no. 7, below, could be due to an aural scribal error. See also the next note.

7. See Frankena, in *GSL,* p. 122, col. vi, l. 9′; Gurney, *STT* 1:1, on no. 15. Note such errors as: *u-tul-la/lu₄* > *ta-bu-la,* VI, 58; also Fr; *ú-ni-qi-ti* > *ni-qé-e-ti,* VI, 60 (Fr); *ga-me-er* > *mi-gir,* VI, 51 (Fr) (cf. *gamir abāri,* etc., *CAD* A₁, p. 38c); *i-na-saḫ* > *i-na-as-ḫar,* VIII, ii, 22 (Gu). Note the aural errors pointed out by Gurney, *JCS* 8:90, n. 18; further errors in *GE* VIII pointed out by Diakonoff, p. 64, n. 18; and in *GE* VI pointed out by Frankena, in *GSL,* pp. 113–18.

4. *ul/lā,* "not," VIII, ii, 14–16 (Gu).
5. *aššu/ša,* "because," XI, 119.
6. *ana pāni/ana muḫḫi,* "toward," VI, 161 (Fr).
7. *ina puḫur,* "among, in the assembly of" (= OB *Atr.* III, iii, 36: *ina puḫri ša*) / *ina maḫar,* "in the presence of," XI, 119–20.
8. *id-di / is-suk,* "he tossed," VI, 161 (Fr).
9. *be-el ḫi-ṭi / be-el ar-ni,* "sinner," XI, 180.[8]
10. *ḫa-'i-ir* or *ḫa-me-er,* "lover, husband" / *ḫa-ta-ni,* "my husband," VI, 7.[9]
11. *u-tu-lu,* etc. "lie down" / *ṣa-lil,* etc., "went to sleep," VI, 190–91.[10]
12. *lu-u ú-še-mi-ki,* "I would make you become" / *lu-u e-pu-uš-ki,* "I would do to you," VI, 163 (Fr).
13. *iš-taq-qu-u,* "gave to drink" / *it-taq-qu-u,* "libated," VII, iv, 44.
14. *iz-za-az,* "he stands (in groves)" / *a-šib,* "he sits (in groves)," VI, 50 and Fr.
15. *nišī,* "people" / *eṭlūtu,* "men," VI, 179.[11]
16. *nišī,* "people, mankind" / *mātu,* "the land, world" or "the populace," XI, 185.[12]
17. *āli-šú,* "his city" / *māti-šú,* "his land," XI, 244.[13]
18. *i-šat-ti,* "he drinks (at the watering place)" / [*i-ṭà*]*p-pir,* "he jostles (at the watering place)," I, iv, 4.[14]
19. *pi-ḫi bāb-ka,* "batten up your entrance" (to the boat) / *pi-ḫi elippa,* "batten up the boat," XI, 88.[15]
20. In one case the variation is between an unusual expression,

8. The reading *be-el ḫi-ṭi* agrees with the following *ḫi-ṭa-(a-) šu;* for *be-el ar-ni,* cf. OB *Atr.* III, vi, 25.

9. The readings *ḫa-'i-ir* and *ḫa-me-er* agree with lines 42 and 46; contrast lines 9, 44. This is the only passage where *CAD* Ḫ (p. 148) recognizes a meaning "bridegroom" for *ḫatānu,* which elsewhere means simply "relative by marriage." In Hebrew, *ḥātān* has the meaning "bridegroom"; is this, then, a west-Semitism? Cf. Goetze, *Or.* 16:246–47, which should be modified to the effect that the meaning, rather than the word itself, is west-Semitic (cf. Bauer, *OLZ* 24:74).

10. The readings *ṣal-li, ṣa-lil* agree with *ṣal-lu* at the end of line 190.

11. The reading *nišī* makes room for the females mentioned in the next line, while *eṭlūtu* excludes them but agrees with lines 182, 184, 190.

12. The reading *niši* agrees with lines 182–83, while *mātu* agrees with line 184. Cf. *Atr.* S, iv, 39.

13. The reading *mātišu* agrees with lines 208, 260, 265.

14. The reading [*i-ṭà*]*p-pir* agrees with ii, 40.

15. The reading *pi-ḫi elippa* repeats a word from the preceding phrase, but both readings are paralleled in related texts; cf. lines 93–94; OB *Atr.* III, ii, 51; *Atr.* U, rev. 3; *Atr.* W, 4, 6; cf. Heidel, p. 84, n. 103.

*šab-ba šap-ta-šú-nu,* "their lips burned," and a better-known one, *kat-ma šap-ta-šú-nu,* "their lips were 'covered' (i.e., constricted)," XI, 126.[16]

In some cases, one of the variants agrees with nearby passages,[17] but lacking a manuscript genealogy it is rarely possible to decide whether these are secondary assimilations or original consistent or redundant readings.

21. A substitution of another type is found in the account of Gilgamesh's lament for Enkidu in VIII, ii, 16–21, which describes Gilgamesh's mourning. In the Nineveh text, the description is phrased in the third person, while in the Sultantepe text it is phrased in the first person.[18]

## B. PLUSSES AND MINUSES: WORDS, SUFFIXES, PHRASES, AND LINES

In addition to substitutions, a small number of variants involves plusses and minuses of single words, suffixes, phrases, and lines[19]:

### *Single Words and Suffixes*

1. The copula *u* between pairs of nouns, verbs, and clauses in about a dozen passages.[20]
2. The particle *ša*, VI, 167 and Fr; VI, 190; VIII, i, 17 (Gu); XI, 282.
3. The preposition *ana,* VI, 173; X, ii, 14 (*CT* 46, 30); XI, 278.
4. The preposition *ina,* X, v, 29 (Wi).

16. Cf. the discussion in Lambert and Millard, pp. 161–62. Note the few examples of *šabābu, AHw,* p. 1118 bc (cf. *Or.* 25:242, n. 1) and, in contrast, the parallels to *katāmu* with parts of the body as a medical symptom in *BWL,* pp. 44–45, l. 87; pp. 52–53, l. 24; *Iraq* 31:31, l. 41, cf. Biggs, *ša-zi-ga,* p. 45, l. 9′ (dul = *katāmu*); on the meaning of *katāmu,* cf. *CAD* K, p. 301a.

17. See nn. 8–15 above, and note *GSL,* p. 120, col. ii, 31 (= *GE* VI, 65) and the comment of Frankena, in *GSL,* p. 116 *ad loc.*

18. Gurney, *JCS* 8:93, ll. 12b–15; note the sudden reversion to first person in line 16 (cf. Gurney, ibid., p. 95, n. 130); on the other hand, note the first-person suffix on *ib-ri* in the Nineveh text (ii, 17).

19. Gurney raises the possibility of a whole section omitted in one of the Sultantepe MSS (*JCS* 8:90).

20. *GE* I, i, 19; iv, 21; III, i, 15; VI, 16, and Fr; VI, 54 (Fr), 90; VIII, i, 4 (Gu), 8 (Gu); ii, 22 (Gu); X, ii, 29 (Wi); v, 27(?) (Wi); cf. X, ii, 22 (Wi).

5. The asseverative particle *lū*, XI, 165.

6. Simple, as opposed to compound, prepositions: *kî/kî pī*, "like," X, vi, 33 (*CT* 46, 30); *ana /ana libbi*, "into," XI, 93.

7. ^Id^*En-ki-dù i-lit-ta-šu šá-d*[*u-um-ma*], "Enkidu, whose birth was [in] the steppe," GEH i, 6 / *a-lid ina šá-di*, "he who was born in the steppe," GEUW i, 17.[21]

8. *al-la-la*, "the roller bird" / *al-lal-la-ki*, "your roller bird," VI, 48 (Fr).[22]

9. *bu-li-šú / bu-lim*, "his / the wild beasts," I, iv, 23 (Wi).

10. *rē'â u-tul-la*, "a shepherd, a herdsman," / *re-'a-a na-qid-da ú-tul-lu*$_4$, "a shepherd, a herder, a herdsman," VI, 58 (Fr).

11. *ki-iz-re-e-ti šam-ḫa-a-ti u ḫarimāti*, "courtesans, hierodules, and prostitutes" / *k*[*i-i*]*z-re-*[*t*]*i u ḫa-ri-me-ti*, "courtesans and prostitutes," VI, 165–66 (Fr).[23]

12. *ul-tu u*$_4$*-um ṣa-at*, "since days of yore" / *ul-tu ṣa-a-tú*, "since of yore," X, ii, 22 (*CT* 46, 30).

13. *eb-bir man-nu*, "who crosses?" / *e-bir tam-tim man-nu*, "who is the crosser of the sea?" X, ii, 23 (*CT* 46, 30).[24]

14. *ša-a-ru a-bu-*[*bu m*]*e-ḫu-ú*, "the wind, the flood, the storm"/ *ša-a-ru ra-a-du mé-ḫu-ú a-b*[*u-bu*], "the wind, the deluge, the storm, the flood," XI, 128.[25]

### *Phrases*[26]

15. *ši-ma-in-ni ši-bu-tu* [x (x) *ši-ma-i*]*n-ni ia-a-ši*, "Hear me, O elders, [. . . ., hear] me" / *ši-ma-i-ni eṭlūti ši-ma-na-aia-ši ši-ma-i-ni šībūt* [*Uruk*^ki^], "Hear me, O men, hear me, hear me, O elders of [Uruk]," VIII, ii, 1 (Gu).[27]

16. *nam-ṣar šib-bi-ia* [*a-ri-te*] *ša pa-ni-ia*, "the dirk in my belt,

21. Note also the variation between *ilittašu* and *alid*.

22. The reading with *ki* harmonizes the line to line 43, but makes it deviate from lines 51, 53, 58 in its nearer context.

23. The fuller list agrees with *Erra* IV, 52. The precise meaning of the terms is uncertain; see most recently *CAD* K, pp. 314–15.

24. The fuller reading agrees with *e-bir tam-ti* ^d^*Šamaš* at the beginning of the line.

25. The longer reading could be viewed as a conflation of the shorter with OB *Atr.* III, iv, 25, *ra-⌜du⌝ me-ḫu-⌜ú⌝* [*a-bu-bu?*].

26. See also *GE* VI, 5 var. 13; Landsberger, *RA* 62:133, col. vi, 7.

27. *CT* 46, 27 ll. 6–7 appear to agree with the Sultantepe reading: [. . . .]-⌜*ni*⌝ *eṭlūti ši-ma-*[. . . . *Ur*]*uk*^ki^ (correct *GSL*, p. 135, no. 6 accordingly); cf. GEUW rev., 7–8.

[the shield] in front of me" / *nam-ṣar ši-bi-i a-ri-te šá pa-ni-ia mu-kil li-du*[. . . .], "the dirk in my belt, the shield in front of me, holder (of) . . . [. . . .]," VIII, ii, 5 (Gu).

17. *ša mu-ti ul ud-du-ú ūmī-šú,* "they did not reveal the time of death" (X, vi, 39). *CT* 46, no. 30 adds several signs at the end of the line. Wiseman read them as an additional clause, *šá* ⌜*bal-ṭú*(?)⌝ *ud*!-*du-ú*, "they did reveal that of life(?)." However, Lambert reads these signs as merely indicating a variant to *ul ud-du-ú* at the beginning of the line: *šá-niš ul-te-du-ú*, "variant: they have made known."[28]

Note that examples 15, 17 (if relevant), and possibly 16, involve parallel phrases (the first synonymous, the second antithetic).

## *Full Lines*[29]

18. *iš-me-ma* $^{d}$*En-ki-du an-na-a qa-bi* $^{d}$*Iš-tar,* "Enkidu heard this speech of Ishtar" (VI, 160), is absent in the Assur manuscript (after *GSL,* 122: v, 4′).

19. *i/iz-zak-ka-ra a-na ib-ri-šu,* "saying to his friend" (VI, 193), is absent in two manuscripts.

20. [$^{d}$]*En-ki-du* $^{d}$*Gilgameš* [*i-pu-ul*], "Enkidu [answered] Gilgamesh," XII, 6 (Wi) = GEN 177, is missing in the Nineveh manuscript (after XII, "2" in *GETh.*).

Although the absence of No. 18 can be explained as a case of homoeoarchton (the following line also begins with *iš*), the instability of transitional passages and introductions to speeches is a common phenomenon.[30]

28. For this difficult line, see Wiseman, in *GSL*, p. 134, and Jacobsen and Lambert, in Alster, ed., *Death,* pp. 21, 55–56.

29. For missing lines in one of the Sultantepe MSS, see Gurney, *JCS* 8:90. For variant word order in a few lines, see *GE* VI, 52 (Fr), 89 (Fr), and 159 (Fr), 174; VIII, ii, 2 (Gu); and perhaps XI, 138 (see Haupt, pp. 128, 140).

30. For the omission of transitions, see Kramer, *JAOS* 64:21, n. 104; 22–23, n. 113. For other examples, see Shaffer, "Sources," apparatus to *GEN* 206 (=*GE* XII, 31), 224 (note the omission of this line after *GE* XII, 55), 231–32 (232 is also omitted after *GE* XII, 69). For examples from *GLL,* note the transition missing after *GSL,* p. 71, l. 86 (see van Dijk's translation there, p. 73, and Falkenstein, *JNES* 19:68–69); after *GLL* A 20 (Kramer, *JCS* 1:32); after *GLL* A 105 (including MS F; present in Shaffer's unpublished edition as l. 102); in one MS, *GLL* A 16 is absent (Kramer, *JCS* 1:32, n. 206). Cf. OB *Atr.* I, 105–6 (absent in one MS?). On introduced versus unintroduced speeches, see Hecker, pp. 48–49.

21. [*ul*]-*te-ziq ra-ma-ni ina da-la-pu: ši-ir-a-ni-ia nissati um-tal-li,* "[I f]retted myself with wakefulness; I filled my joints with misery" / *ul-te-ziq ra-ma-ni da-la-pi: ši-ir-a-ni-ia ni*[*ssati um-tal-li*] *mi-na-a ak-te-šìr* . . . [. . . .], "I fretted myself with wakefulness; [I filled] my joints with mi[sery]; what have I achieved? . . .," X, v, 29 (Wi).[31]

22. VII, iv, 33–39 parallel *Ishtar,* obv. 4 through 10; one manuscript adds after line 39 the succeeding line of *Ishtar* (obv. 11).[32]

## THE SIGNIFICANCE OF THE VARIANTS

In number and character, these differences between the manuscripts are so minimal as to indicate that we are dealing with a single version and several slightly variant witnesses thereto. The relationship between the witnesses cannot be explained without a thorough review of the individual manuscripts (which is not possible on the basis of Thompson's edition) and the construction of a manuscript genealogy. It is far from certain that such a study would show the variants to be based on differing *local* manuscript traditions,[33] as one might infer from such scholarly sobriquets as "the Nineveh recension or version" or "the Assur recension or version." There are cases where Nineveh manuscripts agree with those from other sites, but differ from other Nineveh manuscripts.[34] The fact that a manuscript has come to us from Nineveh by no means shows that it belongs to a "Ninevite recension," since Ashurbanipal had manuscripts gathered or copied for his library in Nineveh from many other cities.[35]

The failure of the epic to reach a completely standardized form

31. The copy in *CT* 46, no. 32, makes the end of the line clearer. The additional passage is partly translated in *CAD* K, p. 285c.

32. *GETh.,* p. 46, n. 9.

33. Cf. Tsevat, pp. 225–26. Similarly, Falkenstein denies that variant recensions of the Sumerian *GLL* (see above, p. 30) are based on varying local text traditions (*JNES* 19:70), and Hallo and van Dijk make a similar point about the MS families of *The Exaltation of Inanna* (p. 42). Lambert and Millard, p. 34, note the presence of three widely different recensions of OB *Atr.* in one town.

34. For example, VI, 52 (MS C and *GSL,* p. 120, col. ii, 18 vs. main text); VI, 58 (MS F and *GSL,* p. 120, col. ii, 24 vs. main text); VI, 161 (MS B and *GSL,* p. 122, col. v, 5′ vs. main text); VI, 191 (MS B vs. main text and *GSL,* p. 122, col. vi, 3′).

35. See Streck, pp. 67–68; Pfeiffer, *State Letters,* no. 256.

is partly reflected in its formal or "Masoretic"[36] characteristics, too. Only the division of the epic into twelve (presumably originally eleven) tablets and the delimitation of their contents seems to have been uniform everywhere.[37] It is less certain that the division of the tablets into six columns was universal.[38] The number of lines in a column and the numbering of lines clearly varied,[39] as did the use of horizontal lines between sections, the writing of two verses on a single line,[40] orthography, and grammar.

In Chapters 2 and 4 we noted a number of major additions to the epic after the Old Babylonian version known to us: the prologue (*GE* I, i, 1–26), the flood story in *GE* XI, and the twelfth tablet. These are first attested in the manuscripts of the late version. There is no evidence for determining whether the prologue and Tablet XII were first added in this version or earlier, at some intermediate stage. Indeed, Tablet XII is so poorly integrated with the rest of the epic that some scholars believe it was appended to the rest of the epic some time after the late version was created.[41] What the addition of this tablet may have been intended to contribute to the epic was discussed in Chapter 4. The contribution of the prologue will

36. For the term, cf. Hallo, *JAOS* 88:74.

37. Note duplicate tablets from different sites ending with the same line or bearing the same number: I (*GETh.*, p. 16, l. 30 and *GSL*, p. 127, l. 30(15′) with colophon identifying the latter as Tablet I); VI (*GETh.*, pl. 26, l. 193 and *GSL*, p. 122, col. vi, 5′, with colophons identifying both as Tablet VI); X (*GETh.*, pl. 43, l. 39 and *GSL*, p. 134, l. 2′, with colophons identifying both as Tablet X). Whether the MSS of *GE* V all began at the same point is debated by Kinnier Wilson, in *GSL*, p. 105, and Landsberger, *RA* 62:104–5, n. 27.

38. For the division of most tablets into six columns, cf. Böhl in *RLA* 3:367, § 9a, p. 368, § 10; Heidel, *JNES* 11:140; for a possible exception, see Gurney, *JCS* 8:87; von Soden, *ZA* 53:227; Landsberger, *RA* 62:123. The tablets from Sultantepe have only one column on each side, but they are unofficial school texts, rather than library texts (cf. Kupper, in *GSL*, p. 98).

39. For different column division, see *GETh.*, p. 13, n. 8; note also that in *CT* 46, no. 20, l. 1, the equivalent of *GE* I, ii, 31b is the first line of a column, and in *CT* 46, 23 the equivalent of *GE* VII, iii, 1 is line 10′ of the fragment. Different line divisions are indicated in the apparatus of *GETh.* by 1) "ten marks," which indicate that the number of the line to which they are affixed is a multiple of ten; these marks often appear in the apparatus for lines whose numbers are not multiples of ten in the main text (see *GETh.*, p. 14, n. 11; p. 17, n. 6; p. 41, n. 9); 2) the notes ". . . makes two lines," ". . . ends line," and ". . . adds to preceding line," e.g., *GETh.*, p. 12, n. 5; p. 41, passim; pp. 60–66 passim.

40. For two verses on a single line, see 2 at the end of the preceding note. For horizontal lines, see *GETh.*, p. 30, n. 6; p. 34, n. 5; p. 39, n. 1; p. 41, n. 3; p. 42, n. 13; p. 45, n. 4; p. 61, nn. 7, 24; p. 62, n. 16; p. 63, n. 25; p. 64, n. 26; p. 65, nn. 10, 40; cf. Gadd, *Iraq* 28:106, n. 2 (and cf. n. 3).

41. Matouš, in *GSL*, pp. 93–94; Böhl, *RLA* 3:368, Jacobsen, *Treasures*, pp. 214–15.

be discussed in Chapter 7. That the full rehearsal of the flood story was first added in the late version is argued in Chapter 12.

The development of the epic from its Sumerian sources of the twenty-first century through the late version current in the first millennium shows a pattern of decreasing degrees of adaptation and revision of earlier sources and versions. The original composition of the epic on the basis of Sumerian sources was carried out with great flexibility. The Old Babylonian author felt free to include some of the Sumerian themes and tales in the epic and exclude others, to draw in material originally unconnected with Gilgamesh, to organize the material according to a plot of his own, to transform the roles of characters and episodes, and to stress themes that were important to him. He or an earlier Akkadian paraphraser felt free to word the epic as he saw fit without any reliance on the wording of the Sumerian sources. Subsequent editors took much less liberty with the epic this author left to them. So far as we can tell, they left its basic form unchanged, although they did add some new material and episodes. The god Shamash, already important in the Old Babylonian version, was credited with more initiative in the late version of the Cedar Mountain episode, but deities who became prominent after the Old Babylonian Period were not inserted into the Akkadian epic (as they were in the Hittite and Hurrian versions). Within a few centuries of the Old Babylonian version—by the Middle Babylonian Period, if not earlier—much of the text began to undergo reformulation, but the final wording remained manifestly related to that of the Old Babylonian version. Once the contents of the late version were settled upon and the text formulated, the epic became stabilized (with the possible exception of the later addition of Tablet XII). Although the manuscripts of this version apparently span some six to seven centuries,[42] they exhibit minimal variation in wording. The late version had become nearly a *textus receptus* or authorized version in wording and content, and different copies or editions differed from each other almost entirely in matters of orthography, grammar, and format.

42. Or more; see n. 1 of this chapter.

# 7

# *The Introduction and Framework of the Late Version*

In the preceding chapters we have traced the development of the epic from its Sumerian forerunners through its various Akkadian versions down to the final Akkadian version of the first (and presumably late second) millennium. While much of our attention has been devoted to developments in the wording of the epic, we have also noted the addition of larger units, such as the prologue, the flood story, and Tablet XII. In this chapter, we want to take a close look at the introduction to the late version (*GE* I, i, 1–ii, 6), which includes the prologue (i, 1–26) and an older hymnic introduction (i, 27–ii, 6) to which the prologue is prefixed. We must consider at the same time the passage at the end of Tablet XI (303–7) which echoes part of the prologue (I, i, 16–21) and, together with the latter, forms a framework around Tablets I through XI.

Our discussion will focus on two issues: the meaning of the text, and the literary affinities of each section. The prominent positions of the prologue and framework suggest the importance that the editor of the late version must have ascribed to their contents. Hence a study of their themes can suggest what the editor wanted them to contribute to the late version. In this respect, our discussion continues the inquiry of Chapters 1 through 6. The study of literary affinities will enable us to see what kinds of traditional literary materials the editor was able to draw upon to express his ideas. In this respect, the discussion begins the kind of inquiry to be pursued in Chapters 8 through 12.

The introduction of the epic is as follows:

i, 1. [Him who] saw everything, let me [make kno]wn to the land,
2. [Who all thing]s experienced, [let me tea]ch i[t] ful[ly].
3. [He searche]d (?) the l[ands(?)] entirely,
4. [Was granted al]l (?) wisdom, ex[perienced(?)] all things.
5. [The hi]dden he saw, the undisclosed he discov[ered].
6. He brought back information from before the flood,
7. Achieved a long [j]ourney, exhausted, but at peace.
8. All his toil he [engra]ved on a (stone) stela / an inscription.
9. He had the wall of Uruk (of?) the sheepfold built,
10. Of hallowed Eanna, the holy storehouse.
11. Behold its outer wall, which/whose. . . . is like bronze.
12. Peer at the inner wall, which none can equal!
13. Touch the threshold, which is from of old!
14. Draw near to Eanna, the dwelling of Ishtar,
15. Which no future king, no one, can equal.
16. Go up onto the wall of Uruk, and walk about,
17. Inspect the base, examine the brickwork:
18. Is not its brickwork of burnt brick?
19. And did not the Seven [Sages] lay its foundations?
20. [(One) *sar* (in area) is city, (one) *sar* or]chards, (one) *sar* lowland, (further) the un[built land of the Temple of Ishtar];
21. [Three *sar*] and the unbuilt land com[prise] Ur[u]k.
22. [Find] the cop[per]. . . . (tablet or tablet box),
23. [Undo the. . . .] of its lock, which is of bronze,
24. [Open] the aperture to its secret contents (or: its secret aperture);
25. [Take out] and read aloud from the lapis-lazuli tablet
26. [How/that] Gilgamesh went through all hardships.
27. [Sur]passing the rulers, renowned, possessing stature,
28. [The he]ro, offspring of Uruk, the butting bull,
29. He goes in front as the leader,
30. He also marches at the rear as the one in whom his brothers trust.
31. The mighty [*tr*]*ap,* protector of his troops,
32. The furious [fl]ood-wave, who destroys (even) stone walls,
33. [The off]spring of Lugalbanda—Gilgamesh is perfect in strength,
34. [The son] of the august cow, Rimat-Ninsun,
35. . . . . Gilgamesh, perfect in awesomeness.
36. [Open]er of the mountain passes,
37. [Digg]er of wells on the flank of the mountain,
38. [Cros]ser of the ocean, the vast sea, to where the sun rises,
39. [Sur]veyor of the (world) regions; seeker of life.

40. [The one who re]ached (participle), by his strength(?) Utnapishtim the Faraway,
41. [He/who rest]ored(?; participle). . . . to their place which the flood had destroyed
42. . . . . for numerous mankind.
43. [Who(?)] can be compared with him in kingship,
44. [Who like] Gilgamesh can say, "I am king indeed!"?
45. [Gilg]amesh was summoned by name from the very day of his birth.

ii, 1. Two-thirds of him is god, one-third of him is human.
2. The image of his body Dingirmaḫ (the mother-goddess) desig[ned(?)].
3. . . . . [com]pleted his form (. . . . ?) like(?). . . .
4. . . . . [fa]ir, most glorious [among heroes].
5. . . . . perfect. . . .
6a. . . . . [he] chased/defeated/approached?. . . .

(*GE* I, i, 1–ii, 6a)[1]

The introduction consists of three parts which are distinct on both chronological and thematic grounds: Section a (1–8) gives pride of place to what Gilgamesh saw and learned, culminating in his engraving "all (his) toil" *(kalu mānaḫti)* in an inscription; the events mentioned occurred after the death of Enkidu (cf. XI, 259, 264). Section b (9–26) refers to his building the walls of Uruk and the temple Eanna (which took place before the events of the epic[2]), invites the reader or listener[3] to behold the walls with wonder (16–21, partially repeated in XI, 303–7), and to search for Gilgamesh's inscription, which tells of "all the hardships" *(kalu marṣāti)*[4] he underwent. For ease of reference, we shall refer to these two sections (which were added later than section c; see Chapter 2) as the *prologue,* distinguishing them from the *introduction* as a whole. Section c (i, 27–ii, 6) is a hymnlike description of Gilgamesh, consisting of a series of heroic epithets and allusions to

1. Text and notes in Appendix, no. 3.
2. See above, p. 6.
3. There is little hard evidence for determining whether the epic was intended for an audience of readers or listeners. The opening line addresses "the land," which could refer to a group of listeners, while the imperatives in lines 11 through 25 are gramatically singular and could refer to a single reader or to a single exemplary member of a group of listeners; line 25 urges the addressee to read the stele which is presumably meant to be understood as the source of the epic's information (see below). See Oppenheim, *Or.* 17:17–20; *AM,* pp. 258–59; Nougayrol, "L'épopée," pp. 853–54; Wilcke, *ZA* 67:209–10; cf. above, chap. 2, n. 6 and pp. 102–3.
4. For the phrase, cf. Gilg. Me. ii, 1, 3; *GE* X, v, 12 (*GETh.,* p. 42) and restored parallels.

some of his exploits, followed by a description of his birth and endowments. This hymn, or at least an Old Babylonian version of its nucleus, formed the introduction to the Old Babylonian version of *Gilgamesh.*[5] Each of these passages warrants closer examination.

## THE PROLOGUE: SECTION A

This section opens with the poet's declaring (in cohortative verbs) his intention to tell about Gilgamesh, who is described in a series of phrases and sentences summarizing his experiences. Both of these elements—the cohortative declaration of the poet's intention ("let me sing," etc.) and the series of phrases describing the hero—are common in the introductions of epics and hymns.[6]

What is unusual about the descriptive phrases in this section is their virtual ignoring of the kind of themes that would normally be stressed in epics and hymns, namely, Gilgamesh's quest to overcome death and the heroic adventures which occupy the first half of the epic,[7] which Gilgamesh himself frequently alludes to in his retrospective speeches (VIII, ii, 10–12; X, ii, 35–37, 39–42; etc.). In place of these, section a mentions the outcome of Gilgamesh's quest, the understanding that he gained. The importance of the latter theme is underlined by the frequency of the verbs "see" and "know," and the nouns "wisdom," "secret(s)," "hidden thing(s)".[8]

5. See above, p. 48.

6. For a study of the introductions to Akkadian epics, see Wilcke in *ZA* 67: 153–216, where similarities and differences between the introduction to *Gilgamesh* and those of hymns and other epics are observed. Note also Wilcke's comments on introductions to Sumerian literary texts in *Jacobsen AV,* pp. 243–44.

7. Cf. Gressmann and Ungnad, pp. 85–86.

8. Oppenheim, *Or.* 17:18; cf. also Borger, *Bi. Or.* 14:192b for a suggestion that the opening line refers to "deep wisdom" (reading *naqba*). Bringing back information from "before the flood" (*lām abūbi,* l. 6) is also a sign of wisdom. I do not believe that this refers to Gilgamesh's hearing the flood story in Tablet XI (Oppenheim, *Or.* 17:18). The only thing that story mentions from before the flood is the preparations for it, and although technically this period of preparation can be described as "before the flood sets out" (*lām abūbi waṣê, Atr.* J rev. 4 in Lambert and Millard, pp. 126–27), the term *lām abūbi* normally refers to the entire antediluvian epoch. This was when, according to Mesopotamian tradition, the ancient sages (*apkallus*) taught men the arts and sciences of civilization, teachings to which nothing material was added after that time. According to Berossus (third century B.C.E.), the antediluvian writings were buried for safekeeping during the flood and then recovered and disseminated to mankind. An astronomical text was attributed to the first of these sages, Adapa, and an Assyrian medical text was said to be "according to the sages from before the

The great deeds which were traditionally regarded as the means of perpetuating one's name, by which Gilgamesh himself had sought in the course of the epic to achieve this goal, are ignored in favor of the wisdom he acquired.[9] It is this aspect of Gilgamesh which the author of the introduction prizes above the quest for immortality and the heroic exploits that dominate the body of the epic.[10]

The culmination of this section is the description of Gilgamesh's engraving a record of "all his toil" in an inscription *(narû).*[11] The lapis-lazuli tablet mentioned at the end of section b may be identical with this inscription; in any case, its contents must have been essentially the same. The epic itself, a third-person narrative, is not a piece of *narû*-literature, which typically is a first-person narrative.[12] It has been suggested that the epic was understood to be based on Gilgamesh's *narû,*[13] and this is perhaps the point of lines 8 and 25. Such an inscription also represents a device for achieving an indirect sort of immortality. Inscriptions were one of the means by which rulers hoped to perpetuate their names[14] and also to receive the blessing of future rulers. Thus the autobiographical inscription of Idrimi, a Syrian king of the fifteenth century, ends: "I wrote my achievements on my statue. Let people [read it] and ble[ss me]."[15] The *narû* inscription of Naram-Sin, king of Akkad,

flood." Ashurbanipal boasted that he studied inscriptions from before the flood. (See Lambert and Millard, pp. 18–19, 25–26, 135–37; Lambert, *JCS* 11:8–9; *ANET,* p. 314c; Komoróczy, *Act. Ant.* 21:137–38; and below, p. 205.) Accordingly, it seems that *GE* I, i, 6 means that Gilgamesh had learned some of this antediluvian wisdom, as implied by Lambert, *JCS* 16:66 *sub* VI, 15.

9. Cf. Ben Sira (Ecclus.) 40:19, which finds wisdom a better source of lasting fame than progeny or building a city.

10. Cf. Shaffer, "Sources," p. 12. In its didactic aspect, the epic is comparable to Sumerian didactic myths described by Wilcke, "Sumerische Lehrgedichte"; like *Gilgamesh,* especially the OB version, a number of these have hymnic introductions to their narratives (Wilcke, ibid., p. 2136).

11. A *narû* is usually a stele, but not always; see Ellis, *Foundation Deposits,* pp. 145–47.

12. Grayson and Lambert, p. 8; Hallo, *HUCA* 33:2, n. 18, 9, n. 63. On the genre, see Güterbock, *ZA* 42:19–21, 62–86; Gurney, *An. St.* 5:93. This would seem to rule out the inference that the epic itself is represented as Gilgamesh's *narû* (Wilcke, *ZA* 67:211).

13. Gressmann and Ungnad, p. 85; *AM,* p. 258.

14. Kraus, *JNES* 19:128–31; Ellis, *Foundation Deposits,* pp. 166–67; McBride, chap. 2. Given the presumed didactic content of Gilgamesh's inscription (see immediately), one may perhaps also compare an Egyptian wisdom text counseling the writing of books as the best means of perpetuating one's name (J. Wilson in *ANET,* pp. 431–32).

15. Oppenheim, in *ANET,* p. 558b.

begins with the appeal: "[. . . .] read the inscription."[16] Reading aloud a deceased king's foundation inscription was an act of reverence due to him from future kings who came upon it.[17] The introduction to *The Gilgamesh Epic* seems to imply that Gilgamesh's inscription told of the wisdom he had gained as a result of all his struggles. That wisdom would presumably have resembled the teachings about the impermanence of life, and the advice to enjoy its benefits, which Gilgamesh heard from the barmaid and Utnapishtim in Gilg. Me. iii and *GE* X, vi.[18] Another example of an inscription which includes lessons its author learned from his life's experiences is that of Naram-Sin; his inscription also shows the role of such a didactic inscription in perpetuating its author's name. Naram-Sin wrote this inscription so that his successors might learn the lessons of his own sad experience[19]:

Whosoever you are, whether governor or prince or anyone else,
Whom the god shall call to rule over a kingdom,
I have made for you a *tupshennu* (ivory tablet or tablet-box) and inscribed a stele for you,
And in Cuthah, in E-meslam,
In the shrine of Nergal I have deposited it for you.
Read this document and
Listen to its words.
Be not bewildered, be not confused,
Be not afraid, do not tremble.
Establish yourself firmly,
*Enjoy yourself* in the bosom of your wife;
Strengthen your walls,
Fill your trenches with water;
Your chests, your corn, your money, your goods, and your possessions
Bring into your stronghold;
Bind up your weapons and put (them/yourself) into a corner.
Spare your warriors and take heed for yourself.
Though he wander through your land, go not out to him;

16. Gurney, *An. St.* 5:98–99, l. 1; Labat, *Religions,* p. 309.

17. *AKA,* pp. 171–72, ll. 13–22.

18. For the latter, note the additions in *CT* 46, no. 32, translated in *ANET,* p. 507.

19. For the text, see Gurney, *An. St.* 5:106–9; *An. St.* 6:163–64; modifications by Hoffner, *JCS* 23:18–20. Compare especially *"enjoy yourself* in the bosom of your wife" to Gilg. Me. iii, 13. On the third line, see the note on *GE* I, i, 22 in Appendix, no. 3; to the problematic *šipir* in the phrase translated "enjoy yourself," cf. *GE* I, iv, 13, 19; Gilg. Me. iii, 14, and chap. 8, n. 17.

Though he *slay* your cattle, go not near him;
Though he eat the flesh of your . . .
Though he . . .
Be meek, be hum[ble],
Answer them (!), "Here am I my lord,"
Respond to their wickedness with kindness,
To kindness with gifts and *exchanges,*
But do not go forth before them.
Let wise scribes read aloud your stele.
You who have read my stele and *kept out of trouble,*
You who have blessed me, may a future king bless you.

Thus, leaving an inscription containing such advice will not only perpetuate the author's name, but will also secure for him the grateful blessing of future rulers who benefit from the advice. This is underlined by Naram-Sin's earlier statement[20] that the failure of Enme(r)kar to leave a similar inscription had cost him Naram-Sin's blessing, as a result of which Enmerkar and his family were not faring well in the netherworld. Gilgamesh's own inscription, with its similar didactic content, as reflected in the epic, would have had the same purpose as Naram-Sin's; it was one way in which Gilgamesh hoped to achieve a kind of immortality.

## THE PROLOGUE: SECTION B

Section b describes another way in which Gilgamesh sought immortality—building the walls of Uruk. The building of enduring structures, with their accompanying foundation inscriptions (such as that of Gilgamesh, mentioned in ll. 22–25) served to perpetuate the name of the royal builder.[21] Thus Takil-ilišśu of Malgium (ca. 1840) wrote: "(The temple) Enamtila . . . all around with a great mantle of baked brick I surrounded, and (thereby) I surely established the eternal name of my kingship."[22] In the Sumerian poem *The Death*

20. In lines 23–30 of his inscription; cf. Gurney's comment, *An. St.* 5:109 *sub* 27.

21. For the limitation of inscriptions and building deposits to temples and royal and public buildings, see Ellis, *Foundation Deposits,* pp. 163–65. Cf. the denigration of this approach to immortality in an Egyptian text in *ANET,* pp. 431–32, and in Ben Sira (Ecclus.) 40:19.

22. Jacobsen, *AfO* 12:364–65, ll. 12–21; Kutscher and Wilcke, *ZA* 68:127. The concept of an eternal name is discussed by Kraus, *JNES* 19:128–31, and McBride, chap. 2.

*of Urnammu,* a promise is made to that dead ruler that his name will be spoken, that the speaker will summon Sumer and Akkad to Ur-nammu's palace, show them the canals he dug, the fields and fortified settlements for which he had been responsible, and (thus) cause them to speak his name.[23] In section b of the introduction to *Gilgamesh,* we see the narrator doing the same thing for Gilgamesh: perpetuating his name by showing his enduring achievements to later generations.

It is this section which is partially repeated at the end of Tablet XI (303–7). It has often been noted that the reference to the walls points to "the only work of the hero that promised, even guaranteed, his immortality."[24] In fact, Gilgamesh was remembered as the builder of the wall of Uruk in the latest historical inscription known to mention him, a Sumerian inscription of AN-àm, king of Uruk in the late nineteenth century.[25] As a literary device, the reversion to this theme at the end of the epic, ending Gilgamesh's adventures on the note with which they began, shows the futility of all the intervening efforts.[26] By placing the words in Gilgamesh's own mouth upon his return to Uruk, the editor shows us the change in Gilgamesh himself, "the movement from heroic idealism to the everyday courage of realism."[27] He whose adventures consisted of attempts to overcome death in ever more unconventional ways ultimately points with pride and acceptance to one of the most conventional ways—the way with which his own career had begun and the rejection of which had first motivated those adventures.[28]

The invitation to behold[29] the walls of Uruk, to approach Eanna,

23. Wilcke, CRRAI 17:90–91, ll. 221–30. Whether *The Death of Gilgamesh,* which may be of the same genre (ibid., pp. 82, 84), ended with a similar promise cannot be determined.

24. *AM,* p. 257; Ellis, *Foundation Deposits,* p. 167, n. 27.

25. See Introduction, n. 56. Since none of the known Sumerian literary texts mentions that Gilgamesh built the wall of Uruk, this information, which is so far mentioned in the late version only, could go back to the nonliterary tradition reflected in AN-àm's inscription.

26. *AM,* p. 257. For the futility of that which is recurring and cyclical, cf. Eccles. 1:9.

27. Jacobsen, *Treasures,* p. 218. Cf. Böhl, *Gilgamesj-Epos,* pp. 148–49; Stamm, *Asiatische Studien* 6:21.

28. Cf. David, p. 155.

29. At least some of the verbs in lines 11 through 17 are also used in Akkadian royal inscriptions to describe the archaeological activities of kings who excavate ancient temples. See Ellis, *Foundation Deposits,* App. A, No. 33 *(amāru),* no. 39 *(palāsu* N); *CAD Ḫ,* p. 161b *(ḫâṭu).*

and the poet's praise of Uruk and Eanna in section b also resemble themes known from hymns to temples and temple cities. For example, the Sumerian hymn to the temple at Kesh concludes:

> To the city, to the city, man, approach!
> To the Kesh temple, to the city, man, approach!
> Its hero Ashshir, man, approach!
> Its lady Nintu, man, approach!
> (Well-)constructed Kesh, Ashshir, praise!
> . . . Kesh, Nintu, praise![30]

Temple Hymn No. 10, describing the house of Asarluhi in Kuar, begins:

> City, from/*in* the Abzu . . . like grain,
> Plain (with) heavy clouds, taking the m e s from its midst,
> Kuar, to the foundation of your shrine
> The lord, who does not *hold back his goods,* goes amazed,
> The Seven Wise Ones have *enlarged* it for you everywhere(?).[31]

The last line recalls *GE* I, i, 19: "Did not the Seven [Sages] lay its (Uruk's) foundations?" Uruk's Eanna temple itself is the subject of Temple Hymn No. 16, which begins:

> House with the great m e s of Kulaba, . . . , (its) . . . has made the temple flourish,
> Well grown with fresh fruit, marvelous, filled with ripeness,
> Descending from the midst of heaven, shrine, built for(?) the steer,
> Eanna, house with seven corners, lifting the "seven fires" at night,
> Surveying the seven . . .[32]

Hymns to temples and their cities are also found among the Old Sumerian literary texts (twenty-fifth or twenty-sixth century).[33] Passages modeled upon them appear in the Neo-Sumerian (ca. twenty-first century) epics about the early dynastic kings of Uruk. Two of the epics about Enmerkar begin with paeans to Uruk, while *Lugalbanda* ends with one to Aratta.[34] A similar passage appears twice,

30. Gragg, in Sjöberg and Bergmann, p. 175, ll. 126–31 (slighty modified).
31. Ibid., p. 25, ll. 135–39. On the m e s and the Seven Sages, see pp. 204–6.
32. Ibid., p. 29, ll. 198–202.
33. Biggs, *JCS* 20:80–81; *Inscriptions,* pp. 45–56; Sjöberg and Bergmann, p. 6.
34. Cohen, *Enmerkar,* pp. 15–16; 65–112, ll. 1–5; Wilcke, *Lugalbandaepos,* p. 221 *sub* 413.

in the middle and (in abridged form) near the end of *Gilgamesh and Agga:*

> Uruk, the *handiwork* of the gods,
> Eanna, the house descending from heaven—
> It is the great gods who have fashioned its parts—
> Its great wall touching the clouds,
> Its lofty dwelling place established by Anu.[35]

Since hymns of this type are also known in Akkadian in the first millennium, there is no difficulty in supposing that such hymns served as models for this section of the prologue.[36]

## EFFECT OF THE PROLOGUE

Since the two sections comprising the prologue (a and b) are a late addition to the epic,[37] the question arises as to what they add that was lacking in the Old Babylonian version. These sections and the doublet of part of section b at the end of Tablet XI stress the wisdom acquired by Gilgamesh in the course of his adventures, and the indirect immortality by reputation which he achieved by his inscription(s) and building projects. In the Old Babylonian version, the message that true immortality is inaccessible to humans was accompanied by the doctrine of carpe diem (Gilg. Me. i, iii). Although the carpe diem passage was not demonstrably preserved in the late version, its emphasis on enjoying the pleasures life offers was (see chap. 11). On the other hand, the message of Gilgamesh's newly acquired wisdom and his reconciliation to indirect immortality through inscriptions and building projects appears to have had no place in the Old Babylonian version.[38] This message is the contribution of the prologue and framework of the late version in I, i, 1–26 and XI, 303–7. While not contradicting the values of the Old Babylonian version, it adds a new dimension to the epic.

35. *ANET,* p. 46, ll. 30–35; 47, ll. 107–9.
36. See Ebeling, *JKF* 2:274–82; Köcher, *ZA* 53:236–40.
37. See above, pp. 48, 103–5.
38. If *GE* XI, 303–7, were present in the OB version (see above, pp. 104–5), they probably would have expressed Gilgamesh's reconciliation to indirect immortality. In that case, the contribution of the late version to that theme would be only in highlighting it by giving it a prominent place in the introduction.

## SECTION C: THE HYMN

Section c, the description of Gilgamesh and some of his exploits, is hymnic in character. The opening phrase in the late version, *šūtur eli* . . . , "surpassing . . ." (27), was also the opening phrase of the Old Babylonian version[39] and is the only part of section c definitely known to have been present in the Old Babylonian version.

This hymn falls roughly into three parts: 1) descriptive phrases and heroic epithets of a general character (27–35); nothing is specific to Gilgamesh here except his name, city, and ancestry (28, 33–35)[40]; 2) Specific achievements and attributes of Gilgamesh (36–41); 3) Gilgamesh's creation and the endowment of his qualities by the gods (i, 45–ii, 6?). The place of lines 42 through 44 in this structure is uncertain, owing to the absence of their beginnings.

### *Part 1*

The phrases and epithets found in part 1 are typical of those found in royal hymns and inscriptions of all periods of Mesopotamian history. Note the following parallels to lines 27 through 35:

27. *šarrum ša in šarrī šūturu anāku,* "I am the king who is surpassing among kings" (Hammurapi)[41]

28. *rīmum kadrum munakkip zā'irī,* "the fiery bull who gores the enemies" (Hammurapi)

29. *ašarid šarrī,* "the leader among kings" (Hammurapi)

30. *tukulti mātišu,* "the one in whom his land trusts" (Sennacherib)[42]

39. See p. 48.

40. Some of these phrases and epithets are used of Gilgamesh elsewhere in the epic. Wiseman *(Iraq* 37:163 *ad loc.)* compares line 29 to *GE* III, i, 6 and Gilg. Y. iv, 11; vi, 23; and line 33 to *GE* I, iv, 38, 45. To line 29, cf. Gilg. Meg. rev. 16 and also *malku-šarru* III, 8, cited in *GSL,* p. 43 (to the entire passage cited there, cf. Klein in *Kramer AV,* pp. 278–79, l. 57, and the note *ad loc.,* p. 288).

41. The Hammurapi selections are from the hymnic prologue and epilogue to *LH,* xxiv b, 79–80; iii a, 7–9; iv a, 23. To line 28, cf. also *šarrum gašrum rīm šarrī,* "the powerful king, the wild bull among kings" (*Inscription of Iahdun-Lim,* Dossin, *Syria* 32:13; Oppenheim, in *ANET,* p. 556b); cf. *SKIZ,* p. 30, l. 9 (Lipit-Ishtar).

42. Seux, p. 346.

31. *sapār nakirī,* "the net (ensnaring) the enemies" (Hammurapi)[43]; *ṣulūl mātim,* "protector of the land (Hammurapi)[44]; *ṣulūl ummānātešu,* "protector of his troops" (Sennacherib)[45]

32. *abūbu šamru,* "raging deluge"; *mu'abbit dūr nakirīšu,* "who destroys the wall of his enemies" (Ashurnasirpal II)[46]

33. *dunni zikrūte emūqī lā šanān ušaršû gattī,* "(the gods) have endowed my body with manly vigor and matchless strength" (Ashurbanipal)[47]

33, 35. *gitmālum,* "perfect" (Hammurapi)[48]

35. *rašubb*[*āku*], "[I am] awesome" (Tukulti-Ninurta II)[49]

## *Part 2*

This part refers to specific achievements and attributes of Gilgamesh. It ignores the heroic adventures of the first half of the epic, as did section a, and mentions only what seem like tangential aspects of the expedition to the Cedar Mountain: opening(?) mountain passes and digging wells on mountainsides (36–37). One might view these lines, along with Gilgamesh's crossing the eastern ocean (38),[50] as typical royal boasts of the extent of the king's conquests and achievements.[51] Gilgamesh himself later mentions scaling the mountains, slaying a lion on the mountain passes, and crossing the seas, in the summaries of his adventures with Enkidu (*GE* VIII, ii, 10; X, i, 34, 55; iii, 17; v, 26–27; Gilg. Me. iv, 10; cf. *GE* IX, i, 8). However, lines 36 and 37 seem charged with greater significance when they are considered the light of the elders' instructions given as Gilgamesh is about to depart for the Cedar Mountain:

43. *LH* iia, 68; cf. Sjöberg, *ZA* 54: 51–52, l. 6.
44. *LH* iia, 48.
45. Seux, p. 266.
46. Seux, pp. 34, 33.
47. Cited in *CAD* E, p. 158b.
48. *LH* iiia, 37.
49. Seux, p. 242.
50. Cf. *GSL,* pp. 71–74, l. 118.
51. E.g., "I who have marched many times on inaccessible paths; who have crossed many times all the depths of the sea," Lyon, no. 2, l. 11, cited in *CAD* E, p. 11b (cf. *GE* X, v, 27); cf. *ARAB* 2, § 54; *The Legend of Sargon* (*ANET,* p. 119), ll. 15–18, cf. ll. 24–27. Similar motifs are cited in *CAD,* articles *ašru, būrtu, ḫuršānu.* Cf. Waldman, "Biblical Echo."

Let Enkidu go before you . . .
[He knows(?)] the passes *(nērebētim)* of the forest . . .
May Shamash . . .
Open for you the barred path,
Keep the road in order for your treading,
The open country in order for your foot!
. . .
In the evening dig a well *(būrtu);*
Let there always be clean water in your waterskin!
Cool water offer to Shamash

(Gilg. Y. vi, 23–42; cf. *GE* IV: *LKU* 39:5 [*RA* 62, 99:e]; V, iii, 46).

The account of these instructions and Gilgamesh's compliance could have been understood as explaining the etiology of the apotropaic *namburbi* ritual performed when digging a well: One recites the words or incantation entitled "well of Gilgamesh" (túl ᵈ*Gilgameš* = *būrti* ᵈ*Gilgameš*) while digging and then libates the water to Shamash, the Anunnaki gods, and to the ghosts of one's family.[52] Another phrase which is related to Gilgamesh's role in Mesopotamian religion is *ḫā'iṭ kibrāti,* "surveyor of the (world) regions" (39). Gilgamesh bears this epithet in an incantation which reflects his role as divine judge and king of the netherworld.[53] Lines 39b and 40 mention themes prominent in the second part of the epic, Gilgamesh's quest for life and his journey to Utnapishtim. The reference of lines 41, 42, and 44 is unknown.[54] The motif of incomparability in line 43 is common in royal inscriptions.[55]

52. *šumma ālu* XVII, rev. 27′–35′, cited by Lambert, in *GSL,* p. 43; Caplice, ed., pp. 149–52. Cf. chap. 4, n. 31. Prof. Jacobsen suggests that this phrase reflects a view that any digging of a well impinges on Gilgamesh's domain, the netherworld.

53. *GSL,* p. 40, l. 3, cf. l. 7. In this role, Gilgamesh shares some of Shamash's atttributes (cf. *BWL,* pp. 126–27, l. 21 end), and perhaps line 38 should also be understood in this light (cf. *tētenebbir tâmatum rapaštum šadilta,* "you (Shamash) cross the wide expanse of the sea unfailingly," *BWL,* pp. 128–29, l. 35; cf. *GE* X, ii, 22–23 as understood by *CAD* Ṣ, p. 119a). Other gods also bear the epithet *ḫā'iṭu,* "surveyor, watchman"; cf. *CAD* Ḫ, p. 160, cf. *CAD* Ṣ, p. 32b.

54. However l. 41 be restored, "returning things (images, rites, scattered people, cities, or lands) to their places" is a standard theme in royal inscriptions (see *LH* i, 64–65 and similar inscriptions; Seux, pp. 340–42; Moran, *RA* 71:190; *AHw,* p. 1334d). Wilcke (*ZA* 67:210) sees lines 42 through 44, especially line 42, as alluding to Gilgamesh's oppression of Uruk. However, lines 43–44 are vague, and line 42's *nišī apâti* refers to the human race, not the population of a specific city (see the use of *apâtu* in *CAD* $A_2$, pp. 168–69).

55. Seux, pp. 286–87, 314, 334–35; cf. *GE* I, ii, 9, 21.

## *Part 3*

The section describing Gilgamesh's creation begins with his name being called—that is, destined by the gods for kingship—on the day of his birth (45). This theme is connected with one frequently found in royal inscriptions, the gods' calling the king's name (for kingship), often before his birth, while he is still in the womb or in his childhood.[56] The next line, "Two-thirds of him is god, one-third of him is human" (ii, 1), is echoed later in the epic, where it follows the statement *šēr ilāni zumuršu,* "his body is the flesh of the gods" (IX, ii, 14, 16). The royal hymn near the beginning of the *Tukulti-Ninurta Epic* contains a similar passage:

> By the fate (assigned by) Nudimmud (Ea) his (Tukulti-Ninurta's) form is reckoned as the flesh of the gods (*šēr ilāni*).
> By the decree of the lord of the lands he was successfully cast into/poured through the channel of the womb of the gods.
> He is the eternal image *(ṣalam)* of Enlil. . . .[57]

The passage describing Gilgamesh's creation and the endowment of his qualities by the gods (i, 45–ii, 6?) is fragmentary in the late version, but it agrees in substance with the better-preserved Hittite version of this part:

> 3. (When he was) created, the heroic god[s(?). . . .-ed]
> 4. Gilgamesh's form. [The great gods (?)] made
> 5. Gilgamesh's form. The heavenly sun-god to him [manliness (?)]
> 6. gave. The storm-god gave him heroism. Cr[eated]
> 7. the great gods Gilgamesh. His stature (lit. form) in he[ight]
> 8. was eleven cubits; his chest was nine *w*[*akshurs*(?)] wide;
> 9. his . . . (part of body) was three(?) [. . . .] long.[58]

The divine shaping of the hero and the endowment of his qualities at birth by the gods is a standard topos in Mesopotamian literature, and there is no reason to doubt that it was present in the Akkadian prototype on which the Hittite version is

56. Seux, pp. 176–79, 370–71.
57. Lambert, *AfO* 18:50–51, ll. 16–18, translation based on Machinist, pp. 465–66.
58. *Hit. Gilg.* I, No. 1, 3–9. Text and notes in Appendix, no. 4.

based.[59] This topos appears as early as the Sumerian royal inscriptions of the pre-Sargonic period.[60] An early example is the description of the birth of Eannatum of Lagash on the *Stele of the Vultures:*

> Ningirsu inserted the germ of Eannatum into the womb. Baba gave birth to him through the vulva. At Eannatum Mother Baba rejoiced. Inanna took him on (her) arm and named him "Worthy-of-the-Eanna-of-Inanna-of-the-Oval." She set him down for Ninhursaga on her (i.e. Ninhursaga's) right knee and Ninhursaga fed him at her right breast. Over Eannatum, the germ inserted into the womb by Ningirsu, Ningirsu rejoiced. Ningirsu laid against him (to measure him) his span, and (up to) five cubits his forearm he laid against him (totalling) five cubits and a span. Ningirsu in great joy gave him the kingship of Lagash . . .[61]

A late example of this topos is found in an inscription of Ashurbanipal, who describes himself as one

> [For whom Ashur], father of the gods, decreed a kingly destiny while I was still in [my] mother's womb,
> [Whose name Nin]lil, the great mother (of the gods), named for the rulership of the land and people,
> [. . . . whose figure] Dingirmaḫ made into the image of a lord . . . ;
> [?] Sin, the holy god, caused me to see good omen[s] that I might exercise sovereignty;
> [Shamash and Adad] entrusted to me the never-failing craft of divination;
> [Mar]duk, sage of the gods, gave me a gift of great intelligence and broad understanding;
> Nabu, the universal scribe, made me a present of the precepts of his wisdom;
> Ninurta and Nergal endowed my body with heroic strength and unmatched physical vigor.[62]

59. The only close parallel which has been pointed out in Hittite literature is found in a myth of Hurrian provenance, *Kingship in Heaven,* where the as yet unborn storm-god declares, "The earth will give me its strength, the sky will give me its valor, Anus will give me his manliness, Kumarbis will give me his wisdom, Naras will give me his . . . , Napsaras will give me his. . . ." (Goetze, in *ANET,* p. 121a). If there is any non-Mesopotamian influence in the creation section of *Hit. Gilg.* I, it is to be found in variant details such as the role of the storm-god, not in the basic topos. Cf. Otten, *Ist. Mit.* 8:119, § 3.

60. See Labat, *Caractère,* p. 61, for Sumerian and OB examples; cf. *ANEH,* p. 49.

61. Jacobsen, in *Kramer AV,* pp. 251–52, 256–57; cf. Jacobsen, *JNES* 2:120–21; Kramer, *Sumerians,* p. 310; Sjöberg, *Or. Suec.* 21:88–89.

62. *Ashurbanipal* $L^4$, in Streck, pp. 252ff.; translation in *ARAB* 2, § 986; both modified by collations in Bauer, *Inschriftenwerk* 2:84, n. 3, and translations in *CAD.*

This inscription has a number of details in common with the descriptions in the Hittite and late version of *Gilgamesh* of Gilgamesh's creation. The creation of the king's form is described thus:

*Ashurbanipal* $L^4$, 7: . . . *-e* DINGIR.MAḪ *alamdimmē bēlūti uṣabbû,* "... , [whose figure] Dingirmaḫ made into the image of a lord"

*GE* I, ii, 2–3: *ṣalam pagrišu* DINGIR.MAḪ *uṣṣi*[*r*], *ušteṣbi gattašu* . . . , "The image of his body Dingirmaḫ desig[ned], completed his form . . ."

*Hit. Gilg.* I, i, 3–5: . . . UR.SAG-iš $^{d}$x [. . . . . . . . . .] $^{d}$GIŠ.GIM.MAŠ-un ALAM-an ša-am-ni-ir-ma [šal-la-uš DINGIR$^{\text{meš}}$-uš(?)] $^{d}$GIŠ.GIM.MAŠ-un ALAM-an . . . , ". . . the heroic god[s(?). . . . -ed] Gilgamesh's form. [The great gods] made Gilgamesh's form."

In the first two passages, note the role of the mother-goddess Dingirmaḫ, the mention of the king's image, and the similar use of two forms of the same verb, *ṣubbû* and *šuteṣbû.* The use of the latter form in *Gilgamesh* is paralleled only in *Enuma Elish,* in a similar context, a description of the birth and endowment of Marduk:

*uštaṣbišum-ma šunnât ilūs*[*su*][63]

"He (Marduk's father or ancestor) completed him
with *a double portion* of [his] divinity"
(*EnEl* I, 91)[64]

Elsewhere this form of the verb refers to the construction of buildings.[65] Royal inscriptions use the form *ṣubbû* in similar contexts.[66]

From this discussion we conclude that the description of the creation of Gilgamesh goes back at least to the Middle Babylonian

63. Thus in the text given by Lambert and Parker, p. 4. Previously the end of the line was read . . . *šunnāt ili uṣṣipšu* or *uṣp*[*a*] (Labat, *Poème,* p. 86; *CAD* Ṣ, p. 227b).

64. The translation here of *šunnât* follows Speiser, in *ANET,* p. 62a; *CAD* Ṣ, p. 227c; for the concept, cf. Gressmann and Ungnad, p. 86, n. 4. Other suggestions are "equality" (Bezold, p. 280a; cf. *CAD* $A_2$, p. 172c, *šinnāt/šunnāt apkalli*) and "different" (in his divinity from other gods; cf. *Erra* I, 23 and Cagni, *ad loc.; AHw,* p. 1166, *šanû* D, 5).

65. *CAD* Ṣ, p. 227b; Lambert, *MIO* 12:49 *sub* 12; cf. *CAD* K, p. 454b; see Speiser, in *ANET,* p. 62, n. 32.

66. See the examples collected in *CAD* Ṣ, pp. 226–27. For other passages of the type we are describing, see the entries collected in *CAD* s. vv. *gattu, bunnanû, lānu, zikrūtu, zumru,* and in *AHw,* s. vv. *lānu, minâtu, mešrêtu, nabnītu.* For the topos in general, see Labat, pp. 57–63; Jacobsen, *ZA* 52:116, 126, with n. 80; Seux, pp. 19–20; Sjöberg, *Or. Suec.* 21:87–112.

period, as reflected in the Hittite version, and that its Akkadian prototype is still reflected in the late version.

Like the hymnic epithets at the beginning of section c, the description of the divine creation and endowment of the hero seems to have been modeled on that topos as it appears in royal inscriptions and hymns.[67] The closest parallels currently known are found in inscriptions. In view of the numerous parallels between royal inscriptions and royal hymns,[68] and of the biographical content of the latter,[69] it would not be surprising to find this topos in royal hymns as well. The hymns do indeed contain numerous formulas of the type "endowed with such-and-such a quality by the god so-and-so." For example, Shulgi describes himself as one who was "granted heroism, might, and life in joy by Sin . . . , endowed with outstanding power by Nunamnir."[70] In a hymn of Lipit-Ishtar[71] we find a series of such epithets which is comparable to the series recited in the Ashurbanipal inscription quoted above: Lipit-Ishtar was given his royal crown by An, his scepter by Enlil, a favorable destiny by Ninlil, enduring charms by Nintu, was spoken to faithfully by Nanna, clothed in fearsomeness by Uta'ulu, granted wisdom and royal power by Enki, and had his head elevated by Inanna. I have not found these epithets in prenatal or birth contexts in the hymns.[72] The hymns do speak of the king possessing certain of his qualities from the womb,[73] and it would not be unexpected for such an endowment scene to be discovered in royal hymns.

67. The same sort of model may be suggested for the description of Marduk's birth in *EnEl.* Such features as Marduk's nursing at the breast of goddesses, his divine father's rejoicing over him, divine endowment of qualities, superiority over his ancestors, and naming by the divine parent (I, 85–102) are typical features of royal inscriptions. The similarity between royal inscriptions and the hymnic introduction to the *Tukulti-Ninurta Epic* is pointed out by Machinist; see n. 57, above.

68. Hallo, CRRAI 17:118–19; cf. the comment in *SAHG,* p. 371 *sub* 28.

69. Hallo, CRRAI 17:118.

70. Falkenstein, *ZA* 50:70–71, ll. 97–99; *SAHG,* p. 118; Kramer, in *ANET,* p. 586.

71. *SAHG,* p. 127, ll. 23–38.

72. *Gilgamesh* also has a few such passages outside of the description of Gilgamesh's birth: ^d^*Gilgameš* ^d^*Šamaš irâmšu-ma* ^d^*Anum* ^d^*Enlil u* ^d^*Ea urappišū uzunšu,* "Gilgamesh—of him Shamash is fond, Anu, Enlil, and Ea have broadened his wisdom" (*GE* I, v, 21–22); *eṭlūta bani balṭa īši zu''na* [*ku*]*zba kalu zumrišu danna emūqa elika īši,* "radiant with manhood, vigor he has, with ripeness gorgeous is the whole of his body; he has greater strength than you" (ibid., ll. 16–18); *šēr ilāni zumuršu,* "his body is the flesh of the gods" (IX, ii, 14); *libbi la sālila tēmidsu,* "you (Shamash) endowed him with a restless heart" (III, ii, 10).

73. E.g., *SAHG,* p. 115, l. 1; p. 126, l. 1; Hallo, *JCS* 20:141, l. 9. Note especially the birth section of the Ur-Nammu hymn published by Castellino, *ZA* 53:122, ll. 43–49, but note that the divine endowment (of wisdom, ll. 60–61) is separated from it by several lines.

The many parallels to royal hymns and inscriptions in section c contrast markedly with its paucity of allusions to the epic itself. Since, as we have said, this hymn, or a form of it, was the introduction to the Old Babylonian version of *Gilgamesh,* it is instructive to compare it to the hymnic introduction of another Akkadian narrative, the Standard Babylonian version of *Anzû.*[74] That introduction mentions the main theme of the myth, Ninurta's victory over Anzû (11), and the first strophe has been characterized as *"in nuce,* the entire myth."[75] On the other hand, parts of the introduction seem intrusive: Some lines refer to exploits and aspects of Ninurta not mentioned in the myth (some are known from other traditions about Ninurta); they are positioned in such a way as to overshadow the central exploit of the myth; and they read more like a general hymn. Moran concludes that an Old Babylonian introduction, consisting of at least the first strophe (1–4) and a transition to the narrative (9), and largely limited to themes appearing in the body of the myth, has been secondarily expanded in its late version. The Old Babylonian introduction to *Gilgamesh* was also expanded by the addition of at least sections a and b. However, section c appears to have developed differently from the introduction to *Anzû.* It seems impossible to find in section c an original nucleus which stressed the main themes of the epic. The only really convincing references to themes of the epic in section c are those connected with the quest for life and the journey to Utnapishtim (parts or all of I, i, 38–40). A similar restriction of allusions was noted in section a, but there the writer's motive was discernible: to stress understanding, rather than heroic exploits. In section c, however, no such motive is evident. On the contrary, several exploits are mentioned, but apart from lines 38 through 40, this is done in a manner which seems, at best, indifferent to the epic. Possible allusions to the Cedar Mountain expedition (36–37) ignore what are in the epic its main points and focus on tangential aspects. Other exploits mentioned in this section (41–42) are not from the epic at all.[76] Furthermore, the statement that Gilgamesh both "goes in front *(illak ina pāni)* as the leader" and marches behind as the rearguard (29–30), while com-

74. Hallo and Moran, pp. 71–79; Wilcke, *ZA* 67:175–79.
75. Hallo and Moran, p. 71.
76. One may recall that traditions about Gilgamesh not known from the epic are mentioned elsewhere in Akkadian literature. See the following note; Introduction, n. 61; and Gurney, *An. St.* 7:127–35.

patible with Gilgamesh's offer to go in front in fighting Huwawa (*lullik-ma ina pānika,* Gilg. Y., iv, 11), can only barely be harmonized with the elders' later instructions that Enkidu march ahead of Gilgamesh (*lillik ina pānika, ālik maḫra,* Gilg. Y. vi, 23, 27; *GE* III, i, 4, 6). Would a writer mindful of the elders' instructions have written line 29? In sum, it seems possible that the hymn about Gilgamesh in section c—perhaps in an earlier form—was originally composed independently of the epic and was secondarily joined to it in the Old Babylonian period as an introduction. The references to Gilgamesh's seeking life and journeying to Utnapishtim (39b–40) could have been added in order to integrate the hymn with the narrative, either when the hymn was first joined to the epic or at a later stage. If, on the other hand, these themes were also known independently of the epic,[77] it is possible that they, too, were part of such an independent hymn.

## A SUMERIAN HYMN TO GILGAMESH

The possibility of an independent hymn to Gilgamesh gains color in the light of a Sumerian hymn to him. One of the hymns of Shulgi, king of Ur (2094–2047), contains two sections addressed to Gilgamesh[78]:

Shulgi, the righteous shepherd of Sumer,
Praises his brother and friend, the lord Gilgamesh
In his might,
Addresses him in his heroism:
"Mighty one in the battle, a devastating flood
Who smites (the enemy) in the heat of the combat,
A catapult(?) of (?) the holy wall, skilled in (hurling) the sling-stone,
Against the 'house' of Kish you brought forth your weapon,
Its seven heroes you captured dead,
[The king of] Kish, Enmebaragesi—
You trampled on his head, [as (if he were) a snake],
You brought over the kingship from(?) Kish(?) to Uruk(?)."
. . .

77. On Gilgamesh's concern with death and desire for immortality in Sumerian sources, see p. 35. On references to Gilgamesh's quest for immortality and perhaps his journey to the survivor of the flood, in terms different from those of the epic, see Lambert, in *GSL,* pp. 44–45, and *CT* 44, no. 18, l. 5′, cited by Civil, *JNES* 28:72.
78. Klein, in *Kramer AV,* pp. 276–81.

Shulgi, the righteous shepherd of Sumer
Praises his [brother] and friend, the lord Gilgamesh,
[In his might],
Addresses [him in his heroism]:
". . . .
In the judgement that you pronounce[. . . .]
Who else, like you, [has proceeded(?) on the] mountain(?) road, [has traveled(?)] on the way to. . . .?
Mighty one, [you felled(?)] the mountain(?)-cedars,
[You penetrated(?) into(?)] the mighty forest,
The ship. . . .
Huwawa [. . . . you captured(?)]
[His(?)] seven 'splendors' . . . .
The small. . . .
From his fortified abode [you removed(?) him]
To Enlil, [in] the Shrine (of) Nippur [you entered(?) with him(?)], as a . . . . [you presented(?) him(?)]
Having. . . . your captured hero,
(To?) the mother of the 'sick man', you brought(?) the son (on? her?) lap.
Your *udug*-mace, whose 'mouth' is wide open, attacks for you the foreign lands.
Gilgamesh, the noble one of Uruk,
The violent storm, at(?) whose oppression. . . .
The inimical rebellious land, like. . . .
You revealed your majesty and greatness, may you [spread(?) over(?) me(?)] (your) protecting arms!"

This hymn shows that hymns were composed to Gilgamesh in Sumerian at least as early as the Ur III period. But this particular hymn shows no real relationship to that in the epic. Like the latter, it consists of general epithets and specific exploits of Gilgamesh, and a few are even similar to those in the epic's introduction (for example, "mighty one in battle, a devastating flood," "[. . . on the] mountain(?)-road"). However, the similarities are too vague to indicate any connection between the Sumerian hymn and that in the epic, and the emphases of the two are quite different. The Sumerian hymn devotes more attention to the specific exploits of Gilgamesh than to general epithets. One of the adventures it mentions, the battle with Kish, is totally overlooked in the Akkadian epic.

To sum up: The introduction to *The Gilgamesh Epic* is based upon a number of standard literary types. It begins with a standard hymnic-epic opening featuring a series of epithets and descriptive phrases about the hero, but modifies this type to stress the wisdom acquired by the hero in the course of the epic, rather than heroic adventures and attributes standard in such introductions. The first section concludes by implying that the epic is based on information recorded by the hero himself in a didactic inscription. The second section features a paean to the walls and temple of Uruk modeled on hymns to temples and temple cities. This paean is partly repeated at the end of Tablet XI (forming a framework around the epic), where it expresses Gilgamesh's ultimate acceptance of his mortality. The paean concludes with an invitation to the reader to recover the inscription buried in the walls, thus leading the reader once again to the epic's alleged source of information. These two sections are a late addition to the epic and, along with the echo of the second section in XI, 303–7, stress the indirect immortality offered by inscriptions and building projects, whereas the Old Babylonian version may have stressed only enjoyment of life in lieu of direct immortality. The third section is a hymnic introduction of the hero modeled on royal hymns, including general epithets and specific exploits and attributes of the hero and a description of his creation by the gods and the qualities with which they endowed him. Here, too, Gilgamesh's major adventures are largely ignored. This section may have originated as a hymn to Gilgamesh which was unconnected with the epic.

# 8

# *Traditional Speech Forms, Literature, and Rituals Reflected in the Epic*

So far we have focused mostly on developments in the Akkadian *Gilgamesh* subsequent to its composition. However, the discussion of literary affinities in Chapter 7 directs our attention to an aspect of the process of composition itself. We saw that the hymnic introduction to the Old Babylonian version was either borrowed or adapted from a hymn to Gilgamesh that was already current in the Old Babylonian period, or else was composed especially for the epic, using other royal hymns and royal inscriptions as literary models. In either case, the Old Babylonian introduction was heavily indebted to literary compositions not originally created for the epic. Similarly we saw that the prologue of the late version was modeled on standard hymnic-epic openings and on Sumerian hymns to temples and cities.

It comes as no surprise to find that an ancient epic draws upon literature originally unconnected with it. Any literary composition, simply by virtue of being composed in a language, makes use of elements that were created independently of that composition itself, such as vocabulary, style, and idioms. Furthermore, a composition, even a fiction, that describes human activities, will tend to base its description on real-life behavior. Writers are often inspired, in addition, by a technique or idea that they find in the work of another writer. All this is true even of modern Western literature, despite the fact that this literature values originality highly. The ancient Near East, in contrast, was a very conservative milieu, and its canons of literary style placed a premium on saying things in conventional ways. On the simplest level, this involved the use of standard formulas, similes, epithets, and the like.[1] But beyond this, ancient writers drew extensively upon larger components, such as topoi, motifs, groups of lines, and episodes, which had their original settings in other compositions. Sometimes they composed passages imitating such elements, and at other times they simply transferred such elements verbatim into their own compositions. By modern Western standards, the style of these writers would seem hackneyed and their procedures would often be considered plagiarism. But by the standards of the ancient Near East, these phenomena reflected a highly valued reliance on tradition, and in order to evaluate ancient Near Eastern literature we ought to set aside our own preferences and try to understand it by its own standards. To help us appreciate those standards, we might keep in mind that even today reliance on conventional forms is considered a virtue in, for example, classical ballet, and is not incompatible with artistic achievement.

In the present chapter, we are interested in a number of brief passages in *The Gilgamesh Epic* which seem to reflect conventional forms of speech, literature, and ritual used in particular life-situations in ancient Mesopotamia. In seeking to identify conventional forms and the life-situations *(Sitz im Leben)* in which they were typically used, the inquiry will be form-critical. In some cases the inquiry will also be source-critical, since some of the passages seem to have been taken into the epic not directly from their original life-contexts, but from other literary compositions. In subsequent chapters, we will seek to identify the literary sources of a number of longer passages in the epic.

The identification of components borrowed from other composi-

1. See, for example, Schott, *Vergleiche;* Kramer, "Sumerian Epic Literature," pp. 825–37; Kramer, *JAOS* 89; Heimpel; Hecker; Limet; Sonneck; Tallqvist, *Götterepitheta;* Seux; Hallo, *IEJ* 12:19–20; Alster, *Dumuzi's Dream;* Wilcke, "Formale Gesichtspunkte."

tions entails certain problems, and since we shall be attempting such identifications in this and the following chapters, we should mention those problems now. Even where we possess a verbatim parallel to a passage, the direction of the borrowing is rarely obvious.[2] We have already encountered the problem of a passage found in virtually identical form in *The Gilgamesh Epic, Ishtar,* and *Nergal and Ereshkigal* (see pp. 125–26). These passages are obviously related, but whether one of the three is the original, or whether the texts exercised a reciprocal influence on each other in the course of their transmission, or whether they relied upon a common source could not be determined. One approach frequently followed is to classify such parallels as representing a topos drawn, not from a particular composition, but from "a stock of phrases, lines, and even whole stanzas at the disposal of a school of poets who created from them ever-new combinations."[3] Even where an element appears to have a more specific source, we shall find that it is rarely possible (as in the case of the flood story in *GE* XI) to point with confidence to a particular composition as its home. More often we can point only to a circle of literary traditions or a type of life-setting from which it was drawn, and sometimes we can point only to a folklore motif as a possible source.

## WISDOM SAYINGS

There are a number of passages in the epic where a character, in trying to convince somebody of something, speaks in a way which resembles wisdom literature in form and content. Presumably this is realistic, and people did quote wisdom sayings to back up their arguments (cf. n. 2). Some examples follow.

2. As it is, for example, in the case of popular proverbs quoted in Akkadian letters and introduced by such phrases as "just like the old proverb" or "as people say" (see *BWL,* pp. 276, 280, 282; cf. Finet, pp. 43–45). Letters also quote or allude to proverbs without such introductions (*BWL,* pp. 232–33). Lambert and Millard, pp. 27–28, argue that a ritual instruction in a letter to a late Assyrian king is a quotation from *Atr.* While this may be correct (*Atr.* is the older of the two texts), in the absence of an explicit statement to this effect in the letter, the possibility could be considered that *Atr.* and the letter were both actually quoting from an ancient ritual text.

3. Hallo, *IEJ* 12:19–20.

## *Who Can Scale Heaven?*

When Gilgamesh proposes journeying to the Cedar Mountain, Enkidu opposes the plan on the basis of his personal knowledge of the dangers posed by Huwawa, whose "breath is death" (Gilg. Y. iii, 12–24). In trying to persuade Enkidu, Gilgamesh argues that fear of the danger should not deter them, since death is man's lot in any case. Part of Gilgamesh's argument is expressed as follows:

> *ma-an-nu ib-ri e-lu-ú ša-m*[*a-i*]
> *i-lu-ma it-ti* $^{d}$*Šamaš da-ri-iš u*[*š-šab*]
> *a-wi-lu-tum-ma ma-nu-ú* $u_4$*-mu-ša*
> *mi-im-ma ša i-te-né-pu-šu ša-ru-ma*
>
> Who, my friend, can scale he[aven]?
> Only the gods l[ive] forever with (i.e., like) the sun.
> As for mankind, numbered are their days.
> Whatever they achieve is but wind!
> (Gilg. Y. iv, 5–8)[4]

A passage similar to the first line of this statement also appears in the Sumerian version of the Cedar Mountain episode, *Gilgamesh and the Land of the Living,* when Gilgamesh seeks the sun-god's permission for the journey. The sun-god is apparently reluctant at first, and in pressing his case Gilgamesh argues that he wants to undertake this journey because he recognizes that man is mortal. He has seen men dying in his city, and he knows that

> lú sukud-da an-šè nu-mu-un-da-lá
> lú dagal-la kur-ra la-ba-an-šú-šú
>
> A man, (even) the tallest, cannot *reach* heaven.
> A man, (even) the widest, cannot *cover* the earth.
> (*GLL* A, 28–29).[5]

Although the Sumerian version of the saying is addressed to a different character than the Akkadian version, the fact that both are

4. Restoration of the first line follows von Soden, *ZA* 53:213. On the sun as a simile for longevity, see chap. 4, n. 56.

5. Kramer, *JCS* 1:10–11 as revised in Shaffer's MS of *GLL* A. For the wording in *GLL* B: MS a, i, 6–8, see Kramer, *JCS* 1:31, n. 25, ll. 6–8. On the translation, cf. *BWL*, p. 327.

quoted by Gilgamesh in similar contexts in the Sumerian and Akkadian version of the same episode indicates that the Akkadian version of the proverb is ultimately dependent on the Sumerian. A form of the Sumerian proverb also occurs in a collection of proverbs "dealing with the supremacy of death over life"[6]:

sukud-da an-na-šè nu-mu-un-da-lá
lú dagal-la kur-ra la-ba-an-šú-šú
kala-ga ki-a NE nu-um-⸢x⸣
ti níg-dùg šà-ḫul-la šu ḫé-ni-ib-kar-kar-re

(Even) the tallest cannot *reach* heaven,
A man, (even) the widest, cannot *cover* the land,
(Even) the strongest cannot . . . . himself(?) on earth.
The pleasant life, let it elapse in joy.[7]

In both *Gilgamesh and the Land of the Living* and Gilg. Y., the proverb is cited to epitomize man's mortality, but the proverb says nothing about death explicitly. It is understandable as a reference to mortality only on the basis of its context in popular usage or in the proverb collection, and one of these is presupposed by its use in the *Gilgamesh* texts.[8]

## *The Three-ply Rope*

In the course of the Cedar Mountain episode, there appears a fragmentary passage in which reference is made to a three-stranded towrope:

6. Alster, *RA* 67:108, n. 1. According to Alster, our proverb is part of the composition n í g - n a m  n u - k a l  z i  k u₇ - k u₇ - d a, "Nothing is precious except a sweet life"; cf. also Alster, *Studies,* p. 86.

7. Alster, *Studies,* pp. 86–89; cf. Kramer, *JCS* 1:35, n. 215. The proverb is echoed in Akkadian in the *Pessimistic Dialogue* (*ANET,* p. 438d[XII] = p. 601d[X] = *BWL,* pp. 148–49, ll. 83–84). Cf. Hallo, *IEJ* 12:20, n. 33.

8. That the proverb does not necessarily refer to mortality outside the context of the proverb collection and dependent passages (including the *Pessimistic Dialogue*) is indicated by the application of its antithesis to gods, where it does not refer to their immortality (*BWL,* p. 327; *ANET,* p. 581d, ll. 123–24 = Hallo and van Dijk, pp. 30–31, ll. 123–24; p. 60; cf. Pope and Tigay, *Ugarit-Forschungen* 3:121–22).

*iš-ten iš-ten-ma u*[*l*(?) x x x]
⌜*ú*⌝*-ba-ra-tu-ma* [x x x x]
*muš-ḫal-ṣi-túm-ma u*[*l* x x x]
2-*ta taš-ka-a-ta/ti* [x x x x]
*áš-lu šu-uš-lu-š*[*u* x x x]
[x x x] *dan-nu* 2 *mi-ra-*[*nu* x x x]

One alone c[annot. . . .]
Strangers [. . . .]
Slippery ground can[not. . . .]
Two . . . . triplets [. . . .]
A three-stranded towrope [. . . .]
Strong. . . . two lion [cubs. . . .]
(*GE* V, ii, 20–25;
*CT* 46, 21, rev.)[9]

According to Landsberger, this is part of a speech by Gilgamesh which appears in both the fourth and fifth tablets of the late version.[10] In fact, at least once the speech is attributed to Enkidu.[11] However, despite the poor state of the text, enough is preserved to permit us to recognize its similarity to a speech of Gilgamesh's in *Gilgamesh and the Land of the Living.*[12] There, when Enkidu's resolve to attack Huwawa falters, Gilgamesh urges him on with a speech about how they can succeed together. The speech begins as follows:

106. gar-ra Enkidu lú-2 nu-ug$_6$-e giš-má-da-lá nu-su-su
107. éš-3-tab-ba lú nu-kud-dè
108. bàd-da-a lú nu-šú-šú
109. é-gi-sig-ga izi nu-te-en-te-en
110. za-e gá-e daḫ-ma-ab gá-e za-e ga-mu-ra-daḫ a-na-me lú ba-an-tum$_4$

106. Stop, Enkidu! Two men will not die; the towed boat will not sink,
107. A towrope of three strands cannot be cut.
108. In the *protection of the wall* one cannot be overwhelmed.
109. In a reed-hut, the fire will not be extinguished.
110. You help me and I will help you, (and) what of ours can anyone carry off?[13]

9. Shaffer, *EI* 9:159–60; Landsberger, *RA* 62:108–9.
10. *RA* 62:108.
11. *GE* V, ii, 20–25. Note also Kramer's comment on the speaker in *GLL* A, 106–19 (*JCS* 1:40).
12. Shaffer, *EI* 9:159–60.
13. This is the composite text presented by Shaffer, *EI* 8:247 (where the lines are numbered 103–7).

The Akkadian and Sumerian passages share references to a three-stranded towrope and to "two," and, if they are indeed related, the Sumerian passage helps us catch the drift of the Akkadian: It speaks of how two people together can overcome obstacles that one cannot overcome alone. The suggestion that this is the meaning of the Akkadian passage, too, is supported by a similar passage in Eccles. 4:9–12, which shows that the three-stranded rope became a standard motif in sayings about the value of a companion:

> Two are better off than one, in that they have greater benefit from their earnings. For should they fall, one can raise the other; but woe betide him who is alone and falls with no companion to raise him! Further, when two lie together they are warm; but how can he who is alone get warm? Also, if one attacks, two can stand up to him. A threefold cord is not readily broken![14]

Kramer noted the proverbial character of the entire Sumerian passage,[15] but these sayings have not been found to date in a Mesopotamian wisdom text from which *Gilgamesh and the Land of the Living* might be said to have borrowed them. That such themes were the subject of wisdom literature is, however, suggested by Eccles. 4:9–12 and by a similar passage in the Akkadian *Advice of Shube-awilum* found at Ras Shamra in Syria, which counsels the wisdom of traveling with a companion.[16]

## *Carpe Diem*

A third passage that resembles wisdom literature is found in the Old Babylonian version of the epic, the barmaid's famous carpe diem speech to Gilgamesh:

14. Ginsberg, ed., *Five Megilloth,* pp. 63–64.

15. *JCS* 1:40; cf. Shaffer, *EI* 8:249, and n. 18. Landsberger, in debating Shaffer's suggestion that the biblical passage Eccles. 4:12 was influenced by lines 106–7, spoke of the internationality and timelessness of such sayings.

16. Nougayrol et al., in *Ugaritica* 5, no. 163, p. 277, ll. 9–16; 280, ll. 9–16. This theme adds color to Speiser's suggestion that the phrase "he who goes in front protects the companion" (Gilg. Y. vi, 27; *GE* III, i, 4; IV, vi, 38) is presented in the form of a commonly known saying (*JQR* 48:212; *Landsberger AV,* p. 390).

6. *at-ta* $^{d}$*Gilgameš lu ma-li ka-ra-aš-ka*
7. *ur-ri u mu-ši ḫi-ta-at-tu at-ta*
8. $u_4$*-mi-ša-am šu-ku-un ḫi-du-tam*
9. *ur-ri u mu-ši su-ur u me-li-il*
10. *lu ub-bu-bu ṣú-ba-tu-ka*
11. *qá-qá-ad-ka lu me-si me-e lu ra-am-ka-ta*
12. *ṣu-ub-bi ṣi-iḫ-ra-am ṣa-bi-tu qá-ti-ka*
13. *mar-ḫi-tum li-iḫ-ta-ad-da-a-am i-na su-ni-*[*k*]*a*
14. *an-na-ma ši-pir* [*šinnisti*]

6. As for you, Gilgamesh, let your belly be full,
7. Make merry day and night.
8. Of each day make a feast of rejoicing,
9. Day and night dance and play!
10. Let your garments be sparkling fresh,
11. Your head be washed; bathe in water.
12. Pay heed to a little one that holds on to your hand.
13. Let a spouse delight in your bosom,
14. For this is the task of [woman].[17]

(Gilg. Me. iii, 6–14)

A parallel to this passage has not so far been discovered in Mesopotamian wisdom literature.[18] Similar sentiments are expressed in many sayings from around the world.[19] The passage has rather explicit parallels from ancient Egypt and Israel.[20] Although the Israelite passage may be dependent on that in *Gilgamesh,*[21] this is not likely to be true of the Egyptian parallels. The notions are conventional, and probably part of popular wisdom.[22]

As an explanation for these documented and presumed parallels between Gilgamesh compositions and wisdom literature, one might

17. The restoration of the last word is based on *GE* I, iv, 13, 19 (cf. Böhl, cited by Diakonoff, p. 65; Speiser, "Mesopotamia," pp. 244, 370, n. 33; cf. Lambert, *MIO* 12:54, ll. 13, 15; 56, ll. 13, 15, as understood by *CAD* K, p. 85d; Hoffner, *JCS* 23:18–19). To l. 12, cf. *SKL* iii, 21–22, which mention Gilgamesh's son and successor.

18. A rough parallel may be *Shube-Awilum* iv, 2–8, as understood by Nougayrol et al., in *Ugaritica* 5:282–83; in a different literary genre, cf. the advice of Naram-Sin in Gurney, *An. St.* 5:106–9, ll. 154–72, quoted above, pp. 145–46.

19. See Gordis, pp. 303–4.

20. Eccles. 9:7–9 (cf. Isa. 22:13); J. Wilson, in *ANET,* pp. 467c, 413d; Lichtheim; Wente. Most of these passages are in contexts dealing with death, as in Gilg. Me.

21. Barton, *Ecclesiastes,* p. 162, following Grimme, pp. 432ff.; cf. Speiser *apud* Ginsberg, "Quintessence," pp. 58–59.

22. Cf. Lichtheim, pp. 200, 207–9; cf. 182.

consider the possibility that the passages were original with the *Gilgamesh* compositions and that, where parallels exist, they were borrowed by the wisdom texts. Narrative texts would not be an implausible origin for some proverbs, but this does not seem especially likely in most of the cases we have discussed. The proverb about reaching heaven is cited by Gilgamesh to epitomize man's mortality, but, as we have noted, it is understandable as a reference to mortality only on the basis of its context in popular usage or in the proverb collection, one of which *Gilgamesh and the Land of the Living* therefore presupposes. The barmaid's advice has so many parallels around the world that its origin in popular wisdom seems assured. This could also be the case with the passage about the value of companionship, although it is not as closely or as widely paralleled as the barmaid's advice, and there is no strong argument against the possibility that it was first composed by the author of *Gilgamesh and the Land of the Living.*[23]

## BLESSINGS, CURSES, AND THREATS

Passages in these categories are sometimes conventional. Three such passages in the epic have affinities elsewhere.

### *Travelers' Blessings and Curses*

In Gilg. Y. vi, 31–33, the elders wish Gilgamesh success on his journey and pray, among other things:

*li-ip-te-kum pa-da-nam pi-ḫi-tam*
*ḫarrana li-iš-ta-siq a-na ki-ib-sí-ka*
*ša-di-a li-iš-ta-si-iq a-na šēpi-ka*

23. In Landsberger's opinion, the references to towing a boat with a three-ply rope fit Gilgamesh and Enkidu traveling to the Cedar Mountain partly by boat (*RA* 62:109, n. 37); cf. Klein, pp. 280–81, l. 94, p. 290 *ad loc.*

Another passage which sounds proverbial is Utnapishtim's advice to Gilgamesh in *GE* X, vi, and at least some of it could be based on current proverbs. Utnapishtim figures as the recipient of advice in *The Instructions of Shuruppak;* see *ANET,* p. 594.

May (Shamash) open for you the barred path,
Keep the road in order for your treading,
The open country in order for your foot![24]

The antithesis of this blessing is found in the Old Babylonian version of *Etana,* where the eagle and the serpent swear friendship before Shamash and pronounce a curse upon whichever of the two should violate the oath. The curse includes the following lines (*Etana* A-2, 1–2):

*li-iḫ-li-iq-šu ṭu-ú-du a-ia ú-ta ḫarranam*
*li-ik-la-šu ne-ri-ib-ta-šu šà-du-ú*

May the path be lost for him that he find not the way!
May the mountain block its entrance for him.[25]

Conceivably, one of these Old Babylonian passages could be modeled on the other, but since they employ mostly different vocabulary, it seems more likely that both are based on a standard motif, probably something like a traveler's blessing, which could be formulated in various ways, and, in the case of *Etana,* was reversed.[26]

## *Curse on a Harlot*

Enkidu's cursing of the harlot in *GE* VII is introduced with a passage resembling the introduction to Ishtar's cursing of the character Asushunamir in *Ishtar.* The latter text is preserved in two versions, which together add up to most of the *Gilgamesh* passage (see the accompanying comparison).[27]

24. On the meaning of *lištassiq,* see von Soden, *ZA* 53:214–15; *AHw,* p. 753bc; contrast *CAD* K, p. 337cd.

25. Cf. NA *Etana,* C-2, 14 (*ANET,* p. 116a).

26. In Gilg. Y., the passage is employed as a traveler's blessing as Gilgamesh and Enkidu set out on their expedition (cf. Gilg. Y. vi, 19; GEUW rev. 11, reading *kur-ba-a-in-ni iṭ-ṭu-di* (= *ina ṭūdi*), "bless me (as I embark) on the path." In *Etana,* there is no expedition, and the curse seems to be invoked simply because it is enforced by the patron of travelers, Shamash (see above, chap. 4, n. 20 and accompanying text), in whose name the eagle and serpent had sworn.

27. For the texts of *Ishtar,* see *BAL* 2:91; for *GE* VII, iii, see *GETh.,* p. 45; *CT* 46:23; Gadd, *Iraq* 28:109; and Schramm, *RA* 64:94.

| ***Ishtar* N, rev.** | ***GE* VII, iii** | ***Ishtar* A, rev.** |
|---|---|---|
| 23a. *al-ka* $^{\mathrm{I}}$*Aṣû-šú-na-mir* | 6. *al-ki* $^{f}$*Šam-ḫat* *ši-ma-tu lu-šim-ki* | 19. *al-kám* ⌜*Aṣ*⌝*-na-me-er šim-ti la ma-še-e lu-šim-ka* |
| | 7. [*ši*]*-mat la i-qat-tu-u ana du-ur da-a-ar* | 20. [*l*]*u-šim-*⌜*ka*⌝*-*⌜*ma*⌝ *šim-ti la ma-še-e ana ṣa-a-ti* |
| 23b. *lu-zir-ka iz-ra rabâ* | 8. *lu-uz-zir-ki iz-ra rabâ* | |
| | 9. *ḫa-an-ṭi-iš ḫar-piš iz-ru-ú-a! lit-ḫu-ki ka-a-ši* | |
| 23a. Come, Asushunamir, | 6. Come, Shamhat, I will decree (your) fate, | 19. Come, Asnamer, I will decree for you a fate not to be forgotten. |
| | 7. A fate that shall not end for all eternity. | 20. A fate I will decree for you not to be forgotten forever. |
| 23b. I will curse you with a great curse. | 8. I will curse you with a great curse. | |
| | 9. With great speed let my curses reach you. | |

The *Gilgamesh* passage could be viewed as a composite of the two versions of *Ishtar,* either created by the editor of *Gilgamesh* or drawn by him from a third, conflate version of *Ishtar.* This seems more plausible than the possibility that the two versions of the latter each drew upon separate parts of the *Gilgamesh* passage.[28] But differences in vocabulary between the *Gilgamesh* passage and those from *Ishtar,* along with the additional line in the *Gilgamesh* passage (9), leave open the possibility that we are dealing with

28. That one version of *Ishtar* borrowed half of a parallelistic passage is not itself implausible (cf. above, chap. 3, § F), but that both versions went to *GE* independently and borrowed different halves seems to assume too much. Oppenheim apparently overlooked the recensional differences in *Ishtar* in arguing for its dependence on *GE* in this passage (*Or.* 19:138, n. 3).

various conventional curse introductions quoted independently by all three texts, with *Gilgamesh* quoting several of the available formulas.

In the body of the curses, two lines are shared by both texts:

*ṣi-il-li dūri lu-ú man-za-zu-ki*

The shadow of the wall shall be your station.
(*GE* VII, iii, 20[29]; *Ishtar* N rev. 26
= *Ishtar* A rev. 23)

[*šak*]-*ru ù ṣam-mu-ú li-im-ḫaṣ li-it-ki*

The [besot]ted and thirsty shall smite your cheek.
(*GE* VII, iii, 22; *Ishtar* N rev. 28;
not present in *Ishtar* A)

In *Gilgamesh,* these lines are part of a lengthy curse which seems mostly tailored to the character and situation of the harlot.[30] The curse mentions her bosom, taverns, her sitting at the crossroads, and the like. In *Ishtar,* the curse passage is shorter, and its other lines reflect conventional curse themes.[31] Since the shared lines fit the character and situation of a harlot but bear no obvious relation to the character and situation of Asushunamir,[32] it seems likely that *Ishtar* borrowed them from *Gilgamesh,* just as it drew upon con-

29. For a possible variant, see Landsberger, *RA* 62:126, l. 25.

30. Oppenheim considers this an etiological curse "designed to explain the peculiar social position of this type of prostitute" (*Or.* 17:40). This does not rule out the possibility that some passages in the curse are conventional.

31. Foul food and drink and lack of a normal dwelling are mentioned in treaty curses, e.g., Reiner in *ANET,* p. 533, § iv, p. 539, § 56. According to Reiner, the curse in *Ishtar* N rev. 24 is simply eating city food, which is disparaged in *Erra* I, 57 (see Hallo, *JCS* 23:57; Reiner, "City Bread," pp. 116–17, followed in *CAD* K, p. 578a).

32. Some scholars think that the *assinnu* and *kulu'u* (the terms applied to Asushunamir in *Ishtar* N, rev. 12 and A, rev. 7) were male prostitutes (see *AHw* on each of these words; cf. Oppenheim, *Or.* 19:135, n. 1). This could require modification of our argument. To do so, however, would require evidence that the *assinnu* and *kulu'u* characteristically sat outside city walls and frequented taverns. This seems unlikely in view of the fact that these men were primarily cultic personnel (see *CAD* on each word). The closest I have been able to come to such evidence is a reference to a *sinnišānu,* "effeminate man," seeking sexual business at a tavern (*BWL,* p. 218, rev. iv, 3–4). The *sinnišānu* is equated with the *assinnu* in a lexical text (*CAD* $A_2$, p. 341b), but the equation cannot be considered definitive: *AHw* cites no references to *sinnišānu* as a cultic functionary.

For harlots frequenting taverns, see *CAD* $A_2$, p. 473, s.v. *aštammu;* Jacobsen, *JNES* 12:184–85, n. 68; *Treasures,* pp. 139–40; Hoffner, in *Studies . . . Güterbock,* pp. 113–21.

ventional curse themes for the rest of the curse of Asushunamir. This seems to be confirmed by the fact that the two shared curses are already found in a Middle Babylonian text of *Gilgamesh* (Gilg. Ur 25, 27), but only one of them appears in the earlier of the two recensions of *Ishtar* (A); the second of the two curses is found only in the younger Nineveh recension of *Ishtar* (N). This suggests that the scribe of the Nineveh recension continued a process, begun earlier, of drawing on *The Gilgamesh Epic* to flesh out the curse.

In sum, whereas *The Gilgamesh Epic* seems either to have borrowed the introduction to the curse from *Ishtar* or to have drawn upon conventional introductions, *Ishtar* seems to have borrowed parts of the curse from *The Gilgamesh Epic.* This reciprocal relationship will be discussed further after the next example.

## *Raising the Dead*

In *GE* VI, 97–100, Ishtar, in another curse, threatens that if Anu refuses her request to send the Bull of Heaven, she will smash the doors of the netherworld and

*u-[še]l-lam-ma [mī]tūti [i]k-ka-lu ba[l-ṭ]u-u-ti*
*eli bal-ṭu-ti ú-šam-[a-d]u mītūti*

I will raise up the dead, and they will devour the living,
I will make the dead outnumber the living!
(*GE* VI, 99–100, from
*GSL,* 121, iii, 34–36)

The latter couplet is found in *Ishtar* N (obv. 19–20), where it is spoken by Ishtar, and in *Nergal and Ereshkigal* (v, 11′–12′, 26′–27′) where it is part of a threat made by Ereshkigal, Ishtar's sister.[33] In *Gilgamesh and the Bull of Heaven,* the Sumerian forerunner of *GE* VI, Ishtar's threat was apparently of a different nature entirely.[34] Since the threat in *GE* VI deals with the realm of the dead and the parallels mentioned both appear in texts dealing with the

33. *ANET,* pp. 107, 511. The parallel passages are set out together in *BAL* 2:87–88. *Ishtar* also contains the threat to smash the doors of the netherworld, whereas *Nergal and Ereshkigal* does not. For the Assur variant of the last line in the *Ishtar* passage, see Heidel, p. 122, n. 65.
34. See chap. 1, n. 9.

netherworld, those texts are more plausible than *Gilgamesh* as the original context of the threat.[35] Since *Ishtar* attributes the threat to the same goddess who utters it in *GE* VI, and also includes the threat to smash the doors of the netherworld, *Ishtar* is the more likely source for the *Gilgamesh* passage.[36]

The conclusion that *GE* VI has borrowed the threat from elsewhere agrees with the fact that this tablet is rife with literary allusions, most relating to Ishtar. Since *Gilgamesh* seems to have drawn some passages from *Ishtar,* while *Ishtar* has borrowed others from *Gilgamesh,* the process of borrowing was probably gradual. The nature of the process is suggested by the fact that some lines appear only in some, not all of the manuscripts of the borrowing compositions: The parallel to *GE* VII, ii, 22 appears only in the Nineveh recension of *Ishtar,* and the parallel to *Ishtar* N obv. 11 is found in only one manuscript of *GE* VII, iv, after line 39.[37] This implies that not all of the parallels were put into the texts by their authors, but that some were added by later copyists. Perhaps on one occasion a copyist of *Gilgamesh* added a line from *Ishtar.* A copyist of *Ishtar,* perhaps many years later, borrowed another line from *Gilgamesh.* The process may have been repeated a few times, and in this way the number of parallels grew.[38]

## MARRIAGE LITERATURE AND CEREMONIES

Another passage in *GE* VI which appears to be modeled on preexistent material is Ishtar's proposal of marriage to Gilgamesh (*GE* VI, 1–21). Within the evolution of *The Gilgamesh Epic,* this passage may be an innovation of the Akkadian version. Nothing in the preserved parts of the Sumerian source of Tablet VI, *Gilgamesh*

35. Cf. the discussion of the epithets for the netherworld in *GE* VII, iv, 33–39 (see chap. 5, pp. 125–26). For further possibly conventional topoi in *GE* VII, cf pp. 124–26, above. For the appearance of a man in Enkidu's dream, cf. Oppenheim, *Dreams,* p. 189. Oppenheim also claims that the *Vision of the Nether World* (*ANET,* pp. 109–10) is modeled on Enkidu's dream (*Dreams,* pp. 213–14), but the differences between the two texts are extensive, and both texts may draw upon conventional material; cf. the "Göttertypen" text published by Köcher.

36. This refers to the Akkadian version of *Ishtar;* in the Sumerian *Inanna's Descent,* 72–76 (*ANET,* p. 54), there is no threat at all.

37. See chap. 5, n. 51.

38. See the list of parallel passages in chap. 5, nn. 51–52.

*and the Bull of Heaven,* resembles the proposal, and, according to Falkenstein, the disagreement between Gilgamesh and Ishtar in that text may have been of an entirely different nature, not involving Gilgamesh's refusal to marry the goddess.[39]

In any case, Ishtar's proposal in the Akkadian version bears a resemblance to texts which describe the sacred-marriage ritual *(hieros gamos)* and appears to be modeled upon such literature or the ritual itself.[40] The texts are part of the liturgy of the ritual sacred marriage in which the king, representing the fertility god Dumuzi/Tammuz, "marries" a female representing the fertility goddess Inanna/Ishtar, in order to promote fertility in the land. These texts describe the king's dressing for the ceremony (cf. *GE* VI, 1–5) and the goddess's bursting into passionate song when she beholds him (cf. 6ff.). She praises the king's charms (cf. 6, 8) and promises him dominion (cf. 16–17), fertility in his reign (cf. 18), and long life.[41] In the epic, Ishtar alludes to the gifts which the groom brought in such marriages, but states that the only gift she desires is Gilgamesh's "fruit" (8).[42] The formula of the proposal proper (*atta lu mutī-ma anāku lu aššatka,* "You be my husband, I will be your wife," l. 9) is not known to be paralleled in sacred-marriage texts, but is identical to the proposal of Ishtar's sister Ereshkigal to Nergal in the myth about those two gods.[43] As ruler of Uruk, the historical Gilgamesh would have taken part in the sacred-marriage ceremony. If Ishtar's proposal was not part of the Sumerian *Gilgamesh and the Bull of Heaven,* it may be another example of a tradition about Gilgamesh that was preserved in the nonliterary tradition for centuries before entering the Akkadian epic, where it was perhaps fleshed out with

39. According to Falkenstein, the occasion for the friction between Gilgamesh and Ishtar in this version may have been Ishtar's denying Gilgamesh the right to pronounce judgement in the Eanna temple (*RLA* 3:361, § c).

40. Cf. van Buren, *Or.* 13:41; van Dijk, *Bi. Or.* 11:84–85. For general discussions of the sacred marriage, see Kramer, *Sacred Marriage* and Jacobsen, *Treasures,* pp. 32–47.

41. See van Dijk, *Bi. Or.* 11:83–88; Kramer, *ANET,* p. 641; *Sacred Marriage,* pp. 63–64; "Shulgi," pp. 378–80; Renger, *RLA* 4:251–59, esp. 255–57. The promise of produce from mountains and plains as tribute (17) resembles passages in royal inscriptions and several other genres cited in *CAD* B, pp. 229c, 235, and *CAD* Ṣ, p. 138d; cf. Waldman, "Wealth."

42. See Greengus, pp. 522–23. The beloved's "fruit" is referred to in love lyrics (Held, p. 8, l. 11; Lambert, *MIO* 12:49–51, l. 8).

43. MB version, A, rev. 82 (*ANET,* p. 104); note that this proposal, too, includes a promise of dominion (cf. also *EnEl* I, 146–57).

passages modeled on the sacred-marriage literature known at the time it was incorporated into the epic.[44]

Another passage concerning marriage ceremonies is the description of the marriage scene at which Gilgamesh first encounters Enkidu (Gilg. P. v, 22–31).[45] Like this passage, sacred-marriage texts describe the public rejoicing, music, and offerings which accompany the ceremony and include the statement that "a bed is laid out" for the goddess, as it is here for the goddess Išḫara, who is apparently personified by the bride.[46] A nearly identical statement is found in the Old Babylonian *Atrahasis Epic,* I, 299–304, in a passage which looks like the prototype of human (not only sacred) marriage ceremonies,[47] and public rejoicing and music (though not necessarily sacrificial offerings) could obviously accompany any marriage. The epic's description of the marriage scene in Gilg. P. is based either on such texts or upon personal observation of one or both types of marriage ceremony.

The discussion in this and the previous chapter indicates that at all stages in the evolution of *The Gilgamesh Epic* writers drew in various ways upon preexistent materials originally unrelated to Gilgamesh for some of their contributions to the texts. The Sumerian *Gilgamesh and the Land of the Living* puts into Gilgamesh's mouth at least one, and possibly two proverbs, apparently drawn from a literary collection or popular usage, proverbs which survive in revised form in one or another of the Akkadian versions of the epic. The Old Babylonian version of *Gilgamesh* began with an introduction either modeled on or borrowed from royal hymns and inscriptions, possibly from an independent hymn about Gilgamesh

44. Bing interprets an Abu Salabikh text as a dialogue between Ninsun and Lugalbanda, with similarities to Ishtar's proposal in *GE* VI (see Introduction, n. 64). If confirmed, this would raise the possibility that a similar text about Gilgamesh and a goddess might also have been written down early and been transmitted in the literary tradition down to the OB or MB Period. It may have been only then that Gilgamesh's response was made into a rejection and the episode was combined with part of the Bull of Heaven story incorporated in *The Gilgamesh Epic.*

45. See above, pp. 91–92, and Appendix, no. 7.

46. Cf. *RLA* 4:255–56; *SKIZ,* p. 133, l. 175 and p. 141, l. 175 = Reisman, p. 190, l. 175; *ANET,* p. 638, l. 40; p. 640, l. 8; p. 642, l. 51. Note that in Gilg. P. v, 26 = *GE* II, ii, 45 the proceedings are "for Gilgamesh as (for?) a god."

47. The passage is characterized as "the myth of the first human wedding" by Landsberger, "Jungfräulichkeit," p. 84, n. 4. See the discussion of the passage by Finkelstein, *RA* 61:133.

himself. It has the barmaid give Gilgamesh advice which looks like it is based on popular wisdom, has the elders bless Gilgamesh before his journey with what looks like a standard traveler's blessing, and may have modeled a scene on the rituals accompanying secular or sacred-marriage ceremonies (the latter scene survives in the late version). The late version of the epic models its prologue on standard hymnic openings and, apparently, hymns to temples and temple cities. Other passages presently known to us only from the late version include a curse introduction and a curse apparently borrowed from *Ishtar,* and a proposal of marriage by Ishtar which looks like it is modeled on sacred-marriage texts or the ritual itself. (Some other curses seem to have been borrowed by *Ishtar* from *Gilgamesh.*) The borrowed and imitated material must have had the effect of making the narratives seem realistic: Characters in various situations speak and act in conventional ways, persuading, advising, blessing and cursing, while the narrator, even when expressing his own unique values, tells of the exploits of his royal hero in ways that court poets had used as long as anybody could remember.

# 9

# *The Oppression of Uruk*

Following the introduction, the narrative of the epic sets in with Gilgamesh's oppression of Uruk, which prompts the gods to create Enkidu. This is part of the chain of events leading to the friendship of Gilgamesh and Enkidu, a chain which, as Kramer concluded, was created ad hoc for the purposes of the Akkadian epic and was not present in the Sumerian sources. As such, the chain is a good example of the Akkadian writer's own creativity. In this and the next two chapters, we seek the raw materials and models out of which the Akkadian writer built three parts of this chain: the oppression of Uruk, the creation of Enkidu, and the early life of Enkidu.

The late version describes the oppression of Uruk and the gods' response as follows:

I, ii, 6b. In the mark of. . . .
7. At/in the sheepfo[ld] of Uruk he (Gilgamesh) did. . . .
8. He establishes himself supreme like a wild bull, lofty is [his] he[ad].
9. He has no rival, and [his] weapons stand (ready).
10. His companions stand (in readiness), heedful of him (i.e., awaiting his command).
11. The men of Uruk are [w]orried in. . . .
12. Gilgamesh does not rel[ease] the son to [his] fat[her].
13. [Da]y and [nigh]t . . . . is overbearing.
14. [Gilga]mesh(?)—h[e is the shephe]rd of Uruk (of?) the shee[pfold]!
15. He is [their(?)] shepherd [. . . . mighty, preeminent, wise!]

16. [Gilgamesh] does not releas[e the young woman to her mother(?)].
17. The war[rior's] daughter, [the man's spouse]—
18. [The gods kept hearing] their outcry.
19. The gods of heaven [called] Uruk's lord (Anu):
20. You indeed created the mighty wild bull. [Lofty is his head.]
21. He has no rival, and [his weapons] s[tand (ready)].
22. [His companions] stand (in readiness), heedful of him (i.e., awaiting his command).
23. Gilgamesh does not release the son to his father. Day and night [. . . . is overbearing].
24. He is the shepherd of Uruk [(of?) the sheepfold]!
25. He is their shepherd and . . . .
26. Mighty, preeminent, wise! . . . .
27. Gilgamesh does not release the young woman to [her mother (?)]."
28. The warrior's daughter, the m[an's] spouse—
29. [Anu] kept hearing their outcry.
30. They called Aruru, the great, (etc.)

(*GE* I, ii, 6b–30)[1]

The Hittite version describes these events more briefly:

I, i, 10. All lands he kept roaming. . . .
11. To the city of Uruk he came. He did . . . .
12. Daily the young men of Uruk
13. he kept on besting. The Moth[er]-goddess. . . .
14. and in/among the winds (of?) Gilgamesh. . . .
15. The [Mo]ther-goddess saw . . . .
Ea, 6. and . . . . in his/her [he]eart [he/she] became [a]ngry.

---

7. Al[l] the gods [went] across/beyond. . . .
8. To the [place(?)] of assembly. . . . she went [and said(?):]
9. "That [Gilgamesh] wh[om] y[ou(?) (pl.)] have [c]reated,
10. I have [c]reated [his equal(?) . . . ."]
11. . . . . mixed [t]ogether. . . .
. . . .

Ec, 1. All [the god]s . . . .
2. [The valian]t Gilgamesh (acc.). . . . :
3. "and [Gilgamesh] the yo[ung] men (acc.). . . ."
4. . . . . thus she heard.

(*Hit. Gilg.* I, i, 10–ii, 4a).[2]

1. For text and notes, see Appendix, no. 3.
2. For text and notes, see Appendix, no. 4. The straight line in frag. Ea, between ll. 6 and 7, is present on the original tablet.

## THE PATTERN OF OPPRESSION, OUTCRY, DIVINE RESPONSE

Gilgamesh's oppression of Uruk and its consequences are described in three stages: an act of oppression (taking place "day and night"), a complaint *(tazzimtu)* by the victims, and a divine response (the creation of someone who will put an end to the oppression). This is a stock pattern, known in several variations in cuneiform literature, in both mythological and historiographic texts.

The earliest examples of this pattern appear in contexts dealing with the creation of mankind or individuals. For example, in the Old Babylonian *Atrahasis Epic*, the Igigi-gods were oppressed night and day with forced labor imposed by the Anunnaki-gods; they complained *(uttazzamū,* verbal form of *tazzimtu)*, and their complaint was ultimately satisfied by the creation of man, who replaced the enslaved gods in their labors.[3] In the *Stele of the Vultures*, in response to a complaint that the city of Umma was encroaching on Lagashite fields, the god Ningirsu engendered the king Eannatum to cope with Umma.[4] A late variant of the pattern in a historical text appears in Cyrus's cylinder inscription. Here the pattern culminates in replacement of the oppressor. Nabonidus, king of Babylon, was committing acts of sacrilege in Babylon, and daily oppressed its inhabitants with corvée labor. As a result of the citizens' complaint *(tazzimtu)*, the gods became angry and abandoned Babylon; however, Marduk's anger abated, and he had mercy on the people and summoned Cyrus to depose Nabonidus.[5] This is a pattern well known in biblical literature, too.[6] Since it often culminates in the creation or sending of a new character, it was a useful device for the introduction of Enkidu, especially because, as we shall see, one form of the pattern (without the creation of a new character) was already found in literature about Gilgamesh.

3. OB *Atr.* I (the parallel between *Gilgamesh* and *Atr.* I continues in the next section of each; see chap. 10). The same pattern is present in *Enki and Ninmah,* the Sumerian forerunner of this part of *Atr.;* see van Dijk, *Ac. Or.* 28:24–30; Benito, pp. 22–25, 35–38. In noncreation contexts, see *Lugal-e* VIII, 1–6 (Radau, nos. 2–3, ll. 1–6). For the outcry of the oppressed in nonliterary texts, cf. PBS 5, no. 74, VI, 14–VII, 17 (Kraus, *JCS* 3:35–36); TCL 15, no. 9, v, 27–28 (*CAD* I–J, p. 144a lex.); ARM 1, no. 6, l. 34. For some biblical examples, see Exod. 21:22; 2 Kings 8:3.

4. See Jacobsen, in *Kramer AV,* pp. 247–48, 251.

5. *ANET,* pp. 315–16.

6. E.g., Exod. 1–4; Judg. 2:14–18; 3:9 (in Judges, this is part of a larger pattern which begins with the nation's guilt).

## THE NATURE OF THE OPPRESSION

Precisely how Gilgamesh oppressed Uruk in the passages quoted is one of the most elusive problems of the epic. The most commonly accepted view is that the oppression involved the imposition of corvée labor,[7] as in some cases of the pattern. Once Gilg. P. became known, most scholars agreed, on the basis of its lines iv, 32–34, that Gilgamesh had been demanding (or had also been demanding) the *jus primae noctis* (or, to use the term more befitting Gilgamesh's status, the *droit de seigneur*).[8] Before searching for the literary antecedents of the oppression of Uruk, we shall have to examine these and other theories.

### *Not Corvée Labor*

On historical grounds, it is entirely plausible that Gilgamesh, like other Mesopotamian kings, imposed forced labor upon the people of his city in the course of building the city's walls. Some of the Sumerian tales about Gilgamesh speak of his impressing the people of Uruk into various types of royal service,[9] and omen literature may picture him as a tyrannical ruler, as we have seen in the Introduction.[10] The Second Early Dynastic Period, in which Gilgamesh lived, is the period in which royal power grew strong in Mesopotamia,[11] and it would be no surprise if the emergent exercise of royal power were remembered as tyrannical. However, it is doubtful whether the epic itself represents Gilgamesh as imposing labor on the city; it uses none of the standard Akkadian terms for corvée labor.[12]

7. So, for example, Oppenheim, *Or.* 17:21–23; von Soden, "Sumer," p. 541; Edzard, "Mythologie," pp. 59, 72.

8. For example, Schott, *OLZ* 36:521–22; *ZA* 42:95; Oppenheim, *Or.* 17:23; Lambert, "Morals," pp. 195–96; *GSL,* p. 51; Korošec, p. 163; von Soden, "Sumer," p. 541; Finkelstein, *JAOS* 90:251–52. Cf. Otten, *Ist. Mit.* 8:122. Others refer more vaguely to sexual demands. The *jus primae noctis* theory was opposed by Ranoszek, p. 210; Landsberger, "Jungfräulichkeit," pp. 83–84; and doubted by Diakonoff, p. 63; see n. 15, below.

9. Kramer, in *GSL,* p. 68 (corvée?); *GLL* B 45 (military draft; cf. Jacobsen's understanding of the oppression in *GE,* in *Treasures,* p. 196).

10. See Introduction, nn. 58–59.

11. Jacobsen, PAPhs 107:479; *ZA* 52:120.

12. Such as *ilku, dullu, abšānu, š/tupšikku, šipru, iškaru, dikûtu, kudurru, zabbilu, allu, marru.* The alleged *tupšakki,* assumedly a form of *tupšikku,* in Gilg. P. iv, 17 (Schott, 2d ed., p. 30, l. 147; Diakonoff, p. 62; Schmöckel, p. 38, l. 24) is now read otherwise (Landsberger, "Jungfräulichkeit," p. 83, with n. 1, and p. 104; *CAD* Ṣ, p. 132).

The forced labor theory seems to have originated with Jensen, when he realized that *GE* I, i, 9 refers to Gilgamesh's building the wall of Uruk.[13] Subsequent advocates of this theory referred to the building of the walls; one remarked how "very skillfully the author . . . links the description of the marvelous . . . walls of Uruk in I, i, 9–19 to the story of their construction [*GE* I, ii, 10–21]. He tells . . . how Gilgamesh compelled the men of Uruk to do villein service."[14] But in fact the passages about Uruk's walls and the oppression are unconnected: They are separated by a full column. As we have seen in Chapters 2 and 7, the passage about the walls is part of a late addition to the epic, and it views the walls with pride, rather than as the product of oppression. It has nothing to do with the oppression of Uruk in *GE* I, ii.

## *Jus Primae Noctis*

It seems clear that the Old Babylonian version (Gilg. P.) mentions the *jus primae noctis.* The man whom Enkidu encounters before entering Uruk says of Gilgamesh:

*aššat šîmātim iraḫḫi*
*šū pānānumma*
*mūtum warkānu*

He cohabits with the betrothed bride—
He first,
The husband afterwards.
(Gilg. P. iv, 32–34)[15]

13. "He had the wall of Uruk (of?) the sheepfold built." Jensen restored the verb *ušēpiš,* "had built," at the beginning of the line; see KB 6(1):116–17, line 9; the restoration was later confirmed by MS evidence. Jastrow and Jeremias, writing before Jensen, did not think that Gilgamesh had imposed corvée (*RBA,* pp. 473–74; Jeremias, *Izdubar-Nimrod,* pp. 15–16).

14. Oppenheim, *Or.* 17:21.

15. On this passage, see Dossin, *Pâleur,* and the review by Schott; Ravn, *Bi. Or.* 10:12–13 and *Ac. Or.* 22:46–47; Landsberger, "Jungfräulichkeit," pp. 82–84, and the review by Finkelstein, *JAOS* 90:251–52. Objections to interpretation of this passage as *jus primae noctis* do not adequately explain the passage, especially since the reading *mūtum* has been confirmed (see Finkelstein, *loc. cit.*). *Jus primae noctis* is best known from the Middle Ages, but it is also mentioned in ancient sources. See Herodotus 4.168, and cf. Jacobs; *Tosefta Ketubot* 1:1 in Lieberman, *Tosefta . . . Nashim,* p. 56, and Lieberman, *Tosefta Kifshutah* 6:186–87.

This passage is not preserved in the late version, but the next scene in the Old Babylonian version is. In this scene, Enkidu prevents Gilgamesh from entering a nuptial chamber, and this leads to a fight between them (*GE* II, ii, 35–50, which abridges Gilg. P. v, 9–vi, 23).[16] The nuptial chamber may connect this scene with the reported exercise of *jus primae noctis.*[17] On the other hand, certain details in this scene call to mind the sacred-marriage ceremony: The proceedings are "for Gilgamesh as (for?) a god" and "a bed is laid out" for the goddess Išḫara (Gilg. P. v, 26–29 = *GE* II, ii, 44–45). The public ceremonies in this scene are compatible with both secular and sacred-marriage ceremonies (see pp. 174–76). Since the text continues by saying that "Gilgamesh (is to) jo[in] wi[th the y]ou[ng wom]an at night" (Gilg. P. v, 30–31, if correctly restored), it may be that every bride at her wedding was thought to personify Išḫara, who was identified with Ishtar, and that by exercising the *jus primae noctis,* Gilgamesh was thought to be performing the role of the god in the sacred marriage.[18] In any case, it is not clear how this scene is related to the oppression described in I, ii. There, ll. 16 and 27 do not speak of an offense committed on or before the first night of a marriage, but of failure to release the young woman at all. Unfortunately the text is broken at the point where it identified to whom Gilgamesh does not release the young woman. Thompson restored *ummiša,* "(to) her mother," which seems to be the most likely restoration.[19] In my notes to the text,[20] I have expressed doubt that in the next line (17) "the daughter of the warrior, the wife of the young man" is part of the direct object of "does not release," thus ruling out the possibility that Gilgamesh was confiscating wives, too. This is not, of course, certain. David's behavior with Bathsheba (2 Sam. 11:4) and Abraham's and Isaac's fears about the kings of Egypt and Gerar (Gen. 12:11–12; 20:11; 26:7) remind us that such high-handed behavior by kings was possible. One must admit that the text does not specify that the purpose for which the

16. Text in Appendix, no. 7; translation on pp. 90–92.

17. This would undermine Oppenheim's assumption that the late version suppressed the charge of *jus primae noctis* (Or. 17:23).

18. On Išḫara as Ishtar and her personification by the bride, see Finkelstein, *RA* 61:133.

19. See Appendix, no. 3, note *ad loc.* (For other restorations, see Oppenheim, *Or.* 17:22; *CAD* B, p. 173d).

20. Appendix, no. 3.

girls are taken is sexual; conceivably they were drafted for domestic service (compare the "law of the king," in 1 Sam. 8:11–18). Without ruling this out, since the late version did include the related nuptial-chamber scene later on, it is hard to believe that *jus primae noctis* is not at least part of what is suggested in I, ii, 7–28.[21]

## *Athletic Contests*

One of the first to doubt the corvée theory was Jacobsen. Since the available text does not make the nature of the oppression clear, Jacobsen reasoned that in view of the gods' creating Enkidu to put a stop to the oppression, our starting point must be in asking what Enkidu did with Gilgamesh.[22] The Hittite version offers important evidence on this question.

In the Hittite version, the oppression of Uruk is condensed into two lines (*Hit. Gilg.* I, i, 11b–13a), of which only one and one-half (12–13a) are clear: "Daily the young men of Uruk he kept on besting." This implies an ongoing contest between Gilgamesh and the young men of Uruk. As early as 1898, Jastrow had stated that Gilgamesh was apparently the conqueror of Uruk and triumphed over its warriors in single combat.[23] There is some evidence which accords with a view of Gilgamesh as an outside conqueror of Uruk.

21. Somewhat reminiscent of Gilgamesh's behavior is that of Shahryar in *The Arabian Nights*. This king married a new girl every night and executed her the next morning, until, after three years, "folks raised an outcry against him and cursed him, praying Allah utterly to destroy him and his rule; and women made an uproar and mothers wept and parents fled with their daughters till there remained not in the city a young person fit for carnal copulation" (Burton, trans., *Arabian Nights*, p. 13).

22. *Ac. Or.* 8:72. Jacobsen concluded that Enkidu became Gilgamesh's homosexual lover, and that the oppression of Uruk had consisted of sexual demands on both sexes (ibid., pp. 69–72). While we understand the oppression differently (as does Jacobsen now; see *Treasures*, p. 196), that Gilgamesh's relationship with Enkidu had homosexual aspects is possible. Note the statements in Gilgamesh's dreams that he will caress Enkidu like a wife (Gilg. P., i, 34, etc.; note especially the comment in the Appendix (this volume) on the use of the verb *ḫabābu* in this passage) and perhaps the implication that in place of his beloved Enkidu, Gilgamesh's wife should delight in his bosom (see above, pp. 50–51). I do not believe that the friends' grasping each other's hands and sleeping together (see Introduction, n. 20) has homosexual overtones. To this day, one can see young Arab men in the Near East walking with interlocked fingers without any implication of homosexuality. Eccles. 4:12 (quoted in chap. 8) mentions lying together for warmth as one of the advantages of companionship, and in the rabbinic treatise *Aboth de-Rabbi Nathan*, 8:3, whose authors shared the biblical opposition to homosexuality, sleeping together is mentioned as a mark of friendship (see Goldin, p. 50).

23. *RBA*, pp. 473–74; also YOR 4(1):27, 30. For a suggestion that Agga of Kish installed Gilgamesh as his vassal ruler in Uruk, see Jacobsen, *ZA* 52:116–18, n. 55.

The obscurity of his origins, reflected in the statement in the *Sumerian King List* that his father was a *lillu*-demon, suggests that he may not have succeeded to the throne legally.[24] Possible Elamite affinities of the name Gilgamesh,[25] if confirmed, might suggest that he was a foreigner. A possible literary reflex of foreign origins is found in the Hittite version of the epic. There, between Gilgamesh's birth and the oppression of Uruk, appears only the statement "He roams through all the lands and comes to the city of Uruk."[26] However, in the late version, Gilgamesh is termed "offspring of Uruk" (*GE* I, i, 28) and son of an earlier king of Uruk, Lugalbanda (I, i, 33, etc.).

There is a parallel in Hittite literature to the motif of a contest in which the hero bests the young men of a city. In the *Gurparanzahu Tale* Gurparanzahu defeats the men of Akkad in an archery contest.[27] It might be claimed that the Hittite version of *Gilgamesh* borrowed the contest motif from the *Gurparanzahu Tale,* rather than finding it in its own Akkadian prototype. However, since the setting of the story is in Akkad, *Gurparanzahu* is thought to go back to a Mesopotamian original,[28] obviating this objection. Be that as it may, the value of the Hittite version of *Gilgamesh* in this case lies more in its interpretive suggestiveness than in its possible attestation of some more original and explicit version of the Akkadian passage.

In suggesting athletic contests between Gilgamesh and others, the Hittite version accords nicely with the import of *GE* I, ii, 9 and 21, "He has no rival, and his weapons stand (ready)."[29] The simile "like a wild ox" (8) also suggests combat (cf. I, iv, 38–39, 45–46; Gilg. P. vi, 11, 16),[30] as does the verb *gutaššuru,* "show oneself superior in strength," in the same line.[31] This interpretation gives these

24. See *SKLJ,* pp. 90–91, l. 18, and n. 131; *Treasures,* p. 213. Cf. Sjöberg, *Or. Suec.* 21:101, n. 2. Gilgamesh's filiation through Lugalbanda in the Sumerian and Akkadian epic compositions is, in Shaffer's view, a secondary, propagandistic development of the Ur III period (Shaffer, "Sources," p. 11). However, the presence of this filiation in the epic may imply that it, at least, considered Gilgamesh's succession to the throne legitimate.

25. Cf. Lambert, in *GSL,* p. 47.

26. *Hit. Gilg.* I, i, 10–11; cf. Otten, *Ist. Mit.* 8:120. Again, cf. Jacobsen's remarks cited in n. 23 above, and Kramer, in *ANET,* p. 47, n. 23.

27. Güterbock, *ZA* 44:86–87, ll. 18′–23′. Cf. also *The Story of Si-nuhe, ANET,* p. 20bc.

28. Güterbock, "Hittite Mythology," p. 154; cf. Gurney, *Hittites,* p. 194.

29. For parallels, see Seux, s.vv. *šanānu* and *tebû.*

30. Hammurapi terms himself "the fiery bull who gores the enemies" (see, p. 150).

31. Cf. *CAD* G, p. 56ab, for examples with this overtone.

phrases an integral place in the story, functioning as more than simply epithets. Following the lead of the Hittite version, we may take these lines to refer to an ongoing situation, like the Hittite's "daily he kept on besting the young men of Uruk." This implies, as noted, constant matches with Uruk's young men. It also accords with Enkidu's announced intention:

> I will challenge him [and will bo]ldly address him,
> [I will] shout in Uruk: "I am he who is mighty!
> [I am the] one who can alter destinies;
> [(He) who] was born on the steppe is mighty; strength he has."
> (*GE* I, iv, 47–v, 3)

This accords especially with the fact that what transpires at Enkidu's first meeting with Gilgamesh is a wrestling match (Gilg. P. vi = *GE* II, ii, 46ff.). This interpretation satisfies Jacobsen's criterion that the nature of the oppression can be inferred from what Enkidu in fact does with Gilgamesh, and it makes pointed the gods' statement of purpose in creating Enkidu: *lištannanūma Uruk*$^{ki}$ *lištap-*[*šiḫ*], "let them (Gilgamesh and Enkidu) rival each other (in battle), so that (the rest of) Uruk may have peace" (*GE* I, ii, 32 = Gilg. Ni.3′). *lištannanūma* also counters I, ii, 9 and 21, where the same root *šanānu* appears in *ul īšu šaninamma tebû* $^{giš}$*kakkē*[*šu*], "he has no rival, and his weapons stand (ready)."

A picture of Gilgamesh as an inveterate competitor may be reflected in an Assyrian astronomical text of the first millennium, *Astrolabe B,* and in *The Death of Gilgamesh,* which mention wrestling and athletics in his honor. The *Astrolabe* describes the month of Ab in part as follows:

| **Sumerian** | **Akkadian** |
|---|---|
| . . . guruš gešpú-lirum-ma | *araḫ* $^{d}$*Gilgameš tušu'u* |
| itu $^{d}$Giš-bil-ga-meš ká-ne-ne | *ūmi eṭlūtu ina bābānišunu* |
| u$_4$-9-kam a-da-mın | *umāš ubāri ultēṣû* |

> Month of Gilgamesh. For nine days (or: on the ninth day) young men contest in wrestling and athletics in their (city) quarters (lit. "gates").[32]

32. *KAV* 218: A, ii, 5–7, 13–15; Weidner, *Handbuch,* p. 86; *CAD* A$_1$, p. 38 lex.; A$_2$, p. 358 lex.; E, p. 409c; cf. Lambert, in *GSL,* p. 56.

That this text refers to an early practice related to Gilgamesh is shown by a similar passage in *The Death of Gilgamesh.* Although the passage is not entirely clear, it appears to foretell memorial ceremonies for Gilgamesh:

> alan-bi $u_4$-ul-li-a-šè a-ba-da-an-dím-e(!?)
> šul(!)-kalag igi-$du_8$ $u_4$-$sakar_x$-gim zag-$du_8$ ḫu-mu-ta-an-ag-eš
> igi-bi-a gešpú-lirum-ma si a-ba-da-ab-sá
> itu-NE-NE-GAR ezen(?)-gidim(?)-ma-$ke_4$-NE
>
> When their/his image has been made unto eternity,
> Mighty youth(s), observing, like the new moon will verily make (lit. "do," = jump?) the threshhold.
> When before them/him wrestling and athletics are conducted,
> In the month of Ab, the festival(?) of the spirits(?), . . .[33]

Whether these exercises were really thought to reflect Gilgamesh's personality or were of a cultic character and not specific to Gilgamesh is uncertain. Wrestling is attested in the cults of Ninurta and Ishtar.[34] In the case of Ishtar, it is part of the athletic entertainment at the sacred-marriage ceremony at Mari. In these cases, likewise, wrestling could have been understood as befitting the character of the god so honored, since Ninurta and Ishtar had martial qualities.[35]

Be that as it may, with his love of competition Gilgamesh embodies that "ambitious, competitive, aggressive, and seemingly far from ethical drive for pre-eminence and prestige, for victory and success" which Kramer finds pervading Sumerian life.[36] A later personality who expressed these values in similar athletic feats was Shulgi, king of Ur (2094–2047), who boasted in his hymns of his prowess in "wrestling and athletics" (gešpú, lirum) and running, claiming that no one could equal him.[37] Whether Shulgi

33. Kramer, BASOR 94:7 ll. 28–31; see the revised translation in *ANET,* p. 50; Jestin; van Dijk, "VAT 8382," p. 240. In line 28, I take the syllable "a" in the last combination as the prospective preformative (ù) > a before ba; Falkenstein, *Das Sumerische,* p. 50, § 34.43eα).

34. *BWL* p. 120, rev. 6–7; Dossin, *RA* 35:1–13; see the more recent translation by Sasson, "Worship," pp. 152–53, n. 9. Note also the mock-combat ceremonies cited by Gurney, *Hittites,* p. 155; Pope, *Song of Songs,* pp. 602–3; Bickerman, pp. 199–201.

35. Edzard, "Mythologie," pp. 114–15, 85; Jacobsen, *Treasures,* pp. 129, 137–38.

36. Kramer, *Sumerians,* pp. 264–68.

37. *Shulgi A* (*ANET,* pp. 585–86), ll. 36–78; *Shulgi B,* l. 109; *Shulgi C,* ll. 129–44; for the latter two hymns, see Castellino, *Two Šulgi Hymns,* pp. 40–41, 256–59; parts of *Shulgi C* are cited by Landsberger, *WZKM* 57:22 *sub* "Zu 2 S. 116," and van Dijk, *Bi. Or.* 11:87.

strove to emulate Gilgamesh as tradition portrayed him, or whether the traditional character of Gilgamesh was actually modeled upon Shulgi, is a moot question.

It remains to be asked why Gilgamesh's demands that the young men of Uruk compete with him in contests should have been considered oppressive. Are we to assume that his seizure of the sons and daughters of Uruk (I, ii, 11–17 = 21–28) is his prize for winning these contests? Contests of champions[38] often result in the enslavement of the loser and those he represents to the victor.[39] There are also many cases in world literature of contests in which the winner wins a bride. The most famous example is the suitors' archery contest for the hand of Penelope in *The Odyssey* (bk. 21).[40] A practice which may be more relevant to *Gilgamesh* is reported in modern times among the Fulani of northeast Nigeria. The *New York Times* of 6 August 1974 reported the death of seventeen guests at a wedding among the Fulani,

> whose tribal rites call for suitors to engage in physical combat for the bride. . . . Fulani practice is that they first demonstrate their endurance by undergoing a whipping, followed with violence at close quarters. The winner gets the bride—if he is among the survivors.[41]

Whether such contests can be related to the charge of *jus primae noctis* in Gilg. P. is not clear. Did Gilgamesh, by winning such competition, win the right to deflower some bride? If the scene which follows that charge is connected with sacred marriage, a key might be provided by the athletic events and competition which formed part of the festivities at this ceremony.[42] Even if the scene is connected with a private wedding, athletic competition may not be an anomalous feature. We have noted the real combat for the bride among the Fulani. Anthropologists also report mock combat of various types as a part of marriage ceremonies in many cultures; in some the prospective groom is blocked at the entrance to the bride's home (compare Enkidu's blocking Gilgamesh at the en-

38. Cf. Hoffner, *CBQ* 30:220, n. 1.

39. Cf. *En El* IV–V; 1 Sam. 17:9; see de Vaux. At stake in Si-nuhe's fight were the loser's property and cattle (*ANET,* p. 20bc).

40. Cf. *Iliad,* 3. 67–72.

41. For other examples, see *MI,* H326.1.2; 331.2; 331.4; 335.4.3.

42. Cf. the ritual text from Mari published by Dossin, *RA* 35:1–13, and the *Hymn to Inanna* in *SKIZ,* pp. 130/38, ll. 55–69 = Reisman, p. 187, ll. 55–69.

trance to the nuptial chamber).[43] Conceivably Gilgamesh won such contests and demanded as his prize not the bride's hand, but the *jus primae noctis.*

Whether or not *jus primae noctis* can be connected with it, a contest theory is enhanced by a recent interpretation of a related passage in *Gilgamesh, Enkidu, and the Netherworld.* We shall now turn our attention to that passage.

## *The* pukku *and* mikkû *Incident in* Gilgamesh, Enkidu, and the Netherworld

This incident is important because of its similarity to the epic's description of the oppression. Unfortunately the incident is described in a very problematic passage, but enough seems clear to assure a connection.

According to *Gilgamesh, Enkidu, and the Netherworld,* Gilgamesh rid Inanna's *ḫuluppu*-tree of a snake, a bird, and a phantom maid, and then uprooted the tree. Events then proceeded as follows[44]:

147. He gives it (the tree) to his sister, pure Inanna, for her chair.
148. He gives it to her for her bed.
149. As for himself, he has its base made into his pukku,
150. He has its branches made into his mikkû.
151. He works the pukku, he brings it out into the broad square.
152. Working the '. . . .', he brings out the '. . . .' in the broad square.
153. The young men of the city who were playing with the pukku,
154. He, a group of widow's children. . . . ,
155. "Oh, my neck, oh, my hips," they lament.
156. He who has a mother, she brings her son bread.
157. He who has a sister, she pours out water for her brother.
158. After evening had come,
159. He drew a mark at the place where the pukku was set down.
160. His pukku, he carried before him and took it to his house.
161. At daybreak where he had drawn the mark,
162. At the widow's accusation,
163. At the young girl's outcry,
164. His pukku and his mikkû fell down to the realm of the netherworld.

43. Crawley, pp. 353–65; Westermarck, 2:254–61.
44. Translation from Shaffer, "Sources," pp. 105–6.

The text goes on to tell how Enkidu sought to retrieve these playthings from the netherworld for Gilgamesh, but was himself seized by the netherworld during the attempt and forced to stay there.

Kramer realized that this passage was related to the oppression scene in *GE* I, ii.[45] In that scene, Gilgamesh's companions do something which has to do with PU-UK-KI- (10). The young men and sons and daughters of Uruk are somehow adversely affected by his behavior (11–12, 16), and the warrior's daughter and young man's wife protest (17–18; Akk. *tazzimtu,* "outcry" there = Sum. i - $^{d}$U t u in *GEN* 163).

These details seem to confirm the ultimate relationship of the Akkadian and Sumerian passages, but the differences between them point either to a radical evolution of the episode over centuries of literary transmission or to a serious misunderstanding of the Sumerian by the Akkadian author.[46] The Sumerian text appears to involve a game, something like polo or croquet, according to Landsberger's interpretation of p u k k u and m i k k û as playthings, the former round and rollable like a hoop, ball, or puck, and the latter a stick.[47] In the course of this game, a group of widows' children were somehow hurt. The next day, at the accusation and outcry of the widows and young girls, Gilgamesh's playthings fell into the netherworld. In the Akkadian text, however, the word written PU-UK-KI-*šú/šu* is not a noun but a verb, *puqqu,* "pay attention"; the entire passage in *GE* I, ii, 10, 22, means "his companions stand (in readiness), heedful of him," (i.e., awaiting his command).[48] This leads to an outcry by a group of females.

The reference to Inanna's bed at the beginning of the Sumerian episode suggests a possible connection with the sacred-marriage ceremony. We have already noted the role of athletic displays and competition at the sacred marriage, but since the text says nothing more about the subject, it cannot be pursued. It appears that the

45. *JAOS* 64:20.

46. Owing to the similarity of Sum. p u k k u and Akk. *puqqu,* as we shall see. For misunderstanding of Sumerian texts by Akkadian scribes, note the mistranslations sometimes found in the Akkadian part of bilingual texts (cf. e.g., Falkenstein, *Haupttypen,* index, p. 102, s.v. *"Akkadische Übersetzung,* Fehler der").

47. *WZKM* 56:124–26; 57:23; cf. *CAD* $M_2$, p. 7; Grayson, *ANET,* p. 507; Gordon, *JCS* 12:62 *sub* 5.93; Jacobsen, *Treasures,* p. 212.

48. See Appendix, no. 3, on *GE* I, ii, 22. This translation accords well with Jacobsen's view that the problem with Gilgamesh was in part that he maintained a constant military alert in Uruk (*Treasures,* p. 196).

Akkadian epic preserved the motif of athletic competition in this episode, but, ironically, misunderstood the word p u k k u which stood at the center of that episode in the original.

What was important for the purposes of the Akkadian author was that Gilgamesh's actions resulted in an outcry by the people of Uruk. The task confronting the Akkadian author was to account for the introduction of a new hero into the epic. The pattern of oppression, outcry, divine response was a known pattern in accounts of the gods' sending or creating a new character. The p u k k u episode in *Gilgamesh, Enkidu, and the Netherworld* came close to that pattern, lacking only an explicit divine response (instead, it had a response of unstated agency: The p u k k u and m i k k û fell into the netherworld). This was sufficient for the Akkadian author's purpose. He lifted the Sumerian episode from its context, where it accounted for Enkidu's demise, and placed it near the beginning of the Akkadian epic, where it explained the need for Enkidu's creation. At some point in the transmission of this episode it underwent further modification in detail: the meaning of p u k k u was misunderstood, the nature of the contest became blurred,[49] and its consequences were modified. But the pattern remained distinct, and so did its function, accounting in a traditional way for the introduction of a new protagonist.

49. Cf. Otten, *Ist. Mit.* 8:120.

# 10

## *The Creation of Enkidu*

The gods' response to Uruk's outcry was to create Enkidu. This is described in three versions of the epic. The clearest description is in the late version:

30. They (the gods) called (the mother-goddess) Aruru, the great: "You, Aruru, created [mankind];
31. Now create . . . ; let him (Enkidu) be a ma[tch] for the storminess of his (Gilgamesh's) heart.
32. Let them rival each other (in battle), that Uruk may gain pea[ce]."
33. When Aruru heard this, a/the . . . of Anu she conceived within her.
34. [A]ruru washed her hands, pinched off clay and threw it onto the steppe.
35. [On the stepp]e(?) she created Enkidu, the valiant; native/offspring of . . . , strength(?)/strengthened(?) by Ninurta.

(*GE* I, ii, 30–35)[1]

Part of this passage is preserved in an older fragment:

1′. They called. . . . , the grea[t]:
2′. "[You created(?)] numerous mankind;
3′. [Now create(?)] his/its. . . . , who will be mighty in strength(?).
4′. [Let them r]ival each other (in battle), that Uruk may have peace."
5′. . . . . sister (acc.).

1. See Appendix, no. 3.

6′. . . . . said to her.
7′. . . . . *young man,* you created a man.

(Gilg. Ni.)[2]

Though the connection between the lines of this fragment is very uncertain, several similarities with the late version are apparent. Lines 1 through 4 correspond with the late version's lines 30 through 32, though line 3 varies substantially from the late version's line 31. *dan emūqa,* "mighty in strength(?)" (3) recalls *dān emuqī īšu,* "he is strong, he has strength," describing Enkidu (*GE* I, iii, 3–4; v, 3; vi, 2), and *danna emūqa elika īši,* "he has greater strength than you (Enkidu)," describing Gilgamesh (I, v, 18). In the older version, this quality of Enkidu's is prescribed for him before his creation, and the passage is clearly designed to make him like Gilgamesh in this respect. Lines 5 and 6 have no counterpart in the late version, while line 7 may correspond to line 35 of that version.[3]

Finally, the Hittite version describes the creation of Enkidu as follows:

i, 17. Al[l] the gods [went] across/beyond. . . .
18. To the p[lace(?)] of assembly. . . . she went [and said(?)]:
19. "That [Gilgamesh] wh[om] y[ou(?) (pl.)] have [c]reated,
20. I have [c]reated [his equal(?). . . ."].
21. . . . . mixed [t]ogether. . . .
. . . .
ii, 1. All [the god]s. . . .
2. [The valian]t Gilgamesh (acc.). . . . :
3. "And [Gilgamesh] the yo[ung] men (acc.). . . . ."
4. . . . . thus she heard. And the mother-goddess
5. [from. . . .] took away birth(?)/growth(?), and she went (away(?)).
6. [. . . . the va]liant Enkidu she created in the steppe.

(*Hit. Gilg.* I, i, 17–21; ii, 1–6[4])

Jastrow noted many similarities between the creation and early life of Enkidu and the biblical account of Adam and Eve, and concluded that the story of Enkidu was based on an account of the creation and early life of mankind.[5] He called attention especially

2. See Appendix, no. 3.
3. Or to line 30; see the note on Gilg. Ni. 7′ in Appendix, no. 3.
4. See Appendix, no. 4.
5. Jastrow, *Religion,* chap. 23; *AJSL* 15:193–214; YOR 4(3):32–47; *ZA* 13: 288–301.

to Enkidu's creation from earth[6] and his creation by Aruru, who is known as the creatress of mankind elsewhere in cuneiform literature.[7]

These shared themes were too common to justify a claim of literary relationship between the description of the creation of Enkidu and any cuneiform creation text then known. However, a passage discovered since Jastrow's time displays enough verbal similarity to the description of the creation of Enkidu to raise just this possibility. The passage is from the first tablet of *The Atrahasis Epic* and, just as here in *Gilgamesh,* it is part of the divine response in the oppression, outcry, divine response pattern. In *Atrahasis,* the gods instruct the mother-goddess to create mankind in terms nearly identical to their instructions to her to create Enkidu in *Gilgamesh:*

| ***GE* I, ii, 30–31** | **OB *Atr.* I, 194–95** |
|---|---|
| *attī* $^{d}$*Aruru tabni* [*amēlūta*]<br>*eninna binî zikir* ŠÚ | *attīma šassūru bāniat awēlūti*<br>*binîma lullâ . . .* |
| You, Aruru, | You are the womb/the birth-goddess, |
| Created [mankind]:<br>Now create . . . | Creatress of mankind:<br>Create man . . . |

In *Atrahasis,* the command is followed by the statement of purpose *lībil abšānam,* "that he may bear the yoke" of the gods' labor,[8] thus establishing the gods' freedom (*andurāram,* OB *Atr.* I, 243). Similarly, in *Gilgamesh,* the address to Aruru culminates with a statement of the ultimate purpose of Enkidu's creation, *Uruk lištapšiḫ,* "that Uruk may gain peace" (I, ii, 32; Gilg. Ni. 4′) from the tyranny of Gilgamesh.

This verbal correspondence is part of a larger structural similarity between the first part of *Atrahasis* and the events culminating in the creation of Enkidu. Both poems, as noted, reflect the oppression, outcry, divine response pattern. Each of the sec-

6. Like Adam's: Gen. 2:7; other biblical passages speak more explicitly of clay, e.g., Job 33:6. Since Jastrow, examples of this theme have appeared in cuneiform literature: OB *Atr.* I, 189–289 (cf. Otten, *Ist. Mit.* 8:120–21); van Dijk, *Ac. Or.* 28:26/30, l. 33 (see p. 30, n. 77); Lambert, *BWL,* p. 88, l. 277; Heidel, *Babylonian Genesis,* p. 65, l. 26.

7. Ebeling, in *RLA* 1:160; Zimmern, *ZA* 39:252–53; Edzard, "Mythologie," p. 105; Hallo, CRRAI 17:124, l. 8.

8. Cf. OB *Atr.* I, 191, 197, 240, etc.

tions being compared opens with oppression; the victims then complain to the gods; the mother-goddess then creates, at the gods' command, a man/mankind to relieve (in different ways) the victims of their suffering. Beyond the parallelism of structure, there are a number of similar details, as the following paraphrases show:

| ***GE* I, ii** | ***OB* Atr. I** |
|---|---|
| 7–16. Urukites oppressed by Gilgamesh day and night. | 1–38. Igigi-gods oppressed by Anunnaki-gods, forced to labor day and night. |
| 17–29. Complaint of Urukites brought to [Anu], who is (by inference) sympathetic. | 39–191. Igigi-gods complain, go to Enlil; complaint eventually brought to Anu and Enki, who are sympathetic. |
| 30a. Gods summon mother-goddess. | 192–93. Gods summon mother-goddess. |
| 30b–31a. They instruct her to create someone. | 194–95. They instruct her to create mankind *(lullû).*[9] |
| 31b–32. They state the purpose. | 195b–97. They state the purpose. |
| 33b. Mother-goddess makes plans or preparations. | 198–219. Gods make plans. |
| 34a. Mother-goddess washes hands. | 221–22. Enki makes purifying bath. |
| 34b. Mother-goddess nips off clay. | 225–26. Mother-goddess mixes clay. |
| 34c. Mother-goddess casts *(ittadi)*[10] it into the steppe. | 233–34. Gods spit *(iddû)* on clay. |
| | 256. Mother-goddess nips off clay. |
| 35. Mother-goddess creates Enkidu. | S obv. iii, 8–13. Birth-goddesses create seven couples. |

The Hittite version of the creation of Enkidu also preserves details similar to the *Atrahasis* creation narrative, and in some

9. N.B. that Enkidu is described as *lullû-amēlu* in *GE* I, iv, 6, 13, 19. On *lullû-amēlu,* see below, chap. 11.

10. Lacking the direct object *ru'tam,* "spittle," *ittadi* cannot mean "spit" as in the parallel passage from *Atr.* *(ru'tam iddû).* But given the overall correspondence of the two texts, the use of forms of the same verb *(nadû)* in both passages raises the possibility that the the wording in *Gilgamesh* is based on that in *Atr.,* the difference being due, perhaps, to misunderstanding.

places is even closer to *Atrahasis* than the late version of *Gilgamesh* is. In the Hittite version, too, the mother-goddess (DINGIR.MAḪ)[11] is the creatress (*Hit. Gilg.* I, i, 13, 15; ii, 4). The reference there (18) to the assembly corresponds to the assembly of the gods in *Atrahasis* at which the decision to create man was made (OB *Atr.* I, 218). The mother-goddess declares that she has created man before actually doing so (*Hit. Gilg.* I, i, 20). She mixes clay before creating Enkidu (21), as the gods do in *Atrahasis* (226). The Hittite version suggests that prior to the late version, this section resembled the *Atrahasis* account of the creation of man even more than it does in the late version.

What is the likelihood of literary dependence of the creation of Enkidu on *Atrahasis?* Despite the similarities, structural and verbal, as indicated by the paraphrases above, there are obviously numerous differences. The question of dependence rests on whether the similarities are so commonplace as to require no close relationship, or whether there are unusual, unexpected similarities which cannot be supposed to have occurred spontaneously.

Some features shared by the two texts are commonplace or very general: creation by the mother-goddess; creation from clay; planning; purifying; nipping off clay; creating. But others are unique, on the basis of present evidence, to *Gilgamesh* and *Atrahasis* or to the circle of creation traditions to which *Atrahasis* belongs.

These features include, as already suggested, the creation's being a response to an outcry of oppressed subjects and its purpose in relieving their suffering. This pattern, culminating in the creation of a new character who relieves or brings relief to the victims, is unique to *Gilgamesh* and creation texts, of which *Atrahasis* and its Sumerian forerunner *Enki and Ninmah* are the loci classici. Outside of these contexts, the closest parallel is found in such passages as the Cyrus cylinder, mentioned in Chapter 9 (p. 180), where the deliverer is sent, not created.[12]

Most impressive, however, are the similar addresses to the mother-goddess. It is interesting to note how these addresses re-

11. For DINGIR.MAḪ and $^{d}$Aruru as variant names of the mother-goddess, see Edzard, "Mythologie," p. 105; cf. Römer, in *Historia Religionum* 1:139.

12. However, Ningirsu's engendering of Eannatum, as explained by Jacobsen, comes very close to this aspect of our pattern, though it differs in other respects (see chap. 9).

semble the invocations in hymns and, especially, incantations.[13] One incantation begins *atti nāru bānât kalâ-ma,* "You, River, are the creator of everything," while another, part of a ritual against spirits of the dead, begins: . . . . *nāru bānât ili u amēli attī-ma,* ". . . O river, creator of god and man are you."[14] In the course of the ritual, this incantation is recited three times and clay is nipped off to make an image of a substitute for the afflicted person.[15] The addresses in *Gilgamesh* and *Atrahasis* could be modeled on such incantations, conceivably on an incantation to implore divine aid in conception or to relieve barrenness,[16] and conceivably involving the shaping of an image of a child. Such an incantation might have read: "You, Aruru, are creatress of mankind; now create a child." In any case, whatever the model for the address, the similarity between *Gilgamesh* and *Atrahasis* points to their interdependence. To deny this, one must believe that these two compositions independently borrowed several details of the creation process from creation texts, similar addresses to the mother-goddess from, perhaps, an incantation for childbirth, and the pattern of oppression, outcry, and creation of an agent of deliverance. This taxes credibility. One must rather assume, at the very least, a source common to both texts in which these details had already been brought together. But since most of the common details, as well as the pattern, are most frequently attested as a group in creation literature, to which genre *Atrahasis* belongs, ultimate inspiration must come from that genre, if not from *Atrahasis* itself.

13. Cf. texts quoted in *CAD* $A_2$, pp. 504d, 512b.

14. For the first, see *TuL,* p. 91, l. 5; *STT,* no. 72, l. 77; *CAD* $N_1$, p. 374c; for the second, see *TuL,* pp. 125–26, no. 30, ll. 14–15 (this ritual also includes an incantation to Gilgamesh, cited above, p. 80. For incantations referring to the past achievements of the gods addressed, in the course of requesting a repetition of those achievements, see Kunstmann, p. 12; cf. Lambert, *Iraq* 31:31ff.

15. *TuL,* pp. 125–26, no. 30, l. 23.

16. Cf. the prayers in Gen. 25:21; 1 Sam. 1:10–11. I do not know of any such incantation from Mesopotamia, but we do have incantations to aid difficult births and to relieve male impotence (*SAHG,* pt. 1, no. 43; Lambert, *Iraq* 31:31–32, 34–35; Biggs, *ŠÀ.ZI.GA;* Strong, *BA* 2:634, cited in *CAD* B, p. 352b; Hoffner, *JBL* 85: 326–34).

# 11

# *The Early Life of Enkidu*

## POSSIBLE MODELS FOR THE EARLY LIFE OF ENKIDU

The model for the epic's description of Enkidu's early life has been subject to more debate than the themes we have examined up to now, because the epic's description of Enkidu bears a resemblance to several different literary topoi.

The late version describes the early Enkidu as follows:

36. [Sha]ggy with hair is his whole body, he is endowed with a head of hair like a woman's.
37. The locks of his hair grow as abundantly as Nisaba('s).
38. He does not know people or civilized land; he is garbed in a garment like Sumuqan.
39. Even with gazelles he feeds on grass;
40. With wild beasts he jostles at the watering place;
41. With wild creatures he sates his thirst with water.

(*GE* I, ii, 36–41)[1]

The Hittite version is characteristically briefer:

1. See Appendix, no. 3.

7. [. . . . the val]iant Enkidu in the steppe
8. [and wild] beasts raise him, and to him
9. they. . . . Wherever the wild beasts to gr[aze]
10. g[o], Enkidu [goes with] them,
11. and [wherever they go] to water,
12. [Enk]idu [goes] with them.

(*Hit. Gilg.* I, ii, 7–12)[2]

This section is not preserved in the known Old Babylonian fragments, but much of that version's picture is inferable from its description of how Enkidu becomes civilized (Gilg. P. ii, iii, and part of v). Enough of the late version of these passages is preserved to indicate that the two versions were in agreement on this picture[3]:

| **Gilg. P.** | **GEUW obv.** |
|---|---|
| ii. 12. Why with wild creatures | 4. Why with [wild creatures |
| 13. Do you keep ranging over the steppe? | do you roam over the steppe?] |
| v. 19. He a[te] spring grass. | |
| 20. The milk of wild creatures | |
| 21. He was wont to suck. | |
| iii. 1. The milk of wild creatures | |
| 2. He was wont to suck. | |
| 3. They placed bread before him. | 19. They placed bread before [him]. |
| | 20. They placed beer befo[re him]. |
| | 21. Enkidu did not eat the bread; |
| 4. He squinted, then he was gaping | he squinted, he was looking. |
| 5. And staring. | |
| 6. Enkidu does not know | |
| 7. How to eat bread. | |
| 8. To drink beer | |

2. See Appendix, no. 4.

3. See Appendix, no. 6. GEUW obv. 19–21 is also partially preserved in GEH i, 8–10.

9. He has not been taught.

22. He rubbed . . . .

23. The hair of his body.

(Gilg. P. ii, 27–30 = GEUW obv. 9–10, where the harlot clothes Enkidu, and Gilg. P. iii, 26, "he put on clothing" [*ilbaš libšam*] imply that he had been naked.)

The general picture conveyed in the Old Babylonian version agrees with that of the late version. There are variations in detail, but none is necessarily contradictory. Both agree that Enkidu ranged the steppe with wild animals and was hairy, ate grass, and was unaccustomed to human food. The available Old Babylonian fragments do not mention that he drank water; they add that he drank the milk of wild creatures, presumably in infancy (see also *GE* VIII, i, 5, quoted just below). The question of clothing is uncertain: The late version's "garbed in a garment like Sumuqan (the god of wild animals and cattle)" has been taken to mean naked,[4] though the phrase "in a garment" seems to imply some sort of rustic garment.[5] If so, the phrase contradicts the passages from both versions quoted at the end of the previous paragraph implying that he was naked.

The Hittite version ignores Enkidu's hairiness and the subject of clothing and specifies, like the late version, that he grazed and drank with the animals. The Hittite version's statement that the wild animals "raised" Enkidu is paralleled in a later passage of the late version: . . . *sí*[*r-ri*(?)-*mu*(?)] *še-zib-bi-šun i-ra-bu-u-ka ka-a-ša,* ". . . ona[gers(?)] raised you with their milk" (*GE* VIII, i, 5).[6]

It has often been suggested that these descriptions reflect the seminomadic Amorites who, from their homeland in the Syrian desert, infiltrated southern Mesopotamia and came to dominate it in the early second millennium.[7] Stock descriptions of the Amorites

4. Jastrow, *AJSL* 15:200; Albright, *JAOS* 40:320; *CAD* L, p. 234c. Note also *KAR* 19, rev.(!), 1–5.

5. Gressmann and Ungnad, p. 87; Oppenheim, *Or.* 17:24, n. 4.

6. Gurney, *JCS* 8:92, 94; *ANET,* p. 506c; see von Soden, *ZA* 53:229; *CAD* $M_2$, p. 107d. The parallel was noted by Otten, *Ist. Mit.* 8:121.

7. For early hints of this view, see Jastrow, YOR 4(3):25; Jensen, *OLZ* 32:651; *GETh.*, p. 7. More recently, see Oppenheim, *Or.* 17:24, n. 5 and *AM,* p. 372, n. 41; Dossin, "Enkidou," p. 589; Gadd, *Iraq* 28:108, n. 13; Reiner, "City Bread," p. 118. Dossin argued that the "bedouin" motif was a Babylonian reinterpretation of an

in the Ur III period mention their habitat, shelter, diet, and dress, and the phraseology generally includes a reference to "not knowing" (Sumerian n u - z u , Akkadian *ul/lā idû*) some feature of civilization.[8] The fullest statement is found in the Sumerian composition *The Marriage of* $^{d}$*MAR.TU,* where $^{d}$MAR.TU, the eponymous deity of the Amorites, is described (in a difficult passage) as follows[9]:

za-lam-gar-ti IM-IM-šeg-[ga. . . .] siskur-siskur-[. . . .]
hur-sag-gá tuš-e. . . .
lú uz[u]-diri kur-da mu-un-ba-al-da dùg-gam-nu-zu-àm
uzu-nu-šeg$_6$-gá al-kú-e
u$_4$-ti-la-na é nu-tuku-a
u$_4$-ba-ug$_x$(BAD)-a-na ki-nu-túm-mu-dam

A tent-dweller [buffeted(?)] by wind and rain. . . .
Dwelling in the mountain. . . .
The one who digs up mushrooms at the foot of the mountain, who does not know how to bend the knee;[10]
Who eats uncooked meat;
Who in his lifetime does not have a house;
Who on the day of his death will not be buried.

Several texts speak of the Amorite's home in the mountains; others state that he does not know city(-life), a house, or grain.[11] One text terms the Amorites "people plotting destruction like beasts, like wolves" (l ú ḫ a - l a m - m [a] d í m - m a u r - r a - g i n$_x$ u r - b a r - r a - g i n$_x$ ).[12]

original picture of Enkidu as an Iraqi marsh Arab *(ma'dān).* Reiner is more cautious than earlier writers on the subject, distinguishing between humanizing and urbanizing as two separate steps in Enkidu's development.

8. Most of the passages are collected, summarized, and analyzed in Buccellati, *Amorites,* pp. 92ff., 330ff.; cf. Kupper, *Les Nomades,* p. 157; Falkenstein, CRRAI 2:16–17; Edzard, *Zweite Zwischenzeit,* pp. 31ff.

9. The translation is based on Buccellati, *Amorites,* pp. 92–93, with some modifications based on Kramer, CRRAI 9:281, with n. 34; Roux, p. 161.

10. To the latter phrase, Roux adds interpretively "(to cultivate the land)" (p. 161), while Chiera took the phrase to mean "he knows no submission" (p. 20, l. 24; cf. *AKA,* p. 64, col. iv, 51; Luckenbill, OIP 2:64, l. 20). Civil takes the phrase to mean "restless" (*apud* Reiner, "City Bread," p. 119, n. 7; cf. *ANET,* p. 586, l. 59).

11. Buccellati, *Amorites,* pp. 330–31 (cf. *EWO,* ll. 129–30, 246–47, and Bernhardt and Kramer, *WZJ* 9:256).

12. Buccellati, *Amorites,* p. 94. In view of Oppenheim's interpretation of Enkidu's garb (above, n. 5), one may also compare *SBH,* p. 107, rev. ll. 3–4, as emended and read in *CAD* A$_2$, p. 94a lex.: [m a r - t u - g ] i n$_x$ e d i n - n a k u š m i - n i - [i n - l a ]: *kīma a-mur*!(text BA)*-ri-i ina ṣēri* [*maška raksāku*], "I have tied a skin around myself in the steppeland like an Amorite."

At first sight it is tempting to relate these passages to *Gilgamesh*'s description of Enkidu as one who "does not know people or (civilized) land" (*GE* I, ii, 38), "a fellow who has come from the hills" (iii, 2 and parallels), who "knows nothing of the eating of bread" (Gilg. P. iii, 6–7). But closer scrutiny brings out significant differences. While the Amorite eats uncooked meat, Enkidu eats grass (*GE* I, ii, 39; Gilg. P. v, 19). Most of Enkidu's characteristics are not found in descriptions of the Amorites. Most important, Enkidu is pictured as living with, and like, wild animals, while the Amorites are described (with the exception of the animal simile just quoted) as uncivilized nomads living in tents. Enkidu needed to become, not simply civilized, but first humanized[13] (*awēliš iwē,* "he became human," or "like a human," Gilg. P. iii, 25, *kīma muti ibašši,* "he is like a human," 27). The description of Enkidu is therefore unlikely to have been modeled on the Amorites.

Since we have found in Chapter 10 that the description of Enkidu's creation was modeled upon accounts of the creation of early man, Jastrow's old suggestion that Enkidu's early life was also modeled on a tradition about primitive mankind seems promising.[14] The late version of the epic itself implies that Enkidu is modeled on primordial man, for it terms him a "primordial man," *lullû amēlu* (I, iv, 6, 13, 19). As an epithet of men, *lullû* appears in Akkadian almost exclusively with reference to man when he is first created.[15] And indeed, Mesopotamian literature describes the life of primordial man as animal-like. The latest witness to this notion is the Babylonian priest Berossus, writing in Greek around 280: "At Babylon an enormous mass of people had settled, and they lived in an unrestrained manner like animals who lack reason and (like) wild

13. Reiner, "City Bread," p. 118.

14. *AJSL* 15:193–214; YOR 4(3):39–47; cf. C.A. Williams, *Oriental Affinities,* § 3.

15. See examples in *CAD* L, p. 242b. The example seen by von Soden (*ZA* 53:231) in *GE* X, vi, 35 is problematic (cf. Oppenheim, *Or.* 17:50, n. 4). Some other examples listed in *AHw,* p. 562c are dismissed by Lambert as belonging to another word or obscure (*JSS* 12:105). However, Lambert's suggestion to translate simply "man" relies exclusively on etymology and overlooks the word's usage. It never appears in noncreation contexts as a synonym of terms such as *tenēšēti, amēlūtu,* etc. Furthermore, the compound form *lullû-amēlu* is of a type widely attested in Akkadian in which the first element functions adjectivally (see Introduction, n. 31). While earlier scholarship may have gone too far in taking *lullû* to mean "savage" (cf. Speiser, in *ANET,* p. 68, n. 86; von Soden, *ZA* 53:231), *AHw*'s "Ursprünglicher Mensch" (p. 562c) is precisely what the evidence calls for.

cattle."[16] Berossus then goes on to narrate how Oannes emerged from the Persian Gulf and taught mankind the arts and sciences of civilization.

The older form of this tradition appears in a Sumerian text which was adduced long ago as a parallel to the description of Enkidu,[17] *The Dispute Between Cattle and Grain* (or *Lahar and Ashnan,* as it is sometimes called after its protagonists).[18] According to this text,

19. nam-lú-u$_x$-lu u$_4$-ri-a-ke$_4$-e-ne
20. ninda kú-ù-bi nu-mu-un-zu-uš-àm
21. tug-gar mu$_4$-mu$_4$-bi nu-mu-un-zu-uš-àm
22. ukù giš-gi-na-a kuš-ba mu-un-gin
23. udu-gin$_x$ ka-ba ú mu-ni-ib-kú
24. a-šar-šar-ra-ka i-im-nag-nag-ne

19. Mankind of that time (i.e., primordial times)[19]
20. Knew not the eating of bread,
21. Knew not the wearing of garments;
22. The people went around with skins on their bodies.
23. They ate grass with their mouths like sheep,
24. Drank water from ditches.[20]

These traditions about primordial mankind represent a likely antecedent to the description of Enkidu. They share these features: not knowing the eating of bread, eating grass, drinking water, and perhaps wearing animal skins (if that is what Enkidu did).[21]

It is possible that this traditional picture of primordial man is modeled on real-life phenomena. Descriptions of suffering in times of calamity bear a strong resemblance to the picture of primordial

16. Translation of the Armenian text by Jacoby, 1:369. The Greek text, ibid., presents insubstantial variants.

17. Driver, *Genesis,* p. 41, n. 2. See now Komoróczy, *Act. Ant.* 21:140–42.

18. For a bibliography of texts, see Gordon, *Bi. Or.* 17:145, n. 210; Borger, *Handbuch,* vols. 1–2, s.v. Barton, *MBI* no. 8; cf. Falkenstein, *Bi. Or.* 5:165; Edzard, "Mythologie," p. 94.

19. Cf. van Dijk, *Ac. Or.* 28:16–34.

20. Line 22 has several variants which have served as the basis of several different translations; see Chiera, p. 29, l. 22; Jean, p. 36, l. 22; Burrows, p. 319; Langdon and Virolleaud, p. 140, l. 22. See most recently Pettinato, pp. 86–90. For l. 24, cf. van Dijk, *Ac. Or.* 28:42 and Cohen, *Enmerkar,* pp. 13–14, n. 22; Cohen, in *Kramer AV,* p. 100, nn. 22–23.

21. The motif of the vegetarian diet of early man (and animals) also appears in Gen. 1:29–30. There it is part of the divine design (until the new order established in Gen. 9:2–3).

man and Enkidu. In a lament over the destruction of Nippur, it is said that when the city was destroyed people "ate all (sorts of) grass like sheep."[22] One of the Sumerian epic poems about Lugalbanda tells how, after he was left for dead in the mountains, he wandered in the highland steppe and survived by eating wild plants and drinking water from a river (as well as by trapping animals).[23] Personal laments and curses mention being driven from society and wandering the steppe like a wild animal.[24] A late text mentions the length of the sage Ahiqar's hair (and nails) after his long incarceration.[25] On the other hand, all of these details call to mind reports of rustic hermits[26] and of children presumed to have been raised in the wilds by animals, who periodically come to the attention of humans.[27] The common denominator of all such persons is their lacking basic traits of human civilization, whether owing to misfortune, choice, or ignorance. But these phenomena do not add up to a literary model for the early life of Enkidu. Only the traditions about primordial man combine in a single context uncivilized behavior, the characteristic term *lullû* (= Sum. n a m - l ú - $u_x$ - l u in *Cattle and Grain,* l. 19), and the motif of "not knowing."

It is on the manner of Enkidu's humanizing and civilizing that the epic parts company with known Mesopotamian traditions about primordial man. These traditions report two ways in which men become civilized. In *Cattle and Grain,* the great gods create the gods of various skills and commodities (for example, cattle, grain, clothing and weaving), present them with necessities for performing their functions (herbs for grazing; plow and yoke), and (thereby?) present men with the implements and products of husbandry which are the bases of civilized life and which are jointly termed

22. Heimpel, p. 224, no. 10.13. Cf. *SP,* no. 1, l. 30: "It is (only) a wild ox in the netherworld which does not eat grass; it is (only) a gazelle in the netherworld which does not drink water"; cf. also Gordon, *JAOS* 74:83, n. 17; Lambert, *BWL,* p. 238. Note also the curse "May he (An) gather grass for (the enemies') mouth to eat, like sheep; may he give their throat water to drink" (Heimpel, p. 224, no. 10, l. 14).

23. Cf. Kramer, "Sumerian Epic Literature," p. 827; for the text and translation, see Cohen, *Enmerkar,* pp. 10–14, n. 22.

24. Ali, no. B7, l. 7; Reiner, in *ANET,* p. 538, § 39; cf. Dan. 4:30 and Tigay, "Paradise," cols. 79–80.

25. Conybeare, pp. lxi, 116, n. 4.

26. Cf. C. A. Williams.

27. For some reflexes of this phenomenon in literature and folklore, see Rudyard Kipling's *Jungle Book* (Mowgli), the legend of Romulus and Remus, and *MI* B 535–38.

"sustenance" (Sum. z i - š à - g á l).[28] The text sums up by saying that the gods of cattle and grain

an(var. unken)-na ḫé-gál mu-un-ne-gál
kalam-ma zi-šà-gál mu-un-ne-gál
me-dingir-re-e-ne si im-sá-sá-e-ne

Brought abundance in heaven (var., the assembly),
Brought "sustenance" on earth,
The m e s of the gods they direct.[29]

The m e s , one of the most elusive concepts in Sumerian literature, are the various norms and traits of civilized life, such as kingship, sexual intercourse, truth, priesthood, crafts, heroism, and so forth.[30] According to another tradition, the m e s of human civilization were mediated to mankind not by gods of the individual skills and commodities, but by a group of semidivine beings (*apkallu*s, roughly "sages") who appeared on earth in the early generations of history, before the flood. According to Berossus, mankind was instructed by Oannes (also known as Adapa, the first *apkallu*) in everything which would tend to domesticate (ἡμέρωσιν, "tame" or "civilize") human life; other versions tell of up to seven such *apkallu*s.[31] In this tradition it is the *apkallu*s who "administer the 'patterns' (Akk. *uṣurātu*) of heaven and earth."[32] The latter passage includes Adapa among these *apkallus*[33] and recalls the statement in the *Adapa* myth that Adapa had been given wisdom "to teach (mankind) the 'patterns' of the land" (*uṣurāt māti kul!-lu-mu, Adapa* frag. A, 3).[34] These "patterns" are roughly equivalent to the m e s which, in *Cattle and Grain,* were administered by the gods of cattle and

28. For this meaning, see Falkenstein, *ZA* 58:10–14, meaning 4; Hallo and van Dijk, p. 95, s.v. z i - š à - g a l $a_7$; cf. also the preceding entry. For the term referring to tools by which man produces food, cf. Sollberger, *JCS* 21:279–91, ll. 11–12, 54–55 (the context is the reestablistment of creation after the flood). Cf. Deut. 24:6; cf. also Deut. 24:15 and *ANET,* p. 409d.

29. Lines 53–55; text according to Falkenstein, *ZA* 58:11–12.

30. See Kramer, *Sumerians,* pp. 115–16; cf. the myth summarized there on pp. 171–83.

31. Jacoby, 1:369–70. On Oannes-Adapa, see Lambert, *JCS* 16:74; van Dijk, UVB 18:47–48; Hallo, *JAOS* 83:176, n. 79.

32. Reiner, *Or.* 30:2, ll. 7′–9′; 4, ll. 7′–9′.

33. See Reiner, ibid., p. 7.

34. Jensen, KB 6(1):92–93, l. 3; Speiser, in *ANET,* p. 101; cf. *Adapa* B 57–58 (Jensen, pp. 98–99, ll. 21–22; Speiser, in *ANET,* p. 102b).

grain.[35] In sum, the *apkallus* represent one tradition of how the m e s were communicated to mankind, while in another tradition individual gods of skills and commodities play that role.[36]

Both traditions present a picture of what is distinctive of human, as against subhuman, life. We have here a conception which is comparable, but not identical, to the concept of humanity (n a m - l ú - $u_x$ - l u) in Sumerian wisdom literature. The latter has been described by van Dijk as equivalent to the Latin *humanitas,* in the sense of "the complete blossoming forth of human values, humanism."[37] This concept is at home in the Sumerian scribal academies. It refers to intellectual achievements[38] and, with its Akkadian equivalent *awīlūtum*[39] as used mainly in Old Babylonian and Old Assyrian letters, to gentlemanly ethical standards.[40] The conception in the traditions about early man is a more basic one, involving those features of civilization which distinguish human behavior from animal behavior.

In the primordial traditions, we have found two different notions of how civilization was transmitted to men. *The Gilgamesh Epic,* similarly, describes how Enkidu becomes human, but this takes place in an entirely different context. Enkidu is humanized and civilized through contact with other human beings who are already civilized. The process involves two stages. The first is mating with the harlot, as a result of which Enkidu "now had wi[sdom, br]oader understanding" (*i-ši ṭé-*[*ma u-r*]*a-pa-aš ḫa-si-sa, GE* I, iv, 29).[41] In the second stage, Enkidu learns the ways of man from the

35. Cf. Lambert's discussion of *uṣurtu* in *Or.* 39:174–75 with the earlier discussions of m e by Jacobsen, *JNES* 5:139, n. 20, and Kramer, *Sumerians,* p. 113. Cf. *ANET,* p. 111, n. 11. The *apkallus* have been described as "mediators between the divine MEs and human knowledge" (*SSA,* p. 20; cf. Lambert and Millard, pp. 18–19).

36. Compare Sanchunyaton's account of the origins of civilization (in Jacoby, 2:803–16; Gifford, pp. 35–47), and see the remarks of Gadd, *Ideas,* p. 11, and Castellino, SVT 4:135 *sub* 14.

37. *SSA,* pp. 23–26; Gordon, *Bi. Or.* 17:123, with n. 17; Gadd, *Teachers,* p. 13; Kramer, *Sumerians,* pp. 243, 264.

38. *SSA,* pp. 23ff.

39. Cf. Gordon, *Bi. Or.* 17:123, n. 17; Oppenheim, *JAOS* 74:11–13; *CAD* $A_2$, pp. 55bc, 57d, 62bc.

40. Cf. also *PRU* 3:20, l. 24, as translated by Moran, in *ANET,* p. 629b, for an example from Ugarit (contrast Nougayrol, *PRU* 3:20, l. 24); cf. *BWL,* p. 267, col. I, 12–15.

41. For a slightly different reading of the line, see von Soden, *ZA* 53:222. Line 34 is often restored with similar meaning as [*en*]-*qa-ta,* "you are wise," but this is far from certain; Oppenheim restores [*dam*]-*qa-ta,* "you are beautiful" (*Or.* 17:27, n. 1).

harlot and the shepherds: wearing clothes, eating bread, drinking beer, anointing himself (Gilg. P. ii, 27–iii, 27).[42] There is nothing unusual about the second stage, but there is about the first. What Enkidu apparently acquired from intercourse with the harlot was the intellectual potential to adopt human ways and the desire to seek human companionship (*GE* I, iv, 29–41).[43] How this was brought about by intercourse we can only speculate. It is possible that a week of intimacy with a human made Enkidu realize where he belonged. This would account for his yearning for a friend, but not for the more extensive physical changes in him:

*pa-ni-šú iš-ta-kan ina ṣēr bu-li-šú*
*i-mu-ra-šu-ma* ᵈ*Enkidu i-rap-pu-da ṣabāti*
*bu-ul ṣēri it-te-si ina zumri-šu*
*ul-taḫ-ḫi-iṭ* ᵈ*Enkidu ul-lu-la pa-gar-šu*
*it-ta-ziz-za bir-ka-a-šú šá il-li-ka bu-ul-šú*
*um-ta-aṭ-ṭu* ᵈ*Enki[du u]l ki-i šá pa-ni la-sa-an-šú*

He set his face toward his wild beasts.
On seeing him, Enkidu, the gazelles run off.
The wild beasts of the steppe drew away from his body.
Startled (var. weakened) was Enkidu, his body was taut,
His knees were motionless—for his wild beasts had gone.
Enki[du] has become weak—his running is [n]ot as it was before.
(*GE* I, iv, 23–28)

The animals now sense that Enkidu is no longer one of them,[44] and Enkidu himself has lost his gazellelike speed. Enkidu's physical as

42. Beer, wine, grain, and fields (as well as water) are termed "the life of people," or "of the land" *(napšat/napišti nišī* or *māti)*: see *CAD* $N_1$, pp. 302–3 *sub* 8; cf. *AHw,* p. 738d (on the reading *napšat* vs. *nablaṭ* (*AHw,* p. 698a), which would mean the same thing, see *BWL,* p. 293, l. 89). This usage is synonymous with that of z i - š à - g á l, z i - g á l, and z i describing the same items in Sumerian (see Falkenstein, *ZA* 58:13–14, and *EWO* 330). Cf. Ecclus. 29:21; 39:26. The epic describes the human practice of using these items as *simat balāṭim,* "that which belongs to life," and *sīmti māti,* "the custom (or: lot) of the land" (Gilg. P. iii, 13–14; see *CAD* B, p. 46d; Finkelstein, *JAOS* 90:251; Lambert, *Or.* 39:175; cf. Gurney, *An. St.* 6:150, ll. 4–5). For bread as a mark of civilization, cf. Shaffer, "Sources," p. 28, n. 3.

43. That Enkidu's earlier manner of life implied the lack of human intellect and his new manner of life its attainment is also suggested by the account of Nebuchadnezzar's similar behavior in Dan. 4, which is attributed to his human heart (i.e., mind) being changed into that of an animal and his being deprived of intelligence (Dan. 4:13, 31–33; 5:21); see Tigay, "Paradise," cols. 79–80.

44. Perhaps Enkidu had now acquired a human odor; cf. Albright, *JAOS* 40:327. For the variant in *GE* I, iv, 26, see *BWL,* p. 333, *sub* 9 (the reference is presumably to *CT* 46, no. 2).

well as his intellectual nature has been transformed. This calls to mind certain folklore motifs. One is the transfer of qualities from one being to another through intimate contact (embracing, kissing, intercourse). The transfer may involve negative qualities (e.g., weakness) or positive ones (e.g., divinity).[45] Enkidu appears to have lost his animal speed and identity and to have contracted human intellectual capacity through intercourse with a human. Another motif is the role of woman as seducer toward civilization. A number of folk tales tell of hermits who lived with animals until they were drawn to civilization by women who seduced them.[46] Apparently the epic has drawn upon both of these motifs here; so far as I know, no other reflexes of them have been found in Mesopotamian literature.

Jastrow's comparison of the Enkidu story to the story of Adam and Eve in the second and third chapters of Genesis implied a biblical reflex of the second motif: By offering Adam the fruit of the tree of knowledge, Eve ultimately drew him to civilized life.[47] In Jastrow's view, both of these stories went back to a common Semitic original which, like the biblical story, dealt with primordial man, but, like the Enkidu story, explicitly included sexual intercourse.[48] But such triangulation back to a common original is not without complication. If the original story dealt with precivilized times, the woman must have been equally uncivilized and could not have contributed to the man's intellect. One might theorize that in the original story the woman was a goddess (N.B. *GE* I, iv, 34; Gilg. P. ii, 11: "You (Enkidu) are like a god," *kima ili tabašši*), but this is pure speculation. Present evidence does not point clearly to a Semitic tale in which all elements of Enkidu's origins and his rise to human culture were already drawn together. It looks rather as if the

45. See Gaster, *Thespis,* pp. 257–59; *Oldest Stories,* pp. 142–43; *Interpreter's Dictionary of the Bible* 1:131; Crawley, vol. 2, index, s.v. "transmission of qualities."

46. Albright, *JAOS* 40:329–30; C. A. Williams, *Oriental Affinities,* 1:12, 30, 35; cf. *MI,* D733.1. That the role of the harlot in bringing Enkidu to civilization was found by the author of the epic in his source is suggested by the superfluity of the role. Why did Gilgamesh need an intermediary to bring himself and Enkidu together? Gilgamesh's dreams imply that Enkidu came to him directly from heaven.

47. See Tigay, "Paradise," cols. 79–80.

48. Rather than euphemistically: In Genesis, instead of simply conferring intelligence through intercourse, Eve gives Adam the fruit of the tree of knowledge; fruit and eating could be taken as euphemisms for sex: cf. *GE* VI, 8; above, chap. 8, n. 42; Prov. 30:20.

compiler of the epic created the episode out of diverse raw materials.[49]

## ENKIDU'S EARLY LIFE AND THE VALUES OF THE EPIC

The question arises as to why the author chose to describe Enkidu's beginnings in this way. Granting the need to account for the origins of Gilgamesh's equal, this literary need did not require so circumstantial an account, and certainly did not require that Enkidu begin his life like an animal.

In keeping with his view that Enkidu represents the Amorite nomad, Dossin held that the friendship of Gilgamesh and Enkidu aimed at expressing and supporting literarily the union of nomadic and sedentary, urban peoples achieved under Hammurapi.[50] In arguing that Enkidu was modeled not on the nomad but on primordial man, whose culture was that of the animal, we perceive the contrast as one between human culture and its absence.[51] Enkidu is first civilized by the harlot Shamhat, who is, it is true, representative of Uruk, called elsewhere " city of courtesans, hierodules, and prostitutes" (*āl kezrēti šamḫātu u ḫarimāti, Erra* IV, 52; cf. *GE* VI, 165–66),[52] and he is subsequently brought to the city. But his civiliz-

49. As did the author of the biblical paradise narrative; Tigay, "Paradise," cols. 81–82.

50. "Enkidou," pp. 592–93.

51. This contrast between human and animal culture was seen by G. Kirk as one of the main themes of the epic:

> One of the main preoccupations of the Central Brazilian Indians was seen to be the relationship between nature and culture, the untamed and the tamed, the raw and the cooked, and the tensions, contradictions, and paradoxes that operated between these extremes. I believe the Gilgamesh epic in its developed Akkadian form to be partly concerned with exploring, consciously or not, something of the same polarity. Men have always been preoccupied with status: with their relations as individuals to families, as families to clans, as clans to tribes—more generally still with their own society's relation to the world outside. That world extends from its broadest cosmological aspects (sky and heavenly bodies, for many the abode of gods or spirits) to the immediate terrestrial environment. It is here that the nature-culture contrast is seen at its most striking, in differences between the organization of the village and its surrounding fields, or the whole cultivated area and the enfolding forest or desert; between the customs and rules of men and women and those applied between animals; between human cultural techniques and the natural processes they seem to imitate, as Aristotle put it, or to counteract (pp. 145–46).

52. See chap. 6, n. 23.

ing experience takes place before he arrives there, and it is summed up in the phrase "he became human" or "like a human" *(awēliš iwē,* Gilg. P. iii, 25), not "a city dweller" *(āšib āli, ālu).* Uruk appears in the epic as the locus of human culture[53]—perhaps even the very best of human culture. What is stressed throughout the epic is the human-ness, rather than the urbanity, of that culture. Even if the culture of Uruk is viewed as higher than that of the shepherds among whom Enkidu was first humanized, the latter representing only the first step in the process,[54] this gradation is of no significance in the epic.

The significance of the contrast between human culture and its absence, as embodied in Enkidu's life, is made clear in Shamash's response to Enkidu's curse of Shamhat, who brought him to civilization and thereby ultimately caused his death:

> Why, O Enkidu, do you curse the harlot Shamhat,
> Who made you eat food fit for divinity,
> Who gave you to drink wine fit for royalty,
> Who clothed you with noble garments,
> And made you have fair Gilgamesh for a comrade?
> And has (not) now Gilgamesh, your bosom friend,
> Made you lie on a noble couch?
> He has made you lie on a couch of honor,
> He has placed you on the seat of ease, the seat at the left,
> That [the prin]ces of the earth may kiss your feet!
> He will make Uruk's people weep over you (and) lament,
> Will fill [joyful] people with woe over you.
> And, when you are gone, he will make himself wear unkempt hair,
> Will don a lion skin and roam over the steppe.
> (*GE* VII, iii, 35–48)

These are the boons of a civilized life as Enkidu experienced them in Uruk,

> Where people are re[splend]ent in festal attire,
> (Where) each day is made a holiday.
> (*GE* I, v, 7–8)

53. Uruk is described as k i - z i - š à - g á l - l a, "the place of z i - š à - g á l - l a"; see Hallo, *Bi. Or.* 23:243:YBC 9859:23, 25; cf. Hallo and van Dijk, p. 26, l. 92. On the significance of this epithet, see above, pp. 204–5.

54. See Reiner, "City Bread," p. 118.

By not denying Enkidu's charges (*GE* VII, iii, 31–32), Shamash implies that the life to which Shamhat brought Enkidu was worth living, despite the untimely death it entailed. Shamash's words are in spirit and in some detail comparable with the barmaid's advice to Gilgamesh in the Old Babylonian version quoted earlier:

As for you, Gilgamesh, let your belly be full,
Make merry day and night.
Of each day make a feast of rejoicing,
Day and night dance and play!
Let your garments be sparkling fresh,
Let your head be washed; bathe in water.
Pay heed to a little one that holds on to your hand;
Let a spouse delight in your bosom,
For this is the task of [woman].
(Gilg. Me. iii, 6–14)[55]

These are the benefits which mortals can hope to derive from life. Their character as marks of human life is also made clear in *GE* XII and its Sumerian source *Gilgamesh, Enkidu, and the Netherworld,* where Enkidu, when he went to the netherworld,

Put on clean raiment,
They marked him as an alien;
With sweet oil from the cruse he anointed himself . . .
(*GE* XII, 33–35 = *GEN* 207–9)

A few lines later there is a passage mentioning Enkidu's acts of affection, as well as hostility, towards members of his family, which recall more indirectly the end of the barmaid's remarks:

He kissed his beloved wife,
He struck his hated wife;
He kissed his beloved son,
He struck his hated son.
(*GE* XII, 42–45 =
*GEN* 217–20)

In the context of *GE* XII, these are signs of the living in contrast with the dead: They are the marks of human life which will provoke the jealous anger of the dead who no longer enjoy them.

55. Akkadian text on p. 168.

These passages confirm the view that the epic explores the meaning of life as well as death.[56] And this is the reason for the epic's describing Enkidu's early life as like that of an uncivilized animal. By contrasting a life devoid of human civilization, the epic underlines the satisfactions that civilized human life offers—in other words, that minimum amount of "meaning" which is available in man's life. This is the epic's message. This is expressed most explicitly in the case of Enkidu, whose rise to humanity is described not only as "becoming human" but also as becoming "godlike" (*kīma ili,* I, iv, 34; cf. VII, iii, 36) in the only way possible for most humans,[57] through intelligence and civilization.

The values expressed in these passages have often been described as hedonistic. Their philosophy is not unique in the ancient Near East.[58] But it is worth contrasting this hedonism to the militaristic heroic ideal stressed elsewhere in the Gilgamesh tradition, but which seems decidedly underplayed in the epic. In the Sumerian *Death of Gilgamesh,* we find a different view of what the gods have granted Gilgamesh in lieu of immortality:

> Enlil . . .
> Has destined your fate, O Gilgamesh, for kingship; for eternal life he has not destined it.
> . . .
> Supremacy over mankind he has granted you,
> Unmatched . . . . he has granted you,
> Battle *from which none may retreat* he has granted you,
> Onslaughts unrivalled he has granted you,
> Attacks from which none may escape he has granted you.
> (*Death of Gilgamesh* A, 33, 35, 41–45)

These are endowments most appropriate to a king; indeed, many phrases in this passage are paralleled in royal inscriptions.[59] The sense of values expressed in the passage is that summed up in *Erra*

56. Landsberger, in *GSL,* p. 33; Shaffer, "Sources," pp. 19–20.

57. Cf. Gen. 3:22–23. When Utnapishtim and his wife are granted immortality, they "become like the gods" (*ēmû kî ilāni, GE* XI, 194). Kings, in their majesty, and conjurers in the exercise of their spells are said to be "the image of the god" (*ṣalam ili;* see *CAD* Ṣ, p. 85c). Note also the use of the latter phrase in an intellectual sense in a statement in the Egyptian *Instruction of Any:* "Men are in the image of the god [in] their custom of hearing a man in regard to his reply" (R. J. Williams, p. 221). Cf. also Gen. 1:26–27; 9:6; *ANET,* p. 417d.

58. Compare Eccles. 9:7–9; Isa. 22:13; *ANET,* pp. 413d, 467c (Egyptian).

59. Cf. Seux, p. 154 s.v. *maḫāru;* p. 345 s.v. *ṭību.*

I, 51: "Taking to the field of manhood is like a holiday" *(alāk ṣēri ša eṭlūti kī ša isinnu-ma).* The same sense of values, subsumed under the concept of manhood, is expressed also in a letter from Shamshi-Adad I, king of Assyria (1813–1781) to his son Yasmah-Addu criticizing him for sleeping with women and urging him, when he goes with his troops to Qatanum, to "be a man!" *(lu awīlāt)* by winning a military victory.[60] This conflict between hedonism and militarism is echoed in literary texts. Yasmah-Addu's pursuit of pleasure rather than a militaristic life has a mythological parallel in the *Erra Epic,* where Ishum and the Divine Seven seek to rouse Erra to battle, while he prefers to sleep and make love to his spouse Mami.[61] Erra is, in fact, following the advice expressed by Naram-Sin. The latter, it will be recalled, advised, "Enjoy yourself in your wife's embrace" and "Bind up your weapons and put (them/yourself) into a corner,"[62] just as Erra orders his weapons into a corner and "makes love with his spouse Mami."[63]

At the beginning of *The Gilgamesh Epic,* we found Gilgamesh pursuing hedonistic pleasures to excess. He also found satisfaction in personal feats of valor, defeating the young men of Uruk in contests of various types. He may have conquered Uruk in the first place. In his pursuit of immortality, he conquered Humbaba and the Bull of Heaven. In the end, these contests brought him no satisfaction and were of no account to the final editor of the epic.[64] To the final editor, Gilgamesh's only enduring achievements were the building of the wall of Uruk and the wisdom he acquired on his journeys and left inscribed for posterity. This inscription must have included something like the advice he received from the barmaid, just as Naram-Sin's stele contained a similar bit of hedonistic advice.

The rise of Enkidu to human culture underlines the values preferred by the epic. This preference may help explain the epic's enduring attraction. While military feats were for the few, the simple pleasures advocated by the barmaid were something many could strive for.

60. ARM 1:69: rev. 13′.
61. *Erra* I, 15–20.
62. Gurney, *An. St.* 5:106–9, ll. 157, 162.
63. *Erra* I, 17, 20.
64. See pp. 143–44.

# 12

# *The Flood Story*

## THE ORIGIN OF THE FLOOD STORY

The outstanding example of material taken from elsewhere into *The Gilgamesh Epic* is the account of the flood in Tablet XI of the late version, lines 15 through 196. There is no evidence that the whole story was recounted in the Old Babylonian version as it is in the late version. Although the Old Babylonian version told how Gilgamesh journeyed to Utnapishtim, the survivor of the flood (see Gilg. Me. iv), the actual retelling of the flood story is not attested in Old Babylonian fragments of the epic, and, as we shall see, there is good reason to believe that the full story was not a part of the epic before the late version.

The discovery of the flood story in *GE* XI in 1872 created a sensation because of the similarity of this story to the biblical account in Genesis, Chapters 6 through 9. The story may have arisen from a specific historical flood that took place in parts of southern Mesopotamia around 2900.[1] The flood came to be regarded as a major turning point in human history,[2] and the story about it was

1. See Hallo, *JCS* 23:61–62; *ANEH,* pp. 35–36.
2. See Lambert and Millard, pp. 15–21, 25–26; Sollberger, *JCS* 21:279–80, and note pp. 280, l. 1, and 282, l. 1.

popular enough to appear in several different versions in ancient Mesopotamia and neighboring areas. The classic Akkadian version of the story was *The Atrahasis Epic,* known in several versions from the Old Babylonian period on.[3] Although the final lines of *Atrahasis* speak of the flood as its main theme ("I have sung of the flood to all the peoples. Hear it!" OB *Atr.* III, viii, 18–19), this epic was actually a history of the human race, beginning with the events leading up to the creation of man and continuing through several calamities down to the flood and its aftermath. A Sumerian counterpart to *Atrahasis* is found in the text named *The Deluge* by modern scholars, although it, too, is really a history of man from his creation through the flood.[4] The story had reached Ras Shamra on the Syrian coast by the Middle Babylonian Period, in an Akkadian version which was probably part of neither *Atrahasis* nor *Gilgamesh.*[5] The story eventually became part of *The Gilgamesh Epic,* and its popularity in this context could be indicated by the fact that, at least for the present, the tablet of the late version in which the story appears (XI) is the tablet of which the largest number of copies has been found, although this could be a coincidence. The story survived into the Hellenistic period and was included in the third-century B.C.E. work *Babyloniaka,* a history of Babylonia written in Greek by the Babylonian priest Berossus.[6] Outside of Mesopotamia, the story had spread earlier to Israel, where it appears in Genesis,[7] and eventually to Greek and Latin writers as well.[8]

Unlike the episodes we studied in Chapters 9 through 11,

3. See the edition of Lambert and Millard.

4. Laessøe, *Bi. Or.* 13:100.

5. Text and translation in Lambert and Millard, pp. 131–33. Cf. above, chap. 5, n. 35, for cuneiform literary texts known west of Mesopotamia in the MB period. Although the hero is called Atrahasis in the Ras Shamra fragment, the fragment consists of a first-person narrative, not a third-person narrative as in *Atrahasis.* Furthermore, the composition is apparently complete in one tablet and contains only the flood story. Since Atrahasis introduces himself in line 6 of this tablet, the composition clearly contained no earlier episodes about him, as did *Atrahasis.* On the other hand, the fragment is not part of *Gilgamesh,* since in *Gilgamesh* the hero had been called Utnapishtim since the OB period.

6. Translations in Lambert and Millard, pp. 134–37; see the discussion by Komoróczy, *Act. Ant.* 21:133–39.

7. Of the voluminous literature on the relationship between the biblical and the Mesopotamian accounts of the flood, one may recommend Sarna, chap. 2; Lambert, "New Look"; Frymer-Kensky; and Millard, *Tyndale Bulletin,* 18:3–18.

8. See Frazer, pp. 66–78; Ovid, *Metamorphoses,* bk. 1 (ed. Innes, pp. 31–43). The Greek and Latin accounts are not necessarily all based on a Mesopotamian account.

where we were unable to point to a specific composition on which *Gilgamesh* was dependent, in the case of the flood story there is no question but that *Atrahasis* served as the source for Tablet XI of the late version. This is crystal clear from the following considerations: 1) Certain lines in *Gilgamesh* and *Atrahasis* are virtually identical,[9] and the two are therefore textually related. 2) The flood story is an integral part of the plot in *Atrahasis,* and it was already part of the plot of that epic in the Old Babylonian period. In *Gilgamesh,* the story is only incidental to the main theme, and, as we shall see, probably did not enter the epic until its late version was created. 3) In Tablet XI, 15–18, Utnapishtim opens his account of the flood with a list of gods (Anu, Enlil, Ninurta, and Ennugi) and their offices which also appears at the beginning of the Old Babylonian *Atrahasis.* In Tablet XI, the list, along with line 19 which may be based on the second tablet of *Atrahasis,*[10] serves to identify the great gods who, according to line 14, decided to bring the flood, but it is really inappropriate for this purpose. Not only does it omit Ishtar, who is explicitly mentioned in lines 119 through 121 as having taken part in the decision, but it mentions Ennugi, who plays no role at all in Tablet XI, and Anu, who is mentioned only in passing, without being involved in the events. In *Atrahasis,* however, all of the gods mentioned in the list play a role in the events surrounding the creation of man, and three of them play a role in the flood as well. Therefore it appears that the editor of the *Gilgamesh* flood story simply took the list over bodily from *Atrahasis,* rather than composing a new one of his own. 4) Finally—and this is the giveaway—although *Gilgamesh* usually calls the survivor of the flood Utnapishtim, in the

9. See the cross-references to *GE* XI in the footnotes and commentary on OB *Atr.* III in Lambert and Millard.

10. *GE* XI, 15–18 = OB *Atr.* I, 7–10; on the last of these lines, see Lambert and Millard, pp. 147–48. This passage is followed in *GE* XI, 19 by a transition introducing Ea which may also be based on *Atr.* Jensen rendered the line "Ea spoke (*ta-mì-ma;* better "was under oath"–J.H.T.) together with them" (KB 6[1]: 231, l. 19), which reflects OB *Atr.* II, vii, 38, 42 (cf. *Atr.* x rev. ii, 47–48). This translation has not generally been accepted (see von Soden, *ZA* 53:232; but cf. Rowton, *JNES* 21:275, no. 332), probably because the *Atr.* passage was not known until recently and the point of Ea's swearing (agreeing to the flood) was unclear. The more commonly accepted rendering "Ea sat (*ta-šib-ma*) together with them" would echo a motif known in *Atr.* but which does not point to literary dependence (cf. OB *Atr.* I, 101, 254; II, iv, 18–19).

flood story he once calls him Atrahasis (XI, 187),[11] the name he bears throughout *The Atrahasis Epic.*

While the flood story in *GE* XI comes from *Atrahasis,* the rest of the narrative about Gilgamesh's encounter with Utnapishtim (*GE* X, iv–vi and the rest of *GE* XI, i.e., ll. 1–14 and 193–307) has no counterpart in *Atrahasis.* The eleventh tablet of the late version (and the Utnapishtim section as a whole) therefore consists of two separate components: the flood story (from *Atrahasis*), and the rest of Gilgamesh's encounter with Utnapishtim (for which no source outside of *Gilgamesh* is presently known, and which was presumably composed by a writer of *Gilgamesh*). In comparing the flood component to its source in *Atrahasis,* it is important to keep in mind that there were several versions and recensions of *Atrahasis.* The best-preserved version of its account of the flood is the Old Babylonian version. Since little more than scraps of the later versions of *Atrahasis* remain, the Old Babylonian text must serve as the main basis for comparison with the *Gilgamesh* version. But enough is known of the later versions of *Atrahasis* to show that at least some details of the *Gilgamesh* version are based on these, and are not the work of the editor of *Gilgamesh.* For example, the changing of the god Enki's name to Ea, the name always used for him in *Gilgamesh,* is typical of the later versions of *Atrahasis* from the Middle Babylonian period on.[12] The line stating that Ea repeated the gods' words to the reed-wall (*GE* XI, 20) is paralleled so far only in the Middle Babylonian fragment from Ras Shamra.[13] The double address "reed-wall, reed-wall!" *(kikkiš kikkiš)* in Ea's statement to the wall (21) is so far paralleled only in the late Assyrian version of *Atrahasis,*[14] as is the "set time" *(adannu)* for the flood (86, 89).[15] The formula used for introducing direct speech in the flood section of *GE* XI is

11. Was this exception a slip or intentional? Millard argues that the name Atrahasis can mean "exceedingly devout" and that this meaning suits Enki's explanation, in line 187, of why he helped Atrahasis survive (*Tyndale Bulletin* 18:13–14). But while *ḫasīsu* by itself could mean "devotion" (see *CAD* Ḫ, pp. 122–23, *sub* 1–2, the combination *atar-ḫasīsa* refers elsewhere to gods and an insightful young eagle, in which cases the meaning must be "wise," rather than "devout."

12. See, for example, *Atr.* S, rev iv, 18ff., in Lambert and Millard pp. 106–9, ll. 18ff.

13. Ibid., pp. 132–33, l. 12.

14. Ibid., pp. 122–23, l. 15.

15. Ibid., pp. 128–29, l. 5.

found in late copies of the *Atrahasis* flood story,[16] not earlier ones. Not enough is known of the later versions of the *Atrahasis* flood story, however, to permit us to describe their relationship to *GE* XI in detail. None of those currently known to us is *on the whole* closer to *GE* XI than the Old Babylonian *Atrahasis* is. To judge only from the texts of *Atrahasis* currently known to us, one might conclude that the flood story in *GE* XI is an eclectic version based on several recensions or versions of *Atrahasis.*[17] This could be the case, but the amount of textual evidence available is too meager to permit a conclusion on this score. All that can be said at present is that some details of the *Gilgamesh* flood story are based on recensions or versions of *Atrahasis* which differ from the Old Babylonian version known to us.[18] Therefore we cannot confidently credit differences between *GE* XI and the Old Babylonian *Atrahasis* to an editor of *Gilgamesh,* except where there is a particular reason for doing so, since the differences may actually derive from some version of *Atrahasis* not presently known.

## DIFFERENCES BETWEEN THE *ATRAHASIS* AND *GILGAMESH* VERSIONS OF THE FLOOD STORY

Differences in wording between the Old Babylonian *Atrahasis* flood story and that in *GE* XI are of the same types encountered among the different versions of *Gilgamesh.*[19] Here are some examples, with passages from *Atrahasis* on the left and the late version of *Gilgamesh* on the right:

### a. DIFFERENT GRAMMATICAL FORMS

| | |
|---|---|
| 1. *pa-aḫ-ru,* "they were gathered" (OB *Atr.* III, v, 35) | *ip-taḫ-ru,* "they gathered" (*GE* XI, 161) |
| 2. *ma-li,* "was filled" (vi, 6) | *im-ta-li,* "became filled" (172) |
| 3. *šu-a-ti,* "it" (acc.; i, 29) | *šá-a-ši,* "it" (dat. for acc.; 31) |

16. See ibid., pp. 122–23, ll. 13–14; pp. 128–29, ll. 11–12; cf. pp. 120–21, ll. 44–45.

17. That the editor of *GE* had several versions or recensions of *Atr.* at his disposal is plausible: Several recensions or versions of a single composition were often present in the same library in Mesopotamia. See chap. 6, p. 137 and nn. 34–35; chap. 1, pp. 30–31 and n. 35; for recensions of *Atr.,* see Lambert and Millard, pp. 31–39.

18. Lambert and Millard, p. 15.

19. And between recensions of *Atr.:* see Lambert and Millard, pp. 32–38.

### b. SUBSTITUTION OF SYNONYMS OR WORDS FUNCTIONING SIMILARLY

| | |
|---|---|
| 1. *er-ṣe-et* $^{d}$*Enlil,* "Enlil's earth" (i, 48) | *qaq-qar* $^{d}$*Enlil,* "Enlil's ground" (41) |
| 2. *uš-te-ri-ib,* "he made enter (the boat)" (ii, 42) | *uš-te-li,* "I made go up (onto the boat)" (84) |
| 3. *i-ša-ag-gu-um,* "(Adad) roars" (ii, 53) | *ir-tam-ma-am-ma,* "(Adad) thundered" (98) |
| 4. *ga-me-er-ta-a*[*m*], "total destruction" (iii, 38) | *lemutti,* "evil" (119) |
| 5. 7 *$u_4$-mi* 7 *mu-š*[*i-a-tim*], "seven days (and) seven nights" (iv, 24) | 6 *ur-ri u* [7] *mu-ša-a-ti,* "six days and seven nights" (127) |
| 6. *qú-ut-ri-ni,* "incense (offering)" (v, 41) | *šur-qi-ni,* "offering" (167) |
| 7. *ik-mi-su,* "collected (for destruction)" (v, 43; also iii, 54) | *im-nu-ú,* "consigned (to destruction)" (169) |

### c. ADDED WORD

| | |
|---|---|
| 1. *i-lu*<br>*it-ti-šá ib-ku-ú*<br>*ana ma-tim* | *ilāni šu-ut* $^{d}$*A-nun-na-ki*<br>*ba-ku-ú it-ti-šá* |
| "The gods<br><br>Wept with her<br>For the land" (iv, 15) | "The gods, those of the Anunnaki,<br>Were in tears with her" (124) |
| 2. *li-ib-ba-ti ma-li*<br>*ša* $^{d}$*I-g*[*i-gi*] | *lib-ba-ti im-ta-li*<br>*šá ilāni* $^{d}$*Í-gì-gí* |
| "He was full of anger<br>At the Igigi" (vi, 6) | "He became filled with anger<br>At the Igigi gods" (172) |

### d. DIFFERENT FORMULATION WITH SAME MEANING

| | |
|---|---|
| *i-ga-ru ši-ta-am-mi-a-an-ni*<br>*ki-ki-šu šu-uṣ-ṣi-ri ka-la*<br>*sí-iq-ri*!*-ia* | *ki-ik-ki-šu ši-me-ma*<br>*i-ga-ru ḫi-is-sa-as* |
| "Wall, listen to me,<br>Reed-wall, observe all<br>my words" (i, 20–21) | "Reed-wall, listen,<br>Wall, pay heed" (22) |

**e. NEW IDEA ADDED**

| | |
|---|---|
| $u_4$*-mu iš-nu-ú pa-nu-ú-šu* | *šá* $u_4$*-mi at-ta-ṭal bu-na-šu*<br>$u_4$*-mu a-na i-tap-lu-si pu-luḫ-ta i-ši* |
| "The look of the weather changed" (ii, 48) | "I watched the appearance of the weather,<br>The weather was awesome to behold" (91–92) |

**f. COMPLETELY CHANGED MEANING**

| | |
|---|---|
| 1. *[ú-ul] ú-te-ed-du-ú*<br>*i-na ka-ra-ši* | *ul u-ta-ad-da-a nišī*<br>*ina šamē* |
| "They were not recognizable<br>in the destruction" (iii, 14) | "The people are not recognizable<br>from heaven" (112) |
| 2. $u_4$*-mu-um*<br>*li-id-da-⌜i⌝-[im]*<br>*li-tu-ur*<br>*li-ki-[il]* | $u_4$*-mu ul-lu-ú*<br>*a-na ṭi-iṭ-ṭi*<br>*lu-ú i-tur-ma* |
| "Let the day<br>Be ever dark,<br>Let it turn<br>Gloomy" (iii, 34–35) | "That day<br>To clay,<br>Alas (lit. indeed) turned" (118) |
| 3. *a-bu-ma-an ul-⌜da⌝*<br>*g[al-la-ta(?)] ti-a-am-ta*<br>*ki-ma ku-li-li*<br>*im-la-a-nim na-ra-am* | *a-na-ku-um-ma ul-la-da*<br>*ni-šu-ú-a-a-ma*<br>*ki-i mārī nūnī*<br>*ú-ma-al-la-a tam-ta-am-ma* |
| "What? Have they given birth<br>To the r[olling (?)] sea?<br>They have filled the river<br>Like dragonflies!" (iv, 5–7) | "When it is I myself who gave birth<br>To my people!<br>They fill the sea<br>Like the spawn of fishes!" (122–23) |

**g. ASSIMILATION**

| | |
|---|---|
| 1. *a-ia-a-nu*<br>*ú-ṣi na!-pi!-iš-tum*<br>*ki-i ib-lu-uṭ ⌜a-wi⌝-lum*<br>*i-na ⌜ka⌝-[r]a-ši* | *[a-ia-(a)]nu-um-ma* (var. *a-a-<nu>-um-ma*)<br>*ú-ṣi na-piš-ti*<br>*a-a ib-luṭ amēlu*<br>*ina ka-ra-ši*[20] |

20. For the text, see Lambert and Millard, p. 164 *ad* col. vi, 9.

| | |
|---|---|
| "Wherefrom (i.e., how) | "Wherefrom (i.e., how) |
| Has life escaped? | Has life escaped? |
| How did | No (Akk. sounds like |
| a man | "wherefrom") man |
| Survive | Was to survive |
| In the destruction?" (vi, 9–10) | In the destruction!" (173) |
| 2. [*be-el ar-n*]*im* | *be-el ár-ni (var. ḫi-ṭi)* |
| *šu-ku-un še-re-et-ka* | *e-mid ḫi-ṭa-a-šú* |
| [*ù*] ⸢*a*⸣*-iu-ú ša* | *be-el gíl-la-ti* |
| *ú-ša-a*[*s*]*-sà-ku* | *e-mid gíl-lat-su* |
| *a-wa-at-ka* | |
| "On the criminal | "On the criminal |
| Visit your penalty, | Impose his crime, |
| [And] on whoever disregards | On the transgressor |
| Your command" (vi, 25–26) | Impose his transgression" (180) |

A few of the readings in the *Gilgamesh* version appear to use later terminology. In the meanings and expressions for which they are used in *GE* XI, *šulû,* "to load on a ship" (b, 2, above), *ramāmu,* "to thunder" (b, 3), and *manû,* "to consign" (to destruction; b, 7) are so far attested in the dictionaries only from the Middle Babylonian period on[21] (although their counterparts in *Atrahasis* are not all limited to the Old Babylonian Period[22]). *gamertu,* in the meaning "total destruction" (literally "termination," b, 4), is attested only once outside *Atrahasis* and was probably replaced because it was uncommon.[23] The replacement of *ūmi* by *urri* in the expression

21. See 1) *CAD* E, pp. 129–30; *AHw,* p. 209c; Salonen, pp. 66–68; 2) *AHw,* pp. 949bc, 950d, 986a, 677a; 3) *AHw,* p. 604d.

22. *šūrubu* is not a normal term for "loading on a ship," and it is unparalleled in that use outside of OB *Atr.,* although its simple stem is used for "entering a ship" in *Atr.* W, 6 and *GE* XI, 88, 93. *šagāmu* continues to be used of Adad's (and other gods') thundering in later texts (*AHw,* pp. 1126a, 1127c). The verb *kamāsu* with the indirect object *karāši* ("collect for destruction") is paralleled only in the OB period, but with similar indirect objects ("net," "weapons") it is paralleled in later texts (see *CAD* K, pp. 115c, 214c).

23. This meaning (for which see Lambert and Millard, p. 158) is questioned by von Soden, *Or.* 38:430–31 (cf. Hallo, *JCS* 23:62, n. 74), but cf. *CAD* G, p. 33c. To the replacement "evil" *(lemutti)* in *GE* XI, 119, cf. the parallelism *gamertam* // *šipru lemnu,* "annihilation // evil deed," in OB *Atr.* II, viii, 34–35. The replacement of *šuṣṣira . . . siqrīya* with *ḫissas* (d) could also represent the elimination of old and uncommon language, for the use of the Š-stem of *naṣāru* for "heeding words" is thus far paralleled only once, in an OB text (also with *siqru,* see *AHw,* p. 756c), while all examples given in *CAD* Ḫ, pp. 123d–24a, for *ḫasāsu,* in the meaning "be mindful of (something), to listen to (somebody)," are late (note the parallelism with *nāṣir,* cited on p. 124a). But if this is the reason for the substitution, one wonders why the editor used a different word, rather than simply adopting the G-form of *naṣāru,* which is common for this meaning (with *amātu* for the divine word) in all periods

"*x* days and *x* (or *x* + 1) nights" (b, 5) is characteristic of the late *Gilgamesh;* it is not certain whether this switch was made in other epics, too.[24] A few other changes may be due to awkward wording in *Atrahasis* (cf. *GE* XI, 119–20, quoted below) or a corrupt text of *Atrahasis.*[25]

### h. EXPANSION

The account of the flood in *GE* XI both expands and abridges parts of the account in the Old Babylonian *Atrahasis.* Some of the expansion seems to have come about through the addition of parallel lines. For example, Ea/Enki's warning to the flood hero reads as follows in the two accounts[26]:

| **OB *Atr.* III, i, 15–29** | ***GE* XI, 20–31** |
| --- | --- |
| 15. [Enki] opened his [mo]uth | |
| 16. [Ad]dressing his servant: | |
| | 20. Their (the gods') words he (Ea) repeats to the reed-wall: |
| 17. " '[*W*]*hat* am I to seek?' you say. | |
| 18. The message that I speak to you, | |
| 19. Observe: | |
| | 21. "Reed-wall, reed-wall, Wall, wall! |

(*AHw,* pp. 755d–756a; cf. *CAD* $A_1$, p. 36a; an answer to this question may be available if Hecker is correct in deriving *šuṣṣuru* from a different root; see Hecker, pp. 77–78, n. 6).

24. See *GE* I, iv, 21 vs. Gilg. P. ii, 6; *GE* X, iii, 23 vs. Gilg. Me. ii, 8; cf. *GE* XI, 199. The Sumerian *Deluge* uses the equivalent of *ūmi* ($u_4$) rather than that of *urri* (u d - d a) in stating the length of the flood (203). In nonnarrative texts, *ūmi* was still used in the first millennium, e.g., Knudtzon, no. 1, l. 3 (cf. p. 14); *PRT* no. 1, l. 5.

25. See Lambert and Millard, p. 163 *ad* col. iv, 18–19a (*GE* XI, 125); p. 160 *ad* col. iii, 9–10 (*GE* XI, 107, for the reading of which see *CAD* Ḫ, p. 171b). For the latter passage, note that idioms like *Atrahasis'* "shattering the noise" seem to be limited to OB sources (see Finkelstein, *JCS* 11:86, col. iv, 5, 16: *ḫuburam . . . kabāsu*), while the simile "shatter (a land, a city, an enemy, etc.) like a pot" is in early and late texts (in Sumerian: Kramer in *JCS* 21:113–18, l. 59; *ANET,* p. 618, l. 409; bilingual and Akkadian texts [apart from Lambert and Millard's restoration in OB *Atr.* III, iii, 10]: see *CAD* Ḫ, p. 171a, lex., and bc; *CAD* K, p. 219c, lex., and p. 220c). For a suggestion regarding *GE* XI, 118, see Appendix, no. 14, *ad loc.*

26. See Appendix, no. 13.

| | |
|---|---|
| 20. Wall, listen to me, | 22. Reed-wall, listen, |
| 21. Reed-wall, observe all my words! | Wall, pay heed! |
| | 23. Shurippakian, son of Ubaratutu: |
| 22. Flee your house, Build a ship. | 24. Dismantle your house, Build a ship. |
| | 25. Give up wealth, seek life. |
| 23. *Spurn property,* and<br>24. Save life. | 26. Spurn [p]roperty, Save life. |
| | 27. [T]ake the seed of all living things aboard the ship. |
| 25. The [s]hip that you shall build, | 28. The ship that you shall build, |
| | 29. Measured shall be her dimensions. |
| 26. . . . . | |
| Equ[al (. . . .)] | 30. Equal [sh]all be her width and her length. |
| 27. . . . . | |
| 28. [. . . . like a c]ircle . . . . | |
| 29. [L]ike the Apsu you shall roof her. | 31. [L]ike the Apsu you shall roof her. |

At this point, Ea/Enki's speech ends in *Gilgamesh,* while in *Atrahasis* it continues with further instructions. The section of the god's speech quoted here is twice as long in *Gilgamesh* as in *Atrahasis.* After each line (or two) which *Gilgamesh* shares with *Atrahasis, Gilgamesh* adds another. Some of the added lines are parallel[27] or essentially equivalent to the shared lines (*GE* XI, 21 with *GE* XI, 22 [ = *Atr.* 20]; *GE* XI, 25 with (part of?) *GE* XI, 24 and 26 [= *Atr.* 22–24].[28] Line 23 of *GE* XI makes it clear that Ea/Enki's words

27. Cf. *GE* XI, 80–83 in contrast to OB *Atr.* III, ii, 30–31; *GE* XI, 159–60 in contrast to OB *Atr.* III, v, 34; *GE* XI, 118–21 in contrast to OB *Atr.* III, iii, 34–37. In the last passage, the wording of *GE* XI, 119 and 120 is so similar as to suggest that they represent variant attempts to render OB *Atr.* III, iii, 36–37 in simpler language; see Appendix, no. 14 *ad loc.*

28. For a different view of the parallelism and meaning of OB *Atr.* III, i, 22–23, and *GE* XI, 24–27, see Hoffner, in *Kramer AV,* pp. 241–45.

were intended for Utnaphishtim, though technically addressed to the wall; this was not clear in lines 21 and 22 of *GE* XI, as it was in the fuller context of *Atrahasis* (15–19). Line 27 of *GE* XI adds the important command to take animals on board. That Atrahasis/Utnapishtim did so is clear from the ensuing narrative in both versions (OB *Atr.* III, ii, 32–37; *GE* XI, 85); the version in *Gilgamesh* makes it clear[29] that he was commanded to do so.[30] Similarly, in the following passage (*GE* XI, 35–47), the *Gilgamesh* version has the god instruct the hero in a ruse to fool the townspeople, whereas the *Atrahasis* version simply described its perpetration by the hero (OB *Atr.* III, i, 40–50).[31]

#### i. ABRIDGMENT

An example of abridgment appears in the scene about the gods' distress during the flood.[32]

| ***OB Atr.* III** | ***GE* XI, 113–26** |
|---|---|
| 30. The Anunnaki, the great gods | 113. The gods |
| 31. [Were sitt]ing in thirst and hunger. | Feared the deluge, |
| | 114. They shrank back, they ascended to the heaven of Anu. |
| | 115. The gods, like dogs, were curled up, crouching outside. |
| 32. The goddess saw it as she wept, | 116. Ishtar cries out like a woman giving birth, |

29. In OB *Atr.* III, i, 24 = *GE* XI, 26 the hero is commanded to "save life" (see Hoffner, in *Kramer AV,* pp. 244–45), whose life remaining unspecified.

30. Conversely, other details of the ship's construction (such as the use of bitumen) are commanded in *Atr.* (OB *Atr.* III, i, 30–33), but are mentioned in *GE* only in execution (XI, 54, 65–66).

31. The paronomastic promise to "shower" down abundance in OB *Atr.* III, i, 34–35 is addressed to Atrahasis and is not part of the ruse (on the pun, see Lambert and Millard, p. 159, *ad loc.*). *GE* XI exploits the ambiguity of the pun and makes it part of the ruse (*GE* XI, 43–44, now addressed to the townspeople), supplementing this pun with another also playing upon the ambiguity of the verb "shower" (see Speiser's notes in *ANET,* p. 93, n. 190, p. 94, n. 202; Heidel, p. 82, n. 170). The dual nature of the rain-shower is paralleled in later Jewish sources which state that God made the rain fall slowly at first, so that if the flood generation should repent at the last moment, he would turn the rain into a shower of blessing (commentary of Rashi at Gen. 7:12). In these sources, the flood hero does not deceive his contemporaries about the flood, but, reshaped in the prophetic mold, warns them and urges repentance; hence God's final delay.

32. See Appendix, no. 14.

| | |
|---|---|
| 33. The midwife of the gods, | 117. Wails the Mistress of the Go[ds], |
| The wise Mami: | The sweet-voiced: |
| 34. Let the day be ever dar[k], 35. Let it turn gloo[my], | 118. That day to clay, alas (lit. indeed), turned |
| 36. When I did/ how could I, in the assembly of the gods, | 119. Because I, in the assembly of the gods, |
| 37. Command | commanded |
| 38. With them total destruction." | calamity. |
| | 120. How could I command, in the assembly of the gods, calamity, |
| | 121. For the destruction of my people, (how could I) command battle, |
| (39–54: Mami continues speech, not paralleled in *GE*) (iii, 55–iv, 3: broken) iv, 4. N[intu] wails . . . | |
| 5. "What? Have they given [birth] to the r[olling(?)] | 122. When it is I myself who give birth to my people? |
| 6. Sea? | |
| Like dragonflies | 123. Like the spawn of fishes, |
| 7. They have filled the river! | they fill the sea!" |
| 8. Like a raft they have put in to the ed[ge], | |
| 9. Like a raft. . . . they have put in to the bank. | |
| 10. I have seen and wept over them; | |
| 11. I have ended my lamentation for them." | |
| 12. She wept, and her feelings she eased; | |
| 13. Nintu wailed | |
| 14. And spent her emotion. | |

| | |
|---|---|
| 15. The gods | 124. The gods—<br>those of the Anunnaki— |
| wept with her<br>for the land. | were in tears with her, |
| 16. She was surfeited with grief | |
| 17. And thirsted for beer. | |
| 18. Where she sat,<br>weeping | 125. The gods humbly<br>sit weeping. |
| 19. Sat they.<br>Like sheep | |
| 20. They filled the trough; | |
| 21. Their lips were athirst | 126. Their lips burn (var. are covered), they have contracted |
| with fever. | fever. |
| 22. From hunger | |
| 23. They were suffering cramp. | |

The omission of lengthy sections like OB *Atr.* III, iii, 39 through iv, 4 and iv, 8–14 (parts of the mother-goddess's lament) in *GE* XI may be due to the fact that the editor of the late version of *Gilgamesh* is not interested in the flood story for its own sake and therefore does not describe it in full detail, unlike *Atrahasis,* where the flood is the main theme. In the passage just quoted from *Atrahasis,* the mother-goddess's lament is related to her creation of mankind earlier in *Atrahasis,*[33] a theme in which *GE* XI had no real interest.

The omission of OB *Atr.* III, iv, 16–17, 19b–20, and 22–23 after *GE* XI, 124, 125, and 126, respectively, at the end of the lament scene, seems to call for a more specific explanation, for the dropping of individual lines right in between others which are preserved but are not synonymous with them appears to be a more deliberate editorial act. The surgery is too delicate to be accidental. These lines share a common theme, the hunger and thirst of the gods during the flood. In fact, every passage in the *Atrahasis* version which mentioned or implied divine hunger has been dropped or modified in *GE* XI. We have already quoted OB *Atr.* III, iii, 30–31 ("the great

33. Lambert and Millard, pp. 54–63; cf. OB *Atr.* III, iii, 44 within the lament itself.

gods . . . were sitting in thirst and hunger"), which were replaced in *GE* XI by a description of the gods' fright (113–15). A more telling passage is that describing the immediate aftermath of the flood[34]:

| **OB *Atr.* III, v, 29–37** | ***GE* XI, 155–62** |
|---|---|
| 29. . . . . | 155. Then I let out (all) |
| 30. To the [four] directions (lit. winds). . . . | To the four directions (lit. winds) |
| 31. He offered [a sacrifice. . . .] | And offered a sacrifice. |
| 32. Providing food. . . . | 156. I poured out a libation on the top of the mountain |
| 33. (illegible) | 157. Seven and seven cult vessels I set up, |
| | 158. And beneath them I poured reed, cedar, and myrtle. |
| 34. [The gods smelled] the savor. | 159. The gods smelled the savor, |
| | 160. The gods smelled the sweet savor. |
| 35. [Like flie]s,<br>about the sacrifice | 161. The gods, like flies,<br>about the one who offered the sacrifice |
| they were gathered. | gathered. |
| 36. [After] they had eaten the sacrifice | 162. When at length |
| 37. [Nin]tu arose<br>To complain against them all. | the Mistress of the Gods arrived . . . |

Note especially the modification of "providing food," in line 32 of the *Atrahasis* passage, to "I poured out a libation" and the dropping of line 36, "After they had eaten the sacrifice." This omission, like those cited above, is especially striking, since in each case what was omitted was immediately adjacent to passages which were preserved. For this reason, it does not seem that we can explain these omissions by the different interests of the writers of the *Gilgamesh* and *Atrahasis* epics, for the adjacent passages which were pre-

34. See Appendix, no. 15.

served could just as well have been dropped: References to the gods' weeping and their feverish lips would be no less dispensable, if the editor's criterion had been merely conciseness, in a context where the interest is not in the flood for its own sake. That the editor was specifically interested in removing references to divine thirst and hunger[35] is borne out by two passages which were modified instead of dropped, for here we can see just what it was that the editor wanted out:

> *ṣa-mi-a ša-ap-ta-šu-nu bu-ul-ḫi-ta,* "their lips were athirst with fever" (OB *Atr.* III, iv, 21), became *šab-ba* (var. *kàt-ma*) *šap-ta-šú-nu le-qa-a bu-uḫ-re-e-ti,* "their lips burn (var. are covered), they have contracted fever" (*GE* XI, 126).

> (*ilū* . . .) [*ki-ma zu-ub-b*]*i e-lu ni-qí-i pa-aḫ-ru,* "(the gods . . .) were gathered [like flie]s over the sacrifice" (OB *Atr.* III, v, 35), became *ilāni ki-ma zu-um-bé-e eli bēl niqî ip-taḫ-ru,* "the gods gathered like flies over the one who offered the sacrifice" (*GE* XI, 161).

The latter passage is especially telling, for the reference to Utnapishtim as "the one who offered the sacrifice" is completely uncalled for in a narrative where Utnapishtim has consistently referred to himself in the first person.[36] These omissions and modifications add up to a systematic elimination of implications that the gods starved and thirsted during the flood. If this was indeed the

35. A reference to the shipboard banquet of Atrahasis' family was also dropped (OB *Atr.* III, ii, 40–44). Was this activity felt to be insensitive on the eve of the catastrophe? Cf. Atrahasis' own mood on that occasion (45–47).

36. Except for the trace of third-person narrative remaining in line 37 (see below, n. 43). Note that the switch in line 161 is not a simple switch from first to third person, accomplished by prefixes alone, such as one finds in MSS of *GE* VIII, ii, 16–21 (see chap. 6, n. 18).

Line 161 has been cited almost since its discovery as an example of the crude anthropomorphism of the Mesopotamian flood story, because it was thought to show divine ravenousness and starvation during and after the flood. Ironically, it turns out that the formulation of this line seeks to soften that impression. The simile of flies, it may be added, simply expresses swarming (cf. *ilū ša Uruk supūri ittūru ana zumbē iḫabbubu ina rebâti,* "the gods of Uruk (of?) the sheepfold became (like) flies buzzing in the squares," K3200:12, in *GETh.*, p. 91 and pl. 59; cf. also Kramer, *JAOS* 89:8). That it was probably not intended in a derogatory way emerges from the discussion of comparisons in Lowth, 1:252–53. Lowth cites *inter alia Iliad* 2:552: "Like the multitudinous nations of swarming insects/Who drive hither and thither about the stalls of the sheepfold/In the season of spring when the milk splashes in the milk pails" (translation from Lattimore, p. 88, where the passage is numbered 2:469–71). Note also that the images there and in the *Atr.* passage, unlike *GE* XI, 161, are realistic: Flies gather about the object of their appetite (the sacrifice, not the sacrificer).

editor's intention, it is, so far as I know, unprecedented and startling, for the dependence of the gods upon man for food is an axiom of Mesopotamian religious thought.[37]

## HARMONIZATION OF THE FLOOD STORY WITH THE REST OF *GILGAMESH*

A few of the modifications in the flood story in the late version of *Gilgamesh* have the effect of harmonizing the story with the content and style of the rest of the epic.

### *The Name of the Flood Hero*

An immediately noticeable difference between *GE* XI and all known versions of *Atrahasis* is the name of the survivor of the flood: Utnapishtim in *Gilgamesh,* as against Atrahasis in the source. Atrahasis means "exceedingly *(atra)* wise *(ḫasis),*" while Utnapishtim is generally understood to mean "he found *(ūta)* life *(napištim).*"[38] The name Utnapishtim is known outside of the epic,[39] and therefore may not have been created for the epic, but only adopted for it by the Old Babylonian author. In fact, the name seems to be an interpretation of the Sumerian version of the flood hero's name, Zi-u$_4$-sud-rá, "life of long days."[40] Reversing the first two elements of the Sumerian name (yielding u$_4$-zi), then giving u$_4$ its value ut; next translating Sumerian zi correctly as *napištim,* "life," and Sumerian sud-rá correctly as *rūqu,* "long, far," yields *Utnapištim rēqu/rūqu,* the standard name and epithet of the flood

37. OB *Atr.* I; *En El; Pessimistic Dialogue,* § 7 (Biggs, in *ANET,* p. 601c).

38. See Heidel, p. 227, n. 5; Speiser, in *ANET,* p. 90, n. 164; cf. *CAD* $A_2$, p. 521a; contrast von Soden, *JNES* 19:165. The OB version apparently uses a slightly different form with perhaps the same meaning, Utanai[sht]im; see Gilg. Me. iv, 6, 13 (see von Soden and *CAD* locc. citt.; in several translations this has been emended to Utanapishtim; see Heidel, p. 71, n. 151).

39. Lambert and Millard, p. 137; for the MA form Utnapushte, see *BWL,* p. 95, ll. 2, 4, and p. 334.

40. Cf. Hallo, *JCS* 20:139–41, ll. 18, 20: zi-u$_4$-sù(SUD) parallel to mu-da-rí, "enduring years" (though the latter phrase is translated otherwise in l. 24). Note that this passage associates zi-u$_4$-sù(SUD) with an attribute similar in meaning to the name Atrahasis: giš-tú$^{\text{geštug}}$ dag[al], "extensive wisdom" (ibid., l. 21).

hero in *Gilgamesh.*[41] The epic probably understands the name as "he, the faraway, found life," as suggested by the frequent references in *Gilgamesh* to "finding life" *(balāṭam atû),* in the course of Gilgamesh's search for and meeting with Utnapishtim.[42] And this must be the reason for *The Gilgamesh Epic*'s preference for this version of the name instead of Atrahasis, for it expresses the reason why Gilgamesh sought out the survivor of the flood: The latter had found life, which Gilgamesh hoped to find.

## *First-person Narration*

The choice of the flood hero's name thus indicates adaptation of the *Atrahasis* flood story to the theme of *The Gilgamesh Epic.* Another important adaptation is the first-person narration of the flood story by Utnapishtim. In *Atrahasis* (and the Sumerian *Deluge*), the narration is phrased in the third person, as is typical of mythical texts. The shift in *Gilgamesh*[43] is due to the fact that Gilgamesh meets with Utnapishtim and hears the story from him firsthand in response to his inquiry about how Utnapishtim became immortal. This adaptation has a precedent in the Ras Shamra fragment of the flood story, where Atrahasis is the narrator.[44] The redactor of *GE* XI did not necessarily have to rely upon a precedent for such a simple and appropriate shift, but since *GE* XI shares another detail with the Ras Shamra fragment,[45] the latter may well reflect a Mesopotamian

41. See Komoróczy, *Act. Ant.* 23:60–61; Oberhuber, pp. 309–10. In this connection it is interesting to note a suggestion by G. R. Driver explaining the biblical name Noah on the basis of Ethiopic *noḫä,* "be long" (cited by Barr, *Comparative,* p. 48, n. 1). However, in view of Akkadian and Amorite personal names based on *nwḫ,* "rest, be satisfied" (*APNM,* p. 237; Stamm, *Namengebung,* pp. 79, 85, 168–69, 291), Noah is more likely derived from the latter root.

42. Cf. Gilg. Me. i, 8; ii, 10; iii, 2; *GE* XI, 198. In view of these puns, I am not persuaded that in the late version the name should be read Ūm-napishtim, "day of life," short for "the day of life is extended" (Ravn, *Ac. Or.* 22:49), although this interpretation has the virtue of accounting for the genitive form of *napištim,* which is otherwise unexplained.

43. A trace of the third-person narrative survives in *GE* XI, 37, *i-zak-ka-ra ana ardi-šú ia-a-tú,* "(Ea) said to his servant, me." Apparently the line originally read "(Ea) said to his servant," as in *Atr.* (OB *Atr.* I, 373; III, i, 16); the editor added "me," but (neglectfully?) did not drop "his servant" (the resulting apposition is not ungrammatical or contrary to accepted style; see *GAG,* § 134b; Hecker, p. 128, n. 1; *LH* prologue, i, 27–31; *GE* I, ii, 24; XI, 28, 194).

44. See n. 5, above.

45. See n. 13 above, and the related part of the text.

text tradition lying behind the *Gilgamesh* version. If so, this is another case where the editor of the late version of *Gilgamesh* was able to choose among available traditions, rather than rewrite freely.

## *Theological Changes*

Unlike the *Atrahasis* version, which shows the reason for the gods' decision to bring the flood, *GE* XI gives none, apparently because this is irrelevant to its purpose of explaining how Utnapishtim became immortal.[46] However, *Gilgamesh* makes certain theological modifications. On the one hand, it introduces Shamash into the narrative, and somewhat abruptly, having him tell Utnapishtim when to board his ship (86).[47] This god had played no real role in the *Atrahasis* version. Since he is an important character in *Gilgamesh,* this change may be the work of an editor of the latter. In another theological modification, *GE* XI exempts Anu from blame for the flood.[48]

## *Stylistic Changes*

On the stylistic level, *GE* XI introduces two scenes with one of the epic's frequently used formulas, "with the first glow of dawn" *(mimmû šēri ina namāri).* Several episodes in *Gilgamesh* begin with this phrase, which does not appear in *Atrahasis* and may, in fact, be unique to *Gilgamesh.*[49]

46. Matouš, *Ar. Or.* 35:12.

47. Noted by Böhl, *RLA* 3:370. In *Atr.* Enki/Ea plays this role (OB *Atr.* III, i, 36; *Atr.* W, 5).

48. Cf. Laessøe, *Bi. Or.* 13:96; Lambert and Millard, p. 163, *sub* col. v, 39–43. Note also how references to Anu in OB *Atr.* III, iii, 53; v, 42; vi, 11–12 are eliminated in *GE* XI, 168, 174, 179. Other gods participated in the flood decision, but *GE* reserves blame for Enlil, perhaps in light of such passages as OB *Atr.* I, 352ff.; II, i, 1ff.; viii, 35.

49. See Introduction, n. 25. According to Hecker, pp. 201–2 (cf. 172), this formula is not attested prior to the MB period. It may be unique to *Gilgamesh,* and if so it would constitute an intentional adaptation of the flood story to the style of *GE* and would not be due simply to the common formulary of Mesopotamian epics.

## NONHARMONIZATION OF THE FLOOD STORY WITH THE REST OF *GILGAMESH*

In contrast to these changes whereby the flood account was adapted to *The Gilgamesh Epic,* a number of stylistic differences remain which reflect the flood story's original independence of *Gilgamesh.*

### *Vocabulary*

*GE* XI, as we have noted, has two components, the part of the tablet concerned with the flood and the "nonflood" portion describing Gilgamesh's encounter with Utnapishtim. During Utnapishtim's account of the flood, his wife is called his *sinništu,* literally "woman" (191, 194), while in the rest of the tablet she is termed his *marḫītu,* "spouse" (202, 205, 209, 258). Since both terms refer to the same woman, and each term is restricted to a separate component of the tablet, the differences clearly represent vocabulary preferences of the components in this particular tablet. Unfortunately, all passages in *Atrahasis* which might have referred to the survivor's wife are missing, and we cannot document the inference that *sinništu* was taken from *Atrahasis.*[50] The *Akkadisches Handwörterbuch* does not cite examples of *sinništu* used with the meaning "wife" in other literary texts,[51] but it cites several examples from Neo-Assyrian and Late Babylonian nonliterary texts.[52] Since the examples are limited to first-millennium texts, we may infer that the word was taken into *Gilgamesh* from a late version of *Atrahasis.*

Although the flood and nonflood components of *GE* XI are thus distinguished from each other by the terms used in each for wife, these preferences are only ad hoc; they are not parts of distinctive vocabularies consistently preferred by the larger sources (*Atrahasis* and *Gilgamesh*) from which these two components, respectively, come. True, within *GE* XI, *sinništu* is used for wife only in the section taken over from *Atrahasis,* but it also appears elsewhere in the late version of *Gilgamesh* in passages which obviously are not from *Atrahasis* (IX, ii, 13, 15). And although only *marḫītu* is used

50. In OB *Atr.* I, 276, 300, the word used for wife is *aššatu.*

51. The only other examples cited on p. 1047d, *sub* 5d, are from *GE* IX, ii, 13, 15.

52. *AHw,* p. 1047c, *sub* 4c.

for wife in that part of *GE* XI composed by a writer of *Gilgamesh,* elsewhere the epic uses other terms for wife.[53]

## *Formulas*

The second difference is formulaic. Outside of the flood narrative, the Utnapishtim section (*GE* X, iv–vi and Tablet XI) consistently uses a single formula for introducing speeches: "A said to him (or her), to B" (A *ana šâšu/šâšima izzakkar(a) ana* B).[54] This formula is used earlier in the epic, too (see p. 61). According to Sonneck, this formula is unique to *Gilgamesh,* but it is found in the Old Babylonian as well as the late version. In fact it is used in the Old Babylonian version of *GE* X, which describes the events leading up to Gilgamesh's meeting with Utnapishtim.[55] The formula was, therefore, presumably taken over from the Old Babylonian version. Within the flood narrative in *GE* XI, on the other hand, a different formula is consistently used: "A opened his mouth to speak, saying to B" (A *pâšu īpušamma iqabbi izzakkara ana* B).[56] According to Sonneck, this particular formula is found only in late texts.[57] Here, then, we have two different formulas, each restricted to one of the component parts of the Utnapishtim section and clearly reflecting the vocabulary of that component. In this case we have an added advantage in that the sources from which these formulas were taken over are preserved. Fragments of the late version of the flood portion of *Atrahasis* employ the formula which is used in the flood portion of *GE* XI[58] (the parallel passages in the Old Babylonian version of *Atrahasis* use older formulas[59]). The formula used in the nonflood part of GE XI is the only one used in the account, in the Old Babylonian version of *Gilgamesh,* of Gilgamesh's journey to Utnapishtim.[60]

53. *sinništu,* as noted; *ḫīrtu,* I, ii, 17, 28; *aššatu,* VI, 9; *marḫītu* is also used in Gilg. Me. iii, 13.

54. *GE* XI, 1, 8, 202, 205, 209, 219, 222, 229, 234, 258, 263, 302. Cf. Sonneck, pp. 225–35; see p. 228, no. 8.

55. Gilg. Me. i, 9; ii, 14; iv, 4, 7, 14; Gilg. Mi. iii, 2, 11; iv, 6.

56. *GE* XI, 36, 37, 174, 177.

57. Sonneck, pp. 227 (no. 3), 234.

58. *Atr.* S, ii, 8; iv, 21–22, 29–30 (different word order); U obv. 13–14; W, 11–12; x rev. ii, [1], 14, 44 (different word order).

59. OB *Atr.* III, vi, 11–12, 16–17; see Sonneck, pp. 226–27, no. 1.

60. See nn. 54 and 55, above.

In this case, too, some of the preferences are only ad hoc, and do not extend throughout the larger sources from which these parts come. Although one of the formulas is unique to *Gilgamesh,* elsewhere in *Gilgamesh* one sometimes finds the formula which in *GE* XI is restricted to the flood story.[61] On the other hand, late *Atrahasis* texts sometimes use other formulas for introducing speeches, in one case even within the flood narrative.[62] Here, too, then, the formulaic difference is restricted to the Utnapishtim section and the formulas are not exclusive and characteristic features of the larger sources by which one could identify a particular source, if and when it should appear elsewhere.

## *Style*

The third difference between the flood portion and the rest of *GE* XI is stylistic in the broadest sense of the word, and in this case the difference is one of degree, rather than kind. Repetitiousness and homogeneity are well-known features of epic style.[63] Akkadian and Sumerian epics, like others, are filled with proposals and their execution, messages and their delivery, repeated speeches, identical introductions to successive episodes, instructions conveyed through third parties followed by their transmission and execution, all repeated in virtually identical terms. The late version of *Gilgamesh,* far more than its Old Babylonian forerunner, is characterized by this kind of style. An outstanding case is found in the tenth tablet of the late version in the descriptions of Gilgamesh's separate encounters with the barmaid, Utnapishtim's boatman, and finally with Utnapishtim himself. The barmaid and Utnapishtim spot the approaching Gilgamesh from afar, and the thoughts of each are introduced in identical terms.[64] Although each encounter begins with unique actions and ends with unique advice, all three contain the same long dialogue in which Gilgamesh is presumably asked who

61. E.g., *GE* I, iii, 1, 13.

62. Lambert and Millard, pp. 122–23, l. 4.

63. For Sumerian epics, see Kramer, "Sumerian Epic Literature," pp. 832–33; for Akkadian epics, see Hecker, esp. chap. 3; Cooper, *JAOS* 97:508–12, and "Gilgamesh." See also above, pp. 100–103.

64. *GE* X, i, 10–12; iv, 12–14. The section which would have contained a similar passage about Urshanabi is missing. See also above, pp. 81–99, esp. 95–99.

he is (to judge from his answer in X, i, 31ff.) and why he appears so worn and sad; in response he describes his achievements, his adventures with Enkidu, Enkidu's death, and his own fear of dying. In at least two of the encounters, Gilgamesh asks for directions to Utnapishtim, in identical terms.[65] The meeting with Utnapishtim's boatman includes instructions which Gilgamesh follows to the letter.[66]

When we come to Utnapishtim's account of the flood in Tablet XI, based on *Atrahasis,* this homogenized, repetitious style appears only sporadically and in short passages. Earlier in this chapter, in passages where comparison with the text of *Atrahasis* was possible, we noted two cases of assimilation (sec. g, pp. 220–21). The formula "with the first glow of dawn" introduces two sections (XI, 48, 96), as do "when the seventh day arrived" (128, 145) and "when at length (the deity so-and-so) arrived" (162, 170). Several passages have series of lines with identical beginnings or endings: "three *šar* . . ." (65–67); "whatever I had . . . I laded upon her" (80–93); "Mount Niṣir held the ship fast, allowing no motion; one day, a second day, Mount Niṣir, (etc.)" (141–44); "the gods" (used as subject, ll. 159–61, with the same verb and object in two of the three lines); "instead of your bringing the deluge, would that . . . had risen up to diminish mankind" (183–86). But the only sequence of identical actions identically described is the releasing of the birds (146–54), and only once is there a sequence of instruction followed by exact execution (86–90, 93, the stated time for boarding the ship and Utnapishtim's doing so). Most telling, there is no coordination at all between Ea's instructions about the ship and its passengers and the actual building and loading (27–31, 50–85), and no description of Utnapishtim's carrying out the ruse in which Ea instructed him (38–47). Only the last two lines of Ea's speech are later repeated, in the passage about boarding the ship (87, 90), but there they are spoken by Shamash, and not to the audience for whom they were originally intended (note the second-person-plural dative suffix in l. 47 and its absence in ll. 87 and 90).

But as soon as the flood story is over, *GE* XI reverts to large-scale repetition and homogeneity. Four examples appear in rapid

65. See above, p. 99, n. 60.
66. *GE* X, iii, 40–46.

succession: Utnapishtim's instructions to his wife to bake wafers and her compliance (211–14); the aging of the wafers and Utnapishtim's account of this to Gilgamesh (215–18, 225–28); Utnapishtim's instructions to Urshanabi and the latter's compliance (239–55); and the speeches of Utnapishtim's wife and Utnapishtim about a consolation prize for Gilgamesh (259–60, 264–65). Utnapishtim introduces his description of the rejuvenating plant with the same couplet with which he introduced the flood story: "I will reveal (to you), O Gilgamesh, a hidden matter, and a secret of the gods I will tell you (9–10, 266–67). The nonflood portion of *GE* XI was thus written in the style characteristic of the late version of *The Gilgamesh Epic,* which rarely missed an opportunity to homogenize related passages,[67] while little was done to revise the flood story so that it would conform more completely to that style.

Here again, the style displayed in the nonflood parts of *GE* XI cannot be said to be distinctive of the late version of *The Gilgamesh Epic* as against *The Atrahasis Epic,* on the whole. *Atrahasis* is filled with repetition and homogenization. Only in its version of the flood, so far as we can tell, does this style appear but minimally. For example, the account of the building of the boat in *Atrahasis* goes far beyond anything Atrahasis could have been instructed to do by Enki.[68] This kind of deviation from the normal homogenized style of *Atrahasis* is reflected in the minimal repetitiousness of the *Gilgamesh* flood story. But since this style is otherwise the rule in *Atrahasis,* one could not use repetition and homogenization for assigning other passages besides the flood story in *The Gilgamesh Epic* to the editor of the late version nor their absence for assigning other passages to the author of *The Atrahasis Epic.* Within *GE* XI, however, there is a clear quantitative divergence in the pursuit of this style, and along with the use of different words for wife and a different formula for introducing speeches, this is another indication that the flood account found in *GE* XI was not extensively

67. An exception is found in *GE* X, iv, 1–8, where there is no description of Gilgamesh's compliance with Urshanabi's instructions. In I, iii, 25–39, the hunter's compliance does not match his father's advice exactly (14–24). Note also *GE* I, vi, 16 in comparison to v, 39.

68. Though the text of the instructions and their execution is extensively damaged in the OB version, one can see that the latter (OB *Atr.* III, ii–iii) is far longer than the former (OB *Atr.* III, i, 22–33). The later versions are also incomplete at these points.

revised when it was incorporated into the epic. It retained several features of its original style, even though these differed from the style of its new locus in *Gilgamesh.*

The *Atrahasis* flood story has thus been incorporated into *The Gilgamesh Epic* in a form which differs considerably, in wording, style, content, and apparently ideology, from the Old Babylonian version of that story. At least some of these changes are due to the editor of the late version of *Gilgamesh* having relied upon a late version (or versions) of *Atrahasis.* We have noted a few cases where the changes assimilate the story to the needs and interests (and, in one case [sec. b, 5, p. 219] vocabulary) of *The Gilgamesh Epic,* but even some of these cases may have been based on late versions of *Atrahasis* or other flood traditions. We have also noted areas where the editor has failed to adapt the flood narrative to the style and formulation of the rest of the late version of *Gilgamesh.* On the whole, there is very little evidence for changes on the part of the editor of the late version of *Gilgamesh,* and one gets the impression that he incorporated the story largely as he found it in one or more versions that were available to him.

## ARTISTIC UNITY IN THE UTNAPISHTIM SECTION

Despite this, the flood story in *GE* XI displays verbal and thematic ties with the rest of the Utnapishtim section which lend a degree of artistic unity to the section as a whole. Ea's command that Utnapishtim "seek life" (*še'i napšati,* XI, 25) echoes Gilgamesh's own quest and that which he attributes to Utnapishtim (*balāṭam še'û/ bu'û/erēšu/saḫāru,* "seek/seek/ask for/pursue life," *GE* I, i, 39; XI, 7, 198, 203; Gilg. Me. i, 8; iii, 2), as well as Utnapishtim's own name ("He Found Life"). Utnapishtim's name is also echoed paronomastically in Enlil's angry demand "Wherefrom (i.e. how) has life escaped?" (*ūṣi napišti,* XI, 173). The theme of revealing the gods' secret to Utnapishtim (186–87) is echoed twice as the latter reveals secrets of the gods to Gilgamesh (9–10, 266–67). Twice crying is described with the formula "tears running down the side of his/my nose" (*eli dūr ap-pi-ia/šú il-la-ka di-ma-a-a/šú;* 137, 291).[69] Week-long sequences figure both in the flood account (76[?], 127–29, 142–

69. This formula is also found in *Nergal and Ereshkigal, STT,* no. 28, col. iv, 52′ (*ANET,* p. 510).

45) and in Gilgamesh's slumber afterwards (199–208).[70] Two of these items are already attested in pre-*Gilgamesh* flood accounts: the week-long duration of the flood in the Sumerian *Deluge* (203) and the phrase *ūṣi napištim* in the Old Babylonian *Atrahasis* (III, vi, 9). The other passages just cited from the *Gilgamesh* flood story are not present in known texts of *Atrahasis* (the late version of the *Atrahasis* flood story survives, however, only in brief fragments). While this leaves open the possibility that these lines were composed by the editor of the late version of *Gilgamesh* for the very purpose of creating literary links between the components of Tablet XI, this does not seem to be the case. The links are mostly not verbatim repetitions,[71] whereas verbatim repetition of motifs and formulas is the hallmark of the late version of *Gilgamesh* outside of the flood story.[72] The verbal and thematic links between the components of Tablet XI seem to be due, not to the free hand of the editor, but to vocabulary, formulas, and motifs shared by many Akkadian epic texts, not just *Gilgamesh* and *Atrahasis,*[73] and to the fact that the flood story was relevant to *Gilgamesh* precisely because it shared a theme with *Gilgamesh* (seeking life).

## THE ADDITION OF THE FLOOD STORY TO *GILGAMESH*

The use of a late formula for introducing speeches in the flood narrative of *GE* XI provides a clue to when this narrative was introduced into the epic. As we have noted, already in the Old Babylonian version of *The Gilgamesh Epic,* Gilgamesh traveled to meet Utnapishtim and presumably reached him, but this does not necessarily imply that Utnapishtim recounted the whole flood story in the Old Babylonian version. In fact, the use of the late formula in *GE* XI implies that the flood story was joined with the rest of the epic only in the late version (which dates to the last half or quarter of the second millennium). The use of the late formula in the flood narrative in *GE* XI shows that this portion of the tablet underwent

70. See Introduction, n. 23.

71. Two exceptions are the formulas "with the first glow of dawn" and "tears running down the side of his/my nose."

72. Allowing for slight variation. See Hecker, pp. 157ff.

73. See von Soden, "Hymnisch-epische Dialekt"; Hecker, chap. 6.

a particular modernization which the rest of *GE* XI escaped. It is scarcely plausible that *after* the flood story was joined to the epic, only that story had its speech introductions modernized while the rest of the tablet did not.[74] We must therefore infer that prior to the late version of *Gilgamesh,* the flood narrative was not part of the Utnapishtim section and that it was taken into *Gilgamesh* from a late version of *Atrahasis,* one dating from a time when the late formula was in vogue.[75] (This conforms to our inference above that the *Gilgamesh* flood story is based on late versions of *Atrahasis,* not on the Old Babylonian version.) The rest of *GE* XI, on the other hand, must have reached its present form, at least with respect to its speech introductions, in isolation from these conditions.

The late entry of the flood narrative into the epic raises the question of why it was added. In the context of the epic the story serves a purpose quite different from what must have been its original purpose[76]: By telling his story to Gilgamesh, Utnapishtim shows him that his own attainment of immortality was due to a set of unique, unrepeatable circumstances. But one wonders whether this necessitated so detailed an account. If this account was first added in the late version, the Old Babylonian version was presumably able to make the point without a full rehearsal of the flood. This only makes more acute the question of why a late editor felt he needed it, especially since the story was available to readers and listeners in *The Atrahasis Epic.*

Perhaps the contribution of the full account to *Gilgamesh* is not to be found in its meaning, but in its artistic function as a digression within the epic. With Gilgamesh having finally reached Utnapishtim, the epic's audience is anxious to know whether he will at long last learn the secret of immortality, a secret the audience, too, would no doubt like to learn.[77] Depending on individual members

74. The late formula appears elsewhere in *GE* (see n. 61 above) in a sporadic manner which suggests natural evolution, rather than systematic revision.

75. Sonneck, p. 232, notes that the switch from formula no. 1 to no. 3 is found in the late version of *Gilgamesh* and *Atr.,* as compared to their OB versions; cf. the texts cited in n. 16, above.

76. Presumably at one time the story was told because of the intrinsic interest of the flood (this may be reflected in the Ras Shamra fragment; see n. 5, above). In *Atrahasis* it has already been subordinated to an etiological purpose: to help explain human infertility, infant mortality, and the existence of women who may not give birth. See Kilmer; Leichty, "Demons," p. 26.

77. *GE* XI tantalizes the audience by having Utnapishtim introduce his account as if he is about to give Gilgamesh the help he wants: "I will reveal to you, Gilgamesh, a hidden matter,/And a secret of the gods will I tell you" (ll. 9–10).

of the audience, the digression may have the effect of building suspense or relaxing it. Perhaps at the beginning of the flood narrative the suspense would be heightened, but as the narrative continues, its own intrinsic interest would begin to distract attention from Gilgamesh's quest and ultimately relax the suspense over that quest. Such relaxation might help prepare the audience's mood for Utnapishtim's disappointing answer and the subdued conclusion of the epic. Like all such suggestions, this one is obviously speculative.

The way in which the flood story was taken into the epic contrasts markedly with the way in which the traditional and borrowed materials discussed in Chapters 7 through 11 were incorporated. With the exception of a few brief passages which seem to have been borrowed literally from other compositions or from popular usage, in those chapters we were, on the whole, unable to point to passages borrowed textually from other compositions. This could be due in part to the incompleteness of our knowledge. Perhaps there was, for example, an Akkadian hymn to Gilgamesh, undiscovered by modern scholars, from which the hymnic introduction to the Old Babylonian version was borrowed virtually verbatim. But in most cases it seems no accident that we find no direct textual source for traditional and borrowed material. Much of the borrowed material we have studied entered the epic in the Old Babylonian version, and the author of that version seems to have exercised the greatest amount of freedom in recasting his source material. Furthermore, much of the material discussed in Chapters 9 through 11 was not originally about characters or situations in *The Gilgamesh Epic,* and it required extensive modification before it could be used in the epic. None of this applies to the flood story. Not only was this story added to the epic by a late editor, who took considerably less liberty with his source material, but prior to its appearance in *Gilgamesh,* this was already a story about the survivor of the flood who tells it to Gilgamesh. Hence the story needed relatively little modification to render it suitable for its new context in *The Gilgamesh Epic.*[78]

78. The editor who added a translation of the second half of *GEN* as *GE* XII modified his source even less; see pp. 105–7.

# *Summary: The Evolution of* The Gilgamesh Epic

We may summarize the development of *The Gilgamesh Epic* as follows.

The historical Gilgamesh was a king of Uruk during the Second Early Dynastic Period in Sumer (ca. 2700–2500). Later inscriptions credit him with building the wall of Uruk and rebuilding a shrine in Nippur. This by itself is hardly the stuff of which epics are made, and Gilgamesh's place in epic tradition is presumably due to more colorful achievements which have not come down to us in sources of a historical character. The adventures of Gilgamesh mentioned in the Sumerian stories and the Akkadian epic are so overlaid with legendary and mythical motifs that one can only speculate about their possible historical basis. They may reflect certain aspects of the magical/priestly and military roles that Gilgamesh would have played as the ruler of Uruk, and conceivably a real preoccupation of his with death. On the other hand, some elements in these stories may be anachronistic projections of later events, and some are due to folkloristic and mythological imagination.

By the twenty-fifth century, Gilgamesh was regarded as a god. It is possible that the transition from oral to written transmission of stories about Gilgamesh may have begun by about this time. The Old Sumerian texts from Abu Salabikh date from approximately this period. Although none of them is about Gilgamesh, some are forerunners (in one case, virtually identical) of other literary works which, like the Sumerian Gilgamesh texts, are known to us in Old Babylonian copies (ca. 2000–1600). It is therefore not implausible that tales of Gilgamesh had likewise been put into writing by the twenty-fifth century (a tale about Gilgamesh reportedly found among the tablets from Ebla would confirm this). This would considerably reduce the period of exclusively oral transmission, but for the present, apart from the reported Ebla text, the earliest compositions about Gilgamesh known to us are the Sumerian tales, attested in Old Babylonian copies, but currently presumed to have been composed in the Ur III Period (ca. twenty-first century), something like half a millennium after Gilgamesh's lifetime.

At least seven separate Sumerian compositions about Gilgamesh are known, four of them highly mythical in character. These four were drawn on in different ways in the course of the development of the Akkadian *Gilgamesh Epic.* The Akkadian epic was given its original shape in the Old Babylonian Period by an Akkadian author who took over, in greater or lesser degree, the plots and themes of three or four of the Sumerian tales *(Gilgamesh and the Land of the Living; Gilgamesh, Enkidu, and the Netherworld; The Death of Gilgamesh;* and possibly *Gilgamesh and the Bull of Heaven).* Either translating freely from Sumerian or working from available Akkadian paraphrases, the author combined these plots and themes into a unified epic on a grand scale. As the central idea in this epic, the author seized upon a theme which was adumbrated in three of the Sumerian tales, Gilgamesh's concern with death and his futile desire to overcome it. The author advanced this theme to a central position in the story. To this end, Enkidu's death became the pivotal event which set Gilgamesh on a feverish search for the immortal flood hero (whose story existed in Sumerian, but had nothing to do with the tales about Gilgamesh), hoping to learn how he had overcome death. The author separated the themes of Enkidu's death and Gilgamesh's grief from their original context in the Sumerian *Gilgamesh, Enkidu, and the Netherworld* and placed them after the friends' victory over Huwawa (and possibly over the Bull of Heaven). To increase the emotional impact that Enkidu's death had on Gilgamesh, and perhaps to make the depth of Gilgamesh's grief more plausible, the author seized upon one or two references to Enkidu in the Sumerian sources as Gilgamesh's friend, rather than servant, and treated him consistently as Gilgamesh's friend and equal. He even went so far as to compose accounts of Gilgamesh's oppression of Uruk, and Enkidu's creation and early life, in order to explain why Enkidu was created and how he became Gilgamesh's friend.

The Sumerian tale that the Old Babylonian author drew upon most directly was *Gilgamesh and the Land of the Living,* which became the basis of the Cedar Mountain episode in the Akkadian epic. Among the important changes introduced in the Old Babylonian version of this episode are a complete reshaping of Gilgamesh's plans for the expedition, a new understanding of the role of Shamash and of the significance of Huwawa, and a new location for the Cedar Forest. Several of these changes reflected the new geographical orientation of Mesopotamian affairs in the Old Babylonian Period and the roles of Gilgamesh, Shamash, and Huwawa in Mesopotamian religion. Another Sumerian tale which was drawn upon in the Akkadian epic was *Gilgamesh and the Bull of Heaven,* which became the basis of the Bull of Heaven episode in Tablet VI. However, it is uncertain whether this story was incorporated into the epic in the Old Babylonian Period, or not until later. The Akkadian version of this story appears to have preserved traces of the anti-Ishtar tendencies of the Sumerian original and even added to them. Drawing upon sacred-marriage literature or rituals, the Akkadian version of this episode gave an entirely new cause for the conflict between Gilgamesh and Ishtar: Gilgamesh's spurning of Ishtar's proposal of marriage.

In addition to what he borrowed from the Sumerian tales about Gilgamesh, the Old Babylonian author added a hymnic introduction, in the style of Sumerian hymns about Gilgamesh and other kings (this hymn is still reflected, possibly in expanded form, in part c of the introduction in the late version). He further unified the epic with recurrent thematic and verbal motifs. He continued the process, already begun in the Sumerian tales, of drawing upon conventional formulas and wisdom sayings. One such saying, telling Gilgamesh how to enjoy his earthly life, since only the gods are immortal, looks like the author's message to the epic's audience.

By the Middle Babylonian Period (1600–1000), the epic was known internationally, both in Akkadian and in Hittite and Hurrian translations, with a little adaptation to the interests of the translators. The Akkadian version(s) of this period, as attested by fragmentary remains and, indirectly, by the Hittite translation, retained some similarities to the wording of the Old Babylonian version, but these witnesses also indicate that the wording of the epic was moving in the direction of the late version, at times coming quite close.

Toward the end of the Middle Babylonian Period, by the last half or quarter of the second millennium, the epic had attained a form which thereafter became standard throughout Mesopotamia. Although this late version is textually related to the Old Babylonian version and although its basic form, plot, and apparently its message do not differ from those of the Old Babylonian version, the late version displays considerable divergence from the Old Babylonian. Lines are reworded in degrees varying from negligible to complete, with some lines being dropped and many more added. In some cases the reformulation modernizes the language of the epic, and in a few cases the older text has been simplified, corrupted, or misunderstood; in many other cases, the editor seems to have simply revised according to his taste. Lines and sections are revised so as to be much more similar to related lines and sections in the late version, resulting in a repetitious, pedantic, and homogenized style. Numerous thematic and verbal motifs recur throughout the epic. In addition, entire sections or episodes are restructured. Certain theological changes occur. In one section, the sun-god is given a more direct role. Hostility to Ishtar seems to have run its course, to the extent that her claim to the Inanna temple is recognized, but that hostility is still reflected atavistically in the Bull of Heaven episode. The national gods Marduk and Ashur have not been admitted to this version, presumably because they had not attained sufficient prominence by the time that this version was formulated, and later, when they had, the epic had attained its standardized form and was no longer subject to theological revision.

Three major additions, attested at least for now only in copies of the late version, but not necessarily all added at the same time by the same editor, are the prologue, the flood story, and Tablet XII. The prologue, modeled on conventional literary forms, stresses the didactic significance of the epic, underscores its message with a passage that frames the first eleven tablets, and suggests that the epic is based on an inscription written by Gilgamesh himself. The flood narrative spells out at length what Utnapishtim presumably told Gilgamesh more briefly in the Old Babylonian version; this narrative is based on a late version of *Atrahasis* and was taken into *The Gilgamesh Epic* without too much modification (although the version in *Gilgamesh* seems to have intentionally suppressed references to divine thirst and hunger). Tablet XII brings the epic's picture of Gilgamesh closer to the role of ruler of the netherworld in which he was familiar in Mesopotamian religion. This tablet is a literal translation of part of a Sumerian composition, with minimal but significant deviations from the original. The addition of Tablet XII could be connected with the interest of incantation priests, like Sîn-leqi-unninnī, in Gilgamesh as ruler of the netherworld. With the late version, the epic achieved its maximal stability in content and wording, with only a small number of relatively insignificant variants separating its manuscripts.

There is no way of determining how many stages the epic went through between the Old Babylonian version known to us and the late version. Revision could have begun as early as the Old Babylonian Period and could be reflected in some of the fragments of the Middle Babylonian Period. Those fragments may reflect two or three different intermediate stages. They do not demonstrably represent the penultimate stage on which the final editor based his work, but since these fragments are at times quite close to the wording of the late version, it is possible that the final revision which produced that version was not very extensive. A comparison of the Middle Babylonian fragments with the late version permits a rough characterization of the changes which took place between the former and the latter, although we cannot identify the editor responsible for any particular change. Where the Middle Babylonian fragments are fairly well preserved, we get the impression that the changes in the late version did not involve extensive reformulation, but were generally limited to the substitution of equivalent words. But other fragments of this period, unfortunately less well preserved, at times indicate that more extensive reformulation went into producing their later equivalents. In the late version, apart from the wording, the order of some lines was rearranged, a few lines were dropped, and lines and entire passages were added. Many additions do not give the impression of originality: They include lines synonymously parallel to those to which they are adjoined; traditional and conventional descriptions; and some material modeled upon or related to other passages in the epic and contributing to its homogenized style.

In the evolution of the epic, a pattern of decreasing freedom of revision is discernible. The greatest degree of liberty is reflected in the composition of the Old Babylonian version, the only one which constitutes a really new composition in comparison to its forerunners. This version took from the Sumerian Gilgamesh tales at most plot outlines, and sometimes no more than an idea or theme; its wording of these tales is a completely free Akkadian paraphrase. It added to the tales many motifs from other compositions, and probably much that was original. No later version of *Gilgamesh* took as much liberty with its forerunner. The Hittite and Hurrian translations adapted the epic a little to Hittite and Hurrian interests, and the Hittite abridged the narrative, but the Hittite told the same story as the Akkadian epic (the Hurrian is too poorly attested to permit us to judge). The wording of the Hittite shows affinities with both the Old Babylonian and the late version. The Middle Babylonian Akkadian fragments also reflect the same story, worded in a way which approaches the wording of the late version. The late version, although it restructured the episodes, reworded the text extensively, and added supplementary material, is textually related to its Old and Middle Babylonian forerunners and also tells the same story. This version became so widely accepted in the first millennium that scribes were no longer able or willing to modify it in any substantial way (apart from the possibly later addition of Tablet XII as an appendix which was not integrated into the epic). In content and wording, this version became practically a *textus receptus*, which, so far as we can tell, was accepted as long as the epic was known.

Where Sîn-leqi-unninnī fits in this process we cannot say. Since he probably lived in the Middle Babylonian Period, he cannot have been the author of the Old Babylonian version. The first-millennium catalogue of cuneiform literature which says that "the series *Gilgamesh* (is) according to Sîn-leqi-unninnī the ex[orcist-priest]" (ÉŠ.GÀR ^d*Gilgameš ša pī* ^Id*Sîn-leqi-unninnī* LÚ.M[AŠ.MAŠ])[1] was

1. Lambert, *JCS* 11:11; *JCS* 16:66 (K9717, etc., rev. 10). The meanings of the phrase *ša pī,* here translated "according to," and of related idioms consisting of a preposition followed by *pī,* are elusive. Since *pī* means literally "mouth," these idioms are sometimes used to refer to an oral source (see, e.g., Lambert, in *GSL,* p. 44), but they are often used simply to mean "according to," and this usage is sometimes found with reference to written sources (see *AHw,* pp. 873–74, *sub* 11). On the reference to "the series *Gilgamesh,*" see Lambert, *JCS* 16:77 and Shaffer, "Sources," p. 3, n. 1.

doubtless understood to mean that Sîn-leqi-unninnī was the author of the late version, since that was the only version known in that period. The very fact that the epic is attributed to him indicates that Sîn-leqi-unninnī must have made some important, perhaps definitive, contribution to its formulation. It is certainly possible that he was the editor of the late version, but this is not necessarily the case. It often happens that a work of literature is attributed to a figure who made a decisive contribution to its development, even though a later form of that work is the one actually in use, as is the case, for example, with *The Iliad* of Homer, the *Mishnah* of Rabbi Judah the Prince, or—to cite a modern example—*Gesenius' Hebrew Grammar.*[2] It is possible that Sîn-leqi-unninnī produced a Middle Babylonian form of *Gilgamesh* which had a substantial enough influence on the final form of the epic to associate his name with it permanently, but that the form found in the first-millennium copies was a later revision of Sîn-leqi-unninnī's text. Still, it is equally possible that he was the editor of the late version.

*The Gilgamesh Epic* drew heavily upon Mesopotamian literary tradition. Not only did the author of the Old Babylonian version base his epic on older Sumerian tales about Gilgamesh, but he and the editors who succeeded him made extensive use of materials and literary forms originally unrelated to Gilgamesh. The epic opens with a standard type of hymnic-epic prologue, and parts of the introduction and end of the epic are modeled on royal hymns and inscriptions, and on hymns in praise of temples and their cities. Royal hymns supplied the model for the description of the creation of Gilgamesh, while Enkidu's creation was modeled on that of mankind in creation myths. Mythical motifs about primitive man also supplied the model for the description of Enkidu's early life. The description of how Gilgamesh oppressed Uruk may have been modeled upon folklore motifs or ancient royal practices. This is not certain, but it is clear that the outline of the description is based on a stock literary pattern and that this pattern is used to account for the creation of Enkidu. Ishtar's proposal of marriage to Gilgamesh

2. Without entering into the Homeric question, I am assuming that Homer composed an early version of *The Iliad;* the vulgate text in use since, apparently, shortly before the Christian era, is certainly later than Homer (see Murray, chap. 12). On the *Mishnah,* see Urbach, col. 104. The work published under the English title *Gesenius' Hebrew Grammar* is a revision by A. E. Cowley of the twenty-eighth German edition, revised by E. Kautzsch (1909), of Gesenius' original work published in 1813.

appears to be modeled on sacred-marriage texts or the sacred-marriage ritual. A curse introduction and a curse in the epic seem to be modeled on passages in *Ishtar,* and Enkidu's deathbed vision of the netherworld, which certainly draws upon some conventional material, may also be indebted to that poem. The flood story is based on the account in *Atrahasis.*

Only rarely is it possible, as in the case of the flood story, to point to a particular non-Gilgamesh text as the very source from which *The Gilgamesh Epic* drew a motif or pattern. The parallels are in some cases too numerous, and in most cases insufficiently detailed to permit this.[3] The parallels permit us, at most, to identify certain circles of tradition (or customs) in which particular motifs were at home and from which they were drawn into the epic.

The present study lends a measure of vindication to the theoretical approach by which Morris Jastrow recognized the diversity of the sources, some about Gilgamesh and some not, which underlay the epic, and succeeded in identifying some of them in a general way. Of course Jastrow could hardly give a precise, detailed description of the sources, since they were not then available. Now that we have so many more texts of the epic and of its sources, we can see how extensively the late version, and even the much earlier Old Babylonian version, differ from the Sumerian sources, for example, and how much room there would be for error in trying to reconstruct those sources from the texts of the epic alone. For the literary critic, this is sobering. But the theoretical approach did not lead Jastrow so very wide of the mark in his general conception of elements the epic was composed from. Hopefully the knowledge gained about literary history in cases where the evolution of a composition can be studied empirically, coupled with a fuller knowledge of ancient history in general, will enable us to use the theoretical approach in a more sophisticated and realistic way, when we must.

What is perhaps most useful about our ability to consult the sources of a composition is the opportunity it gives us to see what was borrowed and what was changed. It is, of course, possible for a writer to borrow without modifying his source in any thoughtful way, and undoubtedly there were hacks who did just this in ancient Mesopo-

3. Cf. Wellek and Warren, *Theory of Literature,* p. 258, on the pitfalls of "parallel-hunting."

tamia. But in the case of *The Gilgamesh Epic,* the use of traditional materials shows rather that the author and editors reflected seriously on their literary heritage and found in it new possibilities for themselves and their audiences. What they borrowed, they modified and put to use in novel ways. The epic's prologue is of a type standard in hymns and epics, but in listing the hero's virtues, it replaces the usual heroic epithets with phrases describing the wisdom Gilgamesh acquired. The hymnic description of Uruk looks like a standard temple-city hymn, but placed in the mouth of Gilgamesh, at the end of Tablet XI, it expresses the futility of his quest to overcome death and his reconciliation to immortality-by-reputation-and-achievement only. The pattern of oppression, outcry, and divine response in the sending of an agent of deliverance appears in the epic with a new and more complex twist in which the agent of deliverance distracts the oppressor and then becomes his friend. Motifs from early human history in the creation and early life of Enkidu are used to advance the epic's message by exemplifying the benefits of human life which the epic stresses in lieu of immortality. The flood story, presumably told in the first place because of its intrinsic interest, and serving in *Atrahasis* to explain the origin of infant mortality and other problems, is used in the epic to help explain why the gods' gift of immortality to Utnapishtim is not repeatable. In most cases, the traditional material has been freely recast in accordance with the writers' purposes. As a result, what were originally tales about a particular hero's life and exploits became a vehicle for exploring the problem of mortality and the way to live with the knowledge of ultimate death.

Such creative use of borrowed material nicely illustrates the remarks of Wellek and Warren on the role of "commonplaces (topoi), recurrent themes and images" in literary history:

> No author felt inferior or unoriginal because he used, adapted, and modified themes inherited from tradition and sanctioned by antiquity. . . . To work within a given tradition and adopt its devices is perfectly compatible with emotional power and artistic value. The real critical problems in this kind of study arise when we reach the stage of weighing and comparing, of showing how one artist utilizes the achievements of another artist, when we watch the transforming power.[4]

4. Ibid., p. 259.

Thanks to the ample documentation available for the evolution of *The Gilgamesh Epic,* we can trace the steps by which its author and editors turned a group of commonplace tales into a powerful epic which expressed universal fears and aspirations so well that the epic lasted for well over a thousand years.

# ΓΙΛΓΑΜΟϹ

## *Excursus: The Afterlife of the Epic*

Since the decipherment of *The Gilgamesh Epic,* speculation has abounded about its influence on world literature.[1] This is a subject which would take us too far afield to pursue in the present volume. Here I wish to simply take note of the few explicit references to the main characters in the epic which have been found outside, and mostly after the cessation, of cuneiform literature.

The latest-dated tablet of *Gilgamesh* is apparently from the second or first century B.C.E., and the latest-dated cuneiform reference to Gilgamesh himself is from the second century.[2] One would expect Gilgamesh to have been mentioned in Berossus' *Babyloniaka* in the early third century, B.C.E., and perhaps he was. However, no such references have been found in the surviving fragments of Berossus. This may be due to the limited interests of the excerpters to whom we owe our knowledge of the *Babyloniaka.*[3]

1. Peter Jensen produced a flood of studies finding echoes of *Gilgamesh* in literature around the world, including the Hebrew Bible, the New Testament, the Homeric epics, and Indo-Germanic literature (see L. de Meyer, "Introduction bibliographique," in *GSL,* pp. 1–30, and the index, s.v. "Jensen, P." on p. 29). For a critique of this work, see Gunkel; but note the comment of Kramer, *JAOS* 64:8, n. 1.

2. See Oelsner, pp. 262–64; van Dijk, *UVB* 18, pp. 44–45, ll. 12, 24 (year 147 of the Seleucid era = 165–164 B.C.E.).

3. Although Berossus recounts the flood story, he calls the hero Xisuthros, a Grecization of Ziusudra, which indicates that his source was not *Gilgamesh.* See Komoróczy, *Act. Ant.* 21:133–35 (cf. 139).

Outside of cuneiform sources, there are only three, late references to characters important in *The Gilgamesh Epic.* Two of them are brief. The first is found in Mandaic and Aramaic versions (the latter from the Dead Sea scrolls found at Qumran) of the so-called "Giants" texts related to the account of the "Sons of God," or angels, in Gen. 6:1–4 and En. 6:7. These texts mention the names of Gilgamesh and Humbaba in the consonantal forms *glgmys/š* and *ḥwb'byš* / *ḥwbbš* (Hobabish).[4] Some centuries later, the Nestorian Theodor bar Qoni (ca. 600 C.E.), writing in Syriac, mentions Gmigmos/Gligmos "as the last of ten kings from Peleg to Abraham and contemporaneous with the latter."[5] Neither of these references necessarily presupposes knowledge of *The Gilgamesh Epic;* both Gilgamesh and Humbaba were known outside of the epic as well.[6]

The third reference is an account of Gilgamesh's birth, but it apparently has confused Gilgamesh with some other character. This account is found in Claudius Aelianus' (ca. 200 C.E.) *De Natura Animalium* (12.21)[7]:

> A love of man is another characteristic of animals. At any rate an Eagle fostered a baby. And I want to tell the whole story so that I may have evidence of my proposition. When Seuechorus[8] was king of Babylon the Chaldeans foretold that the son born to his daughter would wrest the kingdom from his grandfather. This made him afraid and (if I may be allowed the small jest) he played Acrisius to his daughter: he put the strictest of watches upon her. For all that, since fate was cleverer than the king of Babylon, the girl became a mother, being pregnant by some obscure man. So the guards from fear of the king hurled the infant from the citadel, for that was where the aforesaid girl was imprisoned. Now an Eagle which saw with its piercing eye the child while still falling, before it was dashed to the earth, flew beneath it, flung its back under it, and conveyed it to some garden and set it down with the utmost care.

4. See Milik, pp. 311, 313. The form of Humbaba's name with final *š* is reminiscent of the Hittite form Huwawaiš (Kammenhuber, p. 51), although the phonetic value of Hittite /š/ is debated.

5. *SKLJ,* p. 89, n. 128. Note also the curious rendition of the Levite "Gerson" as "Golgom(es)" in Josephus, *Antiquities,* bk. 2, § 178 (Thackeray, ed., 4:240–41). Postbiblical Hebrew and Aramaic sources mention a type of cedar known as *golāmiš, galmāšā* (Jastrow, *Dictionary,* 1:222).

6. See Lambert, in *GSL,* pp. 39–56; Wilcke, "Huwawa/Humbaba;" and see above, pp. 13–15 and 79.

7. English translation by Scholfield, 3:38–41.

8. Apparently Enmerkar. See *SKLJ,* p. 87, n. 115 (cf. Hallo, *JCS* 17:52). This text makes Gilgamesh the immediate successor of Enmerkar, a conception appearing also in the scholia of Theodore bar Qoni (see *SKLJ,* ibid.).

But when the keeper of the place saw the pretty baby he fell in love with it and nursed it; and it was called Gilgamos[9] and became king of Babylon.

Jacobsen suggested that Aelian's account "probably derives ultimately from Berossus."[10] Zimmern suggested that in substance the account probably went back to *Etana,* whose hero was carried to heaven by an eagle, but that it contained also an admixture of the Greek Danae legend[11] (Aelian himself, in his "jest" comparing Seuechorus to Acrisius, recognized the affinity to the latter legend[12]). Most recently, Edzard stated that there was no Babylonian prototype for this legend about Gilgamesh.[13]

The story is certainly older than Aelian himself, since he incorporated it only to exemplify the kindness of eagles to mankind—a motif which must therefore have been in his source. But when this story is compared with numerous other stories about the birth and abandonment of future heroes,[14] one notes that many of its motifs are paralleled in classical sources which could have been known to Aelian, so that an assumption of ultimate dependence on a Mesopotamian original does not seem compelling. The prophecy of usurpation,[15] the child's mother being the threatened king's daughter,[16] her isolation,[17] impregnation by an unseen father,[18] casting from a tower,[19] rescue by an eagle,[20] rearing by a gardener,[21] ultimate fulfillment of the prophecy[22]—all these motifs appear elsewhere, mostly in classical sources. One, however, is ap-

9. A few have expressed reservations about whether "Gilgamos" is really "Gilgamesh": Gadd, *apud* Budge, *Babylonian Story,* p. 41, n. 1; Höfer, p. 789; Jeremias, in Roscher, p. 774, denies it outright.

10. *SKLJ,* p. 87, n. 115.

11. In *KAT,* p. 565, and n. 3; cf. Jastrow and Clay, p. 26.

12. See Scholfield, 3:39, n. a; Binder, *Aussetzung,* § 8.

13. Edzard, "Mythologie," p. 73.

14. See Redford; Binder, § 8; Rank; *MI,* R 131, S 300–399.

15. Redford, § 2 (nos. 15–27).

16. E.g., Binder, § 8 (Perseus), § 7 (Telephos), and Cyrus.

17. E.g., Binder, §§ 7–8.

18. Binder, § 8.

19. Pausanias, *Description of Greece,* 4.18.5 (about Aristomenes).

20. Binder, § 60; cf. the preceding note. Compare also Gaster, *Myth,* pp. 319–20. *Etana* (cited by Zimmern [above, n. 11]) is irrelevant, since Etana's flight on an eagle is not a rescue.

21. *MI,* R 131.8.2. All cases listed there of the foster parent's being a gardener are from India and Indochina.

22. Redford, § 2, passim.

parently paralleled only outside of classical sources: the child's foster parent's being a gardener. Apart from Indian and Indochinese examples of this motif, which are not likely to have influenced Aelian, there is one source which immediately comes to mind—the birth legend of Sargon of Akkad (2334–2279).

The Sargon legend begins as follows[23]:

Sargon, the mighty king, king of Akkad am I.
My mother was an *ēntu*-priestess,[24] my father I knew not (var.: a father I had not).
The brother(s) of my father *loved* the hills.
My city is Azupiranu, which is situated on the banks of the Euphrates.
My mother, the *ēntu*-priestess, conceived me, in secret she bore me.
She set me in a basket of rushes, with bitumen she sealed my lid.
She exposed[25] me in the river, which rose not over me.
The river bore me up and carried me to Akki, the gardener.
Akki, the gardener, lifted me out as he dipped his e[we]r.
Akki, the gardener, [took me] as his son (and) reared me.
Akki, the gardener, assigned me to gardening for him.
While I was gardening, Ishtar granted me her love,
And for four and. . . . years I exercised kingship.

The legend terms Akki, who reared Sargon, *dālû* (LÚ.A.BAL),[26] "water drawer, gardener." Sargon himself is later appointed by Akki "to his gardening service" (*ana nukarribbūtišu* [LÚ.NU.-GIRI$_{12}$-*ti-šu*]). Much earlier, the *Sumerian King List* had described Sargon as one "whose . . . . was a gardener" (. . . . -b a - n i n u - g i r i$_{12}$).[27] There have naturally been many suggestions for restoring the beginning of this line, among them a b, "father," and (ì) - d i b, "foster-father" or "Aufnehmer," but they remain conjec-

23. *CT* 13, nos. 42–43; *CT* 46, no. 46; edited by King, *Chronicles* 2:87–96; cf. Jensen, in *RLA* 1:322–24; Güterbock, *ZA* 42:62–64; *CAD* D, p. 57d (on ll. 8–11); translated by Speiser, with revisions by Grayson, in *ANET*, p. 119. On the text's genre, cf. Grayson and Lambert, p. 8; on its relationship with Moses' birth story, see Childs, pp. 109–10; Greenberg, pp. 198–99.

24. The earlier interpretation of *ēnetum* as *ēntu*, "high priestess" (Jensen, in *RLA* 1:322; Meissner, *Babylonien* 2:70), rejected for a time (Güterbock, p. 62, n. 2; Speiser, in *ANET*², p. 119: "changeling[?]"), is now widely accepted (*CAD* E, p. 173a; Hallo and van Dijk, p. 6; Lambert and Millard, p. 165 *sub* vii, 8–9; Astour, p. 193).

25. See Cogan, pp. 133–34.

26. *CAD* D, p. 57b lex.

27. *SKLJ*, p. 110, l. 32. On the term l ú - n u - g i r i$_{12}$, see Gadd, *RA* 63:2; Edzard, *ZA* 55, pp. 91ff.

tural.[28] The Neo-Assyrian sources are sufficient to offer themselves as sources of the later tradition, which, transferred to Gilgamesh, is reported by Aelian. Another feature of the Sargon legend may also be relevant in this regard, the statement "my father I knew not" (2). This resembles Aelian's statement that Gilgamos' father was "some obscure man"—the Greek term *aphanous* literally meaning "invisible," and thus referring to his simply having been undetected, rather than to humble circumstances. In similar classical legends, the father's not being seen is due to his being a god who succeeds in impregnating the mother because he is able to enter invisibly.[29] The Gilgamos story is somewhat exceptional in not accounting for the father's "invisibility" in this way, and in this detail, too, could therefore go back to the Sargon legend. However, there is another plausible explanation, proposed by Langdon, which connects the "obscure man" mentioned by Aelian with the statement in the *Sumerian King List* that Gilgamesh's father was a *lillu*-demon.[30]

This is the extent of explicit references to important characters in *Gilgamesh* known to us from outside of cuneiform sources. Two of them could reflect knowledge of the epic, but not necessarily. The third apparently is really a form of Sargon of Akkad's birth story mistakenly transferred to Gilgamesh at some point in the history of transmission to Aelian. The confusion is symptomatic of Gilgamesh's gradual disappearance into literary oblivion, from which he did not emerge until modern times.

28. It has recently been suggested that the term *gardener* may have been applied as an epithet to kings or their substitutes in the sacred marriage of the New Year's ritual (Hallo and van Dijk, p. 6). If the original meaning was technical, it was nevertheless taken literally by the later tradition, which clearly considers Akki a real gardener (*Legend of Sargon, ANET,* p. 119, ll. 8–12). Cf. Speiser, *Genesis,* p. 27, for "derivative material . . . sometimes [being] taken more literally than the original sources intended."

29. E.g., Redford, § 2, nos. 21–22, 26; cf. no. 2.

30. Langdon, *Weld-Blundell* 2:12; cf. *GETh.*, pp. 9–10; Shaffer, "Sources," pp. 10–11. See also Sjöberg, *Or. Suec.* 21:101, n. 2.

# *Appendix: Texts and Notes*

As a rule, the texts quoted in translation above are accompanied by the original languages only when the passages are brief. In this appendix, the lengthier texts are presented in the original languages, along with philological notes. New editions of *Gilgamesh and the Land of the Living* and of the Akkadian *Gilgamesh* are expected from A. Shaffer and W. G. Lambert, respectively, and I have not sought to duplicate their efforts. However, the existing editions and translations, especially of the Akkadian epic, are out of date and could not be used without revision in the light of more recent studies. I have generally restricted the philological notes to explaining substantial deviations from the standard editions and translations. In general I have sought to translate the texts literally, rather than literarily, in order to facilitate comparison among similar texts.

In the translation of *Gilgamesh and the Land of the Living,* I owe several suggestions to Prof. T. Jacobsen. For the Akkadian texts, I owe much to Profs. B. L. Eichler and W. L. Moran, to Prof. A. Shaffer and Dr. A. Westenholz for the use of their unpublished copies of Old Babylonian *Gilgamesh* texts, and to Prof. E. V. Leichty for collations. In the case of the Hittite material, I am almost entirely dependent on translations, and these texts are provided simply for the reader's convenience. Prof. H. A. Hoffner, Jr., was kind enough to review text No. 4 with me and provided me with a rough translation of that passage. Prof. R. Stefanini generously helped by reviewing the Hittite parts of Nos. 11 and 12 with me. Many of the readings and translations adopted here are based on *CAD* and *AHw* and on special studies listed at the beginning of each selection below. These studies are cited in the notes by author's name alone. Final responsibility for all readings (except for the Hittite, which follows published editions), translations, and comments is mine.

In this appendix, the forms of Gilgamesh's name are transliterated as written in the various texts, but they are uniformly rendered by the conventional form *Gilgamesh* in the translations. For the pronunciation of the name as *Bilgamesh* in Sumerian, see Falkenstein, *An. Or.* 28:8 and *RLA* 3:357. For Akkadian forms of the name, see Falkenstein, *RLA* 3:357–58; Lambert, in *GSL,* p. 39, n. 1. (Falkenstein's interpretation of the Sumerian form as "The old man is a young man" is strikingly reminiscent of the name given by Gilgamesh to the plant of rejuvenation, *šību iṣṣaḫ(ḫ)ir amīlu,* "as-an-old-man-a-man-becomes-young" [*GE* XI, 281].)

Sumerian texts are presented first. For ease of reference, the Akkadian and Hittite texts are given in the order of their appearance in the epic, rather than the order of citation in the present study.

## *Index to Texts*

| Number (in Appendix) | Text(s) |
|---|---|
| 1 | *GLL* A 153–61 and *GLL* B, MS a, rev. iv, 2–22 |
| 2 | *GEN* 147–64 |
| 3 | *GE* I, i, 1–ii, 41 and Gilg. Ni. |
| 4 | *Hit. Gilg.* I, 1, 3–end, and 2, 1–12 |
| 5 | Gilg. P. i, 1–ii, 1 and *GE* I, v, 26–vi, 27 |
| 6 | Gilg. P. ii, 12–13, 27–30; iii, 1–9, 22–27, and GEUW obv. 4, 9–10, 19–21 |
| 7 | Gilg. P. v, 9–vi, 23 and *GE* II, ii, 35–50 |
| 8 | Gilg. Y. iii, 14–24, 38–iv, 2 and *GE* II, v, 1–6 |
| 9 | Gilg. Bo. obv.! 6–12 and *GE* V, iv, 7–13 |
| 10 | Gilg. Meg. obv. 9b–rev. 1; Gilg. Ur 60–67; and *GE* VII, iv, 14–20 |

| | |
|---|---|
| 11 | Gilg. Mi. iv, 1–10 and *Hit. Gilg.* 11, 1–5 |
| 12 | Gilg. Mi. iv, 11–14; *Hit. Gilg.* 10, rev. iii, 5–21; and *GE* X, ii, 26–27; iii, 40–50 |
| 13 | OB *Atr.* III, i, 15–29; iii, 30–iv, 23; v, 30–38 and *GE* XI, 20–31, 113–26, 155–62 |

## *Reverse Index*

| Text | Number (in Appendix) |
|---|---|
| ***Sumerian Gilgamesh Tales*** | |
| *GLL* A 153–61 | 1 |
| *GLL* B MS a, rev. iv, 2–22 | 1 |
| *GEN* 157–64 | 2 |
| ***Old Babylonian Akkadian* Gilgamesh** | |
| Gilg. Ni. | 3 |
| Gilg. P. i, 1–ii, 1 | 5 |
| ii, 12–13, 27–30 | 6 |
| iii, 1–9, 22–27 | 6 |
| v, 9–vi, 23 | 7 |
| Gilg. Y. iii, 14–24 | 8 |
| iii, 38–iv, 2 | 8 |
| Gilg. Mi. iv, 1–10 | 11 |
| iv, 11–14 | 12 |
| ***Middle Babylonian Akkadian* Gilgamesh** | |
| Gilg. Bo. obv.! 6–12 | 9 |
| Gilg. Meg. obv. 9b–rev. 1 | 10 |
| Gilg. Ur 60–67 | 10 |
| ***Late version Akkadian* Gilgamesh** | |
| *GE* I, i, 1–ii, 41 | 3 |
| v, 26–vi, 27 | 5 |
| GEUW obv. 4, 9–10, 19–21 | 6 |
| *GE* II, ii, 35–50 | 7 |
| v, 1–6 | 8 |
| V, iv, 7–13 | 9 |
| VII, iv, 14–20 | 10 |
| X, ii, 26–27 | 12 |
| X, iii, 40–50 | 12 |
| XI, 20–31, 113–26, 155–62 | 13 |
| ***Hittite* Gilgamesh** | |
| I, frag. 1, 3–end; 2, 1–12 | 4 |

| | |
|---|---|
| No. 10, rev. iii, 5–21 | 12 |
| No. 11, 1–5 | 11 |

**The Atrahasis Epic**

| | |
|---|---|
| OB *Atr.* III, i, 15–29 | 13 |
| iii, 30–iv, 23 | 13 |
| v, 30–38 | 13 |

# 1. *GLL* A, 153–61 and *GLL* B, MS a, rev. iv, 2–22

Translations on pp. 31–32.

*GLL* A from Kramer, *JCS* 1:20–21.

*GLL* B from ibid., p. 25, and pp. 43–44, n. 250, as revised by A. Shaffer in an unpublished manuscript.

| *GLL* **A** | *GLL* **B, MS a, rev.** |
|---|---|
| 153. arad-da-ni-$^{d}$En-ki-du$_{10}$-ra<br>gù mu-na-dé-e | iv, 2. arad-da-na-E[n-ki-du$_{10}$-ra]<br>3. gù mu-un-na-dé-e |
| 154. En-ki-du$_{10}$ mušen-dab$_5$-ba<br>ki-bi-šè ḫa-ba-du | 4. gá-nam-ma ur-sag-ra<br>5. šu ga-àm-bar-re-en-dè-en |
| 155. guruš-dab$_5$-ba<br>úr-ama-na-šè ḫe-gi$_4$-gi$_4$ | |
| | 6. lú-zu-me ḫé-a |
| | 7. dúr-kaskal-la<br>igi me-eb-du$_8$-dè-a |
| | 8. lú-zu-me ḫé-a |
| 156. En-ki-du$_{10}$ $^{d}$Bìl-ga-mèš<br>inim mu-ni-ib-gi$_4$-gi$_4$ | 9. arad-da-a-ni En-ki-du$_{10}$-e<br>10. mu-un-na-ni-ib-gi$_4$-gi$_4$ |
| 157. sukud-du dím-ma nu-tuku | |
| 158. Nam-tar ì-kú-e<br>Nam-tar nu-zu-zu | |
| 159. mušen-dab$_5$-ba<br>ki-bi-šè du-a-bi | 11. ur-sag-dab$_5$-ba<br>12. šu-bar-ra-àm |

*iv, 6, 8.* lú-zu, "informant." Taking zu as causative.

*iv, 7.* dur-kaskal-la, "highwaymen." Falkenstein, *JNES* 19:69 *sub* 8 with n. 14.

160. guruš dab$_5$-ba
úr-ama-na-šè gi$_4$-gi$_4$-da

161. za-e uru-ama-dú-da-zu
nu-ub-ši-gur-ru-dè-en

*161.* u r u , "city." TLB 2, no. 4, l. 87 (van Dijk, in *GSL,* p. 71) reads ú r , "lap" (cf. the previous line there, = line 160 here).

13. en-dab$_5$-ba
14. gi$_6$-pàr-šè gur-ra-àm
15. gudu$_4$-dab$_5$-ba
16. ḫi-li-šè gur-ra-àm
17. u$_4$-ul-lí-a-ta
18. a-ba-a igi im-mi-in-du$_8$
19. kaskal-kur-ra
mu-e-dè-eb-x x x-e
20. gìr-kur-ra
mu-e-ne-eb-sùḫ-sùḫ-e
21. [uru]-ama-ù-dú-da
22. [nu]-ub-ši-gur-[ru]-dè-en-dè-en

*iv, 15.* g u d u$_4$. *CAD* G, p. 83b. Contrast van Dijk, in *GSL,* p. 76 *sub* 88–89.
ḫ i - l i, "priestly headdress." Cf. Renger, *ZA* 59:161–62 (a head ornament, perhaps a wig), following Falkenstein, *AfO* 14:115–16 *sub* 18; Jacobsen, *PAPhS* 107:477, n. 11. Van Dijk, in *GSL,* p. 73 *sub* 89, renders "jouissance," in accordance with the lexical equation ḫ i - l i = *kuzbu,* "luxuriance" (*CAD* K, p. 614); cf. Falkenstein's rendering of the same idiom in *SAHG* p. 209, l. 348 and Kramer's in *Sumerians,* p. 143, l. 4. The parallel g i p a r (a priestly residence) favors "priestly headdress," but the two renderings are not mutually exclusive, since the headdress may have symbolized elegance.

## 2. *GEN* 147–64

Translation on p. 189.

Text and translation from Shaffer, "Sources," pp. 66–69, 105–6; variants not noted here. For a divergent translation of important passages, see Kramer, *Sumerians,* p. 202.

147. nin$_9$-a-ni-kù-$^{d}$Inanna-ra $^{giš}$gu-za-ni-šè mu-na-ab-sum-mu
148. $^{giš}$ná-da-ni-šè mu-na-ab-sum-mu
149. e-ne úr-bi $^{giš}$ellag-a-ni-šè ba-da-ab-dím-e
150. pa-bi $^{giš}$E.KID-ma-ni-šè ba-ab-dím-e
151. $^{giš}$ellag al-du$_{11}$-du$_{11}$-ge sila-ùr-ra $^{giš}$ellag na-mu-un-è

152. IM.DI du$_{11}$-du$_{11}$-ge sila-ùr-ra IM.DI na-mu-un-è
153. guruš-uru-na-ka $^{giš}$ellag al-du$_{11}$-du$_{11}$-ga-ne
154. e-ne erin dumu-nu-mu-un-su-a-ke$_{4}$-ne íb-ba-u$_{5}$-a
155. a-gú-mu a-íb-ba-mu a-nir-ni im-gá-gá-ne
156. ama-tuku dumu-ni-ir ninda mu-na-ab-túm
157. nin$_{9}$-tuku šeš-a-ni-ir a mu-na-dé-e
158. ú-sa$_{11}$-an-e um-ma-kar-ta
159. ki-$^{giš}$ellag-gar-ra-ka-ni giš-ḫur in-ḫur-re
160. $^{giš}$ellag-a-ni igi-ni-a mu-ni-in-íl é-a-ni-šè mu-un-túm
161. á-gú-zi-ga-ta ki-giš-ḫur-in-ḫur-ra íb-ba-u$_{5}$-a
162. šu-dù-dù-a-nu-mu-un-su-a-ta
163. i-$^{d}$utu-ki-sikil-tur-ra-ta
164. $^{giš}$ellag-a-ni ù $^{giš}$E.KID-ma-ni tuš-kur-ra-šè ba-da-an-šub

## 3. *GE* I, i, 1–ii, 41 and Gilg. Ni.

Translations on pp. 141–42, 178–79, 192–93, and 198.

I, i, 1–19 and ii, 1–3, 7–41 from *GETh.,* pp. 11–12 and pls. 1–2 (BM 34916, covering i, 5–20, is republished in *CT* 46, no. 17), supplemented by *CT* 46, no. 19; i, 7–ii, 6a are from GENim (in Wiseman's edition, ii, 1–6a are numbered i, 46–51). Important study by Wilcke, "Anfänge."

Gilg. Ni. from copy by Westenholz and transliterations by Steele (unpublished) and Shaffer, "Sources," p. 23, n. 3 (see photograph, p. 297).

### *GE* I

i, 1. [*šá*] *nag-ba i-mu-ru lu-*[*še*]*-*⸢*e*⸣*-di ma-a-ti*
2. [*šá kul-la-t*]*i i-du-ú ka-l*[*a-ma lu-šal-m*]*i-s*[*u*]
3. [*ib-r*]*i*?*-ma mit-ḫa-riš m*[*a*?*-ta-ti*]
4. [*šug*?*-m*]*ur né-me-qí ša ka-la-a-mi i-*[*du-ú*]
5. [*ni*]*-ṣir-ta i-mur-ma ka-ti-im-tú ip-t*[*u*]
6. [*u*]*b-la ṭè-e-ma šá la-am a-bu-bu*

*i, 1. nagba,* "everything." Cf. Jensen, KB 6(1):423. For other views, see Oppenheim, *Or.* 17:17; Borger, *Bi. Or.* 14:192b.

*i, 1–2.* Although the restorations (essentially from *GETh.*) are uncertain, the *lu-* in line 1 is preserved, as noted by Wilcke, p. 201, thus confirming that the introduction began in the cohortative style.

*i, 3.* Restorations follow *CAD* M$_{2}$, p. 134b.

*i, 4. i-*[*du-ú*]. For other examples of *kalama idû,* see *CAD* K, p. 65b,c. For alternative restorations of the line, cf. *CAD* N$_{2}$, p. 160c.

7. [*u*]*r-ḫa ru-uq-ta il-li-kam-ma a-ni-iḫ ù šup-šu-uḫ*
8. [*iḫ-ru*]-⌜*uṣ*⌝ *i-na* $^{na_4}$*narî* (NA.RÚ.A) *ka-lu ma-na-aḫ-ti*
9. *ú-še-piš dūra* (BÀD) *šá Uruk*(UNUG)$^{ki}$ *su-pú-ri*
10. *šá* É.AN.NA *qud-du-ši šu-tum*$_4$*-mi el-lim*
11. *a-mur du-ur-šu šá ki-ma qé-e ni-ip-*[x x]
12. *i-tap-la-as sa-me-ta-šu šá la ú-maš-šá-lu mam-ma*
13. *ṣa-bat-ma* $^{na_4}$*askupp(at)i*(KUN$_4$) *šá ul-tu ul-la-nu*
14. *qit-ru-*⌜*ub*⌝ *ana*(DIŠ) É.AN.NA *šu-bat* $^{d}$*Ištar*(15)
15. *šá šarru*(LUGAL) *ár-ku-ú la ú-maš-šá-lu amēlu*(LÚ) *mam-ma*
16. *e-li-ma ina*(AŠ)/*ana*(DIŠ) *muḫḫi*(UGU) *dūri*(BÀD) *šá* *Uruk*(UNUG)$^{ki}$ *i'*!*-tal-lak*
17. *te-me-en-nu ḫi-iṭ-ma libitta*(SIG$_4$) *ṣu-ub-bu*
18. *šum-ma libitti*(SIG$_4$)*-šú la a-gur-rat*
19. *u uš-šú-šú la id-du-ú* 7 [*mun-tal-ki*]

*i, 7. šup-šu-uḫ,* "at peace." For the translation, cf. *OBS,* p. 477. The rest of the line, line 8, and line 26 speak of Gilgamesh's toil and hardship (cf. XI, 259, 264). Hence, apparently, *CAD*'s understanding of the word as standing for *šupsuq,* "in pain" (*CAD* A$_2$, pp. 102d–103a; for *ḫ/q,* cf. von Soden, *Ergänzungsheft,* § 25d). But "at peace" would be an apt summary of the ultimate calming of Gilgamesh's "stormy" and "restless heart" (*GE* I, ii, 31; III, ii, 10 [*la ṣa-li-la;* cf. I, v, 19 and the opposition of *lā ṣalālu* and *pašāḫu/šupšuḫu, En El* I, 38; *CAD* Ṣ, p. 72b]).

*i, 9. ú-še-piš,* "had made." Jensen, KB 6(1):116.
*su-pu-ri,* "sheepfold." See *AHw,* p. 1061b.

*i, 10. šu-tum*$_4$*-mi.* This reading is confirmed (against the variant *ku-tùm-mu,* for which no appropriate meaning is known) by the same epithet of Eanna appearing in a prayer to Ishtar; see Reiner and Güterbock, *JCS* 21:260 NB(28): *É-an-na qud-du-šú šu-tùm-mu el-lu;* cf. Sjöberg and Bergmann, p. 19 l. 50, and pp. 60 and 151 *ad loc.* This epithet rules out the suggestion of Ravn, *Ac. Or.* 22:43, regarding our passage. For another reading of this line, see Borger, *Bi. Or.* 26:75, s.v. *ajakku.*

*i, 11. ni-ip-*[x x]. Suggested restorations are *né-eb-*[*ḫu-šú*], "frieze, cornice" (Oppenheim, *Or.* 17:19, n. 2; *AHw,* p. 773d), *ni-ip-ḫ*[*u-šu*], "its brightness, shining" (Heidel, p. 18, n. 22), and *ni-ip-*⌜*ši*⌝*-*[*šu*], "which is made(?) (as if of bronze)" (*CAD* D, p. 192c). Wilcke emends to *qé-e iṣ-ṣu-*[*ri*], "a bird net."
*bronze.* Others: "thread" (*qû* I; Oppenheim, *loc. cit;* Diakonoff *apud* Matouš, *Ar. Or.* 44:63–64).

*i, 12. i-tap-la-as.* Thus *CT* 46, no. 17; *GETh.*'s ungrammatical (for the imperative) *i-pa-la-as* was due to a miscopy by Thompson (Weidner, *AfO* 16:80).

*i, 15. (la) . . . amēlu mam-ma,* "no one." *CAD* A$_2$, p. 286b, construes as "none among the future kings"; Oppenheim takes the phrase separately: "(or) anybody" (*Or.* 17:19).

*i, 16. i'*!*-tal-lak,* following the parallel text in XI, 303 (*i-tal-lak;* cf. *BWL,* p. 148, l. 76); the tablet's reading *im-tal-lak,* ("take counsel") is apparently the result of a copyist's confusion of the graphically similar signs *i'* and *im* (Speiser, unpublished lecture notes; cf. Wilcke).

*i, 18. šum-ma.* Thus *CT* no. 46, l. 17, in agreement with XI, 304 (and K16024:7, in *GETh.,* p. 67, n. 6 and pl. 54).

*i, 19. mun-tal-ki.* Restored from the parallel passage, *GE* XI, 305.

20. [SÁR *ālu*(URU.KI) SÁR *ki*]*râtu*([KI]RI$_6$.MEŠ) SÁR *is-su-ú* *pi-*[*ti-ir bīt*(É) $^{d}$*Iš-tar*]
21. [3 SÁR] *ù pi-ti-ir Ur*[*u*]*k*(UN[U]G)$^{ki}$ *ta*[*m-ḫu*]
22. [x x x (x)] GIŠ.UM(DUB!?).ŠEN.NA *šá e*[*rí*] (UR[UDU])
23. [x x x] x *ḫar-gal-li-šu šá si*[*parri*] (ZA[BAR])
24. [x x] x *bāba*(KÁ) *šá ni-ṣir-ti-*[*šú*?]
25. [x x]-*ma ṭup-pi* $^{na_4}$*uqnî*(ZA.GÌN) *ši-tas-si*
26. [*ki-i šu*]-*ú* $^{d}$GIŠ.GÍN.MAŠ *ittallaku*(DU.DU$^{ku}$) *ka-lu mar-ṣa-a-ti*

27. [*šu*]-⸢*tu*⸣-*ur eli*(UGU) *šarrī*(LUGAL.MEŠ) *šá-nu-u'-ú-du* *bēl*(EN) *gat-ti*
28. [*qa*]*r-du lil-lid Uruk*(UNUG)$^{ki}$ *ri-i-mu mut-tak-pu*
29. [*i*]*l-lak ina*(AŠ) *pa-ni a-šá-red*
30. [*a*]*r-ka il-lak-ma tukul-ti aḫḫī*(SEŠ.MEŠ)-*šú*
31. [*sa-*]*par-ru dan-nu ṣu-lul um-ma-ni-šú*
32. ⸢*a*⸣-*gu-ú ez-zu mu-ab-bit dúr*(BÀD) *abni*(NA$_4$)
33. [*b*]*u-*[*k*]*ur šá* $^{d}$*Lugal-bàn-da* $^{d}$GIŠ.GÍN.MAŠ *gít-*⸢*m*⸣*a-lu e-mu-qí*
34. [*ma-r*]*u*? *ar-ḫi ṣir-ti* $^{f}$*Ri-mat-*$^{d}$*Nin-sún*
35. [x x] $^{d}$GIŠ.GÍN.MAŠ *gít-ma-lu ra-šub-bu*
36. [*pe-t*]*u*?-*ú né-re-bé-e-ti šá ḫur-sa-a-ni*
37. [*ḫe-ru*]-*ú bu-ú-ri šá aḫ*(GÚ) *šadî*(KUR$^{i}$)
38. [*e-b*]*ir a-ab-*⸢*ba*⸣ [*t*]*a-ma-ti rapašti*(DAGAL$^{ti}$) *adi*(EN) *ṣīt-šamši*($^{d}$UTU.È)
39. [*ḫa*]-*a-iṭ kib-ra-a-ti muš-t*[*e-e*]*'-ú ba-lá-ṭi*
40. [*ka*]-*ši-id dan-nu-*⸢*us*?⸣-*su a-na* $^{I}$*Ut-napišti*(ZI) *ru-ú-qí*

*i, 20. is-su-ú,* "lowland." See Weiss, *JAOS* 95:448–49.

*i, 21. ta*[*m-ḫu*]. From *GE* XI, 307; see Ebeling, cited by Heidel, p. 93, n. 216; *AHw,* p. 1312 *sub* 4b.

*i, 22.* Cf. Wilcke, and Wiseman. The references to a lock and an opening in the next two lines favor the view that a container is mentioned here. Cf. *Naram-Sin, narû-Inscription,* l. 149 (the third line of the passage quoted above, p. 145). According to O. R. Gurney, in light of a discovery by C. B. F. Walker, he would now translate that passage "I have made for you a tablet box and inscribed a stone tablet for you" (letter of 1 Nov. 1981).

*i, 27.* The OB version of the epic began here; see above, p. 48.
*šanūdu,* "renowned." See *AHw,* p. 1167c.

*i, 33.* [*b*]*u-*[*k*]*ur.* Wilcke; for construct followed by *ša,* see *GE* X, ii, 16.

*i, 34.* "Rimat-Ninsun," i.e., "Wild Cow Ninsun" (*AHw,* p. 986, s.v. *rīmtu,* 2). The feminine personal-name determinative before "Rimat" indicates that the latter is part of the goddess's name here. For this epithet of Ninsun, see earlier in this line, Gilg. P. vi, 33–34, and Sjöberg, *Or. Suec.* 21:99–101. Cf. the references to Gilgamesh as a "wild bull" (*rīmu, GE* I, i, 28; ii, 20, cf. 8).

*i, 38. a-ab-*⸢*ba*⸣, "ocean." See *CAD* A$_1$, p. 221bc; cf. perhaps Gilg. Mi. iii, 10.

41. [*mu-ti*]*r*? x x x *ana*(DIŠ) *aš-ri-šú-nu šá ú-ḫal-li-qu a-bu-bu*
42. [x x x x x] *ana*(DIŠ) *nišī*(UKÙ.MEŠ) *a-pa-a-ti*
43. [*šá/mannu it-*]⸢*ti*⸣*-šu iš-šá-an-na-nu a-na sarrūti*(LUGAL$^{ti}$)
44. [*šá kīma*(GIM)] $^{d}$GIŠ.GÍN.MAŠ *i-qab-bu-ú a-na-ku-ma šarru*(LUGAL)
45. [$^{d}$GIŠ.GÍ]N.MAŠ *iš-tu u$_4$-um i'-al-du na-bu šum-šú*

ii, 1. *šit-tin-šú ilu*(DINGIR)*-ma šul-lul-ta-šú a-me-lu-tu*
2. *ṣa-lam pag-ri-šu* DINGIR.MAḪ *uṣ*?*-ṣi*[*r*?]
3. [*uš/l*]-⸢*te*⸣*-iṣ-bi-*⸢*i*⸣ *gat-ta-šú u-ṭàr-ra* [x]
4. [x x x x (x) *da*]*mqu* ([S]IG$_5$) *šá-ru-uḫ eṭl*[*ūti*](GURUŠ.[MEŠ])
5. [x x x x x x x] *gít-ma-l*[*u*? x x x x (x)]
6a. [x x x *ú*]*-kaš-šid* [x x x x (x)]
6b. *i-na si-mat* x [x x x] x*-tum*? [x x x]
7. *i-na su-pu-r*[*u*] *šá Uruk*(UNUG)$^{ki}$ *šú-ú it-t*[*a*-x x x]
8. *ug-da-áš-šá-ár ri-ma-niš šá-qú-ú re-*[*es-su*]
9. *ul i-šu šá-ni-nam-ma te-bu-ú* $^{giš}$*kakkē*(TUKUL.MEŠ)-[*šú*]
10. *ina*(AŠ) *pu-uq-qí-šú te-bu-ú ru-'ú-*⸢*ú*⸣-[*šú*]
11. [*it*]*-ta-ad-*⸢*da*⸣*-ri eṭlūtu*(GURUŠ.MEŠ) *šá Uruk*(UNUG)$^{ki}$ *ina*(AŠ) *ku-u*[*m*-x x]
12. *ul ú-maš-*[*šar* $^{d}$]GIŠ.GÍN.MAŠ *māra*(DUMU) *ana*(DIŠ) *a*[*bi*](A[D])-[*šú*]
13. [*ur-r*]*a ù* [*muš*]*i*([GE$_6^{š}$]$^{i}$) *i-kad-dir še-*x [x (x)]
14. [$^{d}$GIŠ.GÍN.]MAŠ(?) *š*[*u-ú rē'*]*u*([SIPA]D) *šá Uruk*(UNUG)$^{ki}$ *su-*[*pu-ri*]

*i, 41.* For suggested restorations, see Moran, *RA* 71:190–91; Wilcke; Lambert, *RA* 73:89.

*i, 45.* Perhaps restore the beginning of the line, instead of [$^{d}$GIŠ.GÍ]N.MAŠ, either [*ana šarrū* (LUGAL)]*-ti*!, "for kingship," or [*ana da-ra-a*]*-ti*!, "forever" (for the first, cf. *AHw,* p. 1190c, *sub* 3a; for the second, *CAD* D, p. 111). See the discussion of this passage above, p. 153.

*ii, 3.* [*uš/l*]-⸢*te*⸣*-iṣ-bi-*⸢*i*⸣, "completed." See Thompson's copy in *GETh.*, pl. 1; Thompson's reading of the last sign as *t*[*a*] was based on his understanding of the verb as a derivative of *ṣabātu,* with the meaning "he hath forced to take" (Thompson, *Epic of Gilgamesh. A New Translation . . . , ad loc.*); cf. *CAD* Ṣ, p. 39. That reading does not fit the context.

*ii, 4.* [*da*]*mqu* ([S]IG$_5$), "fairest." Cf. *GE* VII, iii, 39; Gilg. Bo. rev. 16. For the rest of the line, cf. *GE* VI, 183, 185.

*ii, 5. gít-ma-l*[*u*], "perfect." cf. *GE* I, i, 33, 35; iv, 38.

*ii, 6a.* Cf. *Hit. Gilg.* I, no. 1, l. 11.

*ii, 8. ug-da-áš-šá-ár ri-ma-niš,* "establishes himself supreme like a wild bull." Cf. I, iv, 39, 46, and the translation in *CAD* G, p. 56a.

*ii, 10.* The reading and translation follow Landsberger, *WZKM* 56:125, n. 49 (earlier, Muss-Arnolt, 2:819b). Cf. discussion on line 22, below.

*ii, 14–15.* For a different restoration of these lines, see Wilcke, p. 207, ll. 59–60a.

15. *šu-ú rē'u*(SIPAD)[*-ši-na-ma*(?). . . . *gaš-ru šu-pu-ú mu-du-ú*]
16. *ul ú-maš-ša*[*r* $^{d}$GIŠ.GÍN.MAŠ *batulta*(SAL.KAL.TUR) *ana*(DIŠ) *um-mi-šá*]
17. *ma-rat qu-r*[*a-di ḫi-rat eṭ-li*]
18. *ta-zi-im-ta-ši-na* [*iš-te-nem-mu-ú ilāni*(DINGIR.MEŠ)]
19. *ilāni*(DINGIR.MEŠ) *šá-ma-mi bēl*(EN) *Uruk*(UNUG)[$^{ki}$ *is-su-ú*]
20. *tul-tab-ši ma-a ri-ma kàd-ra* [*šá-qú-ú re-es-su*]
21. *ul i-šu šá-ni-nam-ma t*[*e-bu-ú* $^{giš}$*kakkē*(TUKUL.MEŠ)*-šú*]
22. *ina*(AŠ) *pu-uq-qí-šu te*!*-bu-ú* [*ru-'ú-ú-šú*]
23. *ul ú-maš-šar* $^{d}$GIŠ.GÍN.MAŠ *māra*(DUMU) *ana*(DIŠ) *abi*(AD)*-šú: ur-ra u muši*(GE$_6$[$^{ši}$]) *i-kad-dir še-*x x (x)]
24. *šu-ú rē'u*(SIPAD)*-ma šá Uruk*(UNUG)$^{ki}$ [*su-pu-ri*]
25. *šu-ú re-'-ú-ši-na-ma u* [x x x x]
26. *gaš-ru šu-pu-ú mu-du-ú* x [x x x x x]
27. *ul ú-maš-šar* $^{d}$GIŠ.GÍN.MAŠ *batulta*(SAL.KAL.TUR) *a-na* [*um-mi-šá*]
28. *ma-rat qu-ra-di ḫi-rat e*[*ṭ-li*]
29. *ta-zi-im-ta-ši-na iš-te-nem-me* $^{d}$[*A-num*]

*ii, 16.* [*ana um-mi-šá*], "[to her mother(?)]." Following *GETh.* (others restore terms for husbands or lover). This restoration seems preferable in view of its counterpart "Gilgamesh does not release the son to his father" in line 12; relating sons to fathers and daughters to mothers is a standard device in ancient Near Eastern literature (see *Erra* IIc, 33–34.; III, 9–10; cf. *Atr.* S, v, 18–21 = vi, 7–10; for west-Semitic examples, see Ruth 1:8; Song of Songs 3:4; 8:2; Gen. 24:28; *Keret* B (=*UT,* no. 128; *ANET,* p. 146b), iii, 23–24. Note, however, line 17, below.

*ii, 17–18.* Line 17 is usually construed as the continuation of line 16, adding to the list of those whom Gilgamesh does not release. But this would unbalance the apparent parallelism of line 16 with 12, which has no such sequel. Following the lead of the Sumerian source *GEN,* lines 152–53 (above, no. 2), where it is females who raise the outcry, it seems best to construe line 17 as *casus pendens,* anticipating line 18. The pronoun in line 18 is in fact feminine (*-šina;* cf. Oppenheim, *Or.* 17:22–23), though this in itself could be dismissed as grammatical imprecision (cf. *tazzimtašina* in contexts where there is no possible feminine antecedent: *STC* 1, pp. 219–20 (= vol. 2, pls. 73–74), l. 10; *Cyrus Cylinder,* Weissbach, *VAB* 3, p. 2, l. 9).

*ii, 19.* "The Lord of Uruk (Anu)." For "Lord of Uruk" as a title of Anu, see Tallqvist, *Götterepitheta,* pp. 56–57.

*ii, 22.* The copy reads *ina pu-*UK KI ŠU UT*-bu-ú,* differing from line 10 only in the signs ŠU UT instead of ŠÚ TE. Since lines 21 through 29 repeat lines 9 and 10 and 12 through 18 verbatim, lines 10 and 22 must be harmonized (*contra* what is implied in *ANET,* p. 503d). This is best done as above, emending line 22 to read as line 10; cf. Wilcke, *ZA* 67:203, note to l. "55." Less likely is von Soden's emendation of line 10 to read as line 22 (*ZA* 53:221), yielding *šú-ut*!*-bu-u* in line 10, for the sign *šú* does not normally appear at the beginning of a word.

| *GE* I | Gilg. Ni. |
|---|---|
| 30. ᵈ*A-ru-ru is-su-ú rabītam*(GAL$^{tam}$): | 1′. [x x x (x)] *is-su-u ra-bi-*[*tam*] |
| *at-ti* ᵈ*A-ru-ru tab-ni-*[*i amēlūta*] | 2′. [x x x (x)] *a-wi-lam ma-a-da* |
| 31. *e-nin-na bi-ni-i* ZI KIR ŠÚ *ana*(DIŠ) *u*$_4$*-um lìb-bi-šú* | 3′. [x x x (x)]-*šu* *ša da-an e-mu-qa* |

*ii, 30. is-su-ú rabītam,* "They called . . . the great." For another possible translation, cf. *BAL* 3:118, on *GE* XI, 116.

[*amēlūta*], "[mankind(?)]." Usually "Gilgamesh" or "the man" have been restored here (Jensen; *GETh.*), providing the expected antecedent for the pronouns in the next two lines. But lines 19 and 20 imply that Gilgamesh was created by Anu (cf. l. 3 of the pseudepigraphic letter of Gilgamesh published by Gurney, *An. St.* 7:128–29). Furthermore, Aruru is normally described as the creatress of mankind, not of particular individuals (see chap. 10, n. 7), hence Oppenheim's restoration of *amēlūta* (*Or.* 17:23, n. 4); this restoration seems to have the support of the parallel "numerous mankind" in Gilg. Ni.

*ii, 31.* The direct object of "create" is usually read *zi-kir-šú* and translated "his (i.e., Gilgamesh's) image, replica, counterpart" (*CAD* Z, p. 116c is typical). However, the meaning of this *zikru* (B) is uncertain, and the reading finds no support in line 33, where the *zikru* (if the reading is correct—see below) is not "of Gilgamesh," but "of Anu." Perhaps one might consider reading here *zi-kir kiššūti* (ŠÚ), "a powerful warrior." Cf. *CAD* Z, p. 112b; *CAD* K, pp. 461–62. Both words fit the idea that Enkidu is to be Gilgamesh's equal, for Gilgamesh is "most famous among warriors *(zikarī)*" (*GE* VI, 183, 185) and the "omen of Gilgamesh" portends ŠÚ (Leichty, *Summa Izbu,* p. 46, II, 6; however, the meaning of ŠÚ in that omen is moot; see Intro-

*Gilg. Ni.* Owing to the fragmentary condition of the text, continuous sense is discernible only in light of the parallel passage in *GE;* this may give an exaggerated impression of the similarity between the two texts.

*3′. ša da-an e-mu-qa,* "Who will be mighty in strength(?)" See discussion above, p. 193. After *ša,* one would expect *dan-nu,* not *da-an.*

*lu-u ma-*[*ḫir*]

32\. *liš-ta-an-na-nu-ma*
*Uruk*(UNUG)$^{ki}$ *liš-tap-*[*šiḫ*]

4′. [*li-iš*]*-ta-an-na-an-ma*
*Uruk*(UNUG)$^{ki}$ *li-iš-tap-ši-iḫ*

5′. [x x]*-zu*? *a-ḫa-tam*

6′. [x x *t*]*i-ma iz-za-kar-ši*

7′. [x x] x *a-a-ru tab-ni-i a-wi-lam*

33\. $^{d}$*A-ru-ru an-ni-ta ina*(AŠ) *še-me-šá:* ZIK RU *šá* $^{d}$*A-nim ib-ta-ni ina*(AŠ) *libbi*(ŠÀ)*-šá*

34\. [$^{d}$*A*]*-ru-ru im-ta-si qatā*(ŠU$^{II}$)*-šá ṭi-ṭa ik-ta-ri-iṣ it-ta-di ina*(AŠ) *ṣēri*(EDIN)

35\. [*ina*(AŠ) *ṣēr*]*i*([EDI]N)? $^{d}$*En-ki-dù ib-ta-ni qu-ra-du i-lit-ti* NUMUN*-ti ki-ṣir* $^{d}$*Ninurta*(NIN.IB)

---

duction, n. 60. *kiššūtu* occurs again in *GE* VI, 68).

*lu-u ma-*[*ḫir*], "let him be a match for . . . ," i.e., be able to face; cf. *ūmu lā maḫiri,* " 'storm' whom none can face," cited in *CAD* $M_1$, p. 99d. The usual translation, "let him match his stormy heart," restoring *ma*[*ḫir*] or *ma-*[*šil*], is implausible. Gilgamesh's stormy heart (termed *libbu lā ṣalilu,* "restless heart," in III, ii, 10), is the cause of the very problem the gods are seeking to obviate, and they would hardly want to duplicate such a heart.

*ii, 32. liš-ta-an-na-nu-ma,* "rival each other (in battle)," i.e., fight with each other. Delitzsch, p. 676b; Muss-Arnolt, p. 1074b; Stamm, *Asiatische Studien* 6:15.

*5′. a-ḫa-tam* (acc.), perhaps "sister" as an epithet of Aruru, Enlil's sister (cf. Sjöberg and Bergmann, p. 22, l. 98, and p. 74, l. 98); under the title "Mistress of the Gods," the mother-goddess is called "sister of the gods" in SB *Anzû* I, 112; cf. OB *Atr.* I, 296 (von Soden, *ZA* 68:68, l. 296/25).

*7′. a-a-ru* "young man." If this is the rare *ajaru* D (*CAD* $A_1$, p. 230); note that the word is connected in lexical texts with *eṭlu, zikru (zikaru),* and *qarradu.* However, a comparison of this line with *GE* I, ii, 30 in the parallel column suggests an emendation to *A-ru*!*-ru.*

*ii, 33.* ZIK RU. This line is hardly clarified by line 31, where even if the reading *zikru* is correct, it is Gilgamesh's *zikru,* not Anu's, which Aruru is asked to create (note Oppenheim's attempt to solve this problem, *Or.* 17:24). Elsewhere Enkidu is like a *kiṣru* of Anu (references in *CAD* K, p. 441d; note also *kiṣir* $^{d}$*Ninurta,* below, l. 35), and I suspect that this may be the intention here (i.e., *zik-ru* < *kiṣ-ru;* note the similarity of the signs *zik* (  ) and *kiṣ* (  ). (Alternatively the reading could be due to a verbal or aural error in dictation, resulting in a metathesis of consonants; cf. *mi-gir* < *ga-me-er* in *GSL,* p. 120 Col. II, l. 17, a variant of *GE* VI, 51, and cf. above, chap. 6, n. 5). The idea would be that Aruru had a *kiṣru* (meteor[?]; see note on Gilg. P., i, 7) of Anu in mind and in some way modeled Enkidu after it.

*ii, 35. ilitti* NUMUN*-ti,* "native/offspring of . . ." No satisfactory reading or meaning has been suggested for NUMUN*-ti.* Elsewhere Enkidu is described as *ilittašu sadûmma,* "offspring of the hills" (*GE* I, iv, 2) and *ina ṣēri iwwalidma,* "born on the steppe" (Gilg. P., i, 18; cf. *GE* I, v, 3; II, iv, 7; GEH, obv. 6 = GEUW, obv. 17).

*ki-ṣir* $^{d}$*Ninurta,* "strength(?) of / strengthened(?) by Ninurta." See *CAD* K, p.

36. [*šu*]-⌜ʼ⌝-*ur šar-ta ka-lu zu-um-ri-šú:*
*up-pu-uš pi-ri-tu kīma*(GIM) *sin-niš-ti*
37. *i-ti-iq pi-ir-ti-šu uḫ-tan-na-ba ki-ma* d*Nisaba*
38. *la i-di nišī*(UN.MEŠ) *u ma-tam-ma:*
*lu-bu-uš-ti la-biš kīma*(GIM) d*Sumuqan*
39. *it-ti ṣabāti*(MAŠ.DÀ.MEŠ)-*ma ik-ka-la šam-mi*
40. *it-ti bu-lim maš-qa-a i-ṭàp-pir*
41. *it-ti nam-maš-ši-e mē*(A.MEŠ) *i-ṭàb lìb-ba-šú*

---

259b *sub* el′ and p. 440d *sub* e, citing Stamm, *Namengebung,* pp. 258, 321–22; *AHw,* p. 489b *sub* 9. If the text really intends *kiṣru* of Ninurta, the word may be given a meaning different from that in *kiṣru ša Anim,* "meteor(?) of Anu." But since Enkidu is consistently *kiṣru* of Anu elsewhere in the epic, one is surprised by the appearance of Ninurta here. Does Ninurta replace an original Anu (as in *GE* XI, 179, replacing Anu of OB *Atr.* III, vi, 11)? If so, *kiṣru* must have the same meaning as in *kiṣru ša Anim.*

*ii, 38. ma-tam-ma,* "civilized land." Cf. Castellino, SVT 4:121: "cultivated land."

## 4. *Hit. Gilg.* I, No. 1, 3–end, and No. 2, 1–12

Translations on pp. 153, 179, 193, and 199.

Texts from Otten, *Ist. Mit.* 8:98–101, as revised and supplemented by Laroche, *RHA* 82:8–10; translation follows Otten where available, and unpublished translation by H. A. Hoffner. Earlier edition of no. 1, ll. 3–14 by Friedrich, *ZA* 39:2–5; translation of no. 1, ll. 3–11 in Heidel, p. 17; Schott and von Soden (1970), pp. 17–18.

The horizontal lines represent section dividers found in the original text.

**No. 1**

---

3. ša-am-ni-ia-an-ta-an UR.SAG-iš dx[. . . .]
4. dGIŠ.GIM.MAŠ-un ALAM-an ša-am-ni-ir-ma [šal-la-uš DINGIRMEŠ-uš(?)]
5. dGIŠ.GIM.MAŠ-un ALAM-an dUTU ŠA.ME.E-iš-[ši LÚ-na-tar(?)]
6. [p]a-a-iš dU-aš-ma-aš-ši UR.SAG-tar pa-a-iš ša[-am-ni-ir-ma]
7. šal-la-uš DINGIRMEŠ-uš dGIŠ.GIM.MAŠ-un ALAM-ši pá[r-ga-aš-ti]
8. 11 AM-MA-TUM GAB-ma-aš-ši pal-ḫa-a-aš-ti 9 w[a-ak-šur(?)]
9. UZUMI!-ni-uš-ma-aš-ši da-lu-ga-aš-ti 3 [. . . .]

---

10. [nu] KUR.KURMEŠ ḫu-u-ma-an-da ú-e-ḫe-eš-ki-iz-z[i na-aš-kán]

11. $^{URU}$U-ra-ga URU-ri a-ar-aš na-aš-za-kán x[. . . .]
12. nu-za UD$^{KAM}$-ti-li ŠA $^{URU}$U-ra-ga LÚ$^{MEŠ}$ K[AL]
13. tar-aḫ-ḫi-iš-ki-u-wa-an da-a-iš nu DINGIR.MA[Ḫ. . . .]
14. na-aš-kán $^{d}$GIŠ.GIM.MAŠ-aš IM$^{MEŠ}$-aš an-d[a. . . .]
15. DINGIR.[M]AḪ-aš-ma(?)[. . . .] x-an a-uš-t[a. . . .]

Frag. Ea, 16. [n]a-a[š-za. . . .Š]À$^{BI}$-iš(?)-š[i(?) ka]r-tim-mi-ia[-at-ta-at]

---

17. nu DINGIR$^{MEŠ}$ ḫu-u-m[a-an-te-eš. . . . p]ár-ra-an-ta[. . . .]
18. tu-li-ia-aš p[í-di(?). . . . -a]n pa-it nu[. . . .]
19. u-ni-in-wa ku-[in $^{d}$GIŠ.GIM.MAŠ-un(?) š]a-am-ni-ia-at-t[e(?)-en(?)]
20. nu am-mu-uk[. . . . š]a-am-ni-ia-nu-u[n. . . .]
21. na-a[š-]x[. . . . a]n-da im-mi-i[a-. . . .]. . . .

**No. 2**

1. [nu DINGIR$^{ME}$]$^{Š}$ ḫu-u-ma-an-te-[eš. . . .]
2. [UR.SAG-i]n $^{d}$GIŠ.GIM.MAŠ-un[. . . .]
3. [$^{d}$GIŠ.GIM.MAŠ-u]š-ša-wa LÚ$^{MEŠ}$ K[AL. . . . ]
4. [. . . . -a]š e-ni-eš-ša-a[n iš-ta]-ma-aš-ta nu-kán DINGIR.M[AḪ-a]š
5. [. . . . -a]z-za mi-i-tar ar-ḫa da-a-aš na-aš-ká[n i-ia]-an-ni-eš
6. [. . . . U]R.SAG-in $^{d}$En-ki-ta-an LÍL-ri an-da š[a-a]m-ni-ia-at

---

7. [. . . . UR.]SAG-iš $^{d}$En-ki-ta-aš LÍL-ri an-d[a]
8. [na-an MÁŠ.]ANŠE$^{ḪI.A}$ šal-la-nu-uš-kán-zi nu-uš-ši x
9. x[-x-x]-zi nu ku-e-ez MÁŠ.ANŠE$^{ḪI.A}$ ú-e-ši-[ia-u-wa-an-zi]
10. i-i[a-at(?)-]ta-ri $^{d}$En-ki-d[u-u]š-ša-ma-aš-ta [GAM-an i-ia-at-ta-ri]
11. š[a-ku-r]u-u-wa-u-wa-an-zi-ia [ku-e-ez i-ia-at(?)-ta-ri]
12. [$^{d}$En-k]i-du-ša-aš-ma-aš GAM-a[n i-ia-at-ta-ri]

---

*13.* tar-aḫ-ḫi-iš-ki-u-wa-an, "besting." The verb is Hit. tarḫ- which, preceded by the particle za (l. 12), means "triumph over, defeat" (*Heth. Wb.,* p. 213). While this verb is frequently used in military contexts, the adverb "daily" suggests a contest or single combat. In the Hittite tale *Gurparanzahu,* the verb is used for winning an archery contest (KUB 17, no. 9, l. 23′ [Güterbock, *ZA* 44:86–87]) According to Friedrich, *Heth. Wb.,* p. 213, the Akkadian equivalent of tarḫ- is *le'û;* the latter is used of both military and athletic contests (*CAD* L, p. 156ab *sub* b).

## 5. Gilg. P. i, 1–ii, 1 and *GE* I, v, 25–vi, 27

Translations on pp. 82–87.

Text of Gilg. P. from Langdon, PBS 10(3), revised in light of subsequent studies; A. Westenholz's unpublished copy; and collation by E. Leichty of a plaster cast of the tablet UM 7771. Important editions and studies include Jastrow and Clay, YOR 4(3):62–86, 103–6; *GETh.,* pp. 20–24; and notes by von Soden, *ZA* 53:210–12.

*GE* I from *GETh.,* pp. 15–16 and pls. 6–8, supplemented (for vi, 16–27) by *CT* 46, no. 18, edited by Wiseman in *GSL,* p. 126; notes by von Soden, *ZA* 53:222.

| **Gilg. P.** | ***GE* I** |
|---|---|
| i, 1. *it-bi-e-ma* $^{d}$GIŠ<br>*šu-na-tam i-pa-aš-šar* | v, 25. *it-bi-ma* $^{d}$GIŠ.GÍN.MAŠ<br>*šu-na-ta ipaššar*(BÚR$^{ár}$) |
| 2. *iz-za-kàr-am*<br>*a-na um-mi-šu* | *izzakkar*(MU$^{ár}$)<br>*a-na ummi*(AMA)-*šú* |
| 3. ⸢*um*⸣-*mi i-na ša-a-at*<br>*mu-ši-ti-ia* | 26. *um-mi šunat*(MÁŠ.GI$_6$)<br>*aṭ-ṭu-lu mu-ši-ti-ia* |
| 4. ⸢*ša*⸣-*am-ḫa-ku-ma*<br>*at-ta-na-a*[*l*]-*la-ak* | |
| 5. [*i-n*]*a bi-ri-it eṭ-lu-*⸢*tim*⸣ | |
| 6. *ib-b*[*a-š*]*u-nim-ma*<br>*ka-ka-bu*<br>*ša-ma-i* | 27. *ib-šu-nim-ma*<br>*kakkabāni*(MUL.MEŠ)<br>*šamê*(AN$^{e}$) |
| 7. ⸢*ki-iṣ*!?⸣-*rum ša A-nim*<br>*im-qú-ut*<br>*a-na ṣe-ri-ia* | 28. *kīma*(GIM) *ki-iṣ-ru ša* $^{d}$*A-nim*<br>*im-ta-naq-qu-ut*<br>*e-li ṣēri*(EDIN)-*ia* |

*i, 6.* Von Soden's reading of the first word as *ip-ḫ*[*u-r*]*u-nim-ma* is not supported by collation; *b*[*a*] seems best.

*i, 7.* I retain the usual reading *ki-iṣ-* (as in the late version) against von Soden's *si-ip-* on the strength of collation; the traces of the first sign are very similar to *ki,* while the second is definitely not *ip.* The translation of *kiṣrum* as "meteor(?)" (*CAD* K, p. 441d; *AHw,* p. 488d *sub* 6) fits the astral context of the dream. However, Dossin argues that since the *kiṣru* has a body and feet (see

*v, 28. ki-iṣ-ru,* "meteor(?)." See note on Gilg. P. i, 7.

8. *aš-ši-šu-ma*
*ik-ta-bi-it e-li-ia*

9. *ú-ni-iš-šu-ma*
*nu-uš-ša-šu ú-ul el-te*$_{9}$*-'i*

10. *Uruk*(UNUG)$^{ki}$ *ma-tum*
*pa-ḫi-ir e-li-šu*

11. *eṭ-lu-tum*
*ú-na-ša-qú še*$_{20}$*-pi-šu*

12. *ú-um-mi-id-ma pu-ti*

13. *i-mi-du ia-ti*

14. *aš-ši-a-šu-ma at-ba-la-aš-šu*
*a-na ṣe-ri-ki*

29. *áš-ši-šu-ma*
*[d]a-an e-li-ia*

30. *ul-tab-lak-ki-is-su-⌜ma⌝*
*ul e-le-'-ia nu-us-su*

31. *Uruk*(UNUG)$^{ki}$ *ma-a-tum*
*iz-za-az eli*(UGU)-[*šú*]

32. [*ma-a-tu pu-uḫ-ḫu-rat*]
*ina*(AŠ) [*muḫ-ḫi-šú*]

33. [*i-ṭàp-pi-ir um-ma*]*-nu*
*e*[*li*(U[GU]) *ṣēri*(EDIN)*-šú*]

34. [*eṭlūtu*(GURUŠ.MEŠ)
*uk*]*-tam-ma-ru eli*(UGU)*-šu*

35. [*ki-i šèr-ri la*]*-'i-i*
*u-na-šá-qu šēpī*(GÌR.MEŠ)*-šu*

36. [*a-ram-šu-ma ki-m*]*a áš-šá-te*
*eli*(UGU)*-šú aḫ-bu-ub*

37. [*u a*]*t-ta-di-šú*
*ina*(AŠ) *šap-li-*[*ki*]

---

l. 11), it must be an animal; he therefore derives *kiṣru* from *kaṣāru* in the sense of "construct" and takes it to mean something like "creature," "offspring" (*Le Muséon* 59:63–66).

*i, 12–13. ú-um-mi-id-ma pu-ti,* "I set my forehead." For pulling by a forehead strap, see Jacobsen, *Ac. Or.* 8:67, n. 3. The line is understood differently in *AHw,* p. 212 *sub* D, 4, a and *CAD* E, p. 145a.

*i, 14. at-ba-la-aš-šu.* Jensen, cited by von Soden.

*v, 29.* [*d*]*a-an,* "mighty." In the context, *dan* means heavy (see chap. 4, n. 39), as the parallel passage reads explicitly *(ik-ta-bi-it).* The translation "mighty" is chosen only to bring out the fact that the line uses the same word found in Gilg. Ni 3′; *GE* I, iii, 3–4; v, 3; and below, in the interpretation of the dreams, vi, 1–3, 21–23. See discussion above, pp. 87–88.

*v, 30. ul-tab-lak-ki-is-su-⌜ma⌝.* Ungnad, cited by Schott, *ZA* 42:102.

*v, 35.* Restored from II, ii, 42 (cf. von Soden; *CAD* L, p. 114b).

*v, 36. aḫ-bu-ub,* "caressed(?)." See notes on Gilg. P. i, 34.

*v, 36, 47; vi, 4, 14.* Grayson's translation in *ANET* implies the restoration of *a/ta-ram-šu-ma* at the beginning of these lines (as in vi, 19); collation by E. Leichty shows that there is room for this on the tablet (though in the case of v, 36 "just barely").

15. *um-mi* $^{d}$GIŠ *mu-di-a-at ka-la-ma*

16. *iz-za-kàr-am a-na* $^{d}$GIŠ

38. [*at-ti tul*]-*ta-maḫ-ri-šu it-ti-ia*

39. [*um-mi* $^{d}$GIŠ.GÍN.MAŠ *em-qet mu*]-*da-at ka-la-ma i-di izzakkar*(MU$^{ár}$) *ana*(DIŠ) *bēli*(EN)-*šá*

40. [$^{f}$*Ri-mat-*$^{d}$*Nin-sún em-qet*] *mu-da-at ka-la-ma i-di*

*izzakkar*(MU$^{ár}$) *ana*(DIŠ) $^{d}$GIŠ.GÍN.MAŠ

41. [*ša ta-mu*]-*ru*!? *kakkabāni*(MUL.MEŠ) *šamê*(AN$^{e}$)

42. [*kīma*(GIM) *ki-iṣ-ru ša* $^{d}$*A*]-*nim šá imtanaqutu*(ŠUB.MEŠ) *eli*(UGU) *ṣēri*(EDIN)-*ka*

43. [*taš-ši-šu-ma da*]-*an eli*(UGU)-*ka*

44. [*tul-tab-lak-ki-is-su-ma ul*] *te-le-'-ia nu-us-su*

45. [*at-ta ta-ad-d*]*i-šu ina*(AŠ) *šap-li-ia*

46. [*a-na-ku ul-ta-maḫ*]-*ḫar-šu it-ti-ka*

47. [*ta-ram-šu-ma ki-i/ma áš-šá-te*] ⌜*e*⌝-*li-šú taḫ*-[*bu-ub*]

*v, 38; vi, 15.* [*at-ti*]. Jensen, cited by von Soden; cf. vi, 20.

*v, 38.* [*tul*]-*ta-maḫ-ri-šu,* "made it compete." See the note on Gilg. P. ii, 1.

*v, 39–40; vi, 16.* Restored from vi, 16–17 (cf. *GE* III, i, 17).

*v, 41.* [*ša ta-mu*]-*ru.* Cf. vi, 18; V, iii, 40; Gilg. Har. B, 12.

*v, 46.* [*a-na-ku*]. See note on v, 38.

17. *mi-in-di* $^{d}$GIŠ
*ša ki-ma ka-ti*

18. *i-na ṣe-ri i-wa-li-id-ma*

19. *ú-ra-ab-bi-šu ša-du-ú*

20. *ta-mar-šu-m*[*a* (x?)]
*ta-ḫa-du at-ta*

21. *eṭ-lu-tum ú-na-ša-qú še*$_{20}$*-pi-šu*

22. *te-ed-di-ra-aš-*[*šu* (?)
(x)]*-šu* ?*-ú-ma*

23. ⌜*ta*⌝*-tar-ra-aš-*⌜*šu a-na*⌝ *ṣe-r*[*i-i*]*a*

24. [*i*]*t-ti-lam-ma i-ta-mar*
*ša-ni-tam*

25. [*i*]*t-bi*
*i-ta-wa-a-am*
*a-na um-mi-šu*

26. [*um*]-⌜*mi a*⌝-[*t*]*a-mar*
*ša-ni-tam*

vi, 1. [*il-la-ka-ak-kúm-ma dan-nu*
*tap*]*-pu-u mu-še-zib* [*ib-ri*]

2. [*i-na māti*(KUR) *da-an*]
⌜*e*⌝*-mu-qí i-*[*šu*]

3. [*ki-ma ki-iṣ-ru šá* $^{d}$*A-nim*
*d*]*un-nu-na e-mu-*[*qa-šu*]

4. [*ta-ram-šu-ma ki-i/ma áš-šá-te*]
*e-li-šu taḫ-b*[*u-ub*]

5. [*u šu-u* (?) *uš-te*]*-né-zib-ka*
*ka-*[*a-ša*]

6. [*dam-qa-at šu-qu-r*]*at*
*šu-na-at-ka*

7. [$^{d}$GIŠ.GÍN.MAŠ *ša-niš*
*izzakkar*(MU$^{ár}$)]
*a-na ummi*(AMA)*-šú*

8. [*um-mi a-t*]*a-mar*
*šá-ni-ta šu-ut-ta*

*i, 20.* According to von Soden, nothing is missing here; cf. line 32. Collation neither confirms nor excludes this.

*i, 25.* [*i*]*t-bi.* Thus Westenholz.

*vi, 1–3.* Restored from vi, 21–23.

*vi, 4. taḫ-b*[*u-ub*], "will caress." Since this is part of the interpretation, the tense should be future, as explicitly in vi, 19. I assume that *taḫbub* is an error for *taḫabbub,* perhaps induced by the proximity of *taḫbub* in v, 47, if not simply a case of scribal indifference to tenses (see chap. 6, n. 4).

On the beginning of this line, see the note on v, 36, 47, etc.

*vi, 5.* [*uš-te*]*-né-zib-ka.* Von Soden.

*vi, 6.* [*dam-qa-at šu-qu*]*-rat.* Landsberger *RA* 62:116–20; cf. *GE* V, iii, 38–39; Gilg. Meg. 10–11; *GE* VII: *STT* no. 14, obv. 20a–21a. On *šūqurat,* see also Speiser, *OBS,* p. 475.

| | |
|---|---|
| 27. [*i-na bāb*(KÁ) *bī*]*t*(⌜É⌝) *e-mi-a i-na su-qí-im* | 9. [*ina*(AŠ) *bāb*(KA) *bīt*(É) *e-mu-tī*] |
| 28. [*ša Uru*]*k*([UNU]G)$^{ki}$ *re-bi-tim* | |
| 29. *ḫa-⌜aṣ-ṣi⌝-nu na-di-i-ma* | *ḫa-ṣi-nu na-di-ma* |
| 30. *e-li-šu pa-aḫ-ru* | *eli*(UGU)-*šú paḫ-ru* |
| | 10. [*Uruk*(UNUG)$^{ki}$ *ma-a*]-*tum izzaz* (GUB$^{az}$) *eli*(UGU)-*šú* |
| | 11. [*ma-a-tum pu-uḫ-ḫu-r*]*at ina*(AŠ) *muḫ-ḫi-šú* |
| | 12. [*i-ṭàp-pi-ir um-ma*]-*nu eli*(UGU) *ṣēri*(EDIN)-*šú* |
| | 13. [*a-na-ku*] *at-ta-di-šu ina*(AŠ) *šap-li-ki* |
| 31. *ḫa-aṣ-ṣi-nu-um-ma ša-ni bu-nu-šu* | |
| 32. *a-mur-šu-ma aḫ-ta-du a-na-ku* | |
| 33. *a-ra-am-šu-ma ki-ma aš-ša-tim* | 14. [*a-ram-šu-ma*] *ki-i áš-šá-te* |
| 34. *a-ḫa-ab-bu-ub el-šu* | *eli*(UGU)-*šú aḫ-bu-ub* |

*i, 27.* The restoration is based on the ultimate realization of the dream, Gilg. P. vi, 12; *GE* II, ii, 46, 48 (below, no. 7). The reading *e-mi-a* is supported by collation (the first and last signs are clearly different from each other, ruling out von Soden's *e-ši-e*).

*i, 34. a-ḫa-ab-bu-ub,* "caressed(?)." For the problematic *ḫabābu,* see *ANET,* p. 75, n. 27, and the literature cited there; *CAD* Ḫ, p. 2b; Moran, *Biblica* 50:31, n. 3; Landsberger, *RA* 62:117, n. 71, l. 19. The word could refer to sexual intercourse, as argued by Jacobsen (*Act. Or.* 8:69, n. 2; cf. Biggs, *ŠÀ.ZI.GA,* p. 33, no. 14:7–8), but like the parallel *râmu* (see the passage in Biggs) it may also be a more general term for "love"; note also the lexical equation with *našāqu,* "kiss," cited by *CAD,* and cf. Gilgamesh and Enkidu's kissing each other in friendship, Gilg. Y. i, 19.

*vi, 9.* See note on Gilg. P. i, 27. Collation shows that there is enough room for the restoration.

*vi, 14.* [*a-ram-šu-ma*]. See the note on v, 36.

| | |
|---|---|
| 35. *el-qí-šu-ma aš-ta-ka-an-šu* | |
| 36. *a-na a-ḫi-ia* | |
| | 15. [*at-ti t*]*ul-ta-maḫ-ḫa-ri-šu* *it-ti-ia* |
| 37. ⸢*um-mi* $^{d}$GIŠ *mu*⸣*-da-at* ⸢*ka-la*⸣*-ma* | 16. ⸢*um-mi* $^{d}$GIŠ.GÍN.MAŠ⸣ [*e*]*m-qet* *mu-da-at ka-lá-ma i-di* *izzakkara*(MU$^{ra}$) *ana*(DIŠ) *māri*(DUMU)-*šá* |
| | 17. $^{f}$*Ri-mat-*$^{d}$*Nin-sún em-qet* *mu-da-at ka-lá-ma i-di* |
| 38. [*iz-za-kar-am a-na* $^{d}$GIŠ] | *izzakkara*(MU$^{ra}$) *ana*(DIŠ) $^{d}$GIŠ.GÍN.MAŠ |
| (break of a few lines) | 18. $^{urudu}$*ḫa-ṣi-in-nu šá ta-mu-ru* *amēlu*(LÚ) |
| | 19. *ta-ram-šu-ma* [*ki*]*-i áš-šá-te* *ta-ḫab-bu-ub eli*(UGU)-*šu* |
| ii, 1. *aš-šum uš-*[*ta*]*-ma-ḫa-ru* *it-ti-ka* | 20. *u a-na-ku ul-ta-maḫ-ḫar-šú* *itti*(KI)-*ka* |

*i, 35. a-na a-ḫi-ia,* "at my side." See chap. 4, n. 36, for a possible double entendre here.

*ii, 1. uš-*[*ta*]*-ma-ḫa-ru,* "he shall compete with you," taking the verb as third-person reciprocal, with Enkidu as the subject (*AHw,* p. 580a *sub* 2; *CAD* $M_1$, p. 70c). Others conform the passage to *GE* I, v, 38, 46; vi, 15, 20, by taking the verb as first person (subject: Ninsun) and assuming that a third-person direct object is implicit. However, unlike the parallel passages in the late version, in this version of the second dream Ninsun plays no role, and there is no accusative suffix. Landsberger takes *šutamḫuru* (and *šumḫuru* in *GE* V, iv, 23) as a technical term for dream interpretation, apparently understanding it as "give the correspondence (between the dream and what it symbolizes)"; see *RA* 62:118, n. 73; cf. *CAD* $M_2$, p. 58 *sub* d. However, the following *ittika,* "with you," seems pointless according to this interpretation, whereas *šutamḫuru itti* is attested in the sense of "compete

*vi, 17.* [*em-qet*]. The word is preserved fully only in *CT* 46, no. 18, which actually reads *en-qet.*

21. *il-la-ka-ak-kúm-ma dan-nu tap-pu-ú mu-še-zib ib-ri*

22. *ina*(AŠ) *māti*(KUR) *da-an e-mu-qí i-šu*

23. *ki-ma ki-ṣir šá* $^{d}$*A-nim dun-nu-na e-mu-qa-šu*

24. $^{d}$GIŠ.GÍN.MAŠ *<a-na> šá-ši-ma izzakkar*(MU$^{ár}$) *a-na ummi*(AMA)-*šu*

25. [x x]-*ma ina*(AŠ) *qibīt*(DUG$_4$) $^{d}$*En-líl ma-lik li-in-qu-ut-m*[*a*]

26. [*ib*]-*ri ma-li-ku a-na-ku lu-ur-ši*

27. [*lu-u*]*r-ši-ma ib-ri ma-li-ka a-na-ku*

---

with," "rival," "act as someone's equal," including contexts where no dreams are mentioned; see *CAD* $M_1$, p. 70 *sub* 11a.

*vi, 25. ma-lik.* The reading in *GETh.*, pl. 8, is KU/[K]I GAL-*i;* owing to the break preceding it, no interpretation can confidently be proposed.

## 6. Gilg. P. ii, 12–13, 27–30; iii, 1–9, 22–27; GEUW obv. 4, 9–10, 19–21

Translations on pp. 199–200.
Bibliography for Gilg. P. as above, no. 5.
GEUW from von Weiher, *ZA* 62:224.

| **Gilg. P.** | **GEUW, obv.** |
|---|---|
| ii, 12. *am-mi-nim it-ti na-ma-aš-te-e* | 4. *am-mi-ni itti*(KI) *n*[*am-maš-še-e* |
| 13. *ta-at-ta-*[*n*]*a-la-ak ṣe-ra-am* | *ta-rap-pu-ud ṣēra* (EDIN)] |
| . . . | . . . |
| 27. *iš-ḫu-uṭ* [*l*]*i-ib-ša-am* | |

*ii, 13.* Von Soden restores *ta-at-ta-*[*na-a*]*l-la-ak,* but collation shows no room for two signs.

*obv. 4.* Restored from *GE* I, iv, 35.

| | |
|---|---|
| 28. *iš-ti-nam u-la-ab-bi-íš-šu* | 9. *istēn*(1$^{en}$) *lu-bu-šú* x [x x x x x x x x x x] |
| 29. *li-ib-⌜ša-am⌝ ša-ni-a-am* | 10. *ù šá-na-a lu-bu-šú* |
| 30. *ši-i* [*i*]*t-ta-al-ba-aš* | *ša*[x x x x x x x x x x] |
| . . . | |
| iii, 1. *ši-iz-ba ša na-ma-aš-te-e* | |
| 2. *i-te-en-ni-iq* | |
| 3. *a-ka-lam iš-ku-nu ma-ḫar-su* | 19. *a-ka-lu iš-ku-nu ma-ḫar-*[*šú*] |
| | 20. *ši-ka-ri iš-ku-nu ma-ḫa*[*r-šú*] |
| | 21. *ul i-kul a-kal* $^{d}$*En-ki-dù* |
| 4. *ip-te-eq-ma i-na-aṭ-ṭal* | *ip-te-eq i-da*[*g-gal*] |
| 5. *u ip-pa-al-la-as* | |
| 6. *u-ul i-di* $^{d}$*En-ki-du*$_{10}$ | |
| 7. *aklam*(NINDA) *a-na a-ka-lim* | |
| 8. *šikaram*(KAŠ) *a-na ša-te-e-em* | |
| 9. *la-a lum-mu-ud* | |
| . . . | |
| 22. *ul-tap-pi-it* [x (x)]-*i* | |
| 23. *šu-ʾu*$_{5}$*-ra-am pa-ga-ar-šu* | |
| 24. *ša-am-nam ip-ta-ša-aš-ma* | |
| 25. *a-we-li-iš i-we* | |
| 26. *il-ba-aš li-ib-ša-am* | (Cf. 9–10) |
| 27. *ki-ma mu-ti i-ba-aš-ši* | |

*iii, 22.* The usual restorations are [*ma-li*]-*i,* "shaggy growth" or "grimy hair" (cf. *GE* VI, 1 and see Schott, *ZA* 42: 105); or [*mi*]-*i,* "(with) water" (von Soden). Renger reads *gallābum* (i.e., SU.I), "barber," and renders lines 22–23 "the barber went over his hairy body" (Renger, "Mesopotamian Epic Literature," p. 43). One wonders whether a barber would have been present at a shepherd's hut, where this scene takes place. However, Westenholz's copy is patient of the reading ⌜ŠU⌝.I.

## 7. Gilg. P. v, 9–vi, 23 and *GE* II, ii, 35–50

Translations on pp. 90–92.

Bibliography for Gilg. P. as above, no. 5; notes by von Soden, *ZA* 53:212; Finkelstein, *JAOS* 90:252.

*GE* II, ii from *GETh.*, p. 17 and pl. 9; notes by von Soden, *ZA* 53:223.

| **Gilg. P.** | ***GE* II** |
|---|---|
| v, 9. *i-ru-ub-ma a-na lib*[*bi*](Š[À]) *Uruk*(UNUG)$^{ki}$ *re-bi*!*-tim* | |
| | ii, 35. . . . *ina*(AŠ) *sūqi*(SILA) *ša* *Uruk*(UNUG)$^{k}$[$^{i}$ *su-pu-ri*] |
| | 36. [x (x)]⌜E⌝ I BI EŠ *dan-nu-ti-ma* [(?)] |
| | 37. *ip-ta-ra-as a-lak-ta* [x x x x x] |
| 10. *ip-ḫur um-ma-nu-*[*u*]*m* *i-na ṣe-ri-šu* | 38. *Uruk*(UNUG)$^{ki}$ *ma-a-tu* *iz-za-az* [*eli*(UGU)*-šú*] |
| 11. *iz-zi-za-am-ma* ⌜*i*⌝*-na sú-qí-im* | 39. *ma-a-tu pu-uḫ-ḫu-rat* [*ina*(AŠ) *muḫ-ḫi-šú*] |
| 12. *ša Uruk*(UNUG)$^{ki}$ *re-bi-tim* | |
| 13. *pa-aḫ-ra-a-ma ni-šu* | 40. *i-ṭàp-pi-ir um-man-nu* [*eli*(UGU) *ṣēri*(EDIN)*-šú*] |
| | 41. *eṭlūtu*(GURUŠ.MEŠ) *uk-tam-ma-ru* [*eli*(UGU)*-šú*] |
| | 42. *ki-i šèr-ri la-'i-i* *u-n*[*a-šá-qu šepī*(GÌR.MEŠ)*-šú*] |
| 14. *i-ta-wa-a i-na ṣe-ri-šu* | |
| 15. *a-na-mi* $^{d}$GIŠ *ma-ši-il* *pa-da-tam* | |
| 16. *la-nam* [*š*]*a-pi-il* | |

*v, 11.* The subject of the singular verb could be either Enkidu or the populace of line 10.

*ii, 35.* Perhaps restore from Gilg. P. i, 27 (and *GE* I, v, 9?).

*ii, 38–42.* Restored from *GE* I, v, 31–35.

17. *e-*⌜*ṣi-im-tam*(?)⌝ [*pu*]*-uk-ku-ul*

18. x [x x x x (x)] ⌜*i*⌝*-*[*w*]*a-*⌜*al*(?)⌝*-du*

19. *i-k*[*u-ul*] *di-i-*⌜*ši*⌝

20. *ši-iz-ba š*[*a n*]*a-*⌜*ma*⌝*-*[*aš-te*]*-e*

21. *i-te-en-*⌜*ni*⌝*-iq*

22. *ka-a-a-na i-na Uruk*(UNUG)$^{ki}$ *ni-qí-a-tum*

23. *eṭ-lu-tum* ⌜*ú*⌝*-te-el-li-lu*

24. *ša-ki-in lu-ša-nu*

25. *a-na eṭlu*(GURUŠ) *ša i-*[*š*]*a-ru zi-mu-šu*

26. *a-na* $^{d}$GIŠ *ki-ma i-li-im*

27. *ša-ki-iš-šum me-eḫ-rum*

28. *a-na* $^{d}$*Iš-ḫ*[*a*]*-ra ma-a-a-lum*

29. *na-*⌜*di*⌝*-i-ma*

30. $^{d}$GIŠ *it-*[*ti w*]*a-a*[*r-da-t*]*im*

43. *ul-la-nu-um-ma eṭ-lu ba-ni* [x x x x x]

44. *a-na* $^{d}$*Iš-ḫa-ra*

*ma-a-a-al* [*aš-šu*]*-ti* [*na-di*]

45. *a-na* $^{d}$GIŠ.GÍN.MAŠ *ki-ma ili*(DINGIR)

*šá-ki-i*[*n-š*]*ú* BU-*rum*(?)

(Note that *GE* II, ii, 44–45 = Gilg P. v, 26–27 and 28–29 in inverse order.)

*v, 18–19.* Cf. GEH i, 6 in a similar context.

*v, 22. ni-qí-a-tum.* Von Soden, supported by collation.

*v, 24. lu-ša-nu.* Finkelstein, following Landsberger; cf. *CAD* L, p. 256c. Collation supports *lu-* over *ur-*.

*v, 27. me-eḫ-rum.* Finkelstein guesses at a musical instrument, though none by this name is known. There is a *meḫru* offering, and the word also refers to the antiphone or refrain of a hymn (*AHw,* p. 641c *sub* 8; p. 641a *sub* 3; *CAD* Z, p. 36 *sub* c). *CAD*'s "warrior of equal rank" (*CAD* M$_2$, p. 57c) does not fit the immediate context.

*v, 30.* Westenholz, supported by collation.

*ii, 43. ba-ni,* "handsome." Cf. *GE* VI, 182 and *CAD* B, p. 81c.

*ii, 44. ma-a-a-al* [*aš-šu*]*-ti.* Cf. OB *Atr.* I, 299–302.

31. *i-na mu-ši in-né-*[*mi-i*]*d*

32. *i-ta-ag-*[*š*]*a-am-ma*

33. *it-ta-z*[*i-iz* $^{d}$*En-ki-du*$_{10}$]
*i-na sūqim*(SILA)

34. *ip-ta-r*[*a-as a-l*]*a-ak-tam*

35. *ša* $^{d}$GIŠ

36. [x x x x x (x)] x *da-nu-ni-iš-šu*

vi, 1–4. (nothing preserved)

5. ⸢*i*⸣*-ḫa* x [x x x x x x (x x)]

6. $^{d}$GIŠ *m*[*a*(?)x x x x x (x x)]

7. *i-na ṣe-ri* [x x x x (x x)]

8. *i-ḫa-an-ni-*⸢*ib*⸣[x x x (x x)]

9. *it-bi-ma* [$^{d}$*En-ki-du*$_{10}$]

10. *a-na pa-ni-*⸢*šu*⸣

11. *it-tam-ḫa-ru i-na re-bi-tu ma-ti*

12. $^{d}$*En-ki-du*$_{10}$ *ba-ba-am*
*ip-ta-ri-ik*

13. ⸢*i-na*⸣ *še*$_{20}$*-pi-šu*

14. $^{d}$GIŠ *e-re-ba-am*
*ú-ul id-di-in*

15. *iṣ-ṣa-ab-tu-ma*
*ki-ma le-i-im*

16. *i-lu-du*

46. $^{d}$*En-ki-dù ina*(AŠ) *bāb*(KÁ)
*bīt*(É) *e-mu-ti*
*ip-te-rik*
*šēpā*(GÌR$^{II}$)-[*šú*]

47. $^{d}$GIŠ.GÍN.MAŠ *a-na šu-ru-bi*
*ul i-nam-din*

48. *iṣ-ṣab-tu-ma*
*ina*(AŠ) *bāb*(KÁ) *bīt*(É) *e-mu-ti*

*v, 31.* Von Soden, *OLZ* 1955: 514; *CAD* E, p. 146c.

*v, 32.* Westenholz; cf. von Soden.

*v, 33. it-ta-z*[*i-iz*]. Jastrow and Clay, YOR 4(3), p. 67, l. 197.

*v, 36.* Westenholz, supported by collation.

*vi, 8. ḫanābu* is used of Enkidu's hair in *GE* I, ii, 37. *CAD* Ḫ, p. 76d reads *i-ḫa-an-ni-*⸢*ip*⸣, from a root of unknown meaning.

*vi, 15–16, 21. le-i-im,* "champions (lit. victors)." This rendering is based on

*ii, 46, 48. bīt e-mu-ti,* "marriage chamber." See Finkelstein, *RA* 61:127–36; note also Civil, *JNES* 23:3, l. 14.

17. *sí-ip-pa-am i'-bu-tu*
18. *i-ga-rum ir-tu-ut*
19. $^{d}$GIŠ *ù* [$^{d}$]⌜*En-ki*⌝-*du*$_{10}$
20. *iṣ-ṣa-ab-tu-ú-ma*
21. *ki-ma le-i-im i-lu-du*
22. *sí-ip-pa-am i'-bu-tu*
23. *i-ga-rum ir-tu-ut*

49. *ina*(AŠ) *sūqi*(SILA)
*it-te-eg-ru-ú* ⌜*ri*⌝-*bit ma-a-tu*
50. [*s*]*ip-*[*p*]*u/i*? *ir-ú*!-*bu*
*i-ga-ra i-tú-uš*

(remainder missing)

---

*CAD* L, p. 36c ("wrestler") and 156a (the verb *le'û* used twice for victory in wrestling); there is no entry for a noun *lē'û* with the specific meaning "wrestler." The usual translation "bulls" is inappropriate after "grappling," unless one assumes that the simile applies only to the following "bent the knee" (cf. Renger, "Mesopotamian Epic Literature," pp. 40–41, for a suggestion that the text is intentionally ambiguous).

*vi, 18, 23. ir-tu-ut.* Alternatively, *ir-tu-ud,* with the same meaning; see von Soden.

*ii, 50. ir-ú*!*-bu.* Collation of Lambert *apud* von Soden.

*i-tú-uš. AHw,* p. 762a; *CAD* N$_1$, p. 114b, reads *i-nu*!*-uš,* with the same meaning.

## 8. Gilg. Y. iii, 14–24, 38–iv, 2; *GE* II, v, 1–6

Translations on pp. 93–94.

Gilg. Y. from Jastrow and Clay, YOR 4(3):87–101 and plates following p. 106; subsequent edition in *GETh.,* pp. 25–29; collation by F. Stephens *apud* Pohl, *Or.* 25:273, n. 1; unpublished copy by A. Shaffer; notes by von Soden, *ZA* 53:212–15.

*GE* II, v, from *GETh.,* p. 18 and pl. 10; notes by von Soden, *ZA* 53:223.

**Gilg. Y.**

***GE* II**

v, 1. *aš-šu šul-lu-mu*
[$^{\text{giš}}$*qist*]*i*([TI]R) $^{\text{giš}}$*erini*(ERIN)

2. *ana*(DIŠ) *pul-ḫa-a-ti ša*
*nišī*(UKÙ.MEŠ)
*i-šim-šu* $^{d}$*En-líl*

*v, 2, 5.* See above, p. 68.

| | |
|---|---|
| iii, 14. *i-di-ma ib-ri i-na* *šadî*(KUR$^{i}$) | |
| 15. *i-nu-ma at-ta-la-ku it-ti bu-lim* | |
| 16. *a-na* 60(I ŠU.ŠI) *bēr* (KAS.BU.TA.ÀM) | 3. $^{d}$*Ḫum-ba-ba rig-ma-šu a-bu-bu:* |
| *til-ma-at qí-iš-tum* | *pi-i-šú girru*($^{d}$BIL.GI)-*um-ma* |
| 17. [*ma-an-nu š*]*a ur-ra-du* | *na-pis-su mu-tú* |
| *a-na libbi*(ŠÀ)-*ša* | 4. *i-šem-mé-*⸢*e-ma a-na* 60(KU)⸣ *bē*[*r*](KAS.B[U]) |
| 18. [$^{d}$*Ḫu-wa*]-*wa ri-ig-ma-šu a-bu-bu* | *ri-mat* $^{giš}$*qišti*(TIR): |
| 19. ⸢*pí*⸣-*šu girru*($^{d}$BIL.GI)-*ma* | *man-nu ša ur-ra-du* |
| 20. *na-pi-iš-šu mu-tum* | *ana*(DIŠ) $^{giš}$*qišti*(TIR)-*šú* |
| 21. *am-mi-nim ta-aḫ-ši-iḫ* | (Note that *GE* II, v, 3–4 = Gilg. Y. iii, 16–17 and 18–20 in inverse order.) |
| 22. *an-ni-a-am e-pe-ša-am* | |
| 23. *qá-ba-al la ma-ḫa-ar* | |
| 24. [*š*]*u-pa-at* $^{d}$*Ḫu-wa-wa* | |

*iii, 16.* I ŠU.ŠI. Clay's copy (YOR 4[3], second plate after p. 106, l. 107) apparently, and Shaffer's definitely, support this reading (Landsberger, *RA* 62:113) against I IGI.GUNU (Ungnad and Schott [cited by von Soden]; *CAD* B, p. 209d).

*til-ma-at.* Landsberger, *RA* 62:113; cf. *CAD* L, p. 70a lex., p. 75d.

*iii, 17.* [*ma-an-nu š*]*a.* Ungnad, cited by von Soden.

*iii, 23. qá-ba-al la ma-ḫa-ar,* "irresistible in (his) onslaught." See Kienast, *JCS* 29:73–77.

*iii, 24. šu-pa-at.* Stephens. For the translation "siege engine" (essentially following Grayson in *ANET,* p. 79), cf. Speiser, *JCS* 12:41–43; *CAD* $A_2$, pp. 428–29. The term recurs in Gilg. Y. v, 19. Von Soden, *ZA* 53:213, understands the word as *šuptu* = *šubtu,* "dwelling" (cf. Römer, in *Falkenstein AV,* p. 197), but since elsewhere it is kings and gods

*v, 4. i-šem-mé-*⸢*e-ma*⸣, "he can hear." Heidel, *JNES* 11:141. Landsberger (*RA* 62:113) took the third-person-singular verb as the impersonal ("one hears"), but this would normally be expressed by the plural (*GAG* §75i).

*ri-mat,* "rustling." Von Soden, *ZA* 53:223; *AHw,* p. 986a.

The deviation of this line (and GEH rev. vi, 8) from the OB version could have been prompted by scribal error: The additional *išemme-ma* was perhaps based somehow on *nišemme-ma* in the elders' version of this speech in Gilg. Y. v, 12 or on a dittography of *i-šim-šu* in *GE* II, v, 2, with the resultant reference to hearing then inducing a word for noise *(rimmat);* or *rimmat* may have entered first, perhaps owing to an aural confusion of TIL for TAL and a subsequent reading of TAL in its value RI, with the resultant word for noise then inducing the additional word for hearing.

. . .

38. *ki-i ni-*[*i*]*l-la-ak* [x x x]

39. *a-na qí-iš-ti* $^{gi}$[$^{š}$*erini*]

40. *na-ṣi-ir-ša* $^{d}$*We-er* [x x]

41. *da-a-an la ṣa-*[*li-il*]

42. $^{d}$*Hu-wa-wa* $^{d}$*We-e*[*r* x x x]

43. $^{d}$*Adad*(IM) *iš-*[x x x x]

44. *šu-ú* [x x x x x x]

iv,1. *aš-šum šu-ul-lu-m*[*u*
*qi-iš-ti* $^{giš}$*erini*(TIR)]

2. *pu-ul-ḫ̮á-tim* 7

⸢*i*⸣-[*din-šu* $^{d}$*En-lil*(?)]

5. *áš-šú šul-lu-mu*
*erini*(ERIN):

*ana*(DIŠ) *pul-ḫa-a-ti šá*
*nišī*(UKÙ.MEŠ)
*i-šim-šú* $^{d}$*En-líl*

6. *u a-rid* $^{giš}$*qišti*(TIR)*-šú*
*i-ṣab-bat-su* ⸢*lu*⸣*-u'-tu*

---

who are characterized as "irresistible in (his) onslaught" (see the examples cited by Kienast, *JCS* 29:73–77), I prefer the interpretation which takes *šupat* in apposition to Huwawa and leaves the latter, not his dwelling, as the subject of the characterization.

*iv, 2.* "7." Contrary to *GETh.*'s "*ša*(?)" (based on the parallel passage in *GE* II, v, 2, 5) the numeral 7 is clear, and the reading is supported by other references to Huwawa's sevenfold terrifying halo (see Kinnier Wilson, in *GSL,* pp. 107–10). See the note on the parallel passage.

## 9. Gilg. Bo. obv.! 6–12; *GE* V, iv, 7–13

Translations on pp. 121–22.

Gilg. Bo. from KUB 4, no. 12 (where the obverse and reverse are incorrectly identified); *GETh.,* p. 43; notes by von Soden, *ZA* 53: 220–21.

*GE* V, iv from *GETh.,* p. 37 and pl. 19.

| **Gilg. Bo. obv.** | ***GE* V** |
|---|---|
| 6. *ši-it-tù ra-ḫi-it mu-ši*<br>*ik-tal-dá-áš-*[*šu*(*-nu-ti*)] | iv, 7. [*ši*]*t-tu*$_4$ *re-ḫat nišī*(UKÙ.MEŠ)<br>*eli*(UGU)*-šu im-qut* |
| 7. *i-na mišil*(MAŠ) *mu-ši-ti*<br>*it-ti-šu ši-it-ta* [. . . .] | 8. [*ina*(AŠ)] *qab-li-ti*<br>*šit-ta-šu ú-qat-ti* |
| 8. *šu-ut-ta iz-za-kàr*<br>*a-na* $^{d}$*En-ki-du*$_4$ *i*[*b-ri-šu*] | 9. [*i*]*t-bi-e-ma i-ta-ma-a*<br>*a-na ib-ri-šu* |
| 9. *ki-i la-a ta-ad-kà-an-ni*<br>*mi-na-a* ⌜*e*⌝-[*re-ku*] | 10. [*i*]*b-ri ul tal-sa-an-ni*<br>*am-mi-ni e-re-ku* |
| | 11. [*u*]*l tal-pu-tan*$^{an}$*-ni*<br>*am-mi-ni šá-šá-ku* |
| | 12. [*u*]*l ilu*(DINGIR) *e-ti-iq*<br>*am-mi-ni ḫa-mu-ú*<br>*šēru*(UZU)*-ú-a* |
| 10. $^{d}$*En-ki-du*$_4$ *ib-ri*<br>*a-tám-mar šu-ut-*⌜*ta*⌝ | |
| 11. *ta-ad-kà-an-ni*<br>*mi-na-am* [. . . .] | |
| 12. *e-li ištēn*(1$^{en}$) *šu-ut-ti-ia*<br>*ša-ni-tù* [*šu-ut-tù a-tam-mar*] | 13. [*i*]*b-ri a-ta-mar šalulta*(3$^{ta}$)<br>*šu-ut-ta* |

*obv. 6. ra-ḫi-it,* "outpouring." Cf. *GE* XI, 220; Speiser, in *ANET,* p. 110, n. 15. Landsberger notes that the verb *reḫû* is used of epileptic seizures (*RA* 62:102, n. 18).

*ik-tal-dá-aš-*[*šu(-nu-ti)*]. Von Soden and *CAD* K, 278d, restore a plural suffix in agreement with line 5, but a singular suffix, in agreement with line 7, is equally possible; cf. the equivalent line in the late version.

## 10. Gilg. Meg. obv. 9b–rev. 1; Gilg. Ur 60–67; *GE* VII, iv, 14–20

Translations on pp. 124–25.

Gilg. Meg. from Goetze and Levy, *Atiqot* 2:121–28 and pl. 18; edition by Landsberger, *RA* 62:119, 131–32.

Gilg. Ur from Gadd and Kramer, *UET* 6:394; edited by Gadd, *Iraq* 28:105–16; Landsberger, *RA* 62:129–30.

*GE* VII, iv: composite text based on Landsberger, *RA* 62:129–30; minor variants within *GE* VII, noted by Landsberger, are omitted here.

| **Gilg. Meg.** | **Gilg. Ur** | ***GE* VII, iv** |
|---|---|---|
| | 60. *š*[*e-em*]*-mu ib-ri*<br>[*šu-ut-ta*]<br>[*š*]*a m*[*u-ši*]*-*⸢*ti*⸣*-ia* | 14. [*ši*]*-*⸢*te-me*⸣*ib-ri*<br>*šu-na-ta aṭ-ṭul*<br><*ša*> *mu-ši-*<br>*ti-ia* |
| 9b. *an-ni-tum*<br>*iz-*[*za-kar*] | | |
| 10. [*da*]*m-qa-at ù*<br>*mi-i*[*t-gu-rat*<br>*šu-ut-tu*] | | |
| 11. [*aq-r*]*at*<br>*dam-qa-at*<br>*ù pa-*[*aš-qat*] | | |
| 12. [x]-x *pa-aš-qàt* | | |
| | 61. *i*[*l-su-ú*]*-ma*<br>*ša-mu-ú*<br>*q*[*aq-qa-ru*<br>*i*]*-pu-ul* | 15. *il-su-ú*<br>*šamê*(AN$^{e}$)<br>*qaq-qa-ru*<br>*i-pul* |
| | 62. ⸢*i*⸣-[*na bi-ri*]-<br>*šu-nu a*[*z*]*-*⸢*za*⸣*-*<br>[*az a-n*]*a-ku* | 16. *ina*(AŠ) *bi-ri-*<br>*šu-nu az-za-*<br>*zu a-na-ku* |
| *i-na šu-ut-*[*ti-ia*<br>*at-ta-mar* | | |
| *eṭla*(GURUŠ)] | 63. ⸢*ša ištēn*(1$^{en}$)<br>*eṭlu uk*⸣*-ku-lu*<br>⸢*pa-nu*⸣*-šu* | 17. *šá ištēn*(1$^{en}$)<br>*eṭ-lu uk-ku-ul*<br>*pa-nu-*[*šu*] |

| | | |
|---|---|---|
| 13. *la-nam ku-ri-e*<br>*ra-bi* [x x x<br>(x x) *ša an-zi-i*] | 64. *a-na ša an-zi-i* x | 18. [*a-na*] *ša an-zi-i* |
| 14. [*pa-nu*]-*šu*<br>*ša-ak-nu* | x *pa*-[*nu-šu*<br>*maš-lu*] | *pa-nu-ša*<br>*maš-lu* |
| *ri*-[*it-ta*<br>UR.MAḪ<br>*ri-it-ta-šu*] | 65. *ri-it-*⸢*ti*⸣<br>*né-ši*<br>*ri-*⸢*it*⸣*-ta*?-[*šu*] | 19. [*ri-i*]*t-ti*<br>*nēši*(UR.MAḪ)<br>*rit-ta-a*?-*šu* |
| 15. *ṣú-up-ru*<br>*ša e-ri-*[*i*<br>*ṣú-pu-ur-šu*] | 66. *ṣu-pu-ur*<br>*e-ri-i*<br>*ṣu-up-r*[*u-šu*] | *ṣu-pur*<br>*a-ri-e*<br>*ṣu-pur-ra-šu* |
| 16. *pa-nu-šu ka-la*<br>x [x x x<br>x x (x)] | | |
| 17. [x x x x]-*ni*<br>*ri-it-ta-*[*šu*<br>*iṣ-bat*] | 67. [*i*]*ṣ-bat-ma* | 20. *iṣ-bat* |
| rev. 1. *qí-im-ma-*[*ti-ia*<br><br>x x x<br>x x] | *qí-im-ta-ti-ia*<br>*na*?-*di*? [x x x<br>x x] | *qim-ma-ti-iá*<br>*ú-dan-ni-na-an-*<br>*ni ia-a-ši* |

## 11. Gilg. Mi. iv, 1–10; *Hit. Gilg.* 11, 1–5

Translations on pp. 114–15.

Gilg. Mi. from *CT* 46, no. 16; edited by Millard, *Iraq* 26:99–105; von Soden, *ZA* 58:188–92.

*Hit. Gilg.* 11 from Laroche, *RHA* 82:20, no. 11b; translation follows Friedrich, *ZA* 39:27, no. 11.

| **Gilg. Mi.** | ***Hit. Gilg.* 11** |
|---|---|
| iv, 1. [x x x<br>*Ú-ta-na-iš-tim*? *r*]*é*?-*qá-am* | 1. [z]i-ga!-an! za-a-ši[. . . .]<br>x[. . . . ] |

*iv, 1.* If *rēqam,* the form is as in Gilg. Me. iv, 13 (cf. 11), as against the usual form *rūqu,* etc. (ibid., iv, 6; *GE* XI, 1, etc.)

| | |
|---|---|
| 2. [x x x<br>*a/ta?-ra?*]-⌜*ka-ba*⌝-*am*<br>*elippa*(MÁ) | 2. [z]i-ik-wa-ra-an-kán ku-iš<br>U[D]-t[i M]I-a[n-t]i za-a-iš-ki-ši |
| 3. [*a-na? š*]*a?-šu iš-ḫi-ṭá-am*<br>*lu-ṭe*$_4$*-eḫ-ḫi ka-ta* | |
| 4. [*pu-ḫu-ur?-m*]*a?*<br>*uš-ta-ad-da-nu*<br>*ki-la-al-la-an* | |
| 5. [*šu-ma?*] *a-wa-tam i-qá-ab-bi*<br>*šu-a-ši-im* | |
| 6. [*S*]*u-ur-su-na-bu*<br>*a-na* ⌜*ša*⌝-*a-šum*<br>*iz-za-kàr-am a-na* $^{d}$GIŠ | 3. [U]M-MA $^{d}$Ur-ša-na-bi |
| 7. *šu-ut ab-nim-ma* $^{d}$GIŠ | am-mu-uk-wa a-pu-u-uš<br>2 ALAM.NA$_4$ |
| *mu*!*-še-bi-ru-ú-ia* | 4. [za-]a-i-nu-uš-kir |
| 8. *aš-šum la a-*⌜*la*⌝*-ap-pa-tu*<br>*me-e mu-tim* | |
| | UM-MA $^{d}$GILGAMEŠ ku-wa-at-wa-mu |
| 9. *i-na uz-zi-*[*k*]*a*<br>*tu-uḫ-te-ep-pí-šu-nu-ti* | 5. [ka]r-tim-mi-ya-at-ta-[a]n i-ya-ši |
| 10. [*š*]*u-ut ab-nim* [*aš*]*-šum*<br>*šu-bu-ri-im šu-nu it-ti-ia* | |

## 12. Gilg. Mi. iv, 11–14; *Hit. Gilg.* 10, rev. iii, 5–21; *GE* X, ii, 26–27 and iii, 40–50

Translations on pp. 115–16.

Bibliography for Gilg. Mi. as above, no. 11.

*Hit. Gilg.* 10 from Laroche, *RHA* 82:20, no. 11a; translation follows Friedrich, *ZA* 39:25.

*GE* X, iii from *GETh.,* p. 57 and pl. 41; notes by von Soden, *ZA* 53:231.

| **Gilg. Mi.** | ***Hit. Gilg.* 10** | ***GE* X** |
|---|---|---|
| | rev. iii, 5. IŠ-TU IṢ-<br>ṢI kat-ta x[. . . .<br>-r]u-uš x[. . . .] | |
| | 6. a-da-an-zi nu $^{I}$Ur-<br>ša-na-bi-iš A-NA<br>$^{d}$GILG[AMEŠ] | |
| | 7. LUGAL-i<br>EGIR-pa<br>me-mi-iš-<br>ki-u-wa-an da-iš<br>[ki-i-wa] | |
| | 8. ku-it<br>$^{d}$GILGAMEŠ<br>nu-wa-kán<br>a-ru-na-an<br>p[a-ri-ya-an<br>GIM-an (?)] | ii, 26. *a-lum-ma*<br>$^{d}$GIŠ.GÍN.MAŠ<br><br>*te-te-bir*<br>*tam-ta* |
| | 9. pa-a-i-ši nu-wa<br>ag-ga-an-na-aš<br>ú-e-te-na[-aš] | 27. *a-na mê*(A.MEŠ)<br>*mu-ú-ti* |
| | 10. ku-wa-bi a-ar-ti<br>nu-wa GIM-an<br>i-ya-ši [. . . .] | *ki-i tak-tal-du*<br>*te-ip-pu-uš mi-na*<br><br>. . . |
| iv, 11. [*le-q*]*é-e-ma*<br>$^{d}$GIŠ<br>*ḫa-ṣí-na-am*<br>*i-na*<br>*qá-ti-ka* | 11. ḪA-AZ-ZI-IN-<br>NU-wa<br>ŠU-za<br>e-ep | iii, 40. *i-ši*<br>$^{d}$GIŠ.GÍN.MAŠ<br>*ḫa-ṣi-in-*⌜*nà*⌝<br>*ana*(DIŠ)<br>*i-*[*di*-*ka*] |
| | *iii, 11.* e-ep, "grasp." This is the verb used in the axe formula elsewhere in the Hittite version (Tablet I, frag. 5, rev. iii, x+4′; iv, 2–3). In a lexical text, Hitt. ep- is equated with Akk. *ṣabātu* (*Heth. Wb.* p. 41b), rather than one of the verbs used for the axe formula in the Akkadian versions (OB *leqû* and late version *našû*). | *ii, 26. a-lum-ma* "where(?)." See *CAD* $A_1$, p. 391d; *AHw,* p. 39d.<br><br>*iii, 40. i-*[*di-ka*]. Jensen, KB 6(1), p. 220, l. 40.<br>[*i-kis*]. Von Soden. On the basis of iv, 8 Jensen restored here the number of poles (120; see KB 6(1), p. 220, l. 41 and n. 4); subsequent translators have accepted both restorations ("[cut down twice-sixty] poles"). |

| | | |
|---|---|---|
| | | 41. *e-rid ana*(DIŠ) |
| | | $^{\text{giš}}$*qišti*(TIR)-*ma* |
| | nu-wa-kán | |
| 12. [*pa-ri*]-*si* | [: wi-na-at] | *pa-ri-si* |
| *ša ṣú-up-pa-a* | 12. ŠA | *šá* |
| 300 (5 ŠU.ŠI) | 40 gi-pé-eš-na-aš | 5 NINDA.TA.ÀM |
| | na-aš-ma ŠA 50 | |
| | g[i-pé-eš-na-aš | |
| *ik-sa-am* | kar-aš] | [*i-kis*] |
| 13. [x x] x-*kum-ma* | | 42. *ku-pur-ma* |
| *šu-ku-un*! | | *šu-kun* |
| *ṣe-re-e-t*[*im*] | | *tu-la-a:* |
| 14. [*bi-la* ?] | | *bi-il-la*-[*šu-nu-ti* |
| ⌜*i-na* | | *ana*(DIŠ) |
| $^{\text{giš}}$*elippim*(MÁ)⌝ | | $^{\text{giš}}$*elippi*(MÁ)] |
| x x [x x] | | |
| | 13. nu GIM-an | |
| | $^{\text{d}}$GILGAMEŠ-uš | 43. $^{\text{d}}$GIŠ.GÍN.MAŠ |
| | ŠA $^{\text{I}}$U-ur-ša-na | *an-ni-ta* |
| | [-bi] | |
| | 14. me-mi-ya-an | *ina*(AŠ) |
| | IŠ-ME | [*še-mi-šú*] |
| | nu ḪA-AZ- | 44. *iš-ši ḫa-* |
| | ZI-IN-NU | *ṣi-in-na* |
| | ŠU-za | *ana* (DIŠ) |
| | e[-ep-ta] | *idi*(Á)-*šú:* |
| | | *iš*-[*lu-up* |
| | | *nam-ṣar* |
| | | *šib-bi-šú*] |
| | | 45. *ú-rid ana* (DIŠ) |
| | | $^{\text{giš}}$*qišti*(TIR)-*ma* |

*iv, 13.* *ṣe-re-e-t*[*im*], "oarlock ropes." Cf. *CAD* Ṣ, p. 135c.

*iv, 14.* [*bi-la*(?)]. Cf. the equivalent line in *GE* X, iii, 42.

*iii, 42, 46.* *ku-pur-ma, ik-pur-ma,* "trim(med)(?)." *CAD* K, p. 180b; *AHw,* p. 442d.

[*ana*(DIŠ) $^{\text{giš}}$*elippi* (MÁ)]. Restoration based on the equivalent Old Babylonian and Hittite texts (Gilg. Mi. iv, 14; *Hit. Gilg.* no. 10, iii, 17).

| | |
|---|---|
| 15. nu-kán: wi-na-at | *pa-ri-si* |
| ŠA 50 | *šá* 5 |
| gi-pé-eš-na-aš | NINDA.TA.À[M |
| [. . . .] | |
| 16. kar-aš-ta | *ik-ki-is*] |
| na-at: | 46. *ik-pur-ma* |
| sap-pa-at-ta: | *iš-ta-kan tu-la-a:* |
| piš[-. . . .] | |
| 17. na-at-kán | *ú-bil-ma* |
| A-NA | [*ana*(DIŠ) |
| $^{\text{giš}}$MÁ ša-ra-a | $^{\text{giš}}$*elippi*(MÁ)] |
| da-a-i[š] | |
| 18. na-at-kán | |
| 2?-e-lu-uš-pít | |
| A-NA $^{\text{giš}}$MÁ | 47. $^{\text{d}}$GIŠ.GÍN.MAŠ *u* |
| ša-ra-a [pa-a-ir?] | $^{\text{I}}$*Ur-šanabí* |
| 19. $^{\text{d}}$GILGAMEŠ-uš | *ir-ka-bu* |
| $^{\text{I}}$Ur-ša-na-bi-iš-ša] | [$^{\text{giš}}$*elippa* (MÁ)] |
| nu $^{\text{I}}$Ur-š[a-na-bi-iš] | |
| 20. : pí-in-ta-an-za | |
| ŠU-za e-ep-ta | |
| $^{\text{d}}$GILGAMEŠ[-uš-ma. . . .] | |
| 21. ŠU-za | |
| | 48. $^{\text{giš}}$*má-gi-il-la* |
| | *id-du-ma šu-nu* |
| | [*ir-tak-bu*] |

*iii, 16.* šap-pa-at-ta, "peeled (?)." *Heth. Wb.*, p. 183 ab.

*iii, 48.* [*ir-tak-bu*]. Restored by Jensen (KB 6(1), p. 220, l. 48) from XI, 257 (note XI, 256–57 // X, iii, 47–48).

| | |
|---|---|
| ŠA [KAS?]-aš-ma-aš-kán? | 49. *ma-lak* |
| ITU 1 KAM | *arḫi*(ITU) *u* |
| UD | *ūmī*(UD) |
| 15 KAM | 15-KAM |
| ša [. . . .] | *ina*(AŠ) |
| | *šal-ši* |
| | *ūme*(UD$^{me}$) |
| | *it-ta-*x[x] |
| | 50. *ik-šu-dam-ma* |
| | $^{I}$*Ur-šanabí* |
| | *mê*(A.MEŠ) |
| | [*mu-ti*] |

*iii, 49. it-ta-. . . . ,* "did/was. . . ." The first two signs are clearly *it-ta-*, the third either *ri/tal* or, as shown by collation, possibly *ḫu.* Elsewhere in the epic this formula occurs with the verb *ṭeḫû,* with which the second sign *(ta,* not *ṭa)* is incompatible, and *kašā-du,* which does not fit here at all (for the first, see the references to *CT* 46, 21, and 22 and *LKU* no. 39, col. i [collated] in Introduction, n. 18, and for the second see *GE* I, iii, 48). Von Soden and *CAD* $A_1$, p. 324a, suggest other readings here (*it-ta-tal-*[*ku*], "they departed"; *it-ta-ri-*[*iṣ*], "[the journey . . .] was completed"), but these leave the formula meaning something different from what it means earlier in the epic.

## 13. Selections from OB *Atr.* III and *GE* XI

Translations on pp. 222–27.

OB *Atr.* III, i, 11–26 from Boissier, *RA* 28:92; remainder from *CT* 46, no. 3 and Lambert and Millard, pp. 88–89, 94–99.

*GE* XI from *GETh.*, pls. 44–45, 47–49; latest edition in Borger, *BAL* 2:95, 97–99.

| **OB *Atr.* III** | ***GE* XI** |
|---|---|
| i, 15. [$^{d}$*En-ki p*]*í-a-šu* *i-pu-ša-am-ma* | |
| 16. [*is*]-*sà-qar a-na ar-di-šu* | |
| | 20. *a-mat-su-nu ú-šá-an-na-a* *a-na ki-ik-ki-šú* |
| 17. [*m*]*a-šu-um-ma lu-uš-te-i* *ta-qá-ab-bi* | |
| 18. *ši-ip-ra ša a-qá-ab-bu-ku* | |
| 19. *šu-uṣ-ṣi-ir at-ta* | |
| | 21. *ki-ik-kiš ki-ik-kiš* *i-gar i-gar* |
| 20. *i-ga-ru ši-ta-am-mi-a-an-ni* | 22. *ki-ik-ki-šu ši-me-ma* |
| 21. *ki-ki-šu šu-uṣ-ṣi-ri ka-la* *sí-iq-ri*!-*ia* | *i-ga-ru ḫi-is-sa-as* |
| | 23. $^{lú}$*Šu-ri-ip-pa-ku-ú* *mār*(DUMU) $^{I}$*Ubara-*$^{d}$*Tu-tu* |
| 22. *ú-bu-ut bi-ta* *bi-ni e-le-ep-pa* | 24. *ú-qur bīta*(É) *bi-ni* $^{giš}$*eleppa*(MÁ) |
| | 25. *muš-šìr mešrê*(NÍG.TUK$^{e}$) *še-'i-i napšāti*(ZI.MEŠ) |
| 23. *ma-ak-ku-ra zé-e-er-ma* | 26. [*m*]*a-ak-ku-ra ze-er-ma* |

*i, 22. ú-bu-ut,* "flee." Hoffner, in *Kramer AV,* p. 243.

*i, 23.* "spurn property" is the usual translation of *makkura zēr-ma* here and in the equivalent line in *GE* XI, 26, where the translation has the support of the parallel *muššir mešrê* in line 25. However Hoffner, noting that Atrahasis/Utnapishtim in fact loads his boat with all sorts of property, has suggested the reading and translation *makkura s/ṣ/zêr-ma,* "construct a boat," at least in the *Atr.* passage, and possibly in the *GE* passage as well (*Kramer AV,* pp. 241–45).

*26.* See the note on the equivalent passage. In the *GE* passage, line 25, which seems to explicate line 26, suggests that whatever the case in the *Atr.* passage, here *makkura zēr-ma* means "spurn property," despite the fact that Utnapishtim takes property on board. If Hoffner is right about OB *Atr.* III, i, 23, the *GE* passage may have misinterpreted that line.

| | |
|---|---|
| 24. *na-pí-iš-ta bu-ul-li-iṭ* | *na-piš-t*[*a/i*] *bul-liṭ* |
| | 27. [*š*]*u-li-ma zēr*(NUMUN) *nap-šá-a-ti ka-la-ma a-na lìb-bi* $^{\text{giš}}$*eleppi*(MÁ) |
| 25. [*e*]*-le-ep-pu ša ta-ba-an-nu-*⌜*ú*⌝*-*[*ši*] | 28. [$^{\text{gi}}$]$^{\text{š}}$*eleppu*(MÁ) *šá ta-ban-nu-ši at-ta* |
| | 29. *lu-ú mìn-du-da mi-na-tu-šá* |
| 26. [x x x x] *mi-it-ḫ*[*u-ra-at* (. . .)] | 30. [*l*]*u-ú mit-ḫur ru-pu-us-sa ù mu-rak-šá* |
| 27. [. . . .] | |
| 28. [. . . . *ki-ma k*]*i*!*-ip*!*-pa-ti* [. . .] | |
| 29. [*k*]*i-ma ap-si-i šu-a-ti ṣú-ul-li-il-ši* | 31. [*k*]*i*!*-ma apsî*(ABZU) *šá-a-ši ṣu-ul-lil-ši* |
| . . . | . . . |
| iii, 30. [$^{\text{d}}$]*A-nun-na i-lu ra-bu-tum* | 113. *ilāni*(DINGIR.MEŠ) |
| 31. [*wa-aš*]*-b*[*u*] *i-na ṣú-mi ù bu-bu-ti* | *ip-la-ḫu a-bu-ba-am-ma* |
| | 114. *it-te-eḫ-su i-te-lu-ú ana*(DIŠ) *šamê*(AN$^{e}$) *šá* $^{\text{d}}$*A-num* |
| | 115. *ilāni*(DINGIR.MEŠ) *kīma*(GIM) *kalbī*(UR.$GI_7$) *kun-nu-nu ina*(AŠ) *ka-ma-a-ti rab-ṣu* |
| 32. ⌜*i*⌝*-mu-ur-ma* ⌜*il-tum*⌝ *i-ba-ak-k*[*i*] | 116. *i-šas-si* $^{\text{d}}$*Iš-tar ki-ma a-lit-ti* |
| 33. *ta-ab-su-ut i-li e-ri-iš-ta* $^{\text{d}}$⌜*Ma*⌝*-m*[*i*] | 117. *ú-nam-ba* $^{\text{d}}$*Be-let-i*[*lī*] (DINGIR.MEŠ] *ṭa-bat rig-ma* |
| 34. $u_4$*-mu-um li-id-da-*⌜*i*⌝*-*[*im*] | 118. $u_4$*-mu ul-lu-ú* |
| 35. *li-tu-ur li-ki-*[*il*] | *a-na ṭi-iṭ-ṭi lu-ú i-tur-ma* |

*i, 28.* For the reading, cf. *Atr.* W, 2 (Lambert and Millard, p. 128).

*118.* $u_4$*-mu ul-lu-ú a-na ṭi-iṭ-ṭi lu-ú i-tur-ma,* "that day to clay, alas (lit. indeed) turned." This is a peculiar expression, for the standard Akkadian expression has human beings (re)turn to clay (*GE* X, ii, 12, etc.; XI, 133), while days (re)turn to darkness, as in the par-

| | |
|---|---|
| 36. *a-na-ku i-na pu-úḫ-ri ša* ⸢*i*⸣-[*li*] | 119. *áš-šú a-na-ku ina*(AŠ) *pu-ḫur ilāni*(DINGIR.DINGIR) |
| 37. *ki-i aq-*[*bi*] | *aq-bu-ú* |
| 38. *it-ti-šu-nu ga-me-er-ta-a*[*m*] | *lemutta*(MÍ.ḪUL) |
| | 120. *ki-i aq-bi ina pu-ḫur ilāni*(DINGIR.DINGIR) *lemutta*(MÍ.ḪUL) |
| | 121. *ana*(DIŠ) *ḫul-lu-uq nišī*(UKÙ.MEŠ)-*ia qab-la aq-bi-ma* |
| (39–54: Mami continues speech, not paralleled in *GE*) | |
| (iii, 55–iv, 3: broken) | |
| iv, 4. *ú-na-ab-ba* $^{d}$*N*[*in-tu . . .*] | |
| 5. *a-bu-ma-an ul-*⸢*da*⸣ *g*[*al-la-ta* ?] | 122. *a-na-ku-um-ma ul-la-da ni-šu-ú-a-a-ma* |

---

*iii, 37. ki-i,* "when I did/how could I . . . ." The first, and preferred, translation is based on the similar curse in Job 3:3–9, which begins: "Let the day perish wherein I was born . . . Let that day be darkness . . . Let gloom and darkness claim it . . ." The second is intended to bring out the ambiguity of the Akkadian, which may have led to variant renderings in *GE* XI, 119–20. For parallels to this curse, see Hecker, pp. 173–74.

*iii, 38. ga-me-er-ta-a*[*m*], "total destruction." See chap. 12, n. 23.

*iv, 5–9.* The passage bristles with difficulties, and the translation is uncertain; cf. the suggestions of von Soden, *Or.* 38:432 (however, the objection that *sapannu* is only a late word is contradicted by Gilg. Mi. iii, 7; cf. von Soden, *ZA* 58:190; *AHw,* p. 1025c).

allel passage in OB *Atr.* (further references in Hecker, pp. 173–74.; cf. *GE* XI, 106). Admittedly this could be a case of poetic license, but the similarity of the words for clay *(ṭiṭṭu)* and darkness *(eṭ ûtu)* suggests that the text may have originally read *ana eṭûti,* "to darkness." Moreover, since a particular day is specified (*ūmu ullû,* "that day"), the reference is probably to the day on which the goddess consented to the destruction, and the passage should be taken as synonymous with the curse in the parallel OB *Atr.* III, iii, 34ff., in which case the verb would have been precative *(litūr-ma).* In sum, the original reading may have been *ana eṭûti litūr-ma,* "let (that day) return to darkness, on which I commanded, etc." The corruption to *ṭi-iṭ-ṭi lu-ú* may have been induced by line 133 and *ul-lu-ú* in this line.

*119–20.* See the note on the equivalent passage.

For *puḫur,* "the assembly," a variant in both lines reads *maḫar,* "the presence."

*122.* For a different suggestion, see Borger, *BAL* 3:118 *ad loc.*

| | |
|---|---|
| 6. *ti-a-am-ta*<br>*ki-ma ku-li-li* | 123. *ki-i mārī*(DUMU.MEŠ)<br>*nūnī*($KU_6$.ḪÁ) |
| 7. *im-la-a-nim na-ra-am* | *ú-ma-al-la-a tam-ta-am-ma* |
| 8. *ki-ma a-mi-im*<br>*i-mi-da a-na s[a-pa]n-[ni]* | |
| 9. *ki-ma a-mi-im i-na ṣe-ri*<br>*i-mi-da a-na ki-ib-ri* | |
| 10. *a-mu-ur-ma e-li-ši-na ab-ki* | |
| 11. *ú-qá-at-ti di-im-ma-ti*<br>*i-na ṣe-ri-ši-in* | |
| 12. *ib-ki-i-ma li-ib-ba-ša*<br>*ú-na-ap-pí-iš* | |
| 13. *ú-na-ab-ba* $^{d}$*Nin-tu* | |
| 14. *la-la-ša iṣ-ru-up* | |
| 15. *i-lu*<br>*it-ti-ša ib-ku-ú*<br>*a-na ma-tim* | 124. *ilāni*(DINGIR.MEŠ)<br>*šu-ut* $^{d}$*A-nun-na-ki*<br>*ba-ku-ú it-ti-šá* |
| 16. *iš-bi ni-is-sà-tam* | |
| 17. *ṣa-mi-a-at ši-ik-ri-iš* | |
| 18. *ši-i*<br>*a-šar uš-bu*<br>*i-na bi-ki-ti* | 125. *ilāni*(DINGIR.MEŠ)<br>*aš-ru áš-bi*<br>*i-na bi-ki-ti* |
| 19. *uš-bu-ma*<br>*ki-ma im-me-ri* | |
| 20. *im-lu-nim ra-ṭa-am* | |
| 21. *ṣa-mi-a ša-ap-ta-*<br>*šu-nu bu-ul-ḫi-ta* | 126. *šab-ba* (var. *kàt-ma*) *šap-ta-*<br>*šú-nu le-qa-a bu-uḫ-re-e-ti* |
| 22. ⌜*i-na*⌝ *bu-bu-ti* | |
| 23. *i-ta-*⌜*na*⌝*-ar-ra-ar-ru* | |
| . . . | . . . |

*iv, 14. la-la-ša iṣ-ru-up,* "spent her emotion." Cf. Lambert and Millard *ad loc* and the differing suggestions of *CAD* L, p. 49d; *AHw,* p. 1084c.

| | |
|---|---|
| | 155. *ú-še-ṣi-ma* |
| v, 30. *a-na ša-a-r[i . . . .]* | *a-na* 4 *šārī*(IM.MEŠ) |
| 31. *[i]t-ta-qí [ni-qa-a]* | *at-ta-qí ni-qa-a* |
| 32. *i-za-an-nu-un* [. . . .] | 156. *áš-kun sur-qi-nu* *ina muḫḫi*(UGU) *ziq-qur-rat šadî*(KUR$^{i}$) |
| 33. (illegible) | 157. 7 *u* 7 $^{dug}$*adagurrī*(A.DA.-GUR$_5$) *uk-tin* |
| | 158. *i-na šap-li-šú-nu at-ta-bak* *qanâ*(GI) $^{giš}$*erīna*(ERIN) *u asa*(ŠIM.GÍR) |
| 34. *[i-ṣi-nu i-l]u* *e-re-ša* | 159. *ilāni*(DINGIR.MEŠ) *i-ṣi-nu* *i-ri-šá* |
| | 160. *ilāni*(DINGIR.MEŠ) *i-ṣi-nu* *i-ri-šá ṭāba*(DÙG.GA) |
| | 161. *ilāni*(DINGIR.MEŠ) |
| 35. *[ki-ma zu-ub-b]i* *e-lu ni-qí-i* | *ki-ma zu-um-bé-e* *eli*(UGU) *bēl*(EN) *niqî*(SIZ-KUR.SIZKUR) |
| *pa-aḫ-ru* | *ip-taḫ-ru* |
| 36. *[iš-tu-m]a i-ku-lu ni-qí-a-am* | 162. *ul-tu ul-la-nu-um-ma* |
| 37. [$^{d}$*Nin*]*-tu it-bé-e-ma* | DINGIR.MAḪ *ina ka-šá-di-šú* |
| 38. ⌜*na-ap*⌝*-ḫa-ar-šu-nu* *ut-ta-az-za-am* | |

*v, 31.* *[i]t-ta-qí* (not: *-di*). Matouš, *Ar. Or.* 35:15; cf. the equivalent passage.

*Gilg. Ni. (2N-T79;* Oriental Institute accession number A29934)
(Courtesy of the Oriental Institute, University of Chicago)

# *Abbreviations: Scholarly Literature and Ancient Texts*

## SCHOLARLY LITERATURE

| | |
|---|---|
| AB | Assyriologische Bibliothek |
| *Ac. Or.* | *Acta Orientalia* |
| *Act. Ant.* | *Acta Antiqua Academiae Scientiarum Hungaricae* |
| *AfO* | *Archiv für Orientforschung* |
| *AHw* | Von Soden, *Akkadisches Handwörterbuch* |
| *AJA* | *American Journal of Archaeology* |
| *AJSL* | *American Journal of Semitic Languages and Literatures* |
| *AKA* | King and Budge, *Annals of the Kings of Assyria* |
| *AM* | Oppenheim, *Ancient Mesopotamia* |
| *ANEH* | Hallo and Simpson, *The Ancient Near East: A History* |
| *ANET* | Pritchard, ed., *Ancient Near Eastern Texts Relating to the Old Testament* |
| An. Or. | Analecta Orientalia |
| *An. St.* | *Anatolian Studies* |
| AOAT | Alter Orient und Altes Testament |

| | |
|---|---|
| *APNM* | Huffmon, *Amorite Personal Names in the Mari Texts* |
| *AR* | Ungnad, *Assyrische Rechtsurkunden* |
| *ARAB* | Luckenbill, *Ancient Records of Assyria and Babylonia* |
| ARM | Archives Royales de Mari |
| *Ar. Or.* | *Archiv Orientální* |
| AS | Assyriological Studies |
| AV | Anniversary Volume (used for Festschriften) |
| *BA* | *Beiträge zur Assyriologie und semitischen Sprachwissenschaft* |
| *BAL* | Borger, *Babylonisch-Assyrische Lesestücke* |
| *BASOR* | *Bulletin of the American Schools of Oriental Research* |
| BE | The Babylonian Expedition of the University of Pennsylvania, series A: Cuneiform Texts |
| *Bi. Or.* | *Bibliotheca Orientalis* |
| BM | Tablets in the collections of the British Museum |
| *BWL* | Lambert, *Babylonian Wisdom Literature* |
| *CAD* | Gelb *et al., The Assyrian Dictionary of the Oriental Institute of the University of Chicago* (each volume is cited by the letter(s) of the alphabet it covers; thus *CAD* B, *CAD* $M_2$, etc.) |
| *CBQ* | *Catholic Biblical Quarterly* |
| CBS | Tablets in the collections of the University Museum, University of Pennsylvania |
| CRRAI | Compte rendu de la Rencontre Assyriologique Internationale |
| *CT* | *Cuneiform Texts from Babylonian Tablets in the British Museum* |
| *EI* | *Eretz-Israel* |
| *Falkenstein AV* | Edzard, ed., *Heidelberger Studien . . .* |
| *GAG* | Von Soden, *Grundriss der akkadischen Grammatik* |
| *GETh.* | Thompson, *The Epic of Gilgamesh: Text, Transliteration, and Notes* |

| | |
|---|---|
| Gressmann and Ungnad | Gressmann and Ungnad, *Das Gilgamesch-Epos* |
| *GSL* | Garelli, ed., *Gilgameš et sa légende* |
| *HBS* | Kramer, *History Begins at Sumer* |
| Hecker | Hecker, *Untersuchungen zur akkadischen Epik* |
| Heidel | Heidel, *The Gilgamesh Epic and Old Testament Parallels* |
| *Heth. Wb.* | Friedrich, *Hethitisches Wörterbuch* |
| *HKL* | Borger, *Handbuch der Keilschriftliteratur* |
| *HUCA* | *Hebrew Union College Annual* |
| ICC | International Critical Commentary |
| *IEJ* | *Israel Exploration Journal* |
| *Ist. Mit.* | *Istanbuler Mitteilungen* |
| *Jacobsen AV* | S. J. Lieberman, ed., *Sumerological Studies . . . Jacobsen* |
| *JANES* | *Journal of the Ancient Near Eastern Society of Columbia University* |
| *JAOS* | *Journal of the American Oriental Society* |
| *JBL* | *Journal of Biblical Literature* |
| *JCS* | *Journal of Cuneiform Studies* |
| *JKF* | *Jahrbuch für Kleinasiatische Forschung* |
| *JNES* | *Journal of Near Eastern Studies* |
| *JQR* | *Jewish Quarterly Review* |
| *JRAS* | *Journal of the Royal Asiatic Society of Great Britain and Ireland* |
| *JSS* | *Journal of Semitic Studies* |
| K | Tablets from the Kuyunjik collection, British Museum |
| *KAR* | *Keilschrifttexte aus Assur religiösen Inhalts* |
| *KAT* | Schrader, *Keilinschriften und das Alte Testament* |
| *KAV* | *Keilschrifttexte aus Assur verschiedenen Inhalts* |
| KB | Keilinschriftliche Bibliothek |
| *Kramer AV* | Eichler, ed., *Kramer Anniversary Volume* |
| KUB | Keilschrifturkunden aus Boghazköi |
| Lambert and Millard | Lambert and Millard, *Atra-ḫasīs* |

| | |
|---|---|
| *Landsberger AV* | Güterbock and Jacobsen, eds., *Studies . . . Landsberger* |
| LCL | Loeb Classical Library |
| *LKU* | Falkenstein, *Literarische Keilschrifttexte aus Uruk* |
| LSS | Leipziger semitistische Studien, Neue Folge |
| *MDOG* | *Mitteilungen der Deutschen-Orientgesellschaft* |
| *MI* | S. Thompson, *Motif-Index of Folk Literature* |
| *MIO* | *Mitteilungen des Instituts für Orientforschung* |
| MVAG | Mitteilungen der Vorderasiatischen (or: Vorderasiatisch-Aegyptischen) Gesellschaft |
| MVEOL | Mededelingen en verhandelingen van het Vooraziatisch-Egyptisch Gezelschap/Gerootschop "Ex Oriente Lux" |
| N.F. | Neue Folge |
| N.S. | New Series |
| *OBS* | Speiser, *Oriental and Biblical Studies* |
| OECT | Oxford Editions of Cuneiform Texts |
| OIP | Oriental Institute Publications |
| *OLZ* | *Orientalistische Literaturzeitung* |
| *Or.* | *Orientalia* (all references to New Series) |
| *Or. Ant.* | *Oriens Antiquus* |
| *Or. Suec.* | *Orientalia Suecana* |
| *PAPhS* | *Proceedings of the American Philosophical Society* |
| PBS | Publications of the Babylonian Section, University Museum, University of Pennsylvania |
| *PRT* | Klauber, *Politisch-religiöse Texte aus der Sargonidenzeit* |
| *PRU* | Nougayrol et al., *Le Palais royal d'Ugarit* |
| *RA* | *Revue d'assyriologie et d'archéologie orientale* |
| *RAcc.* | Thureau-Dangin, *Rituels Accadiens* |
| *RBA* | Jastrow, *The Religion of Babylonia and Assyria* |

| | |
|---|---|
| *RHA* | *Revue hittite et asianique* |
| *RLA* | Ebeling and Meissner et al., *Reallexikon der Assyriologie* |
| *SAHG* | Falkenstein and von Soden, *Sumerische und akkadische Hymnen und Gebete* |
| *SAKI* | Thureau-Dangin, *Die sumerischen und akkadischen Königsinschriften* |
| *SBH* | Reisner, *Sumerisch-babylonische Hymnen nach Thontafeln griechischer Zeit* |
| *SKIZ* | Römer, *Sumerische "Königshymnen" der Isin-Zeit* |
| *SKLJ* | Jacobsed, ed., *The Sumerian King List* |
| *SLTNi* | Kramer, *Sumerian Literary Texts from Nippur . . .* |
| *SP* | Gordon, *Sumerian Proverbs . . .* |
| *SRT* | Chiera, *Sumerian Religious Texts* |
| *SSA* | Van Dijk, *La Sagesse suméro-accadienne* |
| StOr | Studia Orientalia Edidit Societas Orientalis Fennica |
| *STC* | King, *The Seven Tablets of Creation* |
| *STT* | Gurney and Finkelstein, *The Sultantepe Tablets* |
| SVT | Supplements to *Vetus Testamentum* |
| TCS | Texts from Cuneiform Sources |
| TCL | Textes cunéiformes du Louvre |
| TIM | Texts in the Iraq Museum |
| TLB | Tabulae Cuneiformae a F. M. Th. de Liagre Böhl Collectae |
| *TuL* | Ebeling, *Tod und Leben . . .* |
| UET | Ur Excavations, Texts |
| UM | Tablets in the collections of the University Museum, University of Pennsylvania |
| *UVB* | *Vorläufiger Bericht über die von den deutschen Archäeologischen Institut und der deutschen Orient-Gesellschaft aus Mitteln der deutschen Forschungsgemeinschaft unternommenen Ausgrabungen in Uruk-Warka* |

| | |
|---|---|
| VAB | Vorderasiatische Bibliothek |
| VAS | Vorderasiatische Schriftdenkmäler der königlichen Museen zu Berlin |
| *WbM* | Haussig, *Wörterbuch der Mythologie* (see Edzard, "Mesopotamien . . .") |
| WVDOG | Wissenschaftliche Veröffentlichungen der deutschen Orient-Gesellschaft |
| *WZJ* | *Wissenschaftliche Zeitschrift der Friedrich-Schiller-Universität Jena, gesellschafts- und sprachwissenschaftliche Reihe* |
| *WZKM* | *Wiener Zeitschrift für die Kunde des Morgenlandes* |
| YBC | Tablets in the Yale Babylonian Collection |
| YNER | Yale Near Eastern Researches |
| YOR | Yale Oriental Series, Researches |
| YOS | Yale Oriental Series, Texts |
| *ZA* | *Zeitschrift für Assyriologie;* volumes cited according to consecutive numeration from *ZA* 1 (1886), without shifting to New Series (Neue Folge) numbers employed since *ZA* 35 (= *ZA* N.F. 1). |
| *ZDMG* | *Zeitschrift der deutschen Morgenländischen Gesellschaft* |

# ANCIENT TEXTS

## *Gilgamesh Texts*

**Note:** *Gilgamesh, The Gilgamesh Epic* refer to the integrated Gilgamesh epic, irrespective of version.

### SUMERIAN

| | |
|---|---|
| *DG* | *The Death of Gilgamesh,* fragments A and B, Kramer, ed., *BASOR* 94: 2–12; *ANET,* pp. 50–52. |
| *GA* | *Gilgamesh and Agga,* Kramer and Jacobson, eds., *AJA* 53: 1–18; Kramer, trans., *ANET,* pp. 44–47. |

*GBH* — *Gilgamesh and the Bull of Heaven* (out-of-date edition of Witzel, *An. Or.* 6:45–68).

*GEN* — *Gilgamesh, Enkidu, and the Netherworld,* Shaffer, ed., "Sources."

*GLL* — *Gilgamesh and the Land of the Living,* Version A, Kramer, ed., *JCS* 1:3–46 (see translation in *ANET,* pp. 47–50), with Version B cited in footnotes (see *JCS* 1: 7); revised MS of both by Shaffer (unpublished). For additional texts and versions, see literature cited in chap. 1, n. 34.

**OLD AND MIDDLE BABYLONIAN (AKKADIAN)**

Gilg. Bo. — Boghazköi fragment; KUB 4:12; Thompson, ed., *GETh.,* pp. 43–44; Speiser, trans., in *ANET,* p. 82.

Gilg. Har. — Harmal fragments: A, van Dijk, ed., TIM 9: 45; *Sumer* 15:9–10. B, van Dijk, ed., TIM 9:43; *Sumer* 13:66, 91 and 14:114–21; Grayson, trans., in *ANET,* p. 504.

Gilg. Me. — Meissner, ed., MVAG 7; Thompson, ed., *GETh.,* pp. 53–54; Speiser, trans., in *ANET,* pp. 89–90.

Gilg. Me. + Mi. — For the join of these two fragments, see *HKL* 2:162 *sub CT* 46, no. 16; cf. Millard, *Iraq* 26:100–101.

Gilg. Meg. — Megiddo fragment; Goetze and Levy, eds., *Atiqot* 2:121-28.

Gilg. Mi. — *CT* 46, no. 16; Millard, ed., *Iraq* 26:99–105; von Soden, ed., *ZA* 58:188–92; Grayson, trans., in *ANET,* p. 507.

Gilg. Ni. — Nippur fragment 2N-T79, copy by Westenholz, transliterations by Steele, and Shaffer in "Sources," p. 23, n. 3; see Appendix no. 3; photograph, above, p. 297.

Gilg. O.I. — Oriental Institute fragment; Bauer, ed., *JNES* 16:254–62; Grayson, trans., in *ANET,* pp. 504–5; new copies by Westenholz (unpublished) and Greengus, *Ishchali,* p. 277.

Gilg. P. — Pennsylvania tablet; Langdon, ed., PBS 10(3); Jastrow and Clay, eds., YOR 4(3):62–86;

| | |
|---|---|
| | Thompson, ed., *GETh.,* pp. 20–24; Speiser, trans., in *ANET,* pp. 76–78. |
| Gilg. Ur | UET 6:394; Gadd, ed., *Iraq* 28:105–21; Landsberger, ed., *RA* 62:123–30. |
| Gilg. Y. | Yale tablet; Jastrow and Clay, eds., YOR 4(3): 87–102; Thompson, ed., *GETh.,* pp. 25–29; Speiser, trans., in *ANET,* pp. 78–81. |

**HITTITE**

| | |
|---|---|
| *Hit. Gilg.* | The Hittite version(s); Tablet I cited from Otten, ed., *Ist. Mit.* 8:93–125; other fragments from Friedrich, ed., *ZA* 39:1–82; Laroche, *RHA* 82:121–38; part of no. 1 translated in Heidel, p. 17; no. 8, Speiser, trans., in *ANET,* pp. 85–86. |

**THE LATE VERSION (AKKADIAN)**

| | |
|---|---|
| *GE* | The late, standard Babylonian ("canonical") version of *The Gilgamesh Epic,* cited from *GETh.,* except where otherwise noted (for additional texts, see *HKL* 1–2 s.v. "Thompson, EG"); translation by Speiser and Grayson, in *ANET,* pp. 79–99, 503–7. |
| GENim | Nimrud fragment, Wiseman, ed., *Iraq* 37: 160–63. |
| GEH | Heidel, ed., *JNES* 11:140–43; partial translation by Speiser, in *ANET,* p. 79. |
| GEUW | Uruk fragment, von Weiher, ed., *ZA* 62:222–29. |

## *Other Ancient Texts*

| | |
|---|---|
| *Anzû* | *The Myth of Anzû;* citations from Speiser and Grayson, trans., in *ANET,* pp. 111–13, 514–16; Tablet I, Hallo and Moran, eds., *JCS* 31:65–115. |
| *Atrahasis, Atr.* | *The Atrahasis Epic;* Lambert and Millard, eds.; references to the Old Babylonian version are preceded by "OB"; for citations such as "*Atr.* S," see MS symbols in Lambert and Millard, pp. 40–41. |

| | |
|---|---|
| *Deluge* | The Sumerian flood story. See Civil, ed., in Lambert and Millard, *Atra-ḫasīs,* pp. 138–45, 167–72; older translation by Kramer, in *ANET,* pp. 42–44. |
| *ELA* | *Enmerkar and the Lord of Aratta;* Kramer, ed., and Cohen, ed. |
| *EnEl* | *Enuma Elish;* Labat, ed., *Le Poème babylonien;* Speiser and Grayson, trans., in *ANET,* pp. 60–72, 501–3. |
| *Erra* | *The Epic of Erra;* Cagni, ed.; translated in Labat et al., *Religions,* pp. 114–37. |
| *Etana* | *The Legend of Etana;* citations from Speiser and Grayson, trans., in *ANET,* pp. 114–18, 517. |
| *EWO* | *Enki and the World Order;* Benito, ed. |
| *Ishtar* | *The Descent of Ishtar to the Netherworld;* Borger, ed., *BAL* 2:86–93; translation by Speiser, in *ANET,* pp. 106–9. The Nineveh and Assur recensions are cited, respectively, as *Ishtar* N and *Ishtar* A. Line numbers from *Ishtar* N unless otherwise indicated. |
| *LH* | *The Laws of Hammurapi;* Driver and Miles, eds., *Babylonian Laws* 2; Meek, trans., in *ANET,* pp. 163–80. |
| SKL | *The Sumerian King List;* Jacobsen, ed., cited as *SKLJ;* Oppenheim, trans., in *ANET,* pp. 265–66. |
| *Tosefta* | *The Tosefta;* Saul Lieberman, ed. |

# *Works Cited*

*Note:* Abbreviations of books and journals cited in this bibliography and in the footnotes are explained in "Abbreviations, Scholarly Literature," pp. 299–304.


Abusch, T. "Mesopotamian Anti-Witchcraft Literature: Texts and Studies. Pt. 1: The Nature of *Maqlû:* Its Character, Divisions, and Calendrical Setting." *JNES* 33 (1974):251–62.

———. Revised reconstruction of *Maqlû.* Unpublished manuscript.

Aelian. *On the Characteristics of Animals.* 3 vols. Translated by A. F. Scholfield. LCL. Cambridge, Mass.: Harvard University Press, 1958–59; London: Heinemann, 1958–59.

Albright, W. F. *From the Stone Age to Christianity.* 2d ed. Garden City, N.Y.: Doubleday, 1957.

———. "Gilgamesh and Engidu, Mesopotamian Genii of Fecundity." *JAOS* 40 (1920):307–35.

Ali, F. *Sumerian Letters.* Ann Arbor, Mich.: University Microfilms, 1964.

Alster, B. "An Aspect of 'Enmerkar and the Lord of Aratta'." *RA* 67 (1973): 101–9.

———. *Dumuzi's Dream.* Mesopotamia: Copenhagen Studies in Assyriology 1. Copenhagen: Akademisk Forlag, 1972.

———. "The Paradigmatic Character of Mesopotamian Heroes." *RA* 68 (1974):49–60.

———. *Studies in Sumerian Proverbs.* Mesopotamia: Copenhagen Studies in Assyriology 3. Copenhagen: Akademisk Forlag, 1975.

Alster, B., ed. *Death in Mesopotamia.* CRRAI 26. Mesopotamia: Copenhagen Studies in Assyriology 8. Copenhagen: Akademisk Forlag, 1980.

Amiet, P. "Le Problème de la représentation de Gilgameš dans l'art." In *GSL,* pp. 169–73.

Arnaud, M. "La Bibliothèque d'un devin syrien à Meskéné-Emar (Syrie)." In *Comptes rendus des seances de l'Academie des inscriptions et belles-lettres,* 1980. Paris: Klincksieck, 1980, pp. 375–88.

Astour, M. "Tamar the Hierodule." *JBL* 85 (1966):185–96.

Barr, J. *Comparative Philology and the Text of the Old Testament.* Oxford: Clarendon Press, 1968

Barton, G. A. *A Critical and Exegetical Commentary on the Book of Ecclesiastes.* ICC. Edinburgh: T. & T. Clark, 1908.

Bauer, Th. "Bemerkungen zur VI. Tafel des Gilgamesch Epos." *OLZ* 24 (1921):72–74.

———. *Das Inschriftenwerk Assurbanipals vervollständigt und neu bearbeitet.* AB, N.F., 1–2. Leipzig: Hinrichs, 1933.

———. "Ein viertes altbabylonisches Fragment des Gilgameš-Epos." *JNES* 16 (1957):254–62.

Benito, C. " 'Enki and Ninmaḫ' and 'Enki and the World Order'." Ph.D. diss., University of Pennsylvania, 1969.

Bernhardt, I., and Kramer, S. N. " 'Enki und die Weltordnung', ein sumerischer Keilschrift-Text über die 'Lehre von der Welt' in der Hilprecht-Sammlung und im University Museum of Pennsylvania." *WZJ* 9 (1959–60):231–56.

———. "Götter-Hymnen und Kult-Gesänge der Sumerer auf zwei Keilschrift 'Katalogen' in der Hilprecht-Sammlung." *WZJ* 6 (1956–57):389–95.

Bezold, C. *Babylonisch-Assyrisches Glossar.* Heidelberg: Carl Winter's Universitätsbuchhandlung, 1926.

Bickerman, E. J. *Four Strange Books of the Bible.* New York: Schocken, 1967.

Biggs, R. D. "The Abū-Ṣalābīkh Tablets." *JCS* 20 (1966):73–88.

———. "The Ebla Tablets. An Interim Perspective." *Biblical Archaeologist* 43(2) (1980):76–87.

———. *Inscriptions from Tell Abū Ṣalābīkh.* OIP 99. Chicago and London: University of Chicago Press, 1974.

———. *ŠÀ.ZI.GA: Ancient Mesopotamian Potency Incantations.* TCS 2. Locust Valley, N.Y.: Augustin, 1967.

Biggs, R. D., trans. "Akkadian Didactic and Wisdom Literature." In *ANET,* pp. 592–607.

Binder, G. *Die Aussetzung des Königskindes: Kyros und Romulus.* Beiträge zur klassischen Philologie 10: Meisenheim am Glan: A. Hain, 1964.

Bing, J. D. "Gilgamesh and Lugalbanda in the Fara Period." *JANES* 9 (1977):1–4.

———. "On the Sumerian Epic of Gilgamesh." *JANES* 7 (1975):1–10.

Böhl, F. M. Th. de L. "Die Fahrt nach dem Lebenskraut." *Ar. Or.* 18 (1950):107–22.

———. "Gilgameš. B. Nach akkadischen Texten." *RLA* 3:364–72.

———. *Het Gilgamesj-Epos: Nationaal Heldendicht van Babylonië.* 2d ed. Amsterdam: H. J. Paris, 1952.

———. "Het Gilgamesj-epos bij de oude Sumeriërs." MVEOL 7:145–77. Leiden: Brill, 1947.

Boissier, A. "Fragment de la légende de Atram-ḫasis." *RA* 28 (1931):91–97.

Borger, R. *Babylonisch-Assyrische Lesestücke.* 3 vols. Rome: Pontifical Biblical Institute, 1963.

———. *Handbuch der Keilschriftliteratur.* 3 vols. Berlin: de Gruyter, 1967–75.

———. *"niṣirti bārûti,* Geheimlehre der Haruspizin." *Bi. Or.* 14 (1957): 190–95.

———. Review of *CAD* $A_1$. *Bi. Or.* 20 (1969):74–75.

Brünnow, R. E. "Assyrian Hymns, 2." *ZA* 4 (1889):225–58.

Buccellati, G. *The Amorites of the Ur III Period.* Istituto orientale di Napoli, Publicazioni del Seminario di Semitistica, ricerche 1. Naples: Istituto Orientale di Napoli, 1966.

———. "Tre saggi sapienza Mesopotamica, 1." *Or. Ant.* 11 (1972):1–36.

Budge, E. A. W. *The Babylonian Story of the Deluge and the Epic of Gilgamesh, with an Account of the Royal Libraries of Nineveh.* London: British Museum, 1920.

Buren, E. D. van. "The Sacred Marriage in Early Times in Mesopotamia." *Or.* 13 (1944):1–72.

Burrows, E. Review of Chiera, *Sumerian Religious Texts. JRAS* (1926): 318–19.

Burton, R., trans. *The Arabian Nights' Entertainments.* Edited by B. A. Cerf. New York: Random House, 1959.

Buttrick, G. A. et al., eds. *The Interpreter's Dictionary of the Bible.* 4 vols. New York and Nashville: Abingdon, 1962.

Cagni, L. *L'epopea di Erra.* Studi Semitici 34. Rome: Istituto di Studi del Vicino Oriento, Università di Roma, 1969.

Calmeyer, P. "Gilgameš. D. In der Archäologie." *RLA* 3:372–74.

Caplice, R. I. "Namburbi Texts in the British Museum, 5." *Or.* 40 (1971): 133–83.

Castellino, G. "Incantation to Utu." *Or. Ant.* 8 (1969):1–57.

———. "Les Origines de la civilisation selon les textes bibliques et les textes cunéiformes." SVT 4(1957):116–37.

———. *Two Šulgi Hymns.* Studi Semitici 42. Rome: Istituto di Studi del Vicino Oriente, Università di Roma, 1972.

———. "Urnammu. Three Religious Texts." *ZA* 52 (1957):1–57; 53 (1959): 106–32.

Chiera, E. *Sumerian Religious Texts.* Crozer Theological Seminary Babylonian Publications 1. Upland, Pa.: 1924.

Childs, B. S. "The Birth of Moses." *JBL* 84 (1965):109–22.

Civil, M. "The 'Message of Lu-dingir-ra to His Mother' and a Group of Akkado-Hittite 'Proverbs'." *JNES* 23 (1964):1–11.

———. Review of T. Pinches, *CT* 44 (1963). *JNES* 28 (1969):70–72.

———. "The Sumerian Flood Story." In Lambert and Millard, *Atra-ḫasīs,* pp. 138–45, 167–72.

Clay, A. T. *Miscellaneous Inscriptions in the Yale Babylonian Collection.* YOS 1. New Haven: Yale University Press, 1915.

Cogan, M. "A Technical Term for Exposure." *JNES* 27 (1968):133–35.

Cohen, S. *Enmerkar and the Lord of Aratta.* Ann Arbor, Mich.: University Microfilms, 1973.

———. "Studies in Sumerian Lexicography, 1." In *Kramer AV,* pp. 97–110.

Conybeare, F. C. et al. *The Story of Aḥiḳar. . . .* 2d ed. Cambridge, England: Cambridge University Press, 1913.

Cooper, J. S. "Bilinguals from Boghazköi." *ZA* 61 (1971):1–22; 62 (1972): 62–81.

———. "Gilgamesh Dreams of Enkidu: The Evolution and Dilution of Narrative." In M. Ellis, ed., *Essays . . . Finkelstein,* pp. 39–44.

———. "More Heat on the AN.IM.DUGUD Bird." *JCS* 26 (1974):121.

———. "A Sumerian ŠU-ÍL-LA from Nimrud with a Prayer for Sin-Šar-Iškun." *Iraq* 32 (1970):51–67.

———. "Symmetry and Repetition in Akkadian Narrative." *JAOS* 97 (1977):508–12.

Cowley, A. E. *Gesenius' Hebrew Grammar.* Oxford: Clarendon Press, 1910.

Crawley, A. E. *The Mystic Rose: A Study of Primitive Marriage. . . .* Revised by T. Besterman. London: Methuen, 1927.

David, M. "Le Récit du déluge et l'epopée de Gilgameš." In *GSL,* pp. 153–59.

Delitzsch, F. *Assyrisches Handwörterbuch.* Leipzig: Hinrichs, 1896.

Diakonoff, I. M. Review of Böhl, *Het Gilgamesj Epos,* and Matouš, *Epos o Gilgamešovi. Bi. Or.* 18 (1961):61–67.

Dijk, J. J. A. van. *Cuneiform Texts: Texts of Varying Content.* TIM 9. Leiden: Brill, 1976.

———. "Le Dénouement de 'Gilameš au bois de cèdres' selon LB 2116." In *GSL,* pp. 69–81.

———. "La Fête du nouvel an dans un texte de Šulgi." *Bi. Or.* 11 (1954): 83–88.

———. L'Hymne à Marduk avec intercession pour le roi Abī'ešuḫ." *MIO* 12 (1966):57–74.

———. "Incantations accompagnant la naissance de l'homme." *Or.* 44 (1975):52–79.

———. "Le Motif cosmique dans la pensée sumérienne." *Ac. Or.* 28 (1964): 1–59.

———. *La Sagesse suméro-accadienne.* Leiden: Brill, 1953.

———. *Textes divers.* TLB 2. Leiden: Nederlandisch instituut voor het nabije oosten, 1957.

———. "Textes divers du Musée de Baghdad, 2–3." *Sumer* 13 (1957): 65–133; 15 (1959):5–14.

———. "Die Tontafeln aus der Grabung in E-anna." In H. J. Lenzen et al., *UVB* 18:39–62. Berlin: Gebr. Mann, 1962.

———. "VAT 8382: ein zweisprachiges Königsritual." In *Falkenstein AV,* pp. 233–68.

Dossin, G. *Correspondance de Šamsi-Addu et de ses fils.* ARM 1. Paris: Imprimerie Nationale, 1950.

———. "Les deux songes de Gilgamesh." *Le Muséon* 59 (1946):63–66.

———. "Enkidou dans l'épopee de Gilgameš." *Academie royale de Belgique: Bulletin de la classe des lettres . . . ,* series 5, 42 (1956):580–93.

———. "L'Inscription de fondation de Iaḫdum-Lim, roi de Mari." *Syria* 32 (1955):1–28.

———. *Le Pâleur d'Enkidou.* Louvain: Imprimerie Orientaliste M. Istas, 1931.

———. "Un Rituel du culte d'Ištar provenant de Mari." *RA* 35 (1938):1–13.

Driver, G. R., and Miles, J. C. *The Babylonian Laws.* 2 vols. Oxford: Clarendon Press, 1952–55.

Driver, S. R. *The Book of Genesis.* 3d ed. New York: Gorham, 1904.

Ebeling, E. "Aruru." *RLA* 1:160.

———. "Aššur. 3) Hauptgott Assyriens." *RLA* 1:196–98.

———. *Keilschrifttexte aus Assur religiösen Inhalts.* WVDOG 28 and 34. Leipzig: Hinrichs, 1915–23.

———. "Ein Preislied auf die Kultstadt Arba-Ilu aus Neuassyrischer Zeit." *JKF* 2 (1952–53):274–82.

———. *Quellen zur Kenntnis der babylonischen Religion.* Vol. 1. MVAG 23(1). Leipzig: Hinrichs, 1918.

———. *Tod und Leben nach der Vorstellungen der Babylonier.* Berlin and Leipzig: de Gruyter, 1931.

Ebeling, E., and Meissner, B. et al., eds. *Reallexikon der Assyriologie.* Berlin and Leipzig: de Gruyter, 1932– .

Edzard, D. O. "The Early Dynastic Period," "The Third Dynasty of Ur—Its Empire and Its Successor States," and "The Old Babylonian Period." In J. Bottéro, E. Cassin, and J. Vercoutter, eds., *The Near East: The Early Civilizations,* pp. 52–90, 133–231. New York: Delacorte, 1967.

———. "Enmebaragesi, contemporain de Gilgameš." In *GSL,* p. 57.

———. "Enmebaragesi von Kiš." *ZA* 53 (1959):9–26.

———. "Mesopotamien. Die Mythologie der Sumerer und Akkader." In H. W. Haussig, ed., *Wörterbuch der Mythologie.* Vol. 1, *Götter und Mythen in vorderen Orient.* Stuttgart: Ernst Klett, 1965.

———. "Sumerische Komposita mit dem Nominalpräfix nu-." *ZA* 55 (1962):91–112.

———. *Die "zweite Zwischenzeit" Babyloniens.* Wiesbaden: Harrassowitz, 1957.

Edzard, D. O., ed. *Heidelberger Studien zum alten Orient, Adam Falkenstein . . .* Wiesbaden: Harrassowitz, 1967.

Ehelolf, H. *Mythen und Rituale.* KUB 17. Berlin: Staatliche Museen, 1926.
Eichler, B. L., ed. *Kramer Anniversary Volume. Cuneiform Studies in Honor of Samuel Noah Kramer.* AOAT 25. Kevelaer: Butzon & Bercker; Neukirchen-Vluyn: Neukirchner Verlag, 1976.
Ellis, M. de J. "Gilgamesh' Approach to Huwawa's Dwelling: A New Text." *AfO* 1982, in press.
———. "*Ṣimdatu* in the Old Babylonian Sources." *JCS* 24 (1971–72):74–82.
Ellis, M. de J., ed. *Essays on the Ancient Near East in Memory of Jacob Joel Finkelstein.* Memoirs of the Connecticut Academy of Arts and Sciences 19. Hamden, Conn.: Archon, 1977.
Ellis, R. S. *Foundation Deposits in Ancient Mesopotamia.* YNER 2. New Haven: Yale University Press, 1968.
Falkenstein, A. "Gebet I. Das Gebet in der sumerischen Überlieferung." *RLA* 3:156–60.
———. "Gilgameš. A. Nach sumerischen Texten." *RLA* 3:357–63.
———. *Grammatik der Sprache Gudeas von Lagaš.* Vol. 1. An. Or. 28. Rome: Pontifical Biblical Institute, 1949.
———. *Die Haupttypen der sumerischen Beschwörung literarisch untersucht.* LSS, N.F. 1. Leipzig: Hinrichs, 1931.
———. *Literarische Keilschrifttexte aus Uruk.* Berlin: Staatliche Museen, 1931.
———. Review of Kramer, *Sumerian Mythology. Bi. Or.* 5 (1948):163–67.
———. *Das Sumerische. Handbuch der Orientalistik.* Pt. 1, *Der nahe und der mittlere Osten;* vol. 2, *Keilschriftforschung und alte Geschichte Vorderasiens;* secs. 1–2, "Geschichte der Forschung," "Sprache und Literatur." Leiferung 1. Leiden: Brill, 1959.
———. "Sumerische religiöse Texte, 2. Ein Šulgi-Lied." *ZA* 50 (1952): 61–91.
———. "Der sumerische und der akkadische Mythos von Inannas Gang zur Unterwelt." In E. Graf, ed., *Festschrift Werner Caskel . . . ,* pp. 96–110. Leiden: Brill, 1968 (published 1969).
———. "Untersuchungen zur sumerischen Grammatik (Fortsetzung)." *ZA* 48 (1944):69–118.
———. "Zu 'Inannas Gang zur Unterwelt'." *AfO* 14 (1941–44):113–38.
———. "Zu den Inschriftenfunden der Grabung in Uruk-Warka, 1960–61." *Baghdader Mitteilungen* 2 (1963):1–82.
———. "Zum sumerischen Lexikon." *ZA* 58 (1967):5–15.
———. "Zur Chronologie der sumerischen Literatur," In CRRAI 2, pp. 12–27. Paris: Imprimerie Nationale, 1951.
———. "Zur Überlieferung des Epos' von Gilgameš und Ḫuwawa." *JNES* 19 (1960):65–71.
Falkenstein, A., and von Soden, W. *Sumerische und akkadische Hymnen und Gebete.* Zürich and Stuttgart: Artemis, 1953.
Figulla, H. *Letters and Documents of the Old Babylonian Period.* UET 5. London: British Museum; Philadelphia, University Museum, University of Pennsylvania, 1953.

Finet, A. "Citations littéraires dans la correspondance de Mari." *RA* 68 (1974):35–47.

Finkelstein, J. J. "ana bīt emim šasū." *RA* 61 (1967):127–36.

———. "The Antediluvian Kings: A University of California Tablet." *JCS* 17 (1963):39–51.

———. "The Genealogy of the Hammurapi Dynasty." *JCS* 20 (1966):95–118.

———. "A Late Old Babylonian Copy of the Laws of Hammurapi." *JCS* 21 (1967; published 1969):39–48.

———. "Mesopotamian Historiography." In *Cuneiform Studies and the History of Civilization. PAPhS* 107(6):461–72. Philadelphia: American Philosophical Society, 1963.

———. "On Some Recent Studies in Cuneiform Law." *JAOS* 90 (1970): 243–56.

———. "The So-called 'Old Babylonian Kutha Legend'." *JCS* 11 (1957): 83–88.

Frankena, R. "Nouveaux fragments de la sixième tablette de l'épopée de Gilgameš." In *GSL,* pp. 113–22.

———. "The Vassal Treaties of Esarhaddon and the Dating of Deuteronomy." *Oudtestamentliche Studiën* 14 (1965):122–54.

Frazer, J. G. *Folk-lore in the Old Testament.* Abridged ed. New York: Tudor Press, 1923.

Friedrich, J. "Die hethitischen Bruchstücke des Gilgameš-Epos." *ZA* 39 (1930):1–82.

———. *Hethitisches Wörterbuch.* Heidelberg: Carl Winter Universitätsverlag, 1952.

———. "Zur Einordnung hethitscher Gilgamesch-Fragmente." *Or.* 30 (1961):90–91.

Frymer-Kensky, T. "The Atrahasis Epic and Its Significance for Our Understanding of Genesis 1–9." *Biblical Archaeologist* 40 (1977):147–55.

Gadd, C. J. "Ebeḫ-il and His Basket Seat." *RA* 63 (1969):1–10.

———. *Ideas of Divine Rule in the Ancient Near East.* London: Oxford University Press, 1948.

———. "Some Contributions to the Gilgamesh-Epic." *Iraq* 28 (1966):105–21.

———. *Teachers and Students in the Oldest Schools.* London: University of London, School of Oriental and African Studies, 1956.

Gadd, C. J., and Kramer, S. N. *Literary and Religious Texts.* UET 6(1). London: British Museum, 1963.

Garelli, P., ed. *Gilgameš et sa légende.* CRRAI 7. Cahiers du Groupe François-Thureau-Dangin 1. Paris: Imprimerie Nationale and Librarie C. Klincksieck, 1960.

Gaster, T. H. "Angel." In G. A. Buttrick et al., eds., *The Interpreter's Dictionary of the Bible,* 1:128–34. New York and Nashville: Abingdon, 1962.

———. *Myth, Legend, and Custom in the Old Testament.* New York: Harper & Row, 1969.

———. *The Oldest Stories in the World.* New York: Viking Press, 1952.

———. *Thespis: Ritual, Myth and Drama in the Ancient Near East.* Rev. ed. Garden City, N.Y.: Doubleday, 1961.

Gelb, I. J. *Hurrians and Subarians.* Chicago: University of Chicago Press, 1944.

Gelb, I. J. et al., eds. *The Assyrian Dictionary of the Oriental Institute of the University of Chicago.* Chicago: Oriental Institute; Glückstadt, Germany: Augustin, 1956–.

Gifford, E. H. *Eusebii Pamphili Evangelicae Praeparationis.* Vol. 3, pt. 1. Oxford: Typographeo Academico, 1903.

Ginsberg, H. L. "The Quintessence of Koheleth." In A. Altmann, ed., *Biblical and Other Studies,* pp. 47–59. Cambridge, Mass.: Harvard University Press, 1963.

Ginsberg, H. L., ed. *The Five Megilloth and Jonah.* Philadelphia: Jewish Publication Society, 1969.

Goetze, A. "An Incantation against Diseases." *JCS* 9 (1955):8–18.

———. "Short or Long *a*? (Notes on Some Akkadian Words)." *Or.* 16 (1947):239–50.

Goetze, A., trans. "Hittite Myths, Epics, and Legends." In *ANET,* pp. 120–28.

Goetze, A., and Levy, S. "Fragment of the Gilgamesh Epic from Megiddo." *Atiqot* 2 (1959):121–28.

Goldin, J. *The Fathers According to Rabbi Nathan.* Yale Judaica Series 10. New Haven: Yale University Press, 1955.

Gordis, R. *Koheleth: The Man and His World.* 3d ed. New York: Schocken, 1968.

Gordon, E. I. "Mesilim and Mesannipadda—Are They Identical?" *BASOR* 132 (1953):27–30.

———. "A New Look at the Wisdom of Sumer and Akkad." *Bi. Or.* 17 (1960):122–52.

———. "The Sumerian Proverb Collections: A Preliminary Report." *JAOS* 74 (1954):81–85.

———. *Sumerian Proverbs: Glimpses of Everyday Life in Ancient Mesopotamia.* Museum Monographs. Philadelphia: University Museum, University of Pennsylvania, 1959.

———. "Sumerian Proverbs and Fables." *JCS* 12 (1958):1–21, 43–75.

Grafman, R. "Bringing Tiamat to Earth." *IEJ* 22 (1972):47–49.

Grayson, A. K., trans. "Akkadian Myths and Epics." In *ANET,* pp. 501–18; revisions of Speiser, "Akkadian Myths and Epics," in *ANET,* pp. 60–119.

Grayson, A. K., and Lambert, W. G. "Akkadian Prophecies." *JCS* 18 (1964): 7–30.

Greenberg, M. *Understanding Exodus.* New York: Behrman House, 1969.

Greenfield, J. C. "Scripture and Inscription." In H. Goedicke, ed., *Near Eastern Studies in Honor of William Foxwell Albright,* pp. 253–68. Baltimore: Johns Hopkins University Press, 1971.

Greengus, S. "The Old Babylonian Marriage Contract." *JAOS* 89 (1969): 505–32.
———. *Old Babylonian Tablets from Ishchali and Vicinity.* Uitgaven van het Nederlands Historische-Archaeologisch Instituut te Istanbul 44. Istanbul: Nederlands Historische-Archaeologisch Instituut in Het Nabije Oosten, 1979.
Gressmann, H. *Altorientalische Texte zum Alten Testament.* 2d ed. Berlin and Leipzig: de Gruyter, 1926.
Gressmann, H., and Ungnad, A. *Das Gilgamesch-Epos.* Forschungen zur Religion und Literatur des Alten und Neuen Testaments 14. Göttingen: Vandenhoeck & Ruprecht, 1911.
Grimme, H. "Babel und Koheleth-Jojakin." *OLZ* 8 (1905):432–38.
Gunkel, H. "Jensens Gilgamesch-Epos in der Weltliteratur." *Deutsche Literaturzeitung* 15 (1909):cols. 901–11.
Gurney, O. R. *The Hittites.* Baltimore: Penguin, 1966.
———. "The Sultantepe Tablets (continued). 4. The Cuthaean Legend of Naram-Sin." *An. St.* 5 (1955):93–113; 6 (1956):163–64.
———. "The Sultantepe Tablets (continued). 6. A Letter of Gilgamesh." *An. St.* 7 (1957):127–35.
———. "Two Fragments of the Epic of Gilgamesh from Sultantepe." *JCS* 8 (1954):87–95.
Gurney, O. R., and Finkelstein, J. J. *The Sultantepe Tablets.* Vol. 1. Occasional Publications of the British Institute of Archaeology at Ankara 3. London: British Institute of Archaeology at Ankara, 1957.
Güterbock, H. G. "Die historische Tradition und ihre literarische Gestaltung bei Babyloniern und Hethitern bis 1200." *ZA* 42 (1934):1–91; 44 (1938):45–149.
———."Hittite Mythology." In S. N. Kramer, ed., *Mythologies of the Ancient World,* pp. 139–79. Garden City, N.Y.: Doubleday, 1961.
———. "The Song of Ullikumi. Revised Text of the Hittite Version of a Hurrian Myth." *JCS* 5 (1951):135–61; 6 (1952):8–42.
Güterbock, H. G., and Jacobsen, T., eds. *Studies in Honor of Benno Landsberger.* AS 16. Chicago: University of Chicago Press, 1965.
Hallo, W. W. "Antediluvian Cities." *JCS* 23 (1970–71):57–67.
———. "Beginning and End of the Sumerian King List in the Nippur Recension." *JCS* 17 (1963):52–57.
———. "The Coronation of Ur-Nammu." *JCS* 20 (1966):133–41.
———. "The Cultic Setting of Sumerian Poetry." In *Actes de la 17e rencontre assyriologique internationale.* CRRAI 17:116–34. Ham-sur-Heure, Belgium: Comité Belge de Recherches en Mesopotamie, 1970.
———. "The Date of the Fara Period: A Case Study in the Historiography of Early Mesopotamia." *Or.* 42 (1973):228–38.
———. "Individual Prayer in Sumerian: The Continuity of a Tradition." *JAOS* 88 (1968):71–89.
———. "The Lame and the Halt." *EI* 9 (1969):66–70.

———. "New Hymns to the Kings of Isin." *Bi. Or.* 23 (1966):239–47.

———. "New Viewpoints on Cuneiform Literature." *IEJ* 12 (1962):13–26.

———. "On the Antiquity of Sumerian Literature." *JAOS* 83 (1963):167–76.

———. "The Royal Inscriptions of Ur: A Typology." *HUCA* 33 (1962):1–43.

———. "Toward a History of Sumerian Literature." In *Jacobsen AV*, pp. 181–203.

Hallo, W. W., and van Dijk, J. J. A. *The Exaltation of Inanna.* YNER 3. New Haven: Yale University Press, 1968.

Hallo, W. W., and Moran, W. L. "The First Tablet of the SB Recension of the Anzu Myth." *JCS* 31 (1969):65–115.

Hallo, W. W., and Simpson, W. K. *The Ancient Near East: A History.* New York: Harcourt Brace Jovanovich, 1971.

Hansman, J. "Gilgamesh, Humbaba, and the Land of the Erin-Trees." *Iraq* 38 (1976):23–35.

Haupt, P. *Das Babylonische Nimrodepos.* AB 3. Leipzig: Hinrichs, 1884.

Hecker, K. *Untersuchungen zur akkadischen Epik.* AOAT Sonderreihe 8. Kevelaer: Butzon & Bercker; Neukirchen-Vluyn: Neukirchener Verlag, 1974.

Heidel, A. *The Babylonian Genesis.* 2d ed. Chicago: University of Chicago Press, 1965.

———. *The Gilgamesh Epic and Old Testament Parallels.* 2d ed. Chicago: University of Chicago Press, 1963.

———. "A Neo-Babylonian Gilgamesh Fragment." *JNES* 11 (1952):140–43.

Heimpel, W. *Tierbilder in der sumerischen Literatur.* Studia Pohl 2. Rome: Biblical Institute Press, 1968.

Held, M. "A Faithful Lover in an Old Babylonian Dialogue." *JCS* 15 (1961): 1–26.

Herodotus. *The Persian Wars.* Translated by George Rawlinson. New York: Random House, 1942.

Höfer, O. "Seuechoros." In W. H. Roscher, ed., *Ausführliches Lexikon der griechischen und römischen Mythologie.* Vol. 4, col. 789. Leipzig: Teubner, 1909–15; repr. Hildesheim and New York: Olms, 1977.

Hoffner, H. A. "The ARZANA House." In K. Bittel, et al., eds., *Anatolian Studies Presented to Hans Gustav Güterbock,* pp. 113–21. Uitgaven van het Nederlands Historische-Archaeologisch Instituut te Istanbul 35. Istanbul: Nederlands Historische-Archaeologisch Instituut in Het Nabije Oosten, 1974.

———. "Enki's Command to Atrahasis." In *Kramer AV,* pp. 241–45.

———. *Gurparanzaḫu and the Bow.* Unpublished translation.

———. "A Hittite Analogue to the David and Goliath Contest of Champions?" *CBQ* 30 (1968):220–25.

———. "Remarks on the Hittite Version of the Naram-Sin Legend." *JCS* 23 (1970–71):17–22.

———. "Symbols for Masculinity and Femininity: Their Use in Ancient Near Eastern Sympathetic Magic Rituals." *JBL* 85 (1966):326–34.

———. Unpublished translation of *Hit. Gilg* I, nos. 1 and 2:1–12.
Homer. *The Iliad.* Translated by Richmond Lattimore. Chicago: University of Chicago Press, 1951.
Hruška, B. "Das spätbabylonische Lehrgedicht 'Inannas Erhöhung'." *Ar. Or.* 37 (1969):473–522.
Huffmon, H. B. *Amorite Personal Names in the Mari Texts.* Baltimore: Johns Hopkins University Press, 1965.
Hunger, H. *Babylonische und assyrische Kolophone.* AOAT 2. Kevelaer: Verlag Butzon & Bercker; Neukirchen-Vluyn: Neukirchener Verlag, 1968.
———. *Spätbabylonische Texte aus Uruk.* Vol. 1. Berlin: Gebr. Mann, 1976.
Jacobs, J. "Jus Primae Noctis." In I. Singer, ed., *The Jewish Encyclopedia,* 7:395. New York and London: Funk & Wagnalls, 1904.
Jacobsen, T. "Ancient Mesopotamian Religion: The Central Concerns." In *Cuneiform Studies and the History of Civilization. PAPhS* 107(6):473–84. Philadelphia: American Philosophical Society, 1963.
———. "The Battle Between Marduk and Tiamat." *JAOS* 88 (1968):104–8.
———. "Death in Ancient Mesopotamia." In Alster, ed., *Death in Mesopotamia,* pp. 19–24.
———. "Early Political Development in Mesopotamia." *ZA* 52 (1957): 91–140.
———. "How Did Gilgameš Oppress Uruk?" *Ac. Or.* 8 (1930):62–74.
———. "The Inscription of Takil-ili-su of Malgium." *AfO* 12 (1937–39): 363–66.
———. "Mesopotamia." In H. Frankfort and H. A. Frankfort, eds., *Before Philosophy,* pp. 137–234. Baltimore: Penguin, 1959.
———. "New Sumerian Literary Texts." *BASOR* 102 (1946):12–17.
———. "Notes on Selected Sayings," and "Additional Notes (1959)." In *SP,* pp. 447–87, 547–50.
———. "Parerga Sumerologica." *JNES* 2 (1943):117–21.
———. "The Stele of the Vultures, Col. I–X." In *Kramer AV,* pp. 247–59.
———. "Sumerian Mythology: A Review Article." *JNES* 5 (1946):128–52.
———. *Toward the Image of Tammuz and Other Essays.* Edited by W. L. Moran. Harvard Semitic Series 21. Cambridge, Mass.: Harvard University Press, 1970.
———. *The Treasures of Darkness. A History of Mesopotamian Religion.* New Haven: Yale University Press, 1976.
Jacobsen, T., ed. *The Sumerian King List.* AS 11. Chicago: University of Chicago Press, 1939.
Jacobsen, T., and Kramer, S. N. "The Myth of Inanna and Bilulu." *JNES* 12 (1953):160–88.
Jacoby, F. *Die Fragmente der griechischen Historiker.* Pt. 3C, *Autoren ueber einzelne Laender.* 2 vols. Leiden: Brill, 1958.
Jastrow, Marcus. *A Dictionary of the Targumim, the Talmud Babli and Yerushalmi, and the Midrashic Literature.* 2 vols. New York: Pardes, 1950.

Jastrow, Morris. "Adam and Eve in Babylonian Literature." *AJSL* 15 (1899):193–214.
———. "Adraḫasis and Parnapištim." *ZA* 13 (1898):288–301.
———. "On the Composite Character of the Babylonian Creation Story." In C. Bezold, ed., *Orientalische Studien Theodor Nöldeke,* 2:969–82. Gieszen: Töpelmann, 1906.
———. *The Religion of Babylonia and Assyria.* Boston: Ginn, 1898.
Jastrow, Morris, and Clay, A. T. *An Old Babylonian Version of the Gilgamesh Epic.* YOR 4(3). New Haven: Yale University Press, 1920.
Jean, C.-F. "L'Origine des choses d'apres la traduction sumérienne de Nippur." *RA* 26 (1929):33–38.
Jensen, P. *Assyrisch-Babylonische Mythen und Epen.* KB 6(1). Berlin: Reuther & Reichard, 1900.
———. "Aussetzungsgeschichten." *RLA* 1:322–24.
———. Review of Jastrow and Clay, *An Old Babylonian Version of the Gilgamesh Epic. OLZ* 24 (1921):268–70.
———. Review of R. C. Thompson, *The Epic of Gilgamish: A New Translation. OLZ* 32 (1929):643–53.
Jeremias, A. "Izdubar." In W. H. Roscher, ed., *Ausführliches Lexikon der griechischen und römischen Mythologie.* Vol. 2, cols. 773–823. Leipzig: Teubner, 1890–94; repr. Hildesheim and New York: Olms, 1978.
———. *Izdubar-Nimrod. Eine altbabylonische Heldensage.* Leipzig: Teubner, 1891.
Jestin, R. "La Conception sumérienne de la vie post-mortem." *Syria* 33 (1956):113–18.
Kammenhuber, A. "Die hethitische und hurrische Überlieferung zum 'Gilgameš-Epos'." *Münchener Studien zur Sprachwissenschaft* 21 (1967): 45–58.
Kienast, B. *"qabal lā maḫār."* *JCS* 29 (1977):73–77.
Kilmer, A. D. "The Mesopotamian Concept of Overpopulation and Its Solution as Reflected in the Mythologies." *Or.* 41 (1972):160–77.
King, L. W. *Chronicles Concerning Early Babylonian Kings.* 2 vols. Studies in Eastern History 2–3. London: Luzac, 1907.
———. *CT* 13. London: British Museum, 1901.
———. *The Seven Tablets of Creation.* 2 vols. London: Luzac, 1902.
King, L. W., and Budge, E. A. W. *Annals of the Kings of Assyria.* Vol. 1. London: British Museum, 1902.
Kirk, G. S. *Myth: Its Meaning and Functions in Ancient and Other Cultures.* Cambridge, England: Cambridge University Press; Berkeley and Los Angeles: University of California Press, 1970.
Klauber, E. G. *Politisch-religiöse Texte aus der Sargonidenzeit.* Leipzig: Pfeiffer, 1913.
Klein, J. Review of Wilcke, *Das Lugalbandaepos. JAOS* 91 (1971):295–99.
———. "Šulgi and Gilgamesh: Two Brother-Peers (Šulgi O)." In *Kramer AV,* pp. 271–92.

Knudtzon, J. A. *Assyrische Gebete an den Sonnengott.* 2 vols. Leipzig: Pfeiffer, 1893.
———. *Die El-Amarna-Tafeln.* 2 vols. VAB 16. Leipzig: Hinrichs, 1915.
Köcher, F. "Der babylonische Göttertypentext." *MIO* 1 (1953):57–107.
———. "Ein Spätbabylonischer Hymnus auf den Tempel Ezida in Borsippa." *ZA* 19 (1959):236–40.
Kohler, J., and Ungnad, A. *Assyrische Rechtsurkunden.* Leipzig: Pfeiffer, 1913.
Komoróczy, G. "Akkadian Epic Poetry and Its Sumerian Sources." *Act. Ant.* 23 (1975):41–63.
———. "Berosos and the Mesopotamian Literature." *Act. Ant.* 21 (1973): 125–52.
Korošec, V. "Gilgameš vu sous son aspect juridique." In *GSL,* pp. 161–66.
Koschaker, P. "Beiträge zum altbabylonischen Recht." *ZA* 35 (1924):192–212.
Kramer, S. N. "The Death of Gilgamesh." *BASOR* 94 (1944):2–12.
———. "The Death of Ur-Nammu and His Descent to the Netherworld." *JCS* 21 (1967: published 1969):104–22.
———. "Dilmun, the Land of the Living." *BASOR* 96 (1944):18–28.
———. *Enmerkar and the Lord of Aratta.* Museum Monographs. Philadelphia: University Museum, University of Pennsylvania, 1952.
———. "The Epic of Gilgameš and Its Sumerian Sources. A Study in Literary Evolution." *JAOS* 64 (1944):7–23, 83.
———. "Gilgamesh and Agga. With comments by Thorkild Jacobsen." *AJA* 53 (1949):1–18.
———. "Gilgamesh and the Land of the Living." *JCS* 1 (1947):3–46.
———. "Gilgameš: Some New Sumerian Data." In *GSL,* pp. 54–68.
———. *History Begins at Sumer.* Garden City, NY: Doubleday, 1959.
———. "New Literary Catalogue from Ur." *RA* 55 (1961):169–76.
———. "The Oldest Literary Catalogue: A Sumerian List of Literary Compositions Compiled About 2000 B.C." *BASOR* 88 (1942):10–19.
———. *The Sacred Marriage Rite: Aspects of Faith, Myth, and Ritual in Ancient Sumer.* Bloomington, Ind.: Indiana University Press, 1969.
———. "Shulgi of Ur: A Royal Hymn and a Divine Blessing." In A. A. Neuman and S. Zeitlin, eds., *The Seventy-Fifth Anniversary Volume of the Jewish Quarterly Review,* pp. 369–80. Philadelphia: Jewish Quarterly Review, 1967.
———. "Sumerian Epic Literature." In *Atti del convegno internazionale sul tema: La poesia epica e la sua formazione (Roma, 28 marzo–3 aprile 1969).* Accademia Nazionale dei Lincei. Anno CCCLXVII–1970. Quaderno N. 139, pp. 825–37. Roma: Academia Nazionale dei Lincei, 1970.
———. *Sumerian Literary Texts from Nippur in the Museum of the Ancient Orient at Istanbul.* Annual of the American Schools of Oriental Research 23. New Haven: American Schools of Oriental Research, 1944.

———. "Sumerian Literature: A General Survey." In G. E. Wright, ed., *The Bible and the Ancient Near East: Essays in Honor of William Foxwell Albright*, pp. 327–52. Garden City, N.Y.: Doubleday, 1965.

———. *The Sumerians: Their History, Culture, and Character.* Chicago: University of Chicago Press, 1963.

———. "Sumerian Similies." *JAOS* 89 (1969):1–10.

———. "Sumero-Akkadian Interconnections: Religious Ideas." In *Aspects du contact suméro-akkadien.* CRRAI 9. *Genava,* N.S. 8 (1960):272–83.

Kramer, S. N., ed., *Mythologies of the Ancient World.* Garden City, N.Y.: Doubleday, 1961.

Kramer, S. N., trans. "Sumerian Myths and Epic Tales," "Sumerian Hymns," "Sumerian Lamentation," "Sumerian Sacred Marriage Texts," and "Sumerian Miscellaneous Texts." In *ANET,* pp. 37–59, 573–86, 611–19, 637–45, 646–52.

Kraus, F. R. "Altmesopotamisches Lebensgefühl." *JNES* 19 (1960):117–32.

———. "Nippur und Isin nach altbabylonischen Rechtsurkunden." *JCS* 3 (1951).

———. "Zur Liste der alteren Könige von Babylonien." *ZA* 50 (1952): 29–60.

Kunstmann, W. G. *Die Babylonische Gebetsbeschwörung.* LSS, N.F. 2. Leipzig: Hinrichs, 1932.

Kupper, J. R. "Les Différentes Versions de l'epopée de Gilgameš." In *GSL,* pp. 97–102.

———. *Les Nomades en Mésopotamie au temps des rois de Mari.* Bibliothèque de la Faculté de Philosophie et Lettres de l'Université de Liège 142. Paris: 1957.

Kutscher, R., and Wilcke, C. "Eine Ziegel-Inschrift des Königs Takil-Iliššu von Malgium, gefunden in Isin und Yale." *ZA* 68 (1978):95–128.

Labat, R. *Le Caractère religieux de la royauté assyro-babylonienne.* Paris: Librarie d'Amérique et d'Orient, 1939.

———. *Le Poème babylonien de la création.* Paris: Librarie d'Amérique et d'Orient, 1935.

Labat, R. et al. *Les Religions du Proche-Oriente asiatique.* Paris: Fayard/ Denoël, 1970.

Laessøe, J. "The Atraḫasīs Epic: A Babylonian History of Mankind." *Bi. Or.* 13 (1956):90–102.

———. "Literary and Oral Tradition in Ancient Mesopotamia." In *Studia Orientalia Ioanni Pedersen . . . Dicata,* pp. 205–18. Copenhagen: E. Munksgaard, 1953.

Lambert, W. G. "An Address of Marduk to the Demons." *AfO* 19 (1959–60):114–17.

———. "Ancestors, Authors and Canonicity." *JCS* 11 (1957):1–14, 112.

———. *Babylonian Wisdom Literature.* Oxford: Clarendon Press, 1960.

———. "A Catalogue of Texts and Authors." *JCS* 16 (1962):59–77.

———. "Divine Love Lyrics from the Reign of Abi-ešuḫ." *MIO* 12 (1966): 41–56.

———. "Gilgameš in Religious, Historical and Omen Texts and the Historicity of Gilgameš." In *GSL,* pp. 39–56.
———. "Gilg. I i 41." *RA* 73 (1979):89.
———. "History and the Gods: A Review Article." *Or.* 39 (1970):170–77.
———. "Literary Style in First Millennium Mesopotamia." *JAOS* 88 (1968):123–32.
———. "A Middle Assyrian Medical Text." *Iraq* 31 (1969):28–39.
———. "Morals in Ancient Mesopotamia." *Jaarbericht . . . "Ex Oriente Lux"* 15 (1958):184–96.
———. "A New Look at the Babylonian Background of Genesis." *Journal of Theological Studies,* N.S. 16 (1965):287–300.
———. "The Reign of Nebuchadnezzar I: A Turning Point in the History of Ancient Mesopotamian Religion." In W. S. McCullough, ed., *The Seed of Wisdom: Essays in Honour of T. J. Meek,* pp. 3–13. Toronto: University of Toronto Press, 1964.
———. Review of *AHw* Fascicles 5 and 6. *JSS* 12 (1967):100–105.
———. Review of M. Ellis, *Studies . . . Finkelstein. JNES* 39 (1980):172–74.
———. "The Theology of Death." In Alster, ed., *Death in Mesopotamia,* pp. 53–66.
———. "Three Unpublished Fragments of the Tukulti-Ninurta Epic." *AfO* 18 (1957–58):38–51.
———. Two Texts from the Early Part of the Reign of Ashurbanipal." *AfO* 18 (1957–58):382–87.
———. "Zum Forschungsstand der sumerisch-babylonischen Literatur-Geschichte." In W. Voigt, ed., *XIX. Deutscher Orientalistentag . . . Vorträge. ZDMG,* supp. 3(1). Wiesbaden: Franz Steiner Verlag GMBH, 1977.
Lambert, W. G., and Millard, A. R. *Atra-ḫasīs. The Babylonian Story of the Flood,* with "The Sumerian Flood Story," by M. Civil. Oxford: Clarendon Press, 1969.
———. *Babylonian Literary Texts. CT* 46. London: British Museum, 1965.
Lambert, W. G., and Parker, S. *Enuma Eliš: The Babylonian Epic of Creation: The Cuneiform Text.* Oxford: Clarendon Press, 1966.
Landsberger, B. "Einige unerkannt gebliebene oder verkannte Nomina des Akkadischen." *WZKM* 56 (1960):109–29; 57 (1961):1–23.
———. "Einleitung in des Gilgameš-Epos." In *GSL,* pp. 31–36.
———. "Jungfräulichkeit: Ein Beitrag zum Thema 'Beilager und Eheschliessung'." In J. A. Ankum, R. Feenstra, and W. F. Leemans, eds., *Symbolae Iuridicae et Historicae Martino David Dedicatae,* 2:41–105. Leiden: Brill, 1968.
———. "Zur vierten und siebenten Tafel des Gilgamesch-Epos." *RA* 62 (1968):97–135.
Langdon, S. H. *The Epic of Gilgamesh.* PBS 10(3). Philadelphia: University Museum, University of Pennsylvania, 1917.
Langdon, S. H. *Le Poème sumerien du paradis, du déluge et de la chute de l'homme.* Translated by C. Virolleaud. Paris: Leroux, 1919.

———. "The Sumerian Epic of Gilgamish." *JRAS* 1932:911–48.
———. *The Weld-Blundell Collection.* Vol. 2, *Historical Inscriptions* . . . . OECT 2. London: Oxford University Press, 1923.
Laroche, E. "Catalogue des Textes Hittites." *RHA* 14 (1956):33–38, 69–116; 15 (1957):30–89; 16 (1958):18–64. Superceded by his *Catalogue des textes hittites.* Paris: Klincksieck, 1971, and "Premier supplément," *RHA* 30 (1972):94–133.
———. "Mythologie d'origine étrangere. 12. Gilgameš." In E. Laroche, ed., *Textes mythologiques hittites en transcription. RHA* 26 (1968): 121–38.
Leichty, E. V. "The Colophon." In R. D. Biggs and J. A. Brinkman, eds., *Studies Presented to A. Leo Oppenheim,* pp. 147–54. Chicago: University of Chicago Press, 1964.
———. "Demons and Population Control." *Expedition* 13 (1971):22–26.
———. *The Omen Series Šumma Izbu.* TCS 4. Locust Valley, N.Y.: Augustin, 1970.
Levy, S. J. "Two Cylinders of Nebuchadnezzar II in the Iraq Museum." *Sumer* 3 (1947):4–18.
Lichtheim, M. "The Songs of the Harpers." *JNES* 4 (1945):178–212.
Lieberman, Saul. *Hellenism in Jewish Palestine.* New York: Jewish Theological Seminary of America, 1962.
———. *The Tosefta: According to Codex Vienna. . . . The Order of Nashim.* New York: Jewish Theological Seminary of America, 1967.
———. *Tosefta Kifshuṭah: A Comprehensive Commentary on the Tosefta.* Pt. 6, *Order Nashim.* New York: Jewish Theological Seminary of America, 1967.
Lieberman, S. J., ed. *Sumerological Studies in Honor of Thorkild Jacobsen.* AS 20. Chicago: University of Chicago Press, 1976.
Limet, H. "Les Chants épiques sumeriens." *Revue belge de philologie et d'histoire* 50 (1972):3–23.
Lowth, R. *Lectures on the Sacred Poetry of the Hebrews.* 2 vols. London: J. Johnson, 1787.
Luckenbill, D. D. *Ancient Records of Assyria and Babylonia.* 2 vols. Chicago: University of Chicago Press, 1926–27.
———. *The Annals of Sennacherib.* OIP 2. Chicago: University of Chicago Press, 1924.
Lutz, H. F. *Early Babylonian Letters from Larsa.* YOS 2. New Haven: Yale University Press, 1917.
Lyon, D. G. *Keilschrifttexte Sargon's Königs von Assyrien, 722–725 v. Chr.* AB 5. Leipzig: Hinrichs, 1883.
McBride, S. D. "The Deuteronomic Name Theology." Ph.D. diss., Harvard University, 1969.
McCartney, E. S. "Notes on Reading and Praying Audibly." *Classical Philology* 43 (1948):184–87.
McCown, D. E., and Haines, R. C. *Nippur I: Temple of Enlil, Scribal Quarter and Soundings.* OIP 78. Chicago: University of Chicago Press, 1967.

Machinist, P. B. "Literature as Politics: The Tukulti-Ninurta Epic and the Bible." *CBQ* 38 (1976):455–82.
Malamat, A. "Campaigns to the Mediterranean by Iahdunlim and Other Early Mesopotamian Rulers." In *Landsberger AV,* pp. 365–73.
Marszewski, T. "The 'Cedar-Land' Motif in the Sumerian Poem about Gilgamesh. The Problem of Its Origin." *Folia Orientalia* 11 (1969): 201–22.
Matouš, L. "Les Rapports entre la version sumérienne et la version akkadienne de l'epopée de Gilgameš." In *GSL,* pp. 83–94.
———. "Zu neueren Literatur über das Gilgameš-Epos." *Bi. Or.* 21 (1964): 3–10.
———. "Zu neueren Übersetzungen des Gilgameš-Epos." *Ar. Or.* 44 (1976):63–67.
———. "Zur neuern epischen Literatur im alten Mesopotamien." *Ar. Or.* 35 (1967):1–25.
Meek, T. J., trans. "The Code of Hammurabi." *ANET,* pp. 163–80.
Meier, G. "Die zweite Tafel der Serie *bīt mēseri.*" *AfO* 14 (1941–44): 139–52.
Meissner, B. *Ein altbabylonisches Fragment des Gilgamosepos.* MVAG 7(1). Berlin: Peiser, 1902.
———. *Babylonien und Assyrien.* 2 vols. Heidelberg: Carl Winter Universitätsverlag, 1920–25.
———. *Beiträge zum assyrischen Wörterbuch.* Vol 2. AS 4. Chicago: University of Chicago Press, 1932.
Metzger, B. M. *The Text of the New Testament: Its Transmission, Corruption, and Restoration.* 2d ed. New York: Oxford University Press, 1968.
Meyer, L. de. "Introduction bibliographique." In *GSL,* pp. 1–30.
Milik, J. T. *The Books of Enoch.* Oxford: Clarendon Press, 1976.
Millard, A. R. "Gilgamesh X: A New Fragment." *Iraq* 26 (1964):99–105.
———. "A New Babylonian 'Genesis' Story." *Tyndale Bulletin* 18 (1967): 3–18.
Moore, C. A. *Esther.* W. F. Albright and D.N. Freedman, eds., *The Anchor Bible.* Vol. 7B. Garden City, N.Y.: Doubleday, 1971.
Moran, W. L., trans. "Akkadian Letters." In *ANET,* pp. 623–32.
———. "Gilg. I i 41." *RA* 71 (1977):190–91.
———. "New Evidence from Mari on the History of Prophecy." *Biblica* 50 (1969):15–56.
Murray, G. *The Rise of the Greek Epic.* New York: Oxford University Press, 1960.
Muss-Arnolt, W. *A Concise Dictionary of the Assyrian Language.* Berlin: Reuther & Reichard; New York: Lemcke & Büchner, 1905.
North, R. "Status of the Warka Expedition." *Or* 26 (1957):185–256.
Nougayrol, J. "L'Épopée babylonienne." In *Atti del convegno internazionale sul tema: La poesia epica e la sua formazione (Roma, 28 marzo–3 aprile 1969).* Accademia Nazionale dei Lincei. Anno CCCLXVII–1970. Quaderno N. 139, pp. 839–58. Roma: Accademia Nazionale dei Lincei, 1970.

———. "Sirrimu (non **purîmu*) 'âne sauvage'." *JCS* 2 (1948):203–8.
Nougayrol, J. et al. *Le Palais royal d'Ugarit III.* Mission de Ras Shamra 6. Paris: Imprimerie Nationale and Librarie C. Klincksieck, 1955.
———. *Ugaritica V.* Mission de Ras Shamra 16. Paris: Imprimerie Nationale and Librarie Orientaliste Paul Geuthner, 1968.
Oberhuber, K. "Odysseus-Utis in altorientalischer Sicht." In O. Menghin and H. M. Ölberg, eds., *Festschrift Leonhard C. Franz,* pp. 307–12. Innsbrucker Beiträge zur Kulturwissenschaft 11. Innsbruck: Sprachwissenschaftliche Institut der Leopold-Franzens-Universität, 1965.
Oelsner, J. "Ein Beitrag zu keilschriftlichen Konigstitulaturen in hellenistischer Zeit." *ZA* 56 (1964):262–74.
Oppenheim, A. L. *Ancient Mesopotamia: Portrait of a Dead Civilization,* with an appendix, "Mesopotamian Chronology of the Historical Period," by J. A. Brinkman, pp. 335–52. Chicago: University of Chicago Press, 1964.
———. *The Interpretation of Dreams in the Ancient Near East.* Transactions of the American Philosophical Society, N.S. 46(3):177–373. Philadelphia: American Philosophical Society, 1956.
———. "Mesopotamian Mythology, 1–3." *Or.* 16 (1947):207–38; 17 (1948): 17–58; 19 (1950):129–58.
———. "A New Prayer to the Gods of the Night." *Analecta Biblica* 12(3) (1959):282–301.
———. "The Seafaring Merchants of Ur." *JAOS* 74 (1954):6–17.
Oppenheim, A. L., trans. "Babylonian and Assyrian Historical Texts." In *ANET,* pp. 265–317, 556–67.
Otten, H. "Die erste Tafel des hethitischen Gilgamesch-Epos." *Ist. Mit.* 8 (1958):93–125.
———. "Gilgameš. C. Nach hethitischen Texten." *RLA* 3 (1968):372.
———. "Zur Überlieferung des Gilgameš-Epos nach den Boğazköy-Texten." In *GSL,* pp. 139–43.
Ovid. *Metamorphoses.* Translated by M. A. Innes. Harmondsworth, England: Penguin, 1955.
Paul, S. M. "Heavenly Tablets and the Book of Life." *JANES* 5 (1973): 345–53.
———. "Psalm 72:5—A Traditional Blessing for the Long Life of the King." *JNES* 31 (1972):351–55.
———. *Studies in the Book of the Covenant in the Light of Cuneiform and Biblical Law.* SVT 18. Leiden: Brill, 1970.
Pausanias. *Description of Greece.* Translated by W. H. S. Jones and H. A. Ormerod. Vol. 2. LCL. London: Heinemann; New York: Putnam, 1926.
Pettinato, G. *Das altorientalische Menschenbild und die sumerischen und akkadischen Schöpfungsmythen.* Heidelberg: Carl Winter Universitätsverlag, 1971.
———. *Catalogo dei testi cuneiformi di Tell Mardikh-Ebla.* Istituto Universitario Orientali di Napoli. Seminario di Studi Asiatici. Series Major, 1. Materiali Epigrafici di Ebla, 1. Naples: 1979.

———. *Ebla: Un impero inciso nell'argilla.* Milan: Arnoldo Mondadori Editore, 1979.

Pfeiffer, R. H., trans. "Akkadian Observations on Life and the World Order." In *ANET,* pp. 434–40.

———. *State Letters of Assyria and Babylonia.* American Oriental Series 6. New Haven: American Oriental Society, 1935.

Poebel, A. *Historical and Grammatical Texts.* PBS 5. Philadelphia: University Museum, University of Pennsylvania, 1914.

———. *Historical Texts.* PBS 4(1). Philadelphia: University Museum, University of Pennsylvania, 1914.

Pope, M. H. *Job.* W. F. Albright and D. N. Freedman, eds., *The Anchor Bible.* 2d ed. Vol. 15. Garden City, N.Y.: Doubleday, 1973.

———. *Song of Songs.* W. F. Albright and D. N. Freedman, eds., *The Anchor Bible.* Vol. 7C. Garden City, N.Y.: Doubleday, 1977.

Pope, M. H., and Tigay, J. H. "A Description of Baal." *Ugarit-Forschungen* 3 (1971):117–30.

Pritchard, J. B., ed. *Ancient Near Eastern Texts Relating to the Old Testament.* 3d ed. Princeton: Princeton University Press, 1969.

Purvis, J. D. *The Samaritan Pentateuch and the Origin of the Samaritan Sect.* Harvard Semitic Monographs 2. Cambridge, Mass.: Harvard University Press, 1968.

Radau, H. *Sumerian Hymns and Prayers to God "Nin-ib" from the Temple Library of Nippur.* BE 29(1). Philadelphia: Department of Archaeology, University of Pennsylvania, 1911.

Rainey, A.F. *El Amarna Tablets 359–379.* AOAT 8. Kevelaer: Butzon & Bercker; Neukirchen-Vluyn: Neukirchner Verlag, 1970.

Rank, O. *The Myth of the Birth of the Hero and Other Writings,* edited by Philip Freund. New York: Vintage, 1959.

Ranke, H. "Zur Vorgeschichte des Gilgamesch-Epos." *ZA* 49 (1950):45–49.

Ranoszek, R. Review of Schott, *Das Gilgamesch-Epos. ZDMG* 88 (1934): 209–11.

Ravn, O. "Notes on Selected Passages in *Enuma Eliš* and *Gilgameš." Ac. Or.* 22 (1955):28–54.

———. "The Passage on Gilgamesh and the Wives of Uruk." *Bi. Or.* 10 (1953):12–13.

Redford, D. B. "The Literary Motif of the Exposed Child (Cf. Ex. ii, 1–10)." *Numen* 14 (1967):209–28.

Reiner, E. "Die akkadische Literatur." In W. Röllig, ed., *Altorientalische Literaturen: Neues Handbuch der Literaturwissenschaft,* 1:151–210. Wiesbaden: Akademische Verlagsgesellschaft Athenaion, 1978.

———. "City Bread and Bread Baked in Ashes." In *Languages and Areas: Studies Presented to George V. Bobrinskoy,* pp. 116–20. Chicago: 1967.

———. "The Etiological Myth of the 'Seven Sages'." *Or.* 30 (1961):1–11.

———. "Fortune-telling in Mesopotamia." *JNES* 19 (1960):23–35.

———. *Šurpu: A Collection of Sumerian and Akkadian Incantations. AfO,* Beiheft 11. Graz: E. Weidner, 1958.

Reiner, E., trans. "Akkadian Treaties from Syria and Assyria." In *ANET,* pp. 531–41.

Reiner, E., and Güterbock, H. G. "The Great Prayer to Ishtar and Its Two Versions from Boğazköy." *JCS* 21 (1967; published 1969):255–66.

Reisman, D. "Iddin-Dagan's Sacred Marriage Hymn." *JCS* 25 (1973):185–202.

Reisner, G. A. *Sumerisch-babylonische Hymnen nach Thontafeln griechischer Zeit.* Mittheilungen aus dem Orientalischen Sammlungen 10. Berlin: Spemann, 1896.

Renger, J. "Heilige Hochzeit. A. Philologisch." *RLA* 4:251–59.

———. "Mesopotamian Epic Literature." In F. J. Oinas, ed., *Heroic Epic and Saga: An Introduction to the World's Great Folk Epics,* pp. 27–48. Bloomington, Ind.: Indiana University Press, 1978.

———. "Untersuchungen zum Priestertum der altbabylonischen Zeit, 2." *ZA* 59 (1969):104–230.

Roberts, J. J. M. *The Earliest Semitic Pantheon.* Baltimore: Johns Hopkins University Press, 1972.

Römer, W. H. Ph. "The Religion of Ancient Mesopotamia." In C. J. Bleeker and G. Widengren, eds., *Historia Religionum: Handbook for the History of Religions.* Vol. 1, *Religions of the Past*, pp. 115–94. Leiden: Brill, 1969.

———. "Studien zu altbabylonisch epischen Texten, 1." In *Falkenstein A V,* pp. 185–99.

———. *Sumerische "Königshymnen" der Isin-Zeit.* Leiden: Brill, 1965.

Rosenthal, F., trans. "Canaanite and Aramaic Inscriptions." In *ANET,* pp. 653–62.

Roux, G. *Ancient Iraq.* Harmondsworth, England: Pelican, 1966.

Rowton, M. B. "The Date of the Sumerian King List." *JNES* 19 (1960): 156–62.

———. "The Woodlands of Ancient Western Asia." *JNES* 26 (1967):261–77.

Sachs, A., trans. "Akkadian Rituals." In *ANET,* pp. 331–45.

Salonen, A. *Nautica Babyloniaca.* StOr 11(1). Helsinki: Societas Orientalis Fennica, 1942.

Sandars, N. K. *The Epic of Gilgamesh.* Baltimore, Md.: Penguin, 1960.

Sarna, N. M. *Understanding Genesis.* New York: Jewish Theological Seminary and McGraw-Hill, 1966.

Sasson, J. M. "Some Literary Motifs in the Composition of the Gilgamesh Epic." *Studies in Philology* 69 (1972):259–79.

———. "The Worship of the Golden Calf." In H. A. Hoffner, Jr., ed., *Orient and Occident: Essays Presented to Cyrus H. Gordon,* pp. 151–59. AOAT 22. Kevelaer: Verlag Butzon & Bercker; Neukirchen-Vluyn: Neukirchener Verlag, 1973.

Schmöckel, H. *Das Gilgamesch-Epos.* Stuttgart: Kohlhammer, 1966; 2d ed., 1971.

Schollmeyer, A. F. *Sumerische-babylonische Hymnen und Gebete an Šamaš: Studien zur Geschichte und Kultur des Altertums.* Vol. 1, *Ergänzungsband.* Paderborn: Schöningh, 1912.

Schott, A. *Das Gilgamesch-Epos neu übersetzt und mit Anmerkungen versehen.* Leipzig: Reclam, 1934; 2d ed., revised and enlarged by W. von Soden. Stuttgart: Reclam, 1958; 3rd ed., 1970.

———. "Die inschriftlichen Quellen zur Geschichte Eannas." In J. Jordan, ed., *UVB* 1. Abhandlungen der preussischen Akademie der Wissenschaften, philosophisch-historische Klasse, 1929/7. Berlin: Gebr. Mann, 1930.

———. Review of Dossin, *La Pâleur d'Enkidou. OLZ* 36 (1933):519–22.

———. *Die Vergleiche in den akkadischen Königsinschriften.* MVAG 30(2). Leipzig: Hinrichs, 1926.

———. "Zu meiner Übersetzung des Gilgameš-Epos." *ZA* 42 (1934):92–143.

Schrader, E. *Die Keilinschriften und das Alte Testament,* edited by H. Zimmern and H. Winckler. 3d ed. Berlin: Reuther & Reichard, 1903.

Schramm, W. "Zu Gilgameš Tf. VII, III, Z. 9 (Thompson, *EG* S. 45)." *RA* 64 (1970):94.

Schroeder, O. *Keilschrifttexte aus Assur verschiedenen Inhalts.* WVDOG 35. Leipzig: Hinrichs, 1920.

Seux, M.-J. *Épithètes royales akkadiennes et sumériennes.* Paris: Letouzey et Ané, 1967.

Shaffer, A. "The Mesopotamian Background of Eccl. 4:9–12." *EI* 8 (1967): 247–50 (Hebrew; English summary, p. 75*).

———. "New Light on the 'Three-Ply Cord'." *EI* 9 (1969):159–60 (Hebrew; English summary, English section, pp. 138–39).

———. "The Sumerian Sources of Tablet XII of the Epic of Gilgameš." Ph.D. diss., University of Pennsylvania, 1963.

———. Revised texts of *GLL* A and B. Unpublished MS, the University Museum, University of Pennsylvania, Philadelphia.

———. Unpublished copy of Gilg. Y.

Simpson, W. K., ed. *The Literature of Ancient Egypt: An Anthology of Stories, Instructions, and Poetry.* New Edition. New Haven: Yale University Press, 1973.

Sjöberg, Å. W. "Die göttliche Abstammung der sumerisch-babylonischen Herrscher." *Or. Suec.* 21 (1972; published 1973):87–112.

———. "Miscellaneous Sumerian Texts. 1." *Or. Suec.* 23–24 (1974–75; published 1976):159–81.

———. *Der Mondgott Nanna-Suen in der sumerischen Überlieferung.* Pt. 1. *Texte.* Stockholm: Almqvist & Wiksell, 1960.

———. "The Old Babylonian Eduba." In *Jacobsen AV,* pp. 159–79.

———. "Ein Selbstpreis des Königs Ḫammurapi von Babylon." *ZA* 54 (1961):51–70.

Sjöberg, Å., and Bergmann, E. *The Collection of the Sumerian Temple Hymns,* and Gragg, G. G., *The Keš Temple Hymn.* TCS 3. Locust Valley, N.Y.: Augustin, 1969.

Smith, S. *"b/pukk/qqu* and *mekku." RA* 30 (1933):153–69.

Soden, W. von. *Akkadisches Handwörterbuch.* Wiesbaden: Harrassowitz, 1959–.

———. "Als die Götter (auch noch) Mensch waren. Einige Grundgedanken des altbabylonischen Atramḫasīs-Mythus." *Or.* 38 (1969):415–532.

———. "Beiträge zum Verständnis des babylonischen Gilgameš-Epos." *ZA* 53 (1959):209–35.

———. *Ergänzungsheft zum Grundriss der akkadischen Grammatik.* An. Or. 47. Rome: Pontifical Biblical Institute, 1969.

———. "Die erste Tafel des altbabylonischen Atramḫasīs-Mythus. 'Haupttext' und Parallelversionen." *ZA* 68 (1978):50–94.

———. *Grundriss der akkadischen Grammatik.* An. Or. 33. Rome: Pontifical Biblical Institute, 1952.

———. "Die Hebamme in Babylonien und Assyrien." *AfO* 18 (1957–58): 119–21.

———. "Der hymnisch-epische Dialekt des Akkadischen." *ZA* 40 (1931): 163–227; 41 (1933):90–183.

———. "Kleine Beiträge zu Text und Erklärung babylonischer Epen." *ZA* 58 (1967):189–95.

———. "Das Problem der zeitlichen Einordnung akkadischer Literaturwerke." *MDOG* 85 (1953):14–26.

———. Review of Böhl, *Het Gilgamesj-Epos,* 2d ed. *OLZ* 50 (1955):513–16.

———. "Status Rectus-Formen vor dem Genitiv im Akkadischen und die sogenannte uneigentliche Annexion im Arabischen." *JNES* 19 (1960): 163–71.

———. "Sumer, Babylon, und Hethiter bis zur Mitte des zweiten Jahrtausends v. Chr." In G. Mann and A. Heuss, eds., *Propyläen Weltgeschichte,* 1:523–609. Berlin: Propyläen, 1961.

———. "Zum akkadischen Wörterbuch, 81–87." *Or.* 25 (1956):241–50.

Sollberger, E. *Royal Inscriptions.* Pt. 2. UET 8. London: British Museum and University of Pennsylvania, 1965.

———. "The Rulers of Lagash." *JCS* 21 (1967; published 1969):279–91.

———. "The Tummal Inscription." *JCS* 16 (1962):40–47.

Sonneck, F. "Die Einführung der direkten Rede in den epischen Texten." *ZA* 46 (1940):225–35.

Speiser, E. A. *Genesis.* W. F. Albright and D. N. Freedman, eds., *The Anchor Bible.* Vol. 1. Garden City, N.Y.: Doubleday, 1964.

———."Gilgamesh VI 40." *JCS* 12 (1958):41–42.

———. Lecture notes and unpublished essay on *Gilgamesh.*

———. "Mesopotamia: Evolution of an Integrated Civilization." In E. A. Speiser, ed., *At the Dawn of Civilization: The World History of the Jewish People.* First Series: Ancient Times, 1:173–266, 366–72. Rutgers University Press: n.p., 1964.

———. *Oriental and Biblical Studies.* Edited by J. J. Finkelstein and M. Greenberg. Philadelphia: University of Pennsylvania Press, 1967.

———. "PĀLIL and Congeners: A Sampling of Apotropaic Symbols." In *Landsberger AV,* pp. 389–93.

———. "ṬWṬPT." *JQR* 48 (1957–58):208–17.

Speiser, E. A., trans. "Akkadian Myths and Epics." Revised by A. K. Grayson. In *ANET,* pp. 60–119.

Stamm, J. J. *Die akkadische Namengebung.* MVAG 44. Leipzig: Hinrichs, 1939.
———. "Das Gilgamesch-Epos und seine Vorgeschichte." *Asiatische Studien* 6 (1952):9–29.
Steele, F. R. Unpublished transliteration of Gilg. Ni. in the Babylonian collection, University Museum, University of Pennsylvania.
Stefanini, R. "Il Poema di Ghilgames." *Ausonia. Rivista di lettere e arti* 25 (Siena, Italy, 1970):7–39.
———. "Enkidu's Dream in the Hittite 'Gilgamesh'." *JNES* 28 (1969): 40–47.
Stephens, F. J. Collation of Gilg. Y., *apud* A. Pohl, "Personalnachrichten." *Or.* 25 (1956):273, n. 1.
Stephens, F. J., trans. "Sumero-Akkadian Hymns and Prayers." In *ANET,* pp. 383–92.
Streck, M. *Assurbanipal und die letzten assyrischen Könige bis zum Untergang Nineveh's.* VAB 7. Leipzig: Hinrichs, 1916.
Strong, S. A. "On Some Oracles to Esarhaddon and Ašurbanipal." *BA* 2 (1894):627–45.
Tallqvist, K. *Akkadische Götterepitheta.* StOr 7. Helsinki: Societas Orientalis Fennica, 1938.
———. *Sumerisch-Akkadische Namen der Totenwelt.* StOr 5(3). Helsinki: Societas Orientalis Fennica, 1934.
Talmon, S., and Fishbane, M. "Aspects of the Literary Structure of the Book of Ezekiel." *Tarbiz* 42 (1972–73):27–41 (Hebrew with English summary).
Thackeray, H. St. J. *Josephus.* Vol. 4. *Jewish Antiquities,* bks. 1–4. LCL. Cambridge, Mass.: Harvard University Press, 1967.
Thompson, R. C. *CT* 18. London: British Museum, 1904.
———. *The Epic of Gilgamesh: A New Translation* . . . London: Luzac, 1928.
———. *The Epic of Gilgamesh: Text, Transliteration, and Notes.* Oxford: Clarendon Press, 1930.
Thompson, S. *Motif-Index of Folk Literature.* Bloomington, Ind.: Indiana University Press, 1955–58.
Thureau-Dangin, F. "La Fin de la domination gutienne." *RA* 9 (1912): 111–20.
———. "Ḫumbaba." *RA* 22 (1925):23–26.
———. "Notes assyriologiques. 23. Un double de l'inscription d'Utu-Hegal." *RA* 10 (1913):98–100.
———. "Rituel et amulettes contre Labartu." *RA* 18 (1921):161–98.
———. *Rituels Accadiens.* Paris, 1921.
———. *Die sumerischen und akkadischen Königsinschriften.* VAB 1. Leipzig: Hinrichs, 1907.
Tigay, J. H. "An Empirical Basis for the Documentary Hypothesis." *JBL* 94 (1975):329–42.
———. "On Some Aspects of Prayer in the Bible." *Association for Jewish Studies Review* 1 (1976):363–79.

———. "Paradise." In C. Roth, ed., *Encyclopaedia Judaica,* vol. 13, cols. 77–82. Jerusalem: Keter, 1971.

———. "The Stylistic Criteria of Source Criticism in the Light of Ancient Near Eastern Literature." In A. Rofé and Y. Zakovitch, eds., *I. L. Seeligmann AV* (in press).

———. "Was There an Integrated Gilgamesh Epic in the Old Babylonian Period?" In M. Ellis, ed., *Essays . . . Finkelstein,* pp. 215–18.

Tournay, R. J. "Inscription d'Anam, roi d'Uruk et successeur de Gilgamesh." In H. Goedicke, ed., *Near Eastern Studies in Honor of William Foxwell Albright,* pp. 453–57. Baltimore: Johns Hopkins University Press, 1971.

Tsevat, M. "Common Sense and Hypothesis in Old Testament Study." *HUCA* 47 (1976):217–30.

Urbach, E. E. "Mishnah." In C. Roth, ed., *Encyclopaedia Judaica,* vol. 7, cols. 93–108. Jerusalem: Keter, 1971.

Vanstiphout, H. L. J. "A Note on the Series 'Travel in the Desert'." *JCS* 29 (1977):52–56.

Vaux, R. de. "Les Combats singuliers dans l'Ancien Testament." *Biblica* 40 (1959):495–508.

Virgil. *The Aeneid.* Translated by C. Day Lewis. Garden City, N.Y.: Doubleday, 1952.

Waldman, N. "A Biblical Echo of Mesopotamian Royal Rhetoric." In A. I. Katsch and L. Nemoy, eds., *Essays on the Occasion of the Seventieth Anniversary of the Dropsie University,* pp. 449–55. Philadelphia: Dropsie University, 1979.

———. "The Wealth of Mountain and Sea: The Background of a Biblical Image." *JQR* 71 (1981):176–80.

Weidner, E. F. *Handbuch der babylonisch Astronomie.* Vol. 1, AB 23. Leipzig: Hinrichs, 1915.

———. KUB 4. Berlin: Staatliche Museen, 1922.

———. "Zu Gilgamesch-Epos, Tafel 1, I, 12." *AfO* 16 (1952–53):80.

Weiher, E. von "Ein Fragment des Gilgameš-Epos aus Uruk." *ZA* 62 (1972):222–29.

Weiss, H. "Kish, Akkad, and Agade." *JAOS* 95 (1975):434–53.

Weissbach, F. *Die Keilinschriften der Achämeniden.* VAB 3. Leipzig: Hinrichs, 1911.

Wellek, R., and Warren, A. *Theory of Literature.* 3d ed. New York: Harcourt, Brace & World, 1956.

Wente, E. F. "Egyptian 'Make Merry' Songs Reconsidered." *JNES* 21 (1962):118–28.

Westenholz, A. Unpublished copies of Gilg. Ni., UM 29-13-570, Gilg. P., and Gilg. O.I., with annotations.

Westermarck, E. *The History of Human Marriage.* 5th ed. 3 vols. London: Macmillan, 1921.

Wilcke, Cl. "Die Anfänge der akkadischen Epen." *ZA* 67 (1977):153–216.

———. "Formale Gesichtspunkte in der sumerischen Literatur." In *Jacobsen AV,* pp. 205–316.

———. "Ḫuwawa/Ḫumbaba." *RLA* 3:530–35.
———. "ku-li." *ZA* 59 (1969):65–99.
———. *Das Lugalbandaepos.* Wiesbaden: Harrassowitz, 1969.
———. "Politische Opposition nach sumerischen Quellen: Der Konflict zwischen Königtum und Ratsversammlung. Literaturwerke als politische Tendenzschriften." In *La Voix de l'opposition en Mesopotamie*, pp. 37–65. Brussels: Institut des Hautes Études de Belgique, 1975.
———. "Eine Schicksalsentscheidung für den Toten Urnammu." In *Actes de la 17e rencontre assyriologique internationale.* CRRAI 17:81–92. Ham-sur-Heure, Belgium: Comité de Recherches en Mesopotamie, 1970.
———. "Sumerische Lehrgedichte." In *Kindler's Literatur Lexikon* vol. 6, cols. 2135–42. Zurich: Kindler, 1965.
Williams, C. A. *Oriental Affinities of the Legend of the Hairy Anchorite.* 2 vols. University of Illinois Studies in Language and Literature 10(2), 11(4). Urbana: University of Illinois Press, 1925–26.
Williams, R. J. "Scribal Training in Ancient Egypt." *JAOS* 92 (1972):214–21.
Wilson, J., trans. "Egyptian Myths, Tales, and Mortuary Texts," "Egyptian Didactic Tales," "Egyptian Observations," and "Egyptian Secular Songs and Poems." In *ANET,* pp. 3–36, 405–10, 431–34, 467–71.
Wilson, J. V. Kinnier. "Hebrew and Akkadian Philological Notes." *JSS* 7 (1962):173–83.
———. "Lugal ud melambi nirgal: New Texts and Fragments." *ZA* 54 (1961):71–89.
———. "On the Fourth and Fifth Tablets of the Epic of Gilgameš." In *GSL,* pp. 103–11.
———. "Some Contributions to the Legend of Etana." *Iraq* 31 (1969):8–17.
Wiseman, D. J. "Additional Neo-Babylonian Gilgamesh Fragments." In *GSL,* pp. 123–35.
———. "A Gilgamesh Epic Fragment from Nimrud." *Iraq* 37 (1975):157–63.
———. "The Laws of Hammurabi Again." *JSS* 7 (1962):161–72.
Witzel, P. M. "Noch einmal die sumerische Himmelsstier-Episode." In *Keilschriftliche Miscellanea.* An. Or. 6:45–68. Rome: Pontifical Biblical Institute, 1933.
Wolff, H. N. "Gilgamesh, Enkidu, and the Heroic Life." *JAOS* 89 (1969): 392–98.
Yadin, Y. "A Note on the Scenes Depicted on the 'Ain-Samiya Cup." *IEJ* 21 (1971):82–85.
Young, G. D. "Utu and Justice: A New Sumerian Proverb." *JCS* 24 (1972): 132–34.
Zimmern, H. *Sumerische Kultlieder aus altbabylonischer Zeit.* 2nd series. VAS 10. Leipzig: Hinrichs, 1913.
———. "Ein Zyklus altsumerischer Lieder auf die Haupttempel Babyloniens." *ZA* 39 (1930):245–76.
Zwettler, M. *The Oral Tradition of Classical Arabic Poetry. Its Character and Implications.* Columbus, Oh.: Ohio State University Press, 1978.

# *Index*

The index consists of the following parts:

J. Apocrypha and Pseudepigrapha
K. New Testament
L. Rabbinic Literature
M. Aramaic
N. Syriac
O. Arabic
P. Mandaic
VI. Folklore motifs cited

It was not possible to include a comprehensive index of modern authors. A small number whose research marked major milestones in the study of the epic are cited in the subject index (Pt. I).

## I. SUBJECT INDEX

## II. PERSONS

## III. DEITIES AND OTHER SUPERNATURAL BEINGS

## IV. FOREIGN TERMS

### A. *Sumerian and Sumerograms*

## B. *Akkadian and Akkadograms*

C. *Hittite*



D. *Hebrew*



E. *Aramaic*



F. *Ethiopic*



G. *Greek*



H. *Latin*

## V. TEXTS CITED

### A. *Sumerian*



SUMERIAN GILGAMESH TEXTS

## B. *Akkadian*

AKKADIAN GILGAMESH TEXTS

## C. *Bilingual*



## D. *Hittite and Hurrian*

## E. *Egyptian*



## F. *Ugaritic*



## G. *Greek*

## H. *Latin*



## I. *Hebrew Bible*